A Field Guide in Colour to
PLANTS AND ANIMALS

A Field Guide in Colour to

PLANTS
AND
ANIMALS

By Jan Toman and Jiří Felix

Illustrated by Květoslav Hísek

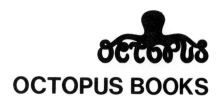

OCTOPUS BOOKS

Translated by Margot Schierlová and Ota Vojtíšek
Graphic design by Milan Albich

English version first published 1974 by
Octopus Books Limited
59 Grosvenor Street, London W1

Reprinted 1975

ISBN 0 7064 0299 5

Printed in Czechoslovakia

CONTENTS

INTRODUCTION

This book is intended for amateur nature lovers who want to know more about the various plants and animals which they see on walks or even in the gardens of their homes. Complicated taxonomic keys and scientific publications are of little help to the man in the street, who usually does not have sufficient time to study specialist books or make personal visits to experts. We have therefore prepared a selection of the most important plants and animals which the reader is most likely to encounter, or which may attract his attention by their striking appearance. Because of the vast quantity of different types of plants and animals, and the limited extent of this book, we were able to describe only certain representatives of the various systematic groups. Our primary aim, however, is to enable the reader to form a general picture of the plant and animal kingdom around him, so that, from the species depicted in this book, he will also be able to identify species not given here and classify them in the proper group according to their characteristic morphological features.

Plants have been arranged according to a scientific system. But to help in the classification we have divided angiosperms into ligneous and herbaceous plants. The species are again grouped in families, i.e. systematic classification is maintained. This emphasizes the relationship of plants which are often different in appearance, but have the same principal characteristics. To make the basic classification principles clearer, preceding each main group we have given a brief characterization and have divided the group into lower systematic units together with their main differentiating characteristics.

The illustrations are accompanied by a concise description of the plants and data on their distribution, incidence, specific habitat requirements, flowering or fruiting time and, where necessary, details of their adaptation.

In the zoological section we have illustrated some 700 species of animals representing 14 main groups (classes). Some classes have been omitted, while in others, the various lower systematic groups, such as orders and families, are not linked strictly systematically. For instance, although ladybirds and leaf beetles are not related, they are often confused and so, for greater clarity, we have illustrated them together.

Since the book covers most of the zoological groups, it is impossible to include all their representatives. In the case of the less numerous groups, such as birds, mammals, reptiles, amphibians and fishes, we were able to include more, or in some cases even the majority of them. In groups like the spiders, crustaceans and, in particular, insects, this was impossible, however, and we therefore chose only their most abundant or striking representatives.

In the text accompanying the illustrations of individual species, we have given their most important morphological features, the manner of their reproduction, the time and place of their appearance and their distribution.

Dr J. TOMAN — Dr J. FELIX

DIVISIONS AND CLASSES OF PLANTS DESCRIBED IN THIS BOOK

FUNGI, LICHENS, LIVERWORTS AND MOSSES —

Mycophyta, Lichenes, Bryophyta

Two types of spore production are common to all fungi. A cross-section of the fruiting body of an *Ascomycetes* reveals the sac-like structure — *ascus* — distinctly visible in the cavity. The spores *(ascospores)* — propagating bodies — are formed in the ascus (plural asci). The *Basidiomycetes* produce spores at the end of special cells — *basidia;* these form in laminar and tube fungi on the *lamellae* (gills under the head of a mushroom) or inside the tubes of a cep or boletus.

1 Fungi

1 *Cross-section of fruit body (a) with asci (b); 2 ascus with spores — propagating bodies of Ascomycetes; 3 cross-section of lamella (a) from fruiting body of a Basidiomycetes (mushroom) with special spore-bearing cells — basidia (b); 4 cross-section of part of a spore-bearing layer of a boletus with tubes (a) and basidia (b).*

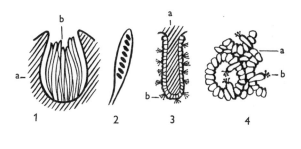

The structure of lichens may be seen in the cross-section of their plant body or *thallus*: they are dual organisms composed on the one hand of the cells of green or blue-green algae; on the other hand of the hyphae of fungi which create layers of unifying fibres. The propagation of lichens may be either separate — alga and fungus multiply separately — or by the propagating bodies consisting of alga cells wrapped in fungus hyphae.

2 Lichens

1 *Cross-section of lichen thallus with algal cells (a) and fungal hyphae (b); 2 lichen propagating body consisting of algal cell wrapped in fungal hyphae.*

3 Liverworts and mosses

1 *Diagram of moss plant: calyptra (a), lid (b), capsule (c), seta (d), stem with leaves (e), rhizoides (f).*

Liverworts and mosses as a rule have their bodies differentiated into root-like fibres *(rhizoids)*, a stem with or without leaves and an unbranched stalk *(seta)* supporting the spore capsule; the latter bearing a lid and often covered with a cap *(calyptra)*.

CLUBMOSSES, HORSETAILS AND FERNS — *Pteridophyta*

Clubmosses have simple green leaves; the fertile ones bearing a solitary *sporangium* at its base. Some species have modified spore-bearing leaves aggregated into cone-like structures.

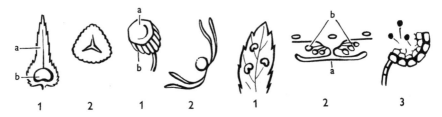

4 Clubmosses
1 *Spore-bearing leaf (a) with sporangium (b); 2 spore.*

5 Horsetails
1 *Spore-bearing leaf consisting of peltate sporangiophore (a) with sporangia (b); 2 spore with hygroscopic spiral bands.*

6 Ferns
1 *Tip of a leaf with sori; 2 cross-section of sori with indusium (a) and stalked sporangia (b); 3 bursting sporangia showing annulus (ring of thickened cells) and ejected spores.*

Horsetails also bear modified spore-bearing leaves in cone-like groups at the end of distinctly articulated stems; these leaves are composed of the sterile peltate sporangiophore which bear the spore-bearing sporangia. Each spore is provided with hygroscopic spiral bands *(elaters)* which enable them to hang together in small clusters, thus aiding eventual fertilization.

Ferns as a rule have sori deposited on the underside of normal green leaves. Sporangia are mostly protected by a skin or *indusium*. Mature sporangia have, in addition to the wall of thin membraneous cells, a ring of thickened cells, the *annulus*. Fluctuations of humidity cause the annulus to straighten, thus rupturing the thin side walls and liberating the spores.

GYMNOSPERMS — *Coniferophyta*
ANGIOSPERMS (FLOWERING PLANTS) — *Angiospermophyta*

Gymnosperms have male 'flowers' or *strobili* with scale-like stamens which bear the pollen sacs. The female strobili are like miniature cones, each scale of which bears one or two, rarely more, ovules. These ovule-bearing scales often grow in the axil of supporting scales known as bracts. The ovules ripen into usually winged seeds.

7 Gymnosperms

1 *Scale-like stamen (a) with pollen sacs (b);*
2 *seed scale (a) with two naked ovules (b)*
and supporting scale (c); 3 *winged seed.*

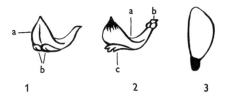

The body of an angiosperm is usually differentiated into a root, stem and leaves, the latter sometimes forming a basal rosette or growing spaced out along the stem; they may also be transformed more or less conspicuously into bracts. In the axil of the bracts or at the end of a stem one to several flowers grow; a cluster of flowers is known as an *inflorescence*.

8 Angiosperms

1 *Diagram of a typical flowering plant: flower (a), sessile upper leaves (b), stem (c), stem leaves with petioles (d), basal leaves (e), root (f);* 2 *Diagram of a flower: pistil — stigma (a), style (b), ovary (c) with ovules (d); stamen — 2 anther lobes (e), connective (f), filament (g); petals or corolla (h) and sepals or calyx (i).*

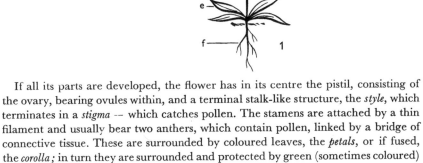

If all its parts are developed, the flower has in its centre the pistil, consisting of the ovary, bearing ovules within, and a terminal stalk-like structure, the *style*, which terminates in a *stigma* -- which catches pollen. The stamens are attached by a thin filament and usually bear two anthers, which contain pollen, linked by a bridge of connective tissue. These are surrounded by coloured leaves, the *petals*, or if fused, the *corolla*; in turn they are surrounded and protected by green (sometimes coloured) leaves, the *sepals* or *calyx* if joined together.

Roots are generally differentiated into the main, mostly spindle-shaped tap root which grows downwards, and secondary, smaller, lateral roots which tend to grow sideways. Roots are usually cylindrical, sometimes swollen (tubers). Sometimes the main root is not developed and is replaced by the roots from the base of the stem

9 Root

1 *Spindle-shaped main root with lateral secondary roots;* 2 *cylindrical root;* 3 *thickened roots (tubers);* 4 *adventitious roots;* 5 *sugar-beet root.*

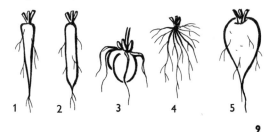

9

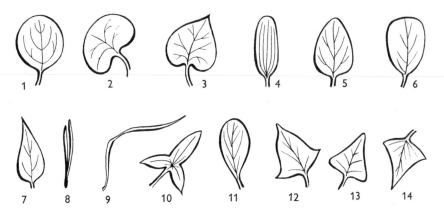

10 Simple leaves
1 *Rounded leaf;* 2 *reniform;* 3 *cordiform;* 4 *elliptic;* 5 *ovate;* 6 *obovate;* 7 *lanceolate;* 8 *acicular;*
9 *linear;* 10 *sagittate or arrow-shaped;* 11 *spathulate;* 12 *hastate;* 13 *triangular;* 14 *rhomboid.*

(adventitious) which are characteristic especially of monocotyledonous plants. The strikingly thickened root, as in the sugar-beet, serves as storage of reserve substances important for the plant nutrition prior to flowering.

Bulbs and corms are modified lowest parts of stems with the fleshy bases of leaves or their sheaths; true bulbs are characteristic of monocotyledonous plants.

According to the shape, outline and pattern of venation, the most common types of dicotyledon leaves are the following: rounded, reniform, elliptic, obovate, ovate, lanceolate, sagittate, with a network or reticulum of veins. Linear or needle-like leaves are characteristic of the gymnosperms. The elongate linear or strap-like leaf

11 Pinnate leaves
1 *Shallowly lobed;* 2 *deeply lobed;* 3 *parted;*
4 *divided.*

12 Palmate leaves
1 *Shallowly lobed;* 2 *deeply lobed;* 3 *parted;*
4 *divided.*

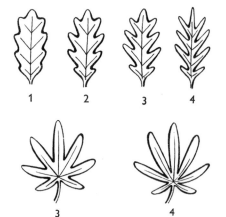

13 Compound leaves
1 *Leaf with one pair of leaflets, the remainder modified as tendrils; 2 trifoliate leaf; 3 digitate; 4 imparipinnate; 5 paripinnate; 6 bipinnate; 7 pinnate with interjected leaflets.*

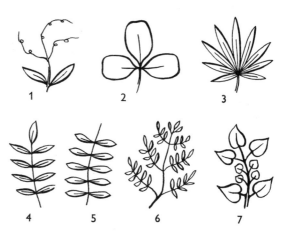

with parallel venation is typical of grasses and many other monocotyledonous plants.

Lobed or divided leaves are, according to the type of venation, either pinnate or palmate but their lobes and segments are continuously connected. Lobed leaves have blades parted to one third at the most, cleft leaves to about one half, divided leaves from two thirds of the blade almost up to the main vein or leaf stalk.

Compound leaves have blades formed by independent leaflets. The illustrated leaf with one pair of leaflets terminates in a branched tendril derived from modified leaflets. Compound palmate leaves may have as few as three leaflets (trifoliate) or up to a dozen or more in some tropical plants. Odd or imparipinnate leaves have the mid-rib always ending with an odd leaflet. Paripinnate leaves on the contrary never have the rhachis with a terminal odd leaflet. Bipinnate (twice pinnate) or even tripinnate (three times pinnate) leaves commonly occur. Pairs of unequally large and small leaflets alternate sometimes (potato) and such a leaf is said to have interjected leaflets.

According to the position of leaves on the stem we distinguish alternate leaves and

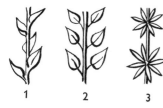 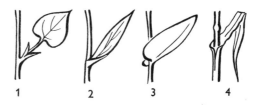

14 Position of leaves
1 *Alternate leaves; 2 opposite leaves arranged in two ranks; 3 whorl.*

15 Attachment of leaves
1 *Petiolate leaf with stipules; 2 sessile leaf; 3 clasping (amplexicaul) leaf; 4 sheathed leaf.*

11

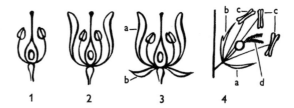

16 Stem
1 *Winged;* 2 *grooved;* 3 *two-edged.*

17 Undergroud stem parts
1 *Creeping rhizome;* 2 *stem tuber.*

opposite ones, the latter often arranged in alternate pairs. Where the leaves are arranged in groups of three or more at each node these are called whorled.

According to the attachment we differentiate petiolate leaves which have the flat blade or *lamina*, attached to a stalk or *petiole*, at the base of which may be a pair of stipules. Leaves without petioles, attached immediately to the stem by the blade, are described as sessile. Sometimes the leaf base embraces the stem; this is known as a clasping or *amplexicaul* leaf. In sheathed leaves, which are characteristic of grasses, the widened base of the linear leaf forms a tube running down a section of the stem known as a sheath.

Stems are mostly rounded but sometimes there are bands or longitudinal ribs, i.e. winged or sharply or bluntly grooved. Stems may be also flattened, with two, three or four sharp edges.

The underground parts of the stem in perennial plants form the creeping rhizomes or stolons or may be thickened into a stem tuber.

18 Flower
1 *Apetalous flower;* 2 *flower with simple perianth;* 3 *flower with perianth differentiated into petals or corolla (a) and sepals or calyx (b);* 4 *grass flower: lemma (a), palea (b), stamens (c), pistil with stigmata (d).*

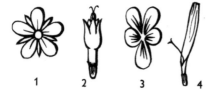

19 Flower symmetry
1 *Regular flower with polypetalous corolla;* 2 *regular flower with gamopetalous, tubular corolla;* 3 *flower with asymmetrical corolla;* 4 *asymmetrical flower with strap-shaped (ligulate) corolla.*

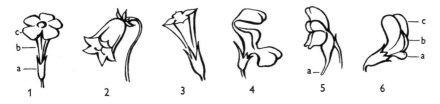

20 Corolla

1 *Tubular corolla with lobes (c) and tube (b), surrounded by calyx (a)*; 2 *bell-shaped corolla;*
3 *funnel-shaped;* 4 *labiate or bilabiate;* 5 *spurred corolla with nectary spur (a)*; 6 *papilionaceous corolla
of vetches: keel (a), wings (b) and standard (c).*

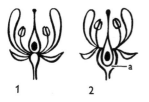

21 Ovary

1 *Ovary superior;* 2 *ovary inferior, showing hollow receptacle (a).*

According to the formation of floral envelopes (sepals and petals or *perianth*) we
distinguish the flower completely without a perianth, with a simple perianth, or one
differentiated into the corolla or petals and sepals or calyx. In grasses the flower
structure is different: the petalless flower grows in the axil of a bract-like *lemma*,
protected by a similar but often pointed or keeled *palea*; there are usually three

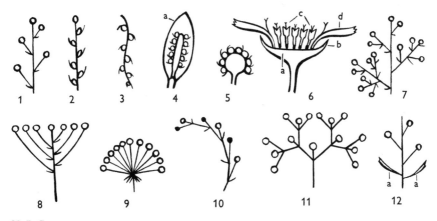

22 Inflorescence

1 *Raceme;* 2 *spike;* 3 *catkin;* 4 *spadix and spathe (a)*; 5 *head;* 6 *capitulum consisting of receptacle(a),
involucral bracts (b), central florets (c) and strap-shaped or ligulate florets (d)*; 7 *panicle;* 8 *corymb;*
9 *umbel;* 10 *monochasial cyme;* 11 *dichasial cyme;* 12 *three-flowered spikelet of grasses with glumes(a).*

13

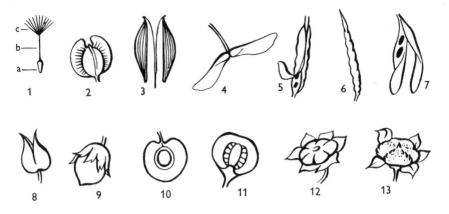

23 Fruits

1 *Achene (a) with elongated beak (b) and pappus (c)* ; 2 *samara;* 3 *schizocarp;* 4 *double samara;* 5 *siliqua;* 6 *loment;* 7 *legume (pod)* ; 8 *capsule;* 9 *nut;* 10 *cross-section of drupe;* 11 *cross-section of berry;* 12 *schizocarpic fruit of mallow;* 13 *fruit of hounds-tongue (Boraginaceae) composed of four nutlets.*

stamens and a pistil with two pinnate stigmata; a proper perianth is missing or reduced to two minute membraneous scales, the *lodicules.*

The symmetry of flowers is most strikingly observed in the corolla. It may have separate petals (polypetalous), or these may be fused together either partially or wholly (gamopetalous). In the latter case, tubular or bell-shaped flowers result.

Tubular flowers may divide at their tips into petal-like lobes or lips and bear at their bases nectar secreting spurs or pouches. Owing to the characteristic shape of the corollas of members of the pea family they are called papilionaceous plants: the two lower petals are fused together to form a keel, the lateral petals form the wings and the upper, largest petal is called the standard.

24 Aggregate fruits
1 *Strawberry, fleshy receptacle with achenes;* 2 *raspberry, cluster of druplets.*

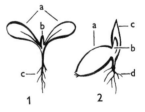

25 Germination
1 *Dicotyledons: cotyledons (a), growing point (b), root (c);* 2 *monocotyledons: seed (caryopsis) of grasses (a), cotyledon (b), first leaf (c), adventitious roots (d).*

14

According to the position of the ovary we distinguish flowers as superior, where the stamens are placed under it, and inferior where the stamens are located above the ovary.

In a diagrammatic representation of an inflorescence, the flowers are indicated as simple circles with the bracts as a short curved line. The most usual types of inflorescence are: *raceme, spike, panicle, corymb, capitulum* and *umbel*. In capitulum, the characteristic inflorescence of the *Compositae* (daisy family), we differentiate a swollen receptacle, protective involucral bracts *(involucre)* and tiny flowers *(florets)*, often of two kinds: central tubular, surrounded by ligulate or strap-shaped ones.

Ovules develop into seeds, the ovary enlarges and forms the fruit. The ovary formed from one carpel matures into an achene or samara, sometimes with a beak, long hairs (pappus), or bearing a wing. The double samaras or schizocarpic fruit, splits into half fruits, sometimes winged. The legume (pod) usually contains several seeds and opens by splitting suddenly into two valves. Capsules also bear many seeds, but open by fissures, toothed pores, holes or lids. The nut is a fruit with hard pericarp. A cross-section of a drupe (stone-fruit) shows three different layers of pericarp: outer skin, pulp and stone; the seed is enclosed inside the stone. The true berry is also fleshy, but contains several seeds. Schizocarpic fruits of mallow plants split radially into many single-seeded nutlets, while dead-nettle or borage have the fruit always formed of four nutlets.

Aggregate fruits represent a tight cluster of fruitlets originating from a single flower with several carpels. In the strawberry, the receptacle becomes swollen and fleshy, but in blackberry and raspberry each carpel develops a fleshy layer. On the other hand the collective fruit originates from a whole inflorescence, e.g. fig, mulberry.

New plants originate from seeds. The dicotyledons germinate with two seed leaves (cotyledons) usually different in shape and size from the true leaves that follow. At the junction of the cotyledons is the growing point which becomes the first stem. As a rule the root is soon differentiated into the main root *(radicle)* and smaller lateral ones. Monocotyledons produce only one cotyledon, and the first leaf often resembles the later adult ones. The radicle soon disappears and is replaced by numerous adventitious roots from the base of the young stem.

Division: **Fungi** — *Mycophyta*

A group of unicellular or multicellular organisms completely lacking the green pigment – chlorophyll. They are mostly colourless but their thallus or fruit body, especially in mushrooms and toadstools, has various pigments except chlorophyll. The photosynthetic process in which organic compounds are formed from inorganic compounds via chlorophyll and sunlight cannot take place in fungi cells. Fungi acquire organic compounds by other means. Either they are parasitic on live organisms — parasitic fungi, or utilize the decaying remains of other organisms — saprophytic fungi. The incoming food supplies of fungi are transformed into such substances as glycogen, oils, etc., unlike green plants whose basic energy and growth supplies are in the form of starch and sugar.

Some fungi live in a beneficial association *(symbiosis)* with other plants; symbiosis of some toadstools with roots of trees, or of some microscopic representatives with the roots of orchids is well known.

The fungal body consists of fibrous tissue. The set of fungal fibres *(hyphae)* forms the *mycelium* on which minute propagating organs or large and conspicuous fruit bodies grow under favourable conditions.

Fungi propagate by spores.

Systematic survey:

Unrepresented class: *Phycomycetes*. Unicellular or with microscopic mycelium; some aquatic, others parasitic on plants and animals.

Class: *Ascomycetes* (p. 18). Multicellular mycelium; spores produced in sporangia — asci.

Subclass: *Protoascomycetidae* (p. 18). Ascus originates by simple transformation of merged cells.

Subclass: *Euascomycetidae* (p. 18). Asci originate by a complicated process, a series of transformations and merging of cells and nuclei.

Class: *Basidiomycetes* (p. 20). Spores are borne naked on conspicuous stalk-like *basidia*.

Subclass: *Heterobasidiomycetidae* (p. 20). Articulated (jointed) basidia.

Subclass: *Homobasidiomycetidae* (p. 20). Non-articulated basidia, unicellular.

Order: *Hymenomycetales* (p. 20). Basidia form a layer on surface of fruiting body; in maturity uncovered.

Order: *Gasteromycetales* (p. 28). Spore-bearing tissue inside fruiting body, enclosed in a skin or *peridium*.

Families are classified according to the characteristics of mycelium, fruiting bodies and the type of spores production.

Division: **Lichens** — *Lichenes*

Dual organisms whose plant body *(thallus)* is composed of fungal hyphae and cells of algae. Both components are in symbiosis forming one organism. In most lichens the fungal component is represented by an *Ascomycetes;* only in some tropical representatives the *Basidiomycetes* are present. As to the algae they are either green or blue-green species. As a rule a certain species of fungi enters into symbiosis with a certain species of algae.

Lichens multiply by the liberation of small groups of algal cells, interwoven with hyphae (gemma) which usually originate in special cup-like structures on the thallus surface. The fungi component also may form independent fruit bodies with spores. A new lichen thallus can develop only if actively growing hyphae encounter the respective alga.

The classification of lichens is mainly artificial.

Represented class: *Ascolichenes* (p. 30). Fungal component is an *Ascomycetes* species.

Unrepresented class: *Hymenolichenes*. Fungal component is a *Basidiomycetes* species.

Division: **Mosses and Liverworts** — *Bryophyta*

Multicellular, green, spore-bearing plants whose body is differentiated into stems with rhizoids and assimilating leaves. Monoecious species have both sexual organs on the same plant, dioecious ones have separately sexed individuals. After fertilization, a stalked capsule *(sporophyte)* develops which remains connected with the plant and from which it draws nutritive substances. On germination, each spore produces green, thread-like structures or *protonema*. From it arises the leafy moss or liverwort plant *(gametophyte)*.

Systematic survey:

Class: **Liverworts** — *Hepaticopsida* (p. 32). Small protonema. Thallus flat, either laminar, sometimes forked, or differentiated into stem and leaves without a mid-rib. Vegetative propagation frequent.

Order: *Marchantiales* (p. 32). Laminar thallus, capsules bursting irregularly.

Unrepresented order: *Jungermaniales*. Small plants consisting of stem with leaves. Simple capsules split into four valves.

Unrepresented order: *Anthocerotales*. Sporophyte generation independently assimilating. Capsule structure is relatively complicated.

Class: **Mosses** — *Bryopsida* (p.32). Distinct protonema, producing erect stems with leaves. Sexual organs at tip of stems or lateral shoots. Capsules with lids.

Subclass: *Sphagnidae* (p. 32). Stems without rhizoids. Leaves of two types. Leaf cells also of two types: some colourless, without chlorophyll, serve as water reservoir, others contain chlorophyll. Simple capsules without cap. Short stalk. Protonema laminar.

Subclass: *Bryidae* (p. 32). Stems with rhizoides. Leaves usually with mid-rib. Capsules with cap, mostly of complicated structure. Stalk often much longer than capsules. Vascular tissue present in some of the larger species. Fibrous protonema.
The classification of families is based on the morphology of capsules and the cell structure of leaves.

Division: **Fungi** — *Mycophyta*

Class: *Ascomycetes*

Subclass: *Protoascomycetidae*

Family: *Saccharomycetaceae*

1 *Saccharomyces cerevisiae*. Unicellular fungus, known as yeast, visible only under microscope. Of considerable economic value as it is used to leaven dough. Other species are used to ferment wine, cider and beer. In the wild it lives on fruits and other parts of many plants. Propagates by budding; the dividing cells mostly remaining together and forming branched strings.

Family: *Taphrinaceae*

2 *Taphrina pruni* (syn. *Exoascus pruni*) ('bladder plum'). Attacks fruits of plum-trees causing them to grow large, lop-sided and bladder-like. *T. deformans* ('peach-leaf cure') causes the leaves of peaches and almonds to curl and swell, finally turning bright red. Dense bunches of twigs — witches brooms — are formed on trees attacked by *T. insititiae*. Related species of this fungus cause similar deformations on birches and hornbeams. The mycelium grows through branches or fruits of host plant and terminal cells develop into asci with spores on surface. Asci grow so close to each other that they appear as fine hoar frost on branches or fruits of afflicted plants.

Subclass: *Euascomycetidae*

Family: *Clavicipitaceae*

3 **Ergot** *Claviceps purpurea*. Parasitic on seeds of grasses, particularly rye. Infection is caused by spores producing hyphae which consume ovary and form a black, horny, seed-like sclerotium. This falls to ground and winters in soil. Red-stalked fruiting bodies *(ascophores)* with club-like tips grow from them the following year and produce more spores which are dispersed by wind or insects when the grasses or grain crops are flowering. Ergot is deadly poisonous; its alkaloids are used in the preparation of valuable medicines.

Family: *Phacidiaceae*

4 *Rhytisma acerinum* ('tar spot'). Parasitic on maple leaves. Forms irregular to rounded, conspicuously large, black, yellow-bordered spots on upper surface of leaves. In spring these black fruiting bodies produce asci full of slender spores. Parasitic also on sow-thistle leaves. Related *Rhytisma punctatum* grows parasitically on sycamore and another member of the genus causes spots on willow leaves.

Family: *Morchellaceae* (syn. *Helvellaceae*)

5 **Morel** *Morchella esculenta*. Fruiting body consists of cap and stalk. Cap mostly ovoid or globose, up to 8 cm. high, yellowish to brownish, with irregular, deep and broad cavities that do not form continuous rows, rather recalling a crumpled honeycomb. Well-known spring mushroom, grows in April and May in open deciduous or mixed forests but also in old gardens, parks and yards. Edible only when young. Old fruit bodies, in which decomposition of albumins takes place, may cause serious poisoning.

Family: *Helvellaceae*

6 *Gyromitra esculenta*. Brown to dark brown hollow cap, irregularly lobed and wrinkled, up to 10 cm. wide. Stalk whitish to yellowish, hollow, sometimes wrinkled on surface and shorter than cap. Grows in spring in sandy pine-woods, also in other coniferous forests. Sensitivity of man to it varies; it is poisonous to some, even deadly. Therefore, this fungus should never be eaten. Related species *Gyromitra gigas* with lighter cap may be eaten without danger after scalding.

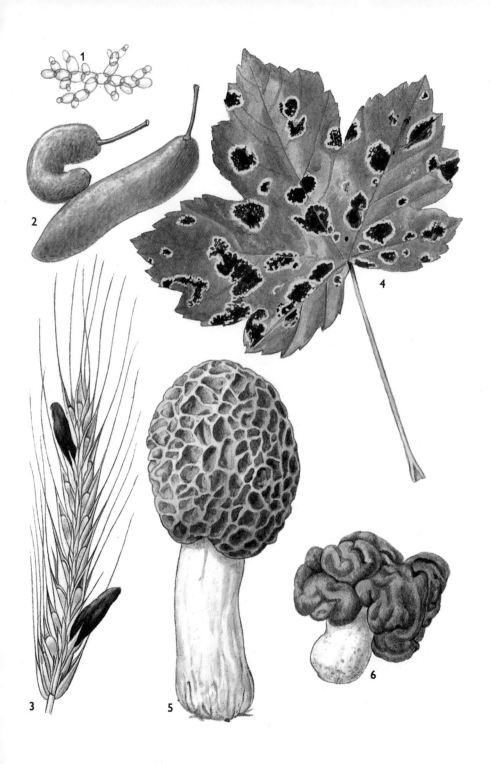

1
2
4
3
5
6

Class: *Basidiomycetes*

Subclass: *Heterobasidiomycetidae*

Family: *Pucciniaceae*

1 *Puccinia graminis.* Parasitic on cereals as well as on barberry. Rusty patches of powdery spores on under surface of barberry leaves. Spores spread by wind on to cereals or other grasses where they germinate. On leaves of these plants so-called summer spores are formed during the growing season. In summer rust spreads by these spores and causes infection of neighbouring plants. At end of the growing season black patches of winter spores form; they overwinter and the following spring each one germinates to produce a basidium with four stalked spores. These are spread by wind and again infect barberry leaves. The sequence of various spore types and alternation of host plants is characteristic of many species of rusts.

Subclass: *Homobasidiomycetidae*

Order: *Hymenomycetales*

Family: *Corticiaceae*

2 *Stereum hirsutum.* Grows on trunks and stumps of deciduous trees. The stemless, shell-like fruiting bodies are yellowish-grey and somewhat leathery, often with a paler zoned striping; the surface varies from soft velvety to shaggy felt in texture. Under surface grey-yellow when dry, reddish in wet weather. A similar species, *Stereum sanguinolentum*, has fruiting bodies with greyish surface. Turns blood-red when injured.

Family: *Polyporaceae*

3 *Trametes versicolor.* Somewhat fleshy to leathery fruiting bodies form fan-shaped, often overlapping clusters, ornamented with concentric dark and light stripes of brown, grey, orange or yellowish velvety hairs; whitish beneath. Abundant on stumps and decayed trunks of deciduous trees and shrubs, also on dry branches. Related species *Trametes zonatus* has no conspicuous striping. Both species are inedible.

4 *Polyporus squamosus.* Young fruiting bodies convex, older ones widely expanded with a depressed centre; stalk (stipe) short and thick. Whitish to brownish-yellow, roughly circular cap thinly covered with darkish, mostly brown, relatively large scales. Flesh white, whitish to yellowish or slightly brown. Grows on branches, trunks, roots and stumps of deciduous trees, especially nut-trees, individually or in groups, from spring to winter. Young, crisp and still not leathery fruiting bodies edible. Strikingly cucumber-like, floury taste.

5 *Grifola sulphurea* (syn. *Laetiporus sulphureus*). Fruiting bodies fleshy, juicy when young, later tough and brittly crumbling. Cap flat against the tree, usually far down densely set one above another. Young fruit bodies bright sulphur yellow, mature even orange, old ones brownish. Grows abundantly on stumps, branches and trunks of deciduous trees in woods but also in parks and gardens. Edible when young, but has a slightly acid, woody taste and seldom eaten.

6 *Phellinus igniarius.* Hoof-shaped fruit bodies on trunks of poplars, willows and other trees where they often grow to large size. Cap flat against the tree without stipe, consists of layers; upper surface greyish to blackish. Fruit bodies of this fungus and of its relative *Fomes fomentarius* served once for making tinder. In poor mountainous regions fruiting bodies of the latter used to be processed to fine, leathery folios of which caps and waistcoats were sewn.

Family: *Hydnaceae*

1 *Sarcodon imbricatus* (syn. *Hydnum imbricatum*). Shallow, funnel-shaped cap with rim in-rolled when young, 6—18 cm. wide, brownish to grey-brown, thickly covered with large, black-grey scales, thickest in centre. Underside of cap thickly covered with greyish to brownish bristles. Grows in coniferous woods, especially pine-woods, in late summer and autumn. In places used for preparing soups and sauces. Only young specimens are suitable, old ones tough.

Family: *Clavariaceae*

2 *Ramaria flava* (syn. *Clavaria aurea*). Edible species with dense coral-like tufts of fruiting bodies. Distinguishable from other inedible *Ramaria* species by yellow colour of branches which do not turn red on bruised spots. The stalk and flesh are white. In places, especially in warm regions, it occurs abundantly in forests at beginning of autumn and end of summer. Related *Sparassis crispa* is edible. Its fruiting body formed by flattened undulate branchlets weighs up to several kilograms.

Family: *Boletaceae*

3 *Boletus felleus* (syn. *Tylopilus felleus*). May easily be mistaken for edible boletus. Differs from it by more striking olive-brown network on stipe. Under surface pinkish, when bruised turning rusty brown. Hot bitter taste, quite inedible, even if not poisonous. Abundant forest mushroom, especially in coniferous woods in higher altitudes; in lowlands and deciduous woods occurs only occasionally.

4 Edible Boletus *Boletus edulis*. Most sought after and most frequent of three similar boleti. Pine boletus and oak boletus are differentiated, apart from colouring, by symbioses with roots of different trees. Stipe of edible boletus has white network in upper part and the smooth cap is pale brown; more frequent summer oak boletus has network with large mesh on whole of stipe; pine boletus has fine, thick network. Edible boletus is found especially in pine-woods from July to October, from lowlands to mountains; oak boletus from spring to September in deciduous forests, occasionally under other trees; pine boletus grows during summer as well as in autumn in sandy pine-woods, rarely in other woods in lower altitudes.

5 *Boletus luteus* (syn. *Ixocomus luteus*). Chocolate brown to brownish-yellow cap with easily peelable, membraneous skin. In wet weather stickily slimy; shiny and smooth when dry. Young fruit bodies have cap connected with stalk by a membraneous skin (volva). After the cap has burst through, the remains of volva appears as a ruff-like ring on the stipe. Stipe above ring whitish-yellow, with a darker speckling. Found in grassy places at outskirts of pine forests, usually during whole summer and autumn, from lowlands to mountains. Excellent edible species.

6 *Boletus chrysenteron*. Cap of young fruiting bodies dark brown, smooth, of older ones yellow-brown with an irregular pattern of reddish cracks. Stalk relatively thin, dirty yellow to yellow-brown with touch of red. Under surface yellow, later olive, taking on a blue tint when bruised. Frequent summer and autumnal mushroom. Grows in all woods, more abundant in pine-woods, from lowlands to foothills. Frequently sought after but not very valuable due to considerable fragility.

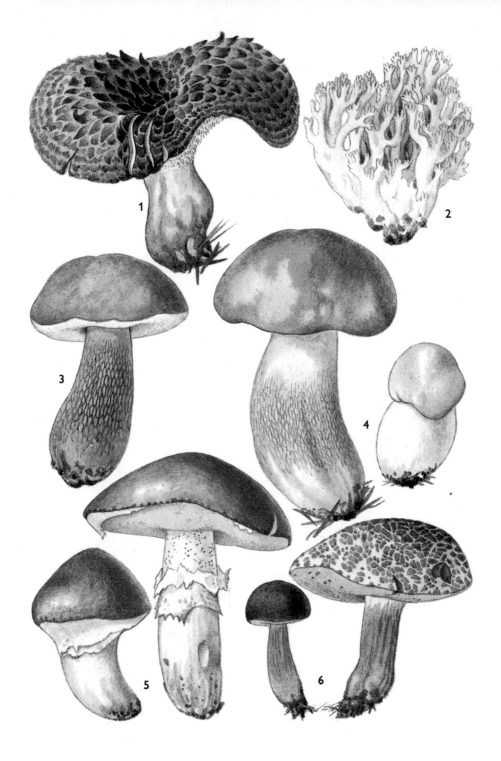

Family: *Boletaceae*

1 *Boletus scaber*. Fleshy cap greyish to dark brown, often cracked in dry conditions, pulp watery whitish, early becomes soft; under surface greyish to buff, also soon becoming soft. Stalk long, tough, whitish to brownish-grey, fibrous, covered with tiny blackish scales, flesh when cut turns faintly rosy. In summer and autumn found frequently under birches or aspens from lowlands to mountains.

2 *Boletus aurantiacus*. Fruit body with dark orange to maroon cap. Stipe long, tough, white to greyish, at first covered with whitish, later with reddish to brownish flaky scales. White flesh turns greyish to black. Occurs abundantly in woodland of various types but usually under aspen and birch. Grows from summer to autumn from lowlands to mountains. A similar species, *Boletus testaceoscaber*, has lighter, rather orange cap; young fruiting bodies have blackish scales on stipe.

Family: *Cantharellaceae*

3 Chanterelle *Cantharellus cibarius*. Young fruit bodies with a convex cap: as it matures, the margins grow up to form a shallow funnel shape. Whole fruit bodies almost yolk yellow, flesh whitish to yellowish. Found from summer to autumn very abundantly in coniferous woods, most frequently in pine-woods. Sought after for preparing fried dishes and pickling in vinegar; not suitable for drying.

Family: *Agaricaceae*

4 *Agaricus campestris*. Young fruit bodies have elongated globose cap, later fibrous, brownish and scaly. Whitish flesh; the gills beneath pinkish, maturing to chocolate brown. Whitish stalk with conspicuous ring encircling it in upper third. Never has sheath at base of stalk as is characteristic of deadly poisonous species such as fool's mushroom *(Amanita verna)* and avenging angel *(Amanita virosa)*. Both differ from *Agaricus campestris* by always white gills and the fact that they grow largely under deciduous trees. *Agaricus campestris* is found in grassy places, mostly out of woods. In forests, especially spruce-woods, it is replaced by horse mushroom *(Agaricus arvensis)*.

Family: *Lepiotaceae*

5 Parasol Mushroom *Lepiota procera*. Stalk up to 35 cm. high; cap at first convex, sometimes with small central swelling or umbo, later widely expanded, brownish with torn scales on surface. Flesh and gills white or whitish. Bulbous based stalk has a loose ring. Grows from summer to autumn in spruce-woods but also in other coniferous or mixed forests and in grassy places from lowlands to mountains. Commonly prepared in various ways for its attractive meaty flavour. Confused perhaps only with relative *Lepiota rhacodes* with a firmly fused ring and flesh turning orange-red when cut.

Family: *Tricholomataceae*

6 St. Georges Mushroom *Tricholoma gambosum*. Popular spring delicacy; grows from April in grass or sparse woods under deciduous trees and shrubs. Cap whitish, yellowish to brownish, gills white or grey-yellow. Short cylindrical whitish stipe. Flesh has a mealy taste and smell. Young fruiting bodies easily mistaken for poisonous *Rhodophyllus sinuatus* (syn. *Entoloma lividum*) which, however, does not grow until summer and has salmon rosy gills when mature.

Family: *Russulaceae*

1 *Russula cyanoxantha*. Cap violet, green, violet-green or greenish with violet tint. Flesh whitish, gills white to yellowish, flexible and not brittle, unlike other members of this genus. Grows abundantly in summer and autumn in mixed or deciduous woods, from lowlands to foothills. Suitable mainly for preparing soups and sauces and for pickling in vinegar in mixture with boleti.

2 Sickener *Russula emetica*. Strikingly red cap hardly confusable with edible mushrooms. Young fruiting body has convex cap, old ones flattened, often shallowly concave in centre. Gills and stipe white to light yellowish, flesh whitish. May cause vomiting if eaten raw. Edible when cooked, but best avoided. Found from summer to autumn in all woods with acid soils, especially in mixed and coniferous forests.

3 Saffron Milk Cap *Lactarius deliciosus*. Young fruiting bodies have convex cap, in maturity expanded, concave in centre, red-orange, as a rule with several dark, mostly green, concentric circles. When cut, flesh releases orange milk, gills become greenish on bruising. Grows mainly in autumn in grassy places in coniferous woods, especially in young spruce-woods. Commonly pickled in vinegar for its characteristic spicy taste. It can hardly be confused with inedible *Lactarius torminosus* which exudes white milk and mostly grows under birches.

Family: *Amanitaceae*

4 Death Cap *Amanita phalloides*. Most poisonous European mushroom. Yellow-green, pure green or brown-green cap is convex at first, later flattened. Stipe, flesh and gills whitish to greenish. Stipe with white skirt-like ring has a cup-shaped base and a conspicuous whitish to greyish sheath, torn at tips. Grows quite abundantly in summer and autumn in deciduous or mixed woods in warmer regions, in coniferous forests especially under pines. Inconspicuous, rather sweetish, treacherous taste. Contains at least two deadly poisonous substances.

5 Blusher *Amanita rubescens*. Fleshy cap is rose to maroon with brownish warty scales. When cut, the flesh is reddish, gills whitish with pink tint. Strong, slender stalk with swollen base. Beneath the cap there is flared whitish to grey-rose ring, usually thickly grooved on upper side. Distinguishable from similar inedible toadstools by reddening of pulp and by ring grooving. *Amanita rubescens* grows in summer and autumn from lowlands to mountains in all types of forests, especially under spruces.

6 Fly Agaric *Amanita muscaria*. Much less poisonous than death cap or avenging angel, being of rather intoxicating character. Cap ornamented with whitish or yellowish warty patches on coral-red surface. Flesh and gills whitish to yellowish, stalk white, with concentric rings of volva remains at base. Ungrooved wide ring under cap. Summer to late autumn in coniferous and birch woods.

Family: *Coprinaceae*

1 *Coprinus micaceus.* Abundant mushroom, growing in gregarious clusters. Occurs on stumps near human dwellings, in gardens, orchards, parks and forests. Cap firstly ovoid, later bell-shaped, often sprinkled with minute, shiny granules. Gills at first white, soon turning grey, later dark brown. Stalk thin, white, without ring. Ripe fruit bodies tend to disintegrate or 'melt' into slimy black substance. Similar *Coprinus* species may be encountered especially near or on old compost and manure heaps etc.

Order: *Gasteromycetales*

Family: *Sclerodermataceae*

2 Earth Ball *Scleroderma aurantium* (syn. *S. citrinum*). Roughly spherical fruiting bodies 3—10 cm. in diameter, sit on the surface of usually peaty soil. Flesh at first whitish, when cut turns pink with violet tint. Young fruiting bodies edible: later become hard and crack into darker scales disclosing the brighter cortical layer. Inside filled with violet-blackish, later black flesh. Finally turns into a black pasty matter that dries up into greyish dust, full of spores. Grows in woods, more often on sandy soils, from summer to autumn.

Family: *Lycoperdaceae*

3 Warted Puffball *Lycoperdon perlatum* (syn. *L. gemmatum*). Narrowed bases of pear-shaped fruiting bodies grow from soil. Surface of young body whitish or creamy, yellowish with pointed warts. Ripe fruiting body smooth with irregularly round aperture on top; when pressed or stepped on, a cloud of brownish spores is puffed out of this opening. Summer and autumnal, growing from lowlands high up to mountains, in meadows, pastures and spruce-woods, often in great numbers. Young fruit bodies with white flesh edible.

4 *Bovista plumbea.* Young fruiting bodies almost globose, slightly compressed on top; outer surface whitish, inside pure white. Ripe ones dark grey, filled with brown dust-like spore mass; when pressed, spores fly out through oval opening on top. In summer and autumn found abundantly in grassy places, at the edges of meadows and pastures and on the outskirts of forests, from lowlands to mountains. Edible when young; has excellent delicate taste.

Family: *Geastraceae*

5 *Geastrum fimbriatum.* Young fruiting bodies more or less globose; in maturity outer layer cracks into four ray-like segments which turn inside out thrusting up the ovoid fruiting 'capsule' on a short stem-like neck. Grows in summer and autumn from lowlands to mountains with other species of earth-stars, often in groups, especially in spruce-woods. Unsuitable for eating.

Family: *Phallaceae*

6 Stinkhorn *Phallus impudicus.* Conspicuous for its appearance and in maturity also for the disgusting smell of decaying flesh. Slightly reminiscent of morel with long, cylindrical stalk and conical, pitted cap. Globular fruiting bodies rather resemble small puffballs when young as they are covered with white-skinned jelly-like layer. In mature specimens only conspicuous sheath at stalk base remains of this layer. Stalk up to 25 cm. high, thickly and shallowly porous. Cap covered with olive greenish slime which attracts insects that normally feed on carrion. Grows from summer to autumn in deciduous woods and in gardens on humus-rich soil. Mature fruiting bodies inedible because of bad odour.

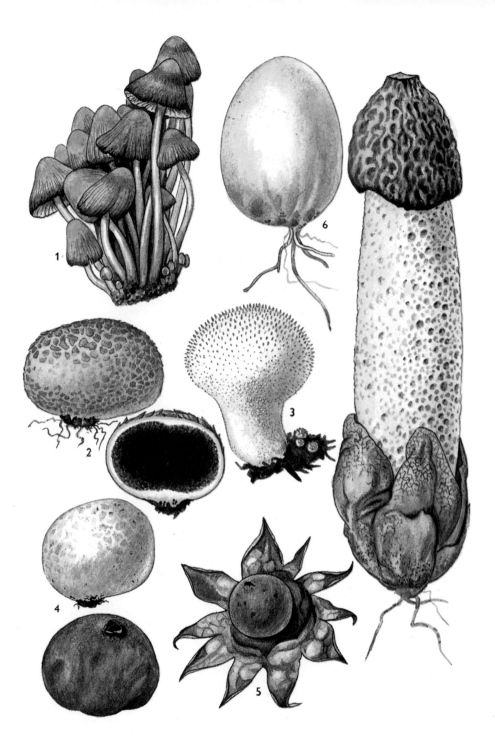

Division: **Lichens** — *Lichenes*

Class: *Ascolichenes*

Family: *Buelliaceae*

1 *Rhizocarpon geographicum*. Appears as yellow-green, black striated patches on non-limestone rocks. Irregularly lobed thalluses form striking designs resembling maps. Thin, corticular thallus contains in addition to algal cells also hyphae of an *Ascomycetes*. (*Basidiomycetes* are a component of tropical lichens.) Tiny fruit bodies of fungal component are black with multicellular spores. Grows mainly in mountains, most often on granite boulders.

2 *Cladonia arbuscula* (syn. *C. sylvatica*). Very abundant species, resembling reindeer moss from which it differs especially in colouring; it is yellow-green or straw-yellow, its podetia are narrower and slightly brownish at the shoot ends. Fungal component sometimes forms tiny maroon thalluses on twig tips. Grows in similar places as reindeer moss, often together forming extensive carpets.

3 Reindeer Moss *Cladonia rangiferina*. Forms conspicuous whitish or greyish bushes, abundantly branched. Twigs bent to one side, with brownish tips. Often grows in great quantity in dry pine-woods and on heathland, from lowlands to mountains. Can survive long periods of drought; in rain takes in moisture very quickly again.

4 *Cladonia fimbriata*. 1—3 cm. high cups, olive or grey-green on upper side, whitish on under side, grow from a basal scaly podetium. Fungal component forms short-stalked, brownish fruit bodies on margins of cups. Cup surface covered with powdery segments, containing alga cells wound around with fungal hyphae. Grows on dry sites, in open woods, heathlands, on decayed stumps and mossy rocks from lowlands to mountains. Related species have fungal fruit bodies scarlet-red and cup rims strikingly notched.

Family: *Peltigeraceae*

5 *Peltigera canina*. Thallus broadly lobed, sometimes with lobes up to 5 cm. wide, upper side grey-white or brownish, finely felt-like, underside whitish, covered with numerous bunches of fungal rhizoids. Fruiting bodies of fungal component brown, tubular, erect at end of lobes. Common lichen from lowlands high up to mountains. Grows in sunny spots, on mossy rocks, on putrefying trunks as well as in meadows.

Family: *Parmeliaceae*

6 *Hypogymnia physodes* (syn. *Parmelia physodes*). Probably the most frequently found lichen. Its rosette-like thallus is greyish to grey-green on upper surface, dark brown to black on underside, bordered with white. Fruiting bodies of fungal component appear only rarely. Grows abundantly from lowlands to foothills; related species also in mountains. In suitable places forms extensive coatings on tree trunks and branches. Also grows on stumps, dead trunks, less often on rocks and earth.

7 Iceland Moss *Cetraria islandica*. Thallus chestnut to dark brown, sinuately branched, spiny margined, ascending, up to 10 cm. high, or more. Grows on moorland and heathland and in forests and peat-bogs; indicator of poor acid soils.

Family: *Usneaceae*

8 *Evernia prunastri*. Grows from lowlands to mountains on bark of deciduous trees, old shrubs, also on trunks of felled trees, in orchards, parks, gardens and open woods; abundant everywhere, rare only on rocks. Soft thallus is many-branched, often more or less pendent, grey-green to yellow-green, lighter on underside, white-spotted edges and upper side. Similar species, *Evernia furfuracea*, with black-violet underside of thallus grows in similar places and on rocks and walls at higher altitudes.

Family: *Teloschistaceae*

9 *Xanthoria parietina*. Brightly coloured thalluses are light to orange yellow, arranged in rosettes, forming neat patches on trees, rocks and walls. Dish-like fruiting bodies of fungal component are very frequently seen. Grows from lowlands to mountains, but particularly near the sea.

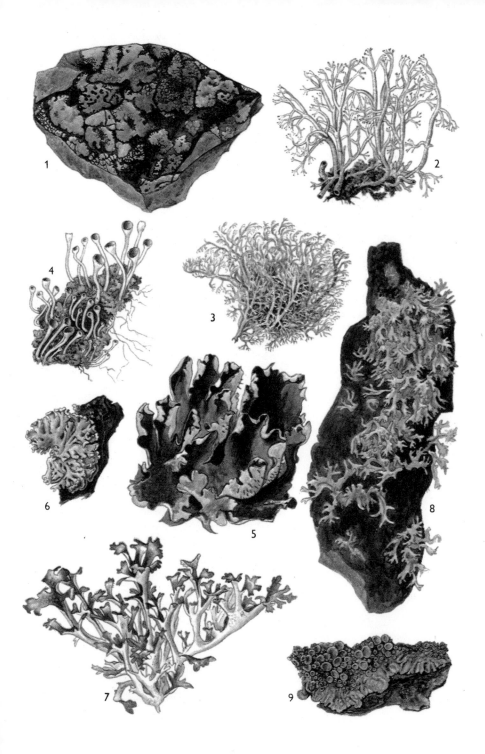

Division: **Mosses and Liverworts** — *Bryophyta*

Class: **Liverworts** — *Hepaticopsida*

Family: *Marchantiaceae*

1 *Marchantia polymorpha.* Lamellar thallus broadly ribbon-shaped, forked, ground hugging. The upper side has conspicuous air chambers just beneath the surface, each having a breathing pore. Dioecious plant with sexual organs on stalked discs; male discs irregularly lobular, female ones star-shaped. Vegetative propagation by special tiny bodies *(gemmae)* embedded in shallow cups. Forms dark green coatings everywhere in moist places; particularly in gardens and greenhouses. Grows from lowlands to mountains in sunny or semi-shaded places.

Class: **Mosses** — *Bryopsida* (syn. *Musci*)

Subclass: *Sphagnidae*

Family: *Sphagnaceae*

2 *Sphagnum palustre.* Requires plenty of light as do majority of bog-mosses. Forms soft pale green carpets. Stems 10—40 cm. high with clustered side branches rosetted towards the tips; more frequently than in other bog-mosses stem bears at apex round brown capsules which explode on ripening. All members of this genus are important for creation of moss peat.

Subclass: **True Mosses** — *Bryidae*

Family: *Polytrichaceae*

3 *Polytrichum commune.* Stout moss whose simple, erect stems can reach a length of 25 cm. Sharply notched leaflets during dry spells thickly overlap and cover stem, standing out and apart in wet weather. Red stalk about 10 cm. long. Large capsule covered with hairy, yellow to reddish brown calyptra. Grows in mountains, hill country, heathland, along forest streams and in clearings. Tiny relative *Polytrichum formosum* is more frequent in lowlands Its leaves stand apart even during dry conditions.

Family: *Dicranaceae*

4 *Dicranum scoparium.* Erect stems up to 10 cm. high, thickly set with sickle-bent, blunt leaflets, finely notched at tip. Stems 2—4 cm. high, reddish, with brown, cylindrical, slightly bent capsule having a long-beaked reddish lid. Cap overlaps from lid to capsule. A moss of coniferous woods, growing abundantly on ground, tree stumps, trunks, boulders and rocks, from lowlands to mountains.

Family: *Ditrichaceae*

5 *Ceratodon purpureus.* Erect stems, sparsely covered with narrow, finely pointed leaves, having inrolled margins; they twist up together in dry weather. Stalk shiny dark red, erect at first, but leaning over horizontally as the capsule ripens. Cap overlaps lid and covers over half of capsule. Grows abundantly from lowlands to mountains, on burnt ground, in clearings, on heathland, rocks and walls.

Family: *Leucobryaceae*

6 *Leucobryum glaucum.* Forms dense rounded hummocks of distinctive grey-green foliage. Stems bear entire leaves with upturned rim that lack a central rib. Dioecious moss, only very rarely fruitful; female plants have dark purple stems 1—2 cm. high. Grows in moist woods and on moorland.

Family: *Funariaceae*

1 *Funaria hygrometrica.* Grows on bare ground, heathland, walls and roofs, and is one of the first colonizers on burnt ground. Simple stems are not more than 3 cm. high, upper leaves rolled and bud-like when dry, short-pointed and entire. Sporophyte stalk is yellow to red, twisted, nodding at the tip with a grooved brown capsule.

Family: *Bryaceae*

2 *Bryum argenteum.* Tiny moss forming pale to silvery-green cushions. Stems only 1—2 cm. high with ovate and pointed leaves. Pendent capsule is red-brown, elongated cylindrical to ovoid, with small pointed lid; the short (about 1 cm.) stalk is also red. Grows from lowlands to foothills but is more frequent in lower altitudes on walls, rocks, along roads, among paving-stones and in similar places. It is one of the very few mosses found in big cities.

Family: *Mniaceae*

3 *Mnium punctatum.* This and other species of *Mnium* are frequent from lowlands to high up in mountains. Reddish stems are up to 5 cm. high with relatively large, almost rounded leaves which are covered with pellucid dots. Stalk 2—4 cm. high, usually reddish, at top yellow, with drooping or horizontal capsule. Capsule with elongated and sharply beaked lid and a shiny brown cap. Grows abundantly in moist woods, on banks of forest streams and in mountains. Often fertile.

Family: *Hypnaceae*

4 *Pleurozium schreberi* (syn. *Hypnum schreberi*). Stems red, up to 15 cm. long, ascending, pinnately branched, in two regular rows; branches at top recurving. Leaves overlapping, convex, broadly ovate, with double veins; those on branches are smaller than on main stems. Dioecious, fertile only in places. Then a thin, corrugated red stalk with elongated, curved capsule develops on female plant. Grows not only in coniferous and mixed forests but also in meadows, on grassy slopes and rocks where acid conditions are found.

Family: *Hylocomiaceae*

5 *Hylocomium splendens.* Stems red, up to 20 cm. long, rigid, bi- to tripinnately branched, conspicuously flattened. Main stem leaves sessile, overlapping, ovate, elongated, abruptly tapering to long points; margins of upper third finely serrate; leaves of branches oval, smaller, abruptly tapering to a fine point, serrate. Dioecious species; female plant up to 4 cm. high, with pendent, ovoid capsules. Grows in forests, on grassy slopes, among rocks overgrown with vegetation and in meadows. Often fertile.

Family: *Rhytidiaceae*

6 *Rhytidiadelphus triquetrus.* Reddish stems are densely leaved, up to 15 cm. long, erect or semi-prostrate, irregularly branched. Leaves lanceolate, pointed, spreading, in upper part finely serrate and grooved. Dioecious plant, stalk about 2—5 cm. high, sinuously corrugated, red. Capsule shortly ovate, pendent, red, with warty navel-shaped lid. Common in shady places in mixed forests, especially on limestone in spruce-beech growths; also on grassy slopes, sand dunes and sometimes on moorland.

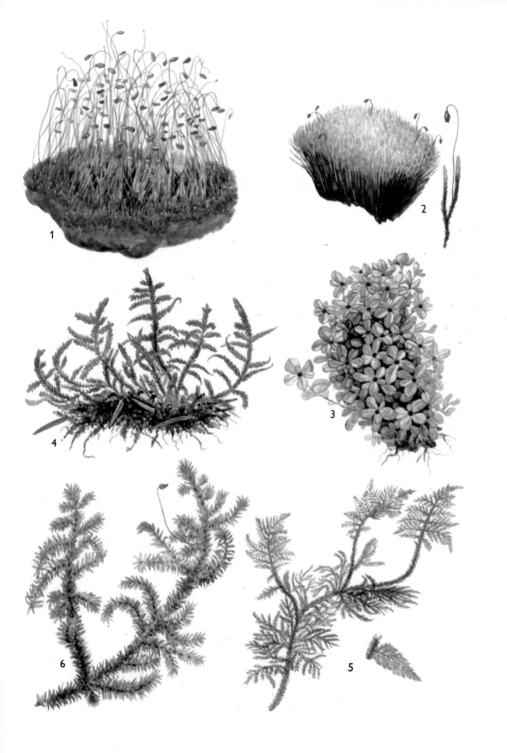

Division: **Vascular Plants** — *Tracheophyta*

Distinct from the preceding groups, the vascular plants form the asexual generation; the sexual generation is as a rule very small, often microscopic. In *Pteridophytina* the sexual generation is independent of the plant proper as regards nutrition, in gymnosperms and angiosperms it is hidden in special organs of the asexual generation and is completely dependant on it for nutrition.

The plant body is distinctly differentiated into root, stem and leaves and is penetrated by a system of water-conducting tissues, or vascular bundles, that ensure transport of water and nutritive substances. The anatomic as well as morphologic structure is more complicated than in fungi and mosses.

Sub-division: **Clubmosses, Horsetails and Ferns** — *Pteridophytina*

Multicellular green, spore-bearing plants, completely adapted to life on dry land. The alternation of sexual and asexual generation is not readily observable. The bodies of clubmosses, horsetails and ferns form the asexual generation while the sexual one is much reduced, often microscopic. Besides assimilating leaves they have sporophylls that sometimes differ from them. These bear the sporangia. Horsetails and clubmosses have conspicuous cone-shaped sets of leaves which bear the sporangia.

Spores may be identical as regards their shape, size and physiological function; in this case they germinate into a *prothallus* with male and female organs — antheridia and archegonia. Heterosporous species have spores of two types which develop into unisexual prothalli either with antheridia or archegonia only.

Pteridophytina are not a uniform group; they only represent a certain stage of development of spore-bearing plants. The extinct *Pterophyta*, abundant in the Paleozoic Era, helped to form the coal measures.

Class: **Clubmosses** — *Lycopodiopsida*

Spore-bearing plants with asexual generation differentiated into root, stem, leaves and sporangia. The stems are not articulated, but usually forked. Small, sessile and single-veined leaves often possess a scaly outgrowth — the ligule — on the upper surface. The sporangia are placed at the base of the upper side of sporophylls which form cone-shaped spikes. Clubmosses have a bisexual or unisexual, very simplified, prothallus. The female spores ripen in the archegonia, the spermatozoids are borne in the antheridia. Some species also produce vegetative buds which are dispersed by wind and water.

Systematic classification (extinct groups not included):

Order: *Lycopodiales.* Spores identical, prothallus bisexual with archegonia as well as antheridia. Leaves without ligule.

Unrepresented order: *Selaginellales.* Sporangia and spores different, prothallus unisexual either with one archegonium or one antheridium. Leaves with ligule.

Unrepresented order: *Isoëtales.* Both spores and sporophylls are heterosexual, prothallus unisexual, very reduced. They are related to the extinct tree-like clubmosses of the Paleozoic Era. Plants associated with wet places or aquatic.

The classification of clubmosses into families is based on the arrangement of sporophylls.

Class: **Horsetails** — *Sphenopsida* (syn. *Equiṣetopsida*)

Spore-bearing plants with the asexual generation differentiated into root, stem, leaves and sporangia. The stems are distinctly articulated, with the lateral branches arranged in whorls. The leaves are tiny, scale or sheath-like, single-veined. Sporophylls are distinctly different from assimilating leaves; they are stalked, shield-like, with several sporangia on the under surface and are arranged in terminal cone-shaped spikes. The horsetails are homo- as well as heterosporous, but even the homosporous species have a unisexual prothallus. Each spore has four hygroscopic spiral bands that during the fluctuation of humidity variously twist and mutually intertwine, thus several spores are held together. This fact guarantees that several dioecious prothalli will grow side by side, ensuring the fertilization of a macrospore in the archegonium by some of the spermatozoids, borne in the antheridia. The horsetails, not to mention extinct groups, are represented by one single order — *Equisetales* — with one family and one genus.

Class: **Ferns** — *Filicopsida* (syn. *Polypodiopsida*)

Spore-bearing plants with an independent asexual generation; they consist of roots, stems, leaves and sporangia. The stems are not articulated. Contrary to the two preceding classes the leaves are large with a rich venation, often pinnate and arranged into rich, fan-shaped groups. Young leaves are usually conspicuously spirally rolled. Sporangia are placed mostly on the underside of assimilating leaf-blades, sometimes the sporophylls are different from assimilating leaves. The ferns are either homo- or heterosporous; in the former the prothalli are bisexual, in the latter unisexual.

Systematic classification (extinct groups omitted):

Unrepresented subclass: *Marattiidae.* Tropical ferns. Several thick-walled sporangia grow always together in special structures. Large multipinnate leaves.

Subclass: *Ophioglossidae* (p. 38). Ferns with a single leaf, differentiated into a flat assimilating part and a stalked, sometimes branched, part with thick-walled, sessile sporangia. Young leaves are not spirally rolled.

Subclass: *Polypodiidae* (p. 40). Young leaves usually spirally rolled. Stalked sporangia, mostly thin-walled, form sori on the edge or on underside of blades. These are usually protected by indusium.

Unrepresented order: *Osmundales.* Partially thick-walled sporangia without indusia and ring. Spores of one form. Prothallus large, living several years, bisexual.

Order: *Polypodiales* (p. 40). Thin-walled sporangia with conspicuous ring (annulus) often with indusium. Spores of one form. Prothallus small, of short duration, bisexual.

Order: *Salviniales* (p. 42). Aquatic ferns. Sporangia without ring, closed in sporocarps, spores of two forms. Prothalli very small, consist only of several cells, unisexual. Young leaves not spirally rolled.

Unrepresented order: *Marsileales.* Plants of wet places or aquatic. Young leaves spirally rolled. Clusters of sporangia enclosed in sporocarps; spores of two forms, prothalli develop inside them. Male prothallus with a single antheridium, female one with a single archegonium.

The classification of families is based on the location of sori, shape and structure of spores, the way sporangia open to release spores, type of venation and the structure of vascular bundles in the leaves.

Division: **Vascular Plants** — *Tracheophyta*

Sub-division: *Pteridophytina*

Class: **Clubmosses** — *Lycopodiopsida*

Family: *Lycopodiaceae*

1 Stag's-horn Clubmoss *Lycopodium clavatum*. Creeping stems of up to 1 m. long, forked into shorter erect stalks. Leaves linear lanceolate, entire to irregularly notched, hairy. Spore-bearing spikes arranged usually in pairs on thin stalks with tiny, sessile leaflets. Sporophylls widely ovate, with colourless, soft spicule. Grows in open forests, on heathland and among rocks in mountains, from lowlands to mountains. Sporangia ripen from June to August.

Family: *Huperziaceae*

2 Fir Clubmoss *Lycopodium selago* (syn. *Huperzia selago*). Erect, tufted, branched stems up to 25 cm. high. Leaves erect, spreading, soft, linear-lanceolate, entire. Sporangia do not form terminal spikes; they are placed mostly in upper part of stem on sporophylls, similar to other leaflets. Often produces bulbils in leaf axils at end of branches. Grows in humid, shady woods, among rocks and on ledges, particularly in mountains. Sporangia mature from July to October.

Class: **Horsetails** — *Sphenopsida* (syn. *Equisetopsida*)

Family: *Equisetaceae*

3 Common Horsetail *Equisetum arvense.* Species with two types of stems: spring stem terminates in spore-bearing spike, summer stem sterile. Spring stems are 10—20 cm. high, yellowish to brownish, with cylindrical, slightly inflated, light green, notched sheaths. Spore-bearing spike up to 3 cm. long, brownish; after spores are released in March and April spring stems die. Summer stems about 50 cm. high, with distinct ribs. Both stems and branches have ribbed brownish sheaths. Common weed in fields and gardens, by the roadside and in open woods from lowlands to mountains.

4 Wood Horsetail *Equisetum sylvaticum*. Stems of two types: spring stem up to 50 cm. high, at first wax-pink, during ripening of sporangia turns green, later resembles summer stems. These grow almost simultaneously with spring stems; are regularly branched, branches are slender and pendent and further branched. Sheaths slightly inflated, funnel-shaped, teeth tinted with red. Grows gregariously in moist places in forests from lowlands to mountains on poor soils. Sporangia ripen from April to June.

5 Water Horsetail *Equisetum fluviatile*. Robust stems over 1 m. high with fine ribs, often unbranched and shiny, submerged parts maroon. Sessile sheaths glossy, lower ones reddish, upper green with black, awl-shaped teeth bordered with white. Spore-bearing spike short and ovoid. Sporangia mature from May to July. Grows from lowlands to mountains, in wet places, bogs, and on muddy banks of rivers and lakes.

Class: **Ferns** — *Filicopsida* (syn. *Polypodiopsida*)

Subclass: *Ophioglossidae*

Family: *Ophioglossaceae*

6 Adder's Tongue Fern *Ophioglossum vulgatum*. Small fern, about 8—20 cm. high, with underground rhizome and one single leaf. Sterile part of leaf leathery, ovoid, entire, yellow-green and mat-shiny; spore-bearing part with sporangia, arranged in two parallel rows close together. Sporangia ripen from June to August. Grows in marshy and mountain meadows, and moist clearings in woods, more frequently on limestone. A very small form *(O. lusitanicum)* is found on grassy cliff tops in the Channel Isles and Scilly Isles and in Mediterranean regions.

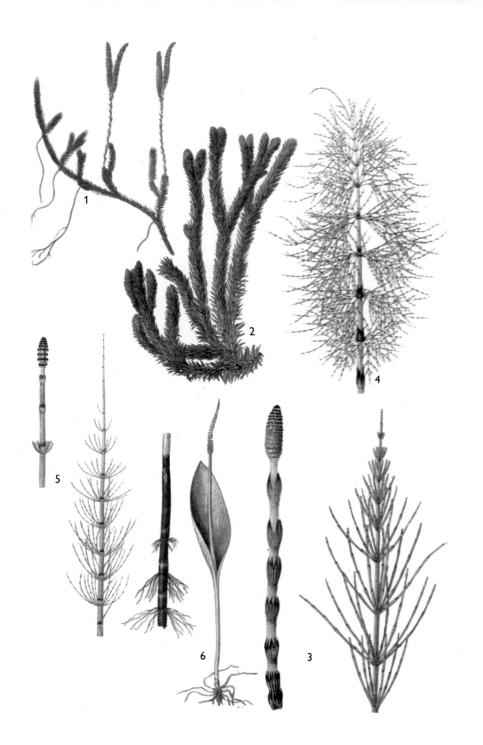

Family: *Ophioglossaceae*

1 Common Moonwort *Botrychium lunaria*. Small fern up to 5—15 cm. or more high. Sterile part of single leaf simply pinnate, spore-bearing part bi- to tripinnate. Sterile part composed of 4—7 or more pairs of fan-shaped, entire or scalopped, leathery segments. Spore-bearing part long-stalked, terminating with sporangia arranged in two rows on linear segments. Sporangia yellow-brown, later of cinnamon shade, ripen from May to June. Grows from lowlands to high up in the mountains, in meadows, pastures and among rocks; generally of localized distribution.

Subclass: *Polypodiidae*

Order: *Polypodiales*

Family: *Matteuciaceae*

2 Ostrich Fern *Matteuccia struthiopteris* (syn. *Struthiopteris germanica*). Fan of up to 150 cm. high, sterile leaves, grows from robust rhizome. Blades simply pinnate, segments fine, linear-lanceolate. Spore leaves only 50—60 cm. high, grow in centre of sterile fronds and have segments at first rolled, later unrolled. Sori ripen from June to August. Grows in moist places, along streams and rivers, in forests, from lowlands to mountains. Also cultivated for ornament.

Family: *Blechnaceae*

3 Hard Fern *Blechnum spicant*. A fern with leaves of two types; the sterile ones over-wintering, leathery, pinnately divided to mid-rib. Segments dark green, linear-lanceolate, entire. Non-leafy sporophylls, growing from centre of tuft, are longer, erect, up to 40 cm. high, with interrupted pinnate to linear segments, bearing sori which ripen from July to September. Grows, often gregariously, in woods, on moors, heaths, mountain grassland and among rocks.

Family: *Aspidiaceae* (syn. *Dryopteridaceae*)

4 Male Fern *Dryopteris filix-mas*. Robust fern over 1 m. high, with rusty-scaly rhizome. Leaf stalks bearing pale brown scales. Leaf blade deeply pinnately divided, pinnules dark green, lighter on underside, with toothed margins. Large sori adhere to mid-rib of pinnules; indusia kidney-shaped. Sporangia ripen from June to September. Grows in shady woods, among boulders and in hedgerows, from lowlands to mountains.

5 Beech Fern *Thelypteris phegopteris* (syn. *Phegopteris polypodioides*). Long-stalked leaves, up to 10—30 cm. or more high, grow from long rhizome. Blades simply pinnate, lanceolate leaflets deeply pinnately lobed, more or less hairy. Conspicuous backwards slant of lowest pair of leaves and fusion of lowest pinnules with mid-rib aid in identifying this fern. Sori rounded, light brown, on border of pinnules; no indusia. Sporangia ripen in June and July. Grows in moist, shady woods, among rocks and on banks of forest streams, from lowlands to mountains.

Family: *Athyriaceae*

6 Brittle Bladder Fern *Cystopteris fragilis*. Long-stalked fronds, 8—25 cm. or more high, grow from short rhizome. Fragile, dark brown petioles usually shorter than bipinnate blades, with deeply lobed and notched leaflets; sori in two rows either side of pinnule mid-rib. Sporangia ovoid pointed, ripening from June to September. Grows on walls, rocks and screes, also in shady woods, from lowlands to mountains. Only found in the north and west of Great Britain.

40

Family: *Athyriaceae*

1 Lady Fern *Athyrium filix-femina*. Leaves 20—100 cm. or more high, with stalk and mid-rib often purplish and bearing a few chaffy scales. Grows from short, dark brown, scaly rhizome. Freshly green, bi- to tripinnate leaves with alternate, lanceolate, long-pointed leaflets; pinnules ovate to lanceolate, toothed. Margins of pinnules with crescent or kidney-shaped sori; sporangia ripen from July to September. Grows abundantly and often gregariously from lowlands to mountains, in moist forests, and shady places on acid soils.

Family: *Aspleniaceae*

2 Forked Spleenwort *Asplenium septentrionale*. Small evergreen fern, 4 to 15 cm. high, short, black-brown scaly rhizome and narrow blades, black-brown at base. Blades have slender, forked pinnules. Sori cover almost whole under surface of pinnules. Sporangia ripen from June to October. Grows in sunny places, in cracks of acid rocks, rarely on walls, from lowlands to mountains. Rare in Britain.

3 Wall Rue *Asplenium ruta-muraria*. Long-stalked evergreen leaves, bipinnate, dark green, up to 3—12 cm. high, grow from creeping rootstock. Pinnules obovate to lanceolate with crenate or dentate margins. Linear, coalescent sori ripen from June to October. Grows in cracks of rocks, walls, and screes, almost always on limestone, from lowlands to mountains. Related maidenhair spleenwort, *A. trichomanes*, has leaves simply pinnate and oval or oblong pinnules.

Family: *Pteridaceae*

4 Bracken *Pteridium aquilinum*. A deciduous fern up to 2 metres high with stout cylindrical petioles up to 1 m. long, which grow from thick, black, creeping rhizomes. Blades triangular bi- to tripinnate, light green, lanceolate to oblong pinnules, lobed at base, with marginal sori. Sporangia ripen from July to September. Grows gregariously in open woods, especially pine-woods, and on heath and moorland, usually on acid soils, from lowlands to mountains. This fern and its subspecies is distributed all over world; important cosmopolitan species.

Family: *Polypodiaceae*

5 Common Polypody *Polypodium vulgare*. Long-petioled evergreen leaves, pinnately divided into alternate, lanceolate and entire, somewhat leathery blunt tipped pinnules, grow from creeping rhizomes. Two rows of relatively large, rounded sori without indusia on under surface of pinnules. Sporangia ripen from May to September. Grows in woods, on shady, mossy rocks, and on trunks and branches of deciduous trees.

Order: *Salviniales*

Family: *Salviniaceae*

6 Water-fern *Salvinia natans*. Tiny floating 'fern'. Stem 5—15 cm. long, bears leaves in whorls of three of which two are always floating, short-stalked with undivided blade, tufted with hair-like papillae on upper surface; third leaf transformed into numerous, root-like submerged segments. Sporangia of two types: small male and large female ones, closed in sporocarps. Ripen in August and September. Grows locally, in lakes and slow flowing rivers, mainly in central and southern Europe. Often grown as aquarium plant.

Sub-division: **Gymnosperms** — *Gymnospermae* (syn. *Coniferophytina*)

Multicellular, green seed-bearing plants; exclusively trees and shrubs. The leaves are mainly small or narrow, often needle-like, rarely broad with fan-shaped venation; mainly evergreen. Vascular bundles are usually formed by tracheids, the true water-conducting vessels are missing. (Tracheids are narrow tubular cells whose transverse partitions are not perforated. Vessels are relatively broad tubes, originated from a series of elongated cells without transverse partitions.) Flowers are unisexual, monoecious or dioecious. True floral envelopes are absent. Male sporophylls are transformed into stamens and form cone-like flowers or strobili, the pollen grains correspond to male spores. Female sporangia are transformed into naked ovules which are borne on the upper surface of the sporophylls. The latter become woody as they mature and form the scales of the characteristic cone. The sexual generation is part of the asexual one, protected in its organs and fully nourished by it. The fertilization of the egg-cell by the male pollen nucleus takes place via the pollen tube germinating from the pollen grain. The fertilized ovule develops into a naked uncovered seed and the whole female inflorescence or strobilus becomes a woody cone.

The *Coniferopsida* (pines, firs, cypresses, etc.) are a very ancient group, perfectly adapted to contemporary climatic conditions; by growing in community they have a decisive influence on the topography and climate of extensive territories.

Unrepresented classes:

Cycadopsida. Palm-like plants with leathery, palmate leaves, spirally rolled when young. Usually dioecious plants; ovules borne on blade margins. Fertilization of egg-cell by mobile spermatozoid. Naked seeds resemble drupes.

Ephedropsida. Shrubby plants with small, scaly leaves; young ones are not spirally rolled. Tiny, unisexual, dioecious flowers, usually with a primitive perianth. Fertilization via male pollen cell. Naked seeds hidden in persistent perianth.

Ginkgopsida. Fan-shaped, bilobed leaves. Dioecious flowers; male pendent, catkin-like, female long-stalked with two small ovoid ovules. Fertilization by mobile spermatozoids. Seed resembles plum in shape and structure.

Represented class: *Coniferopsida* (p. 50). Leaves usually scale- or needle-like, stems and leaves with resin canals. Unisexual, mono- as well as dioecious flowers. Fertilization of egg-cell via male pollen cell.

Order: *Taxales* (p. 50). Dioecious shrubs or trees. Female cones considerably reduced, bud-like, with a single erect ovule, covered at maturity by a fleshy cup-like structure.

Order: *Pinales* (p. 50). Usually monoecious robust trees, plus a few of shrubby habit. Female cones (strobili) have fleshy seed scales, usually with two ovules, in axils of supporting bracts. Seeds rest on upper side of seed scales but are protected by enlarging of scales which grow tightly together, and become tough and woody.

In the classification of families the structure of cones, number of ovules and the leaf attachment and shape are applied.

Sub-division: **Angiosperms** — *Angiospermae* (syn. *Angiospermophytina*)

Multicellular, usually green, seed-bearing plants whose seeds are enclosed in fruits. The bodies of angiospermous plants represent the asexual generation, as a rule differentiated into root, stem and leaves, with perfectly developed vascular bundles, containing usually in addition to tracheids also vessels. The leaves are relatively large, mainly with flat blades, simple or compound. The generative organs are enclosed by a true flower and after pollination and fertilization the seeds develop within a fruit (which may be fleshy or dry). The carpels are often fused together into the pistil in which ovules are contained. The ovule as a rule has two envelopes. The egg-cell is fertilized by a pollen grain nucleus. The fertilized egg-cell develops into the embryo contained within the seed, usually with nutritive tissue, known as *endosperm*. The ovules develop into the seeds simultaneously with the enlargement and swelling of the ovary walls into a pericarp; therefore the seeds are not naked but protected within a fruit. The flowers of angiosperms are predominantly bisexual (hermaphrodite), sometimes unisexual as a result of the disappearance of the other sex organs — stamens or pistil. In a bisexual flower the central pistil is usually surrounded by stamens either in spirals or in one or more circles. Floral envelopes are usually differentiated into an inner, often coloured, corolla and outer, mostly green, calyx; sometimes they remain undifferentiated, forming a perianth; finally the corolla and sometimes also the calyx may not be present.

Stamens are usually formed of a thin filament, and an anther of two pollen sacs joined by connective tissue. As distinct from the preceding groups, the male cells of the germinated pollen grain are not formed as spermatozoids.

The pistil has a hollow ovary containing ovules and is provided with a style bearing a stigma, where the pollen grains, transported by insects or wind during the pollination, are caught. The pollen tubes from grains, germinated on the stigma, penetrate through the style into the ovary cavity to the ovules. Fertilization, therefore, does not take place on the uncovered ovules as in the case of conifers, but in the ovary cavity. Thus we see that in the angiospermous plants, the sexual and asexual generations have reached a state of complete interdependence. The main feature, the fact that the ovules and seeds are covered and that a fruit develops, gives protection from unfavourable environmental effects; it is another adaptation to dry-land life.

Angiospermous plants are known from fossils originating from as early as the Mesozoic Era. They are estimated to originate about 200 million years ago; the territory extending from south-eastern Asia to Pacific Islands and north Australia is considered to be their probable original habitat.

Although angiosperms are a very numerous and varied group of plants, it is possible to assume their common origin from a single, long extinct, group of plants from the sphere of coniferous *Cycadopsida* and *Filicopsida*.

Class: **Angiospermous Plants** — *Magnoliopsida*

Subclass: **Dicotyledones** — *Magnoliidae* (syn. *Dicotyledonae*)

The seed contains two seed leaves or cotyledons between which the growing point is situated. After germination and during further development the first root or radicle stays as the main root, branching to produce lateral roots. Vascular bundles in the stem are circularly arranged and have a special tissue (the *cambium*) whose activities result in the secondary thickening of the stems of woody plants; trees and shrubs have stems with evident annual rings. Leaves are of various shapes and usually have a net-like venation. Flowers usually have floral envelopes differentiated into calyx or sepals and corolla or petals; usually they are tetramerous or pentamerous. Flowers may be borne singly or in clusters of few to many. From the great number of orders and families we include only those which occur most frequently.

Order: *Ranales* (syn. *Ranunculales*). Both herbs (*Nymphaeaceae*, p. 76, *Ranunculaceae*, p. 76 [with few exceptions]) and woody plants (*Berberidaceae*, p. 54). Flowers mostly regular, radiate, sometimes asymmetrical; the more primitive spiral arrangement of floral parts changes into circular or whorled. Usually many stamens; carpels mostly free or imperfectly fused together. Tissues of many species contain a number of poisonous substances, e.g. alkaloids, etc.

Order: *Aristolochiales*. Herbs as well as woody plants, often climbers. Flowers regular or asymmetrical, with unified perianth and usually trimerous (*Aristolochiaceae*, p. 84).

Order: *Papaverales*. Usually herbs. Flowers solitary or in branched inflorescences; calyx often falling as the flower opens, flowers bisexual, regular (*Papaveraceae*, p. 84), or asymmetrical (*Fumariaceae*, p. 86). Arrangement of floral parts usually in two whorls (*Cruciferae*, p. 86, *Resedaceae*, p. 90).

Order: *Cistales*. Herbs and woody plants with a number of foreign families. Common feature: ovary as a rule formed of three carpels, ovules growing on walls of ovary (*Cistaceae*, p. 90, *Violaceae*, p. 96).

Order: *Phytolaccales*. Herbs, trees and shrubs: ovules borne in ovary on central column. (*Caryophyllaceae*, p. 94, *Chenopodiaceae*, p. 96).

Order: *Polygonales*. Herbs and woody plants, including climbers, with unisexual or bisexual flowers. One-celled ovary with a single ovule. Perigone persists on fruit (*Polygonaceae*, p. 98).

Order: *Santalales*. Herbs or woody plants (*Loranthaceae*, p. 54), mostly semi-parasitic. Leaves simple, entire, without stipules; perianth often not differentiated.

Order: *Urticales*. Herbs and woody plants (*Urticaceae*, p. 100, *Cannabaceae*, p. 98, *Ulmaceae*, p. 54). Flowers without a perianth or with scaly perigone; ovary superior with a single ovule.

Order: *Sarraceniales*. Insectivorous herbs, conspicuous for leaf modifications enabling them to catch and digest insects and other small animals (*Droseraceae*, p. 100).

Order: *Rosales*. Woody plants or herbs (*Saxifragaceae*, p. 102, *Crassulaceae*, p. 100, *Rosaceae*, p. 54, 102). Alternate stipular leaves. Regular or asymmetric flowers, pentamerous, rarely 4- or 6-merous. As a rule many stamens (usually multiple of 5), number of carpels similarly different, from many down to a single one. Fruits are achenes, samaras, drupes, pomes, follicles or pods.

Order: *Fabales*. Herbs and woody plants with alternate, stipular, compound leaves. Usually symmetrical flowers, pentamerous, rarely 4-merous; perianths and filaments of stamens wholly or partially fused together. Single pistil; fruit usually a pod (*Fabaceae*, p. 58, 108).

Order: *Hamamelidales*. Woody plants with simple leaves. Usually regular, bisexual flowers; corolla often reduced. Pistil consists of two carpels, fused together (*Platanaceae*, p. 60).

Order: *Juglandales*. Woody plants with alternate, odd-pinnate leaves without stipules. Flowers unisexual, monoecious without a perianth, inflorescence catkin-like, female ones reduced in number. One-celled ovary with single ovule (*Juglandaceae*, p. 62).

Order: *Fagales*. Woody plants with alternate, simple leaves. Unisexual, monoecious flowers. Perianth reduced, small or missing altogether, occasionally replaced by enlarged bracts (*Corylaceae*, p. 60). Of the several ovules in each ovary only one (or two) matures. Flowers always in compound inflorescences, often a catkin (*Betulaceae*, p. 62). Fruit nut or nutlet, sometimes winged *(Betula)* or enclosed in woody cupule (*Fagaceae*, p. 62).

Order: *Salicales*. Woody plants with simple leaves. Dioecious flowers arranged in catkins and lacking a perianth; stamens usually two, one pistil comprising a one-celled ovary with many ovules. Capsules with several seeds (*Salicaceae*, p. 62).

Order: *Geraniales*. Herbs without any common vegetative features. Flowers regular, pentamerous. Various fruit forms occur, often characteristically separating — schizocarps (*Geraniaceae*, p. 112), capsules (*Oxalidaceae*, p. 114, *Linaceae*, p. 114) and others.

Order: *Rutales*. Mostly woody plants (*Simaroubaceae*, p. 66), less frequently herbs of varied appearance, fragrant. Bisexual, pentamerous flowers, sometimes symmetrical, often with glandular disc beneath ovary (*Rutaceae*, p. 114, *Polygalaceae*, p. 66, 114).

Order: *Euphorbiales*. Herbs and woody plants of most varied appearance without any common vegetative features. Flowers simplified, usually unisexual, regular, often without perianth; pistil consists of three carpels, fused together. Frequently conspicuous and coloured bracts surround the inflorescence, imitating a flower (*Euphorbiaceae*, p. 114).

Order: *Celastrales*. Woody plants with alternate, stipular, simple as well as compound leaves. Flowers regular, mostly 4- or 5-merous; free perianth (*Celastraceae*, p. 66).

Order: *Sapindales*. Herbs or more often woody plants. Leaves mostly compound (*Hippocastanaceae*, p. 66), less frequently simple (*Aceraceae*, p. 66, *Impatientaceae*, p. 116). Flowers regular or asymmetrical, bisexual as well as unisexual; corolla and calyx usually developed, often with glandular disc beneath ovary.

Order: *Rhamnales*. Woody plants with alternate, simple as well as compound leaves. Characteristic glandular disc in flowers and sometimes a whorl of stamens before the petals. Flowers regular, tetra- or pentamerous ovary formed of three to five carpels (*Rhamnaceae*, p. 68).

Order: *Malvales*. Woody plants and herbs with a number of representatives in tropics. Flowers perfect, pentamerous; stamens usually in one whorl, often numerous and fused together at base of their filaments (*Tiliaceae*, p. 68), or fused in a staminal tube (*Malvaceae*, p. 116); fruit is capsule or schizocarp.

Order: *Parietales* (syn. *Hypericales*). Mostly tropical woody plants, rarely herbs with simple leaves. Occurrence of oil cells or canals in tissues and twisting of petals in buds is conspicuous. As a rule many stamens, often in bundles; ovary superior, often three-celled (*Guttiferae*, p. 116.)

Order: *Myrtales*. Mostly woody plants, less frequently herbs, usually with opposite leaves, often in opposite pairs. Flowers bisexual, tetra- or pentamerous, regular, rarely asymmetrical, often with conspicuous fusion of floral envelopes into a tube. Ovary consists of four carpels fused together, with single style (*Lythraceae*, p. 116, *Onagraceae*, p. 118, *Eleagnaceae*, p. 68, *Thymelaeaceae*, p. 70).

Order: *Umbelliflorae* (syn. *Apiales*). Herbs, less frequently woody plants. Leaves with sheaths at base, without stipules. Flowers usually in umbels tetra- or pentamerous, marginal flowers usually asymmetrical, others regular, bisexual; calyx reduced. Ovary inferior consists of two to five carpels; schizocarp drupe or berry are most frequent types of fruit. Conspicuous presence of oil cells and canals in tissue (*Araliaceae*, p. 70, *Umbelliferae*, p. 118, *Cornaceae*, p. 70).

Order: *Plumbaginales*. Herbs or shrubs with simple entire leaves, usually arranged spirally. Bisexual, regular, perfect, pentamerous flowers. Ovary superior; fruit achene or capsule (*Plumbaginaceae*, p. 122).

Order: *Primulales*. Herbs of various types; leaves without stipules. Flowers usually pentamerous, regular; sepals and petals grown together, at least at base; stamens in a single whorl, outer circle disappeared or into extra floral organs. Ovary superior, one-celled, as a rule with a large number of ovules, fruit a capsule (*Primulaceae*, p. 122).

Order: *Ericales*. Woody plants (*Ericaceae*, p. 70, *Vacciniaceae*, p. 72), or herbs (*Pyrolaceae*, p. 126) with simple, often evergreen leaves. Flowers bisexual, regular, rarely symmetrical, tetra- to pentamerous; petals mainly fused to form a tube or bell, or sometimes free. Anthers often with horn-like protuberances, pollen grains often sticky and adhering in strings. Single pistil formed of two to five carpels.

Order: *Oleales*. Woody plants or herbs with opposite, simple or pinnate, leaves without stipules. Corolla and calyx tetramerous, two to five stamens. Ovary superior, two-celled, each cell has mostly two ovules. Fruits of various types, capsules, berries, drupes, etc. (*Oleaceae*, p. 72).

Order: *Loganiales*. Herbs or woody plants with opposite, simple leaves (*Gentianaceae*, p. 126), rarely alternate and trimerous (*Menyanthaceae*, p. 128). Flowers tetra- to pentamerous, usually regular, bisexual. Ovary formed of two carpels fused together (*Apocynaceae*, p. 128, *Asclepiadaceae*, p. 128).

Order: *Tubiflorae* (syn. *Lamiales*). Herbs or woody plants of various appearance; rarely parasitic or semi-parasitic. Bisexual, regular or asymmetrical flowers; floral parts in four whorls, as a rule pentamerous, often with reduced number of stamens. Two carpels fused together form ovary with four ovules. Capsule as fruit (*Convolvulaceae*, p. 128), or four single-seeded nutlets (*Boraginaceae*, p. 130, *Labiatae*, p. 132).

Order: *Scrophulariales*. Mainly parasitic herbs (*Orobanchaceae*, p. 144); partially parasitic plants, sometimes with fewer stamens, ovary of two carpels with many ovules, fruit a capsule (*Scrophulariaceae*, p. 140, *Plantaginaceae*, p. 144); flowers regular and fruit a berry or capsule (*Solanaceae*, p. 74, 138).

Order: *Rubiales*. Herbs as well as woody plants. Leaves opposite or in whorls, simple or compound. Flowers regular or asymmetrical, tetra- to pentamerous, calyx sometimes reduced or completely missing. Ovary inferior; fruits are two-seeded drupes (*Rubiaceae*, p. 144, *Loniceraceae*, p. 74, 146, *Valerianaceae*, p. 146, *Dipsacaceae*, p. 148).

Order: *Campanulales*. Mainly herbs, often also with lactiferous ducts; starch replaced by inulin. Leaves alternate, simple, without stipules. Flowers bisexual, mostly regular, pentamerous; anthers mostly connected to form a tube. Ovary inferior. Fruit a capsule with many seeds (*Campanulaceae*, p. 148).

Order: *Asterales*. Plants of various types, herbs, and woody plants including climbers. Common feature: type of inflorescence — capitulum. Flowers with five-lobed ligulate corollas sometimes quite indistinct, sometimes only three teeth. Five stamens, united to the corolla with their filaments; anthers joined into tube. Ovary of two carpels with a single ovule; fruit an achene. Starch replaced by inulin. Oil and resin canals occur in many genera (*Compositae*, p. 150).

Subclass: **Monocotyledones** — *Butomidae* (syn. *Monocotyledonae*)

The seed contains a single cotyledon the base of which encloses the growing point. The main root rarely becomes dominant after germination and is replaced by numerous adventitious roots from the base of the stem. Vascular bundles are dispersed in the stem. The tissue by which the stems of dicotyledonous plants become secondarily thicker is not developed in monocotyledons and therefore no trees with annual rings exist among them. The leaves, mostly alternate, are usually simple and entire with conspicuous parallel venation. Floral envelopes are not always clearly differentiated sepals (calyx) and petals (corolla) looking alike, either green or coloured. Flowers, mostly trimerous, often form large inflorescences.

Order: *Helobiae* (syn. *Butomales*). Aquatic or swamp plants. Floral envelopes in two whorls; flowers somewhat resemble members of the *Ranunculaceae*. Floral envelopes not differentiated (*Butomaceae*, p. 168), sometimes reduced or missing completely (*Potamogetonaceae*, p. 168). Unstable number of carpels, often imperfectly fused in ovary. Fruit usually a folicle or achene.

Order: *Liliales*. Herbs or woody plants, including climbers. Corolla usually in two whorls with three petals each, often fused; similarly the stamens are in two whorls of three, rarely in one whorl (*Iridaceae*, p. 172); flowers rarely tetramerous. Ovary superior (*Liliaceae*, p. 168), or inferior (*Amaryllidaceae*, p. 172).

Order: *Juncales*. Plants of grassy appearance. Scaly perianth, stamens in two whorls. Ovary superior, fruit a capsule (*Juncaceae*, p. 172).

48

Order: *Cyperales*. Plants of grassy appearance characterized by inconspicuous simplified flowers in spikelets. Floral envelope either absent or transformed into bristles or scales. Stamens in one whorl. Unisexual as well as bisexual flowers are mono- and dioecious (*Cyperaceae*, p. 172).

Order: *Poales* (syn. *Graminales*). Grasses with unbranched stems. Leaves without petioles. Bisexual flowers grow in axils of bract-like lemma; palea consists of two petals fused together. Usually three stamens; three carpels form the ovary with two pinnate stigmata (*Poaceae*, p. 174 — provide most of the world's grain and cereal crops).

Order: *Microspermae* (syn. *Orchidales*). Herbs or subshrubs. Flowers often with conspicuously coloured and uniquely formed floral envelopes in two whorls of three with a single stamen. Ovary inferior with large number of minute ovules. It matures to a capsule often with hundreds or even thousands of small, light seeds. Before flowering, ovary as a rule twists through 180°. Flowers often spurred. Pollen grains usually adhere in sticky clusters (pollinia) (*Orchidaceae*, p. 180).

Order: *Arales*. Herbs or woody plants, including climbers, mostly with tiny flowers in a simple spike (spadix) covered with a leafy, sometimes coloured bract (spathe) (*Araceae*, p. 184); or only in twos or threes with a small sheath, corresponding to a spathe (*Lemnaceae*, p. 184). By suppression of one of the sexes inflorescences often become unisexual. Fruit usually a berry.

Order: *Pandanales*. Herbs or woody marsh plants with flowers in globose heads (*Sparganiaceae*, p. 184), or spadix (*Typhaceae*, p. 184); inflorescence unisexual or part male and part female, with or without a scaly perianth. Fruit usually a dry drupe.

Sub-division: **Gymnosperms** — *Gymnospermae*

Class: **Coniferous plants** — *Coniferopsida*

Family: *Taxaceae*

1 Yew *Taxus baccata*. Broad-headed tree to 20 m., either in the open or as an understory tree, mainly on chalk or limestone. Abundantly planted in many cultivated forms, often in parks. Grows slowly; therefore annual rings are very dense and even old trees are rarely very big. Only coniferous tree with resin canals. Wood and needles contain poisonous alkaloid toxin. Dioecious tree, flowers in March and April. Male cones grow in axils of needles and have shield-shaped stamens. Female cones have one ovule ripening into seed, enveloped in fleshy red cupule; only this is not poisonous.

Family: *Pinaceae*

2 Silver Fir *Abies alba*. Tall, stout tree up to 45 m. or more, with pyramidal to cylindrical crown. Young shoots with fine, grey-brown tomentum, gradually changing into whitish, grey-green, smooth or scaly bark. Blunt, flat needles, with two white stripes beneath arranged in two rows, adhere to twig by disc-like bases. After they fall the twig remains almost smooth. Fir is monoecious, flowers from May to June. Male flowers have orange yellow anthers. Female flowers are borne on upper side of preceding year's stronger twigs and develop into erect cones, disintegrating at maturity. Grows in mountain or foothill woods and forms important component of beech-fir forests. Often planted. In parks cultivated in various forms, together with related species from North America, Asia and southern Spain.

3 Norway Spruce *Picea abies* (syn. *P. excelsa*). Tall tree up to 60 m. or more, with shallow roots and slender pyramidal crown; young bark light brown, older greyish or maroon, scaly, changing into cracked bark. Branches in regular whorls, with pointed needles; when these fall they leave peg-like protuberances on twigs. Spruce is dioecious; flowers in April and May. Male flowers grow on preceding year's twigs; at first they are red, later yellowish and ovoid. Pendent female flowers at end of branches in upper part of crown are reddish before pollination. Mature cones also are pendulous and do not disintegrate. Originally native of mountain and foothill forests but generally planted also at lower altitudes; in many cultivated forms commonly planted in parks together with some North-American species. This is the popular Christmas tree of central Europe and Britain.

4 European Larch *Larix decidua*. A deep-rooting tree up to 45 m. tall with spreading branches that droop at the tips in mature specimens. Grey-brown bark later becomes thick and irregularly scaly. The soft light green needles in clusters on shortened lateral shoots are of annual duration. Flowers from April to June; male flowers globose, sulphur-yellow, female ones red, ripening in autumn to small ovoid-globose cones. Larch is a mountain conifer, and needs high light intensity. For its valuable timber it is abundantly cultivated even at lower altitudes, especially on margins of coniferous woods and in parks. The evergreen Douglas fir — *Pseudotsuga menziesii* — is also planted in woods. The pendent cones have trifid scales which project like three-pointed tongues; needles with two white stripes give out pleasant smell when crushed. Also cultivated in parks; native of western North America.

1

2

3

4

Family: *Pinaceae*

1 Scots Pine *Pinus sylvestris*. A tree up to 40 m., with a globose to flattened crown. Bark of young twigs green, later turning rusty; old trunks have a fissured, reddish-brown or grey-brown bark. Needles arranged in pairs on short shoots. Flowers from May to June; male flowers sulphur-yellow, female ones arranged individually or in twos or threes at ends of branches, reddish, ripen two years. Originally grows in lowlands and hills, on sandy soils, rocks and heather moors. Commonly planted in poor, sandy soils. The Weymouth pine — *P. strobus* — with grey-green, long needles in clusters of five, is often cultivated in parks; it is native of North America.

2 Austrian Pine *Pinus nigra*. A variable species ranging in height from 25—45 m., sometimes more. Bark rough, greyish to dark brown. Needles longer than in Scots pine, 8—15 cm. long, dark green, stiff and sharply pointed. Flowers in June and July. Male flowers cylindrical, yellowish, stamens with pink connective. Female flowers red to light violet during flowering, pruinous, ripen as late as third year into large, glossy, yellow-brown cones with seed-scales of dark brown beneath. Grows from limestone foothills of eastern Alps up to Mediterranean region. Often planted in dry forests of central Europe. Also cultivated for ornamental purposes in parks.

3 Mountain Pine *Pinus mugo*. A broad, bushy shrub with irregularly branched trunk, or small tree with erect trunk and pyramidal crown. Mountain pine grows either as knee-pine in central-European mountains above tree line or as bog-pine on peat soils and in hilly country. Needles arranged in pairs, slightly twisted, rich green, under lens distinctly toothed. Male flowers yellow, with conspicuously large stamen connective. Female flowers on ends of shoots, red to light violet. Knee-pine flowers from June, bog-pine as early as May. Cones ripen third year, are conically ovoid to globose. Of compact conical habit is the Arolla pine — *P. cembra*, reaching 20—25 m. in height. Needles usually in fives and cones containing large edible seeds; a native of Alps and Carpathians.

Family: *Cupressaceae*

4 Juniper *Juniperus communis*. A very variable species, ranging in size from a prostrate shrub to a small tree with conical crown up to 10 m. or more tall. Needles stiff, prickly pointed, grey-green, in trimerous whorls; white stripe on upper side. Dioecious flowers; male flowers axillary, ovate, yellowish; female ones individual, greenish. Flowers in April and May. Fruit matures in short-stalked, berry-like cone formed by three fleshy, fused seed scales; at first green, second year blue-black with a whitish 'bloom'. Forms undergrowth of coniferous forests, especially pine-woods, also occurs on slopes and in pastures. Protected in many countries. Savin — *J. sabina* — with scaly, sessile needles, and several American and Asian species, are also often cultivated.

Flowering Trees and Shrubs

Class: **Angiospermous Plants** — *Magnoliopsida*

Subclass: **Dicotyledones** — *Magnoliidae*

Family: **Barberry** — *Berberidaceae*

1 Common Barberry *Berberis vulgaris*. Shrub up to 2.5 m., with smooth bark and alternate leaves. Clusters of obovate sharply serrated leaves with short petioles arise in axils of branched spines (modified leaves). Yellow fragrant flowers in pendent racemes. Stamens sensitive to touch. Flowers during May and June. Fruit red berry. Grows on sunny slopes and open groves from lowlands to foothills; most commonly seen in hedgerows in Britain. Also cultivated in various garden forms.

Family: *Loranthaceae*

2 Mistletoe *Viscum laxum*. Semi-parasitic evergreen shrub, of spreading habit up to 1 m. in diameter in crowns of coniferous trees, especially pines. Branches by repeated forking; twigs brittle. Leaves opposite, yellow-green, elongate obovate, entire, leathery texture. Tiny unisexual flowers are borne in small clusters in forks of branches. Fruits yellowish-white, globose berries. Flowers from March to April; berries mature as late as December. Stouter white mistletoe (common mistletoe in G.B.) — *V. album* — with larger white berries, grows on a wide range of deciduous trees.

Family: **Elm** — *Ulmaceae*

3 European White Elm *Ulmus laevis* (syn. *U. effusa*). Robust tree with wide crown up to 35 m. Leaves with short petioles, sharply serrate, smooth above, usually hairy beneath. Flowers arranged in clusters on long stalks; anthers reddish. Achenes have wide cilious border, notched at tip. Flowers in March and April. Grows in meadows and moist forests; often also planted. Related wych elm *(U. glabra)* — grows in woods, from hilly country to foothills, while *Ulmus carpinifolia* (syn. *U. campestris*) grows in river valleys; both species have flowers in sessile clusters.

Family: **Rose** — *Rosaceae*

4 Wild Raspberry *Rubus idaeus*. Branches somewhat thorny in lower parts, otherwise hairy to smooth. Leaves odd-pinnate, sharply toothed, underside white; terminal leaflet largest, sometimes rounded. Flowers white, arranged in pendent cymes. Fruits a cluster of red druplets — the tasty raspberries; easily separate from the plug-like receptacle when ripe. Flowers in June and July, sometimes later. Grows abundantly on heaths and hills, scrub and open woods. Often cultivated in gardens for its fruit.

5 Bramble *Rubus fruticosus*. A very variable species according to some authorities, split up into hundreds of microspecies. Native to woods, scrub, heaths, open hillsides and hedgerows. Most important common features: thorny branched stems and compound, mostly palmate leaves with 3—5 leaflets. Flowers white or pink. Globose druplets ripen to purple-black, pruinous blackberries. The related, smaller, thin-stemmed *Rubus caesius*, growing along roads, field margins, paths, has mainly trifoliate leaves and fruits with a waxy white 'bloom'.

6 *Cotoneaster integerrimus*. A low, spreading shrub with reddish branchlets. Leaves small, with short petioles, entire, rounded, smooth above, hairy beneath. Flowers in small clusters, somewhat pendent. Calyx maroon, persistent; corollas white or pink flushed, stamens red; fruits subglobose, red. Flowers in April and May. Grows on sunny, bushy, stony or rocky slopes, in open woods and steppes, from lowlands to foothills. Many Asiatic species are cultivated as ornamental shrubs, e.g. *Cotoneaster horizontalis*, *C. microphyllus*, and the tree-sized *C. frigidus*.

Family: **Rose** — *Rosaceae*

1 Dog Rose *Rosa canina.* A variable spreading shrub up to 3 m. tall; best known and most abundant of all wild central-European roses, characterized by arching, spiny branches. Leaves pinnate, with 5 to 7 ovate to elliptical, sharply serrate, smooth leaflets. Flowers solitary or in small clusters at end of branchlet. Sepals glandular on margins, outer ones usually cleft. Corollas white, flushed pink. Fruit an ovoid hip. Flowers from May to July. Grows in thickets on slopes, in hedgerows and forest margins from lowlands to foothills. The similar *Rosa dumetorum* has hairy leaflets and petioles.

2 Alpine Rose *Rosa pendulina* (syn. *Rosa alpina*). Widely expanded shrub up to 2 m. tall, with pendent branches, sparsely covered with fine spines; upper branches are usually spineless. Leaves pinnate, with 7 to 11 elliptic, sharply serrate leaflets, dark green above, somewhat hairy underside. Flowers solitary, rarely in small clusters, on long stalks. Flowers purple-red; hips bottle-shaped, pendent, red. Flowers from May to July. Grows in hill and mountain forests and on bushy slopes.

3 Blackthorn or **Sloe** *Prunus spinosa.* Densely branched thorny shrub or small tree up to 4 m. Leaves elliptic, smooth, obovate with glandular margins. White flowers in small clusters often in profusion, before the leaves. Fruits are globose drupes, dark purple when ripe, usually with a waxy white 'bloom'. Flowers in March and April. Grows abundantly on sunny slopes, in hedgerows, at the edge of forests and in clearings from lowlands to foothills.

4 Gean or **Wild Cherry** *Prunus avium.* Tree up to 20 m. or more tall, with widely expanded crown and smooth, grey branches. Entire, ovate leaves have two small, reddish, globose glands at base; blades serrate, smooth above, hairy beneath. Flowers white, opening from April to May. Fruit a globose drupe, yellow or red, sweet, with agreeable but slightly bitter taste. Found in woods, thickets and hedgerows, often on limestone or chalk soils. The cultivated sweet cherry is derived from this species.

5 Bird Cherry *Prunus padus.* Large shrub or tree up to 15 m. with glossy brown branches. The leaves are obovate, abruptly pointed, finely serrate with two spherical glands on petiole. Flowers white, in pendent racemes; drupes small, black, astringent. Flowers and leaves give out pleasant bitter-almond smell. Flowers open in April and May. Grows in woods, scrub, and in hedgerows at lower altitudes. Sometimes forms of this tree are planted in parks and gardens.

6 Midland Hawthorn *Crataegus laevigata* (syn. *C. oxyacanthoides*). Shrub or small tree up to 10 m., with red-brown, spiny branches. Leaves shallowly lobed and serrate. Flowers arranged in flattened clusters, stalks white or sometimes rosy. Globose to ovoid, red fruits (haws) have two stones each. Flowers in May and June. Grows wild in woods, on bushy slopes and in hedgerows. Several red, pink and double-flowered forms are cultivated in parks and gardens.

Family: **Rose** — *Rosaceae*

1 Wild Pear *Pyrus communis*. Broadly pyramidal tree, sometimes with spiny branches up to 15 m. tall. Leaves with long petioles are ovate, pointed, finely serrate, glossy. Flowers, arranged in rounded corymbs, have long stalks. Corollas white or rarely pink-flushed. Fruits pear-shaped or globose, mature seeds black. Flowers in April and May. Grows wild in deciduous forests, on thickets and hedgerows at low altitudes. An allied species, *P. cordata*, is more bushy and spiny with smaller fruits. All the cultivated varieties of pears are derived from *P. communis*, which some authorities claim to be of multiple hybrid origin.

2 Crab Apple *Malus sylvestris*. Small tree to 10 m. tall. Young branches woolly, hairy, later more or less smooth. Leaves ovate, serrate, finely toothed. Petioles half of blade length. Flowers in small corymbs, pink in bud opening white; anthers yellow, lower half of styles fused together. Fruits almost globose, mature seeds brown. Flowers in May. Grows wild in hedgerows and woods. Cultivated apple-trees *(M. × domestica)* have no spiny branches; leaves are densely hairy on under surface, upper surface scattered with hairs; considered to be of ancient hybrid origin.

3 Mountain Ash or **Rowan** *Sorbus aucuparia*. A spreading tree up to 15 m. or more tall, with felted winter buds. Leaves odd-pinnate, leaflets sessile, elongated, lanceolate, sharply serrate, hairy on underside. Flowers creamy white, arranged in wide, flattened, branched corymbs. Fruits red, berry-like, globose, slightly larger than pea. Rowan grows wild in open woods and on grassy and rocky slopes from lowlands to mountains; often planted in avenues.

4 Common Whitebeam *Sorbus aria*. A large shrub or small tree up to 15 m. or more tall, with glossy, red-brown branches. Leaves irregularly serrate to shallowly lobed, under surface white, petals woolly at base. Fruits orange to reddish with yellow pulp. Flowers in May and June. Grows on sunny slopes and in open woodland from lowlands to mountains. Related wild service tree *(S. torminalis)* has sharply pinnately cut leaves almost hairless beneath and fruits, yellow-brown, spotted with darker lenticels.

Family: *Fabaceae* (syn. *Papilionaceae*)

5 Broom *Sarothamnus scoparius* (syn. *Cytisus scoparius*). Shrub with angular green branches up to 2 m. or more tall. Alternate leaves with short petioles composed of 3 lanceolate to obovate leaflets, silky hairy beneath. Flowers solitary or in small clusters, bright yellow. Style spirally twisted, protruding from keel, pods black, explosive when ripe. Flowers in May. Grows, often gregariously, at forest margins, sandy and stony slopes at lower altitudes, excluding limestone soils.

6 German Greenweed *Genista germanica*. Small shrub to 40 cm. or more, with ascending or erect, hairy, thorny branches. Leaves are ovate-lanceolate, pointed, and hairy. Flowers yellow, in leafy racemes at tips of shoots. Pods black-brown, hairy, exploding when ripe. Flowers from May to July. Grows in dry woods, especially pine-woods and in open sites on sandy soils from lowlands to foothills. Related dyer's greenweed *(G. tinctoria)* has thornless stems and hairless pods.

Family: *Fabaceae*

1 *Cytisus nigricans*. Deciduous shrub up to 2 m. tall, with erect, green, hairy branches. Petiolate leaves of three pointed, obovate, dark green leaflets, paler beneath. Yellow flowers in bractless racemes turn black when dried. Pods brown-black, smooth. Flowers from May to August. Grows on sunny slopes, among rocks and in dry woods from lowlands to foothills. Related common laburnum *(Laburnum anagyroides)*, a tree up to 7 m. tall with pendent racemes of large, yellow flowers, is often cultivated.

2 Spiny Rest-harrow *Ononis spinosa*. Sub-shrub up to 40 cm. or more, with ascending or erect branches, mostly spiny, with one or two rows of hairs. Leaves of three leaflets, each narrowly obovate and serrate. Flowers pink, calyx bilabiate, hairy. One-seeded pods of same length or longer than calyx, softly hairy. Flowers from June to September. Grows in rough grassy places, field boundaries and on sunny slopes in lower altitudes of temperate regions. Related common rest-harrow *(O. repens)* is thornless, creeping or decumbent sub-shrub with underground rhizomes.

3 False Acacia *Robinia pseudoacacia*. Tree up to 27 m. tall with deeply fissured bark. Leaves petiolate, odd-pinnate, stipules transformed into strong, curved thorns. Leaflets petiolate, oval to elliptic, entire. Flowers white, occasionally flushed pink, fragrant, in pendent racemes. Pods strongly flattened, hairless. Flowers in May and June. Native of North America, since 18th century planted in avenues together with other North-American species with pink or violet-rose flowers.

Family: *Platanaceae*

4 *Platanus hispanica* (syn. *P.* × *acerifolia*). Abundantly cultivated hybrid of eastern and western plane-trees, planted only rarely in parks. Robust tree up to 40 m. with striking scaly fawn and grey bark peeling in flakes. Illustrated species differs from its parent species by hairless underside of leaves; central lobes usually longer than their base width; globose inflorescences arranged mostly in strings of one to four. Oriental plane *(P. orientalis)*, native of eastern Mediterranean, has narrower lobes and inflorescences arranged in strings of up to six. Buttonwood or 'sycamore' *(P. occidentalis)*, native of North America, has leaves hairy on underside, central lobes wider and inflorescences in ones and twos. Plane-trees flower in May.

Family: **Hazel** — *Corylaceae*

5 Hornbeam *Carpinus betulus*. Tree up to 30 m. tall, with grey, smooth bark and glossy, brown branches. Leaves narrowly oblong, doubly sharply serrate. Male and female catkins cylindrical, female ones erect, with flowers in axils of trilobed bracts; male pendulous. Ovary, with two red stigmata, develops into a nut, attached to the trilobed bract which enlarges and acts as a wing for wind dispersal. Flowers from April to May. Grows in woods and hedgerows at lower altitudes, also planted for coppicing, hedging and as a specimen tree.

6 Hazel *Corylus avellana*. Tall, well-branched bush up to 6 m. Leaves petiolate, glandular, obovate to rounded, doubly serrate, with short hairs. Male inflorescences are catkins up to 5 cm. long, female ones bud-like with two filamentous, red stigmata. Fruit is small nut enveloped in enlarged bracts, with white seed and cinnamon-brown seed coat. Flowers from January to April. Grows fairly abundantly in open woods and on sunny slopes from lowlands to mountains. Once much planted for coppicing. The cob nut of commerce is a form of this species.

Family: **Walnut** — *Juglandaceae*

1 Common Walnut *Juglans regia*. Robust tree up to 30 m. tall, with grey bark; branchlets at first green-brown, later ash-grey. Leaves odd-pinnate, with usually 5 to 7 pairs of obovate or elliptic, entire, smooth leaflets. Male catkins pendulous on previous year's twigs, female flowers at tips of new twigs with two lobed stigmata. Fruit globose to ovoid drupe with tough, somewhat fleshy exocarp and stony endocarp; seed coat membraneous, lobed seed white. Flowers in April and May. Native of south-eastern Europe and Asia Minor. Often cultivated for its highly edible nuts.

Family: **Birch** — *Betulaceae*

2 Silver Birch *Betula pendula* (syn. *B. verrucosa*). Slender elegant tree up to 25 m. tall with straight trunk and white bark, transversely peeling in paper-thin bands; bark deeply fissured at base. Leaves usually rhomboid to triangular, ovate, slender pointed, smooth, doubly serrate except base. Male as well as female catkins pendent, anthers yellow, stigmata purple. Seeds (nutlets) winged, wings wider than nutlet. Flowers in April and May. Grows abundantly in forests, on slopes and heathland, often planted. Related birch, *Betula pubescens*, has less pendent branches and leaves and twigs hairy when young.

3 Alder *Alnus glutinosa*. Tree up to 20 m. or more tall, with slender, dark grey trunk with fissured bark; young branchlets glandular. Leaves broadly obovate, with notched point, doubly toothed, smooth, rich green; young ones sticky. Male catkins with red scales, female ones long-stalked, ovate, maturing to brown, cone-like fruits. Wingless achenes. Flowers in March and April. Grows in moist meadows and near water. Related grey alder *(A. incana)* has pointed leaves, grey-green on underside, downy; bark light grey and smooth.

Family: **Beech** — *Fagaceae*

4 Beech *Fagus sylvatica*. Robust tree up to 30 m. or more, with slender trunk and smooth, pale grey bark. Buds long, slender, pointed, with red-brown ciliate scales. Leaves petiolate, almost entire, broadly ovate, pointed, with ciliate margins. Male flowers in long-stalked, pendent clusters; perianth red-brown. Female flowers in pairs are at ends of new twigs, enclosed in green cup. These mature red-brown and open by four valves. Fruits are triangular nuts or beech-mast. Flowers in April and May. Grows fairly abundantly from lowlands to highlands. Several forms are known, including red, purple and copper-leaved and the fern-leaved beech with deeply cut leaves.

5 Sweet Chestnut *Castanea sativa*. Tree up to 30 m. or more, dark grey-brown bark often with spiral fissures. Leaves short-petiolate, oblong, lanceolate, stiff, sharply serrate. Flowers in erect spike-like clusters; female ones at the bottom, individual or in threes, enclosed in globose, prickly barbed cupule; male florets whitish, forming bulk of spike. Fruit — chestnuts — dark brown, glossy, leathery skin, with single seed. Flowers in July. Native of southern Europe; often planted for edible seeds and in parks for ornament. Naturalized in some territories, e.g. Carpathians and southern Britain where it was once extensively coppiced for fencing.

Family: **Poplar and Willow** — *Salicaceae*

6 White Poplar *Populus alba*. Rapid growing suckering tree up to 25 m., with pale grey bark. Leaves ovate, orbicular, notched to deeply 5-lobed, undersides felted with white hairs. Male catkins long and thick, female ones shorter; flowers with two red styles and yellow stigmata. Long-haired seeds. Flowers in March and April. Grows in forests and near rivers; also much planted. Related black poplar *(P. nigra)* is often planted in avenues, mainly the Italian form with columnar crown.

Family: **Poplar and Willow** — *Salicaceae*

1 Aspen *Populus tremula*. A suckering tree up to 20 m. tall, with bark at first smooth, yellow-grey, later black-grey and fissured. Young twigs smooth or shortly hairy, buds sticky. Leaves almost round to rhomboid, shallowly notched. Long catkins with bracts palmately cut, anthers before releasing pollen red; purple stigmata in twos. Downy seeds. Flowers in March and April. Grows in open, moist places in woods, clearings, hedgerows, from lowlands to mountains.

2 Goat Willow *Salix caprea*. Large shrub or small tree up to 10 m. tall. Leaves petiolate, ovate-oblong to obovate, pointed, narrowed or rounded at petiole, entire or irregularly toothed, upper side more or less hairy, under side felted with persistent grey hairs. Dioecious catkins appear before the leaves; male ones erect, thick, long silvery-haired, flowers with yellow anthers; female catkins similar, but are less hairy and stay grey-green, elongate when ripe and shed tiny seeds in cotton wool like hair. Flowers from March to May. Grows abundantly at edges of forests, in clearings, on slopes, along brooks and in hedgerows from lowlands to mountains.

3 *Salix purpurea*. Shrub or small tree up to 3 m. tall with thin, flexible and tough branches. Leaves shortly petiolate, obovate-oblong to linear oblanceolate, pointed, finely serrate, entire at petiole; somewhat blue-green above, glaucous beneath. Male catkins have stamens fused to filaments; red anthers, after pollination turning black; female catkins shortly conical. Flowers in March and April. Distinctive by having leaves and buds in sub-opposite pairs. Grows along streams and rivers and in wet meadows from lowlands to foothills. Also cultivated together with osier *(S. viminalis)*.

Family: **Beech and Oak** — *Fagaceae*

4 Common Oak *Quercus robur* (syn. *Q. pedunculata*). Robust tree up to 30 m. or more tall with widely expanded, irregular crown; old branches strong, tortuous, old trunk has brownish-grey, deeply fissured bark. Buds ovoid, brown. Leaves shortly petiolate, pinnately lobed, blades cordate at petiole, hairy when young, soon becoming smooth, leathery, usually with five pairs of lobes. Male flowers in pendent catkins, female ones sessile, globular, in cupule; stigmata red. Acorns in twos to fives on long stalks. Flowers in April and May. Forms main component of oak-woods from lowlands to foothills. At one time commonly planted.

5 Durmast Oak *Quercus petraea* (syn. *Q. sessiliflora*). Differs from preceding species by ovoid crown, long-petiolate leaves, wedge-shaped blades at petiole and sessile acorns. Both species often hybridize and many trees are difficult to identify. In places the hybrid is more abundant than parent species. North-American *Quercus borealis* with red autumn leaves and *Quercus coccinea* with scarlet leaves are cultivated in parks; both have leaves larger than the native species and with bold, sharply pointed lobes.

6 Hairy Oak *Quercus pubescens*. Usually shrub with often distorted trunk and cracked bark. Young twigs and buds white-haired. Leaves obovate, pinnately lobed, blades wedge-shaped or cordate at petiole, lobes rounded or pointed, felted with grey hairs on both sides when young. In maturity upper surface almost smooth. Acorns long ovoid, pointed, in felted cupule. Flowers in April and May. Grows mainly on limestone soils, on sunny slopes in lower altitudes of warm regions.

Family: *Simaroubaceae*

1 Tree of Heaven *Ailanthus peregrina* (syn. *A. altissima*). Robust tree up to 35 m. or more; young branches reddish, hairy. Leaves up to 1 m. long, odd-pinnate, reddish when young. Leaflets lanceolate with one to three glandular teeth at base. Tiny flowers yellow-green, arranged in large panicles; fruit winged, sometimes bright red. Flowers in June and July. Native of eastern Asia; cultivated as ornamental tree and often planted. Sometimes becomes naturalized.

Family: **Milkwort** — *Polygalaceae*

2 Box-leaved Milkwort *Polygala chamaebuxus* (syn. *Chamaebuxus alpestris*). Small sub-shrub, rarely above 20 cm. Stems decumbent, ascending, often rooting. Leaves almost sessile, persistent, evergreen, leathery, smooth, entire, oval, with a small point. Flowers arranged singly or in small groups in leaf axils; winged sepals white, sometimes buff-yellow or carmine. Petals yellow, reddening at tips after fertilization. Fruit a capsule. Flowers from March to September. Grows among rocks and in open forests, mainly pine-woods, on mountain slopes.

Family: *Celastraceae*

3 Spindle Tree *Euonymus europaea*. A shrub up to 3 m. or more; young branches green, somewhat four-winged, smooth. Leaves petiolate, lanceolate to ovate, pointed, smooth. Flowers in axillary clusters; petals greenish. Square pink capsule with orange seeds. Flowers in May and June. Grows at outskirts of forests, on slopes and in hedgerows from lowlands to foothills. Several forms are cultivated in gardens.

Family: *Hippocastanaceae*

4 Common Horse-chestnut *Aesculus hippocastanum*. Robust tree up to 25 m. or more; young branches brown, buds large and sticky. Leaves palmate, compound with 5–7 leaflets, each obovate, up to 20 cm. long and irregularly toothed. Flowers in dense, pyramidal panicle, petals white, spotted with red and yellow. Fruit a somewhat spiny capsule with one or two polished, dark brown seeds. Flowers in May and June. Native of Albania and Greece, but commonly cultivated in avenues, parks and gardens. Related species have red or rose flowers.

Family: **Maple** — *Aceraceae*

5 Sycamore *Acer pseudoplatanus*. Tree up to 30 m. or more with broad crown and scaly bark. Leaves deeply palmately lobed and toothed; grey-green on underside, sometimes reddish flushed on both sides. Flowers yellow-green, in pendent panicles. Fruit a double samara with propeller-like wings. Flowers in May and June. Native of central and southern Europe but well naturalized elsewhere. Grows fairly abundantly from lowlands to mountains in deciduous forests. Several forms are planted in parks and gardens.

6 Norway Maple *Acer platanoides*. Tree up to 30 m., with fissured scaly bark; young twigs release milky juice. Leaves palmate with 5–7 pointed lobes and blunt teeth; in autumn turns yellow or reddish. Corymbs of bright yellow-green flowers are erect, appearing before the leaves expand. Fruit much flattened double samara with long, parallel wings. Flowers in March to May. Grows fairly abundantly from lowlands to mountains in deciduous woods. Several forms are often cultivated (some with purple or variegated leaves) in parks and gardens.

Family: **Maple** — *Aceraceae*

1 Common Maple *Acer campestre*. Shrub or small tree up to 15 m. or more; twigs sometimes with corky ridges. Leaves palmate, with 3 to 5 lobes, entire or bluntly toothed. Flowers yellow-green, downy, in small, erect, corymbose panicles. Fruit a hairy double samara with small blunt wings. Flowers from May to June. Grows in hedgerows on bushy slopes and in open forests mainly at lower altitudes.

Family: *Rhamnaceae*

2 Alder Buckthorn *Frangula alnus*. Smooth-barked shrub up to 5 m. with slender branches. Leaves alternate, shortly petiolate, elliptic, entire, under side hairy when young. Small greenish flowers in axillary clusters; fruit a berry-like, black-violet, three-seeded drupe. Flowers in May and June. Grows in moist forests and near water, from lowlands to mountains. Related *Rhamnus catharticus*, usually with spiny branches, finely serrate opposite leaves and a more bushy habit grows on bushy slopes and in hedgerows on well-drained soils.

Family: **Lime** — *Tiliaceae*

3 Small-leaved Lime *Tilia cordata*. Tree up to 25 m. with long-petiolate leaves, asymmetrically cordate, smooth above, on under side greyish, with tufts of rusty hairs in vein-axils. Flowers yellow-white, inflorescence stalk bearing a large ligulate bract. Fruit a globose capsule, the floral bract persisting as a wing for wind dispersal. Flowers in early July. Grows in deciduous woods from lowlands to foothills; also often planted in parks and avenues.

4 Large-leaved Lime *Tilia platyphyllos*. Often robust tree up to 30 m. with black-brown bark. Leaves petiolate, cordate, usually asymmetric, dark green above, pale green beneath, somewhat hairy. Flowers white-yellow; capsule with three to five ribs, sub-globose. Flowers in late June. Grows in deciduous woods and on stable screes. Planted in parks and gardens, sometimes with other species; silver lime *(T. tomentosa)*, having leaves white felted beneath; and the similar but pendulous branched *T. petiolaris*.

Family: *Elaeagnaceae*

5 Sea Buckthorn *Hippophaë rhamnoides*. Spiny shrub up to 3 m. tall with dense branches, silvery-scaly when young. Leaves alternate, linear-lanceolate, entire, under surface silvery-scaly. Flowers greenish, in axillary clusters; male and female on separate plants. Fruits orange-red, rarely yellow, brown-dotted berries. Flowers from March to May. In Europe native only on sandy, gravelly river banks and stony slopes. In Britain on dunes and cliffs by the sea. Often planted for showy fruit, and as a hedge or windbreak near the sea.

6 Oleaster *Elaeagnus angustifolia*. Shrub, less frequently small tree, usually with spiny branches. Leaves alternate, shortly petiolate, narrow-lanceolate, upper side grey-green, under side silvery white. Tubular flowers silvery yellowish, fragrant. Fruits are pale amber-yellow berries. Flowers in May and June. Native of Mediterranean; often cultivated in parks and gardens. Not to be confused with the allied *E. argentea* (syn. *E. commutata*) with wider leaves, pendent flowers and silvery berries.

Family: *Thymelaeaceae*

1 Mezereon *Daphne mezereum*. Deciduous shrub up to 1 m., mostly with erect, little branched stems. Leaves alternate, lanceolate to oblanceolate, blunt-pointed, smooth, pale green. Strongly fragrant rosy-purple flowers appear before the leaves in lateral clusters. Fruits are globose, orange-red, poisonous drupes. Flowers from February to April. Grows in deciduous woods from lowlands to mountains. *Daphne cneorum* with terminal flowers and evergreen leaves grows at foot of Alps. Both species often cultivated. More common in Britain is the evergreen spurge laurel *(D. laureola)*, with glossy dark green, oblanceolate leaves and yellow-green flowers from the leaf axils of the shoot tips.

Family: *Araliaceae*

2 Ivy *Hedera helix*. Evergreen climber up to 30 m. with stems that cling by pads of shoot adhesive roots. Leaves leathery, opposite, long-petiolate, smooth, glossy, of two basic forms: non-flowering branches have leaves palmately three- to five-lobed, flowering ones have entire leaves, ovate to lanceolate. Flowers with five petals, greenish, arranged in rounded umbels. Fruit a globose, black berry. Flowers in September and October. Grows from lowlands to mountains in forests and thickets, climbs rocks and tree trunks. Flowers and fruits only at the top of its support. Many forms of varying leaf shape and colour are often cultivated for ornament.

Family: **Dogwood** — *Cornaceae*

3 Cornelian Cherry *Cornus mas*. Shrub or small tree up to 8 m. Leaves opposite, shortly petiolate, ovate to elliptic, pointed, with flattened hairs. Profuse yellow flowers in corymbs before leaves unfold. Fruits are oblong-ovoid red drupes. Flowers from February to April. Grows on bushy slopes and in open forests at lower altitudes. For long cultivated in parks and gardens for its distinctive early flowers.

4 Dogwood *Cornus sanguinea* (syn. *Svida sanguinea*). Shrub of bushy habit up to 3 m. tall, with dark red branches especially during the winter. Leaves opposite, petiolate, ovate or oval, pointed, smooth. Flowers white in flat cymes, followed by black drupes. Flowers in May and June. Grows abundantly in deciduous woods, on bushy slopes and in hedgerows from lowlands to foothills. Related *Cornus alba*, with underside of leaves grey-green and hairy and bright red winter stems, a native of North America, is often cultivated.

Family: **Heath** — *Ericaceae*

5 Rusty-leaved Rhododendron *Rhododendron ferrugineum*. Small shrub up to 1 m. Tough, evergreen leaves are oblong-lanceolate, glossy, underside covered with rusty brown scales; margins inrolled. Flowers dark rose. Flowers from May to July. Grows on rocky slopes of Alps and in open woods on lower slopes. Related alpenrose *(R. hirsutum)* with somewhat paler flowers and bristly margins of leaves, green on both sides, grows mainly in calcareous Alps. Many North-American and Asian species and especially their hybrids are cultivated in parks and gardens.

6 Marsh Tea or **Wild Rosemary** *Ledum palustre*. Low evergreen shrub to 1 m. tall, with curious spicy fragrance. Young branches rusty hairy. Leaves alternate, sessile, linear to oblong, entire, the margins inrolled, under side rusty felted. Flowers fragrant, white, in dense terminal umbels; fruit an oblong capsule. Flowers from May to July. Grows in peat-bogs, mossy rocks and at outskirts of wet forests from lowlands to foothills. Avoids limestone soils. Native of northern Europe and Asia. Poisonous, formerly used for protection against moths. In some areas now exterminated; a protected plant in certain countries.

Family: **Heath** — *Ericaceae*

1 Heather or **Ling** *Calluna vulgaris*. Low shrub up to ½ m., rarely to 1 m. tall, sometimes decumbent, rooting and densely leafy. Leaves very small, linear, overlapping, with margins inrolled; glabrous or densely grey hairy in some forms. Flowers in one-sided racemes, drooping, pale purple, sometimes darker or white. Fruit a capsule. Flowers from July to October. Grows abundantly on acid soils, in places dominant over vast areas — heaths and moors — also in open woods, on rocks, and in sandy places, from lowlands to mountain slopes.

2 *Erica carnea*. Decumbent, well branched, small evergreen shrub to 30 cm. tall, with ascending, densely-leaved branches. Leaves linear, in whorls, smooth and glossy. Flowers in dense one-sided racemes. Stalked flowers drooping, rose-red, with narrow, bell-shaped corollas; capsule cylindrical. Flowers from December to May. Grows on screes, among rocks and in pine-woods, in the Alps and on their lower slopes. Many forms also cultivated. Related *Erica tetralix* has pink flowers in umbels and hairy leaves; *Erica cinerea* has flowers in dense racemes in summer.

Family: *Vacciniaceae*

3 Cowberry *Vaccinium vitis-idaea*. Low, densely branched evergreen shrub to 30 cm. with creeping shoots and erect twigs. Leaves alternate, obovate, the apex rounded or with a short point, slightly inrolled, margin dark green, glossy above, gland dotted beneath. Flowers in short terminal drooping racemes, corollas white or light rosy, bell-shaped. Fruit a berry, globose, red and glossy. Flowers from June to August. Grows in dry forests, especially pine-woods, on heaths, moors and peat-bogs, from hilly country to mountains.

4 Common Bilberry *Vaccinium myrtillus*. Low, densely branched deciduous bush with creeping stems and erect branches up to 60 cm. tall. Leaves alternate, ovate, pointed, finely serrate, smooth, bright green, borne on green, angled twigs. Flowers solitary in leaf-axils, stalked, drooping; corolla globose, palest green with rosy flush. Mature berries globose, black, with a waxy 'bloom'; edible and tasty. Flowers from April to July. Grows abundantly in forests, from lowlands high up to mountains; in Britain mainly on heaths and moors, locally abundant, but only on acid soils. Related cranberry (*Oxycoccus quadripetalus*), with evergreen leaves and prostrate stems and the corollas deeply four-parted, grows on peat-bogs.

Family: **Olive** — *Oleaceae*

5 *Forsythia suspensa*. Shrub up to 3 m. tall, with long, pendent branchlets, hollow, angled and warty. Leaves simple or trifoliate, ovate, irregularly serrate, mostly unfold later than flowers. Flowers in lateral clusters before the leaves; bright yellow, bell-shaped with four lobes. Fruit a capsule. Flowers in March and April. Native of eastern China, but frequently cultivated in parks and gardens.

6 Common Privet *Ligustrum vulgare*. A semi-evergreen to deciduous shrub up to 3 m. or more. Leaves opposite, shortly petiolate, lanceolate, entire, mostly pointed, bright green. Flowers in terminal, erect panicles; corollas cream-white and funnel-shaped. Fruit a glossy, black berry. Flowers in June and July. Grows on bushy slopes, in hedgerows and open woods, mainly at lower altitudes. Sometimes grown in hedges. The Japanese *L. ovalifolium*, a taller, more robust species with elliptic leaves, is now a popular hedging shrub.

2

6

1

3

5

4

Family: **Olive** — *Oleaceae*

1 Common Ash *Fraxinus excelsior*. Broad-headed tree up to 25 m. tall. Branches grey-green, buds black-brown, broadly ovate. Leaves opposite, odd-pinnate; leaflets sessile, ovate to lanceolate, long-pointed, finely and sharply toothed, smooth. Flowers tiny, purplish, without petals, in axillary panicles before the leaves. Fruits are narrow, elongated, glossy samaras on slender, pendent stalks. Flowers from April to May. Grows fairly abundantly in woods, meadows, on screes, and in hedgerows, from lowlands to mountains. Also often planted, particularly the weeping form.

Family: **Nightshade** — *Solanaceae*

2 Bittersweet or **Woody Nightshade** *Solanum dulcamara*. Climbing deciduous sub-shrub up to 2 m., sometimes more, with petiolate, entire, ovate, often pinnatifid leaves. Flowers in drooping panicles at end of branches. Corollas blue-violet with reflexed petals. Anthers yellow, a central yellow cone. Fruit a drooping, red, elliptical berry. Flowers from June to September. Grows fairly abundantly in thickets, hedgerows, woods and waste places, from lowlands to foothills.

Family: *Loniceraceae*

3 Common Elder *Sambucus nigra*. A shrub or small tree up to 10 m., with branchlets filled with white pith. Leaves odd-pinnate; leaflets ovate to elliptic, pointed, toothed, except at base. Inflorescence a large, flat-topped cyme with creamy flowers having a rank fragrance. Fruits are black, glossy druplets. Flowers in June and July. Grows abundantly in thickets, forests, on debris and along hedges from lowlands to foothills. Inflorescence and fruits edible and tasty, leaves poisonous.

4 Scarlet-berried Elder *Sambucus racemosa*. Shrub up to 4 m., with branchlets bearing yellow-brown pith. Leaves odd-pinnate, leaflets ovate to elliptic, finely toothed, on under side finely and thinly scalloped. Inflorescence a dense ovoid panicle with flowers greenish yellow. Red druplets. Flowers from April to May. Grows in clearings and at outskirts of woods, from foothills to mountains. Several forms, with deeply cut or golden leaves, are grown in parks and gardens.

5 Guelder Rose *Viburnum opulus*. A deciduous shrub or small tree up to 4 m. tall. Leaves palmate with three to five lobes, sharply pointed and irregularly toothed. Inflorescences flat, cymose; inner flowers small, bell-shaped, hermaphrodite, whitish; outer flowers large, round, white and sterile. Mature drupes subglobose, red. Flowers in May and June. Grows fairly abundantly at woodland margins, in thickets and hedgerows, from lowlands to mountains. Several forms are cultivated in gardens and parks; one (the snowball tree), has all sterile flowers in globose heads. Related wayfaring tree *(V. lantana)* with oval leaves, felt-like on underside, and no showy sterile florets, grows in more open places, especially on chalk and limestone.

6 Snowberry *Symphoricarpos rivularis*. A deciduous suckering shrub up to 2 m., or more, tall. Leaves oval, entire, rarely lobed. Flowers in small racemes; corollas bell-shaped, small, white with rosy tint. Fruit a white berry with spongy flesh. Flowers from June to August. Native of North America; commonly cultivated in woods for game birds, often becomes wild. Also often grown in gardens.

Herbaceous Plants

Class: **Angiospermous Plants** — *Magnoliopsida*

Subclass: **Dicotyledones** — *Magnoliidae*

Family: **Waterlily** — *Nymphaceae*

1 White Waterlily *Nymphaea alba.* Perennial aquatic herb with stout, creeping rhizome. Long-petiolate leaves, narrowly cordate, have circular blades, floating on water surface. Flowers large, cup-shaped, petals white, of same length as four green sepals. Stamens have linear filaments. Flowers from June to August. Grows in lakes and ponds, at low altitudes; often cultivated.

2 Yellow Waterlily *Nuphar lutea.* Aquatic plant with stout perennial rhizome, similar to white waterlily. Long-petiolate leaves with ovate-oblong blades are leathery, smooth, floating on water surface. Flowers yellow, strongly fragrant, with disc-like stigma. Fruits are bottle-shaped, pulpy capsules. Flowers from June to August. Grows in lakes, ponds and slow flowing rivers at lower altitudes. Related least yellow waterlily *(N. pumila)* has smaller flowers, slightly fragrant, with a somewhat lobed stigma.

Family: **Buttercup** — *Ranunculaceae*

3 Marsh Marigold *Caltha palustris.* Perennial, hairless herb 30—40 cm. high with fibrous roots, erect stems, sometimes ascending and rooting. Bottom leaves petiolate, top ones sessile, blades cordate, rounded to bluntly triangular, toothed and glossy. Flowers yellow, glossy, with 5—8 golden yellow petals. Fruit a cluster of beaked follicles. Flowers from March to July. Grows by the waterside, in damp meadows and ditches, from lowlands to mountains.

4 Globe Flower *Trollius europaeus.* Robust perennial herbs with erect stems, 30—60 cm. high, and terminal, solitary flowers. Leaves deeply palmately lobed with 3—5 segments, each deeply cut and toothed; lower leaves long-petiolate, upper ones sessile. Large flowers up to 3 cm. in diameter, globose, light to golden yellow, composed of 5—15 petaloid sepals. Fruit a cluster of beaked follicles. Flowers in May to July. Grows in wet meadows in foothills and mountains; in places extinct through over-picking, therefore it deserves strict protection. Hybrids of this and Asiatic species with orange flowers are cultivated in gardens.

5 Common Baneberry *Actaea spicata.* A somewhat foetid perennial, poisonous herb with erect, unbranched stems, 30—60 cm. high. Basal leaves bi- to tripinnate, leaflets ovate, pointed and toothed. Small flowers, yellowish-white, in long-stalked terminal racemes. Fruit a glossy black berry. Flowers in May and June. Grows in shady, deciduous forests from hills to mountains; in lowlands only rarely.

6 Columbine *Aquilegia vulgaris.* Perennial herb, up to 50 cm. high. Leaves composed of 3 to 9 somewhat glaucous leaflets, ovate, deeply to shallowly lobed; upper stem leaves smaller and less divided. Flowers long-stalked, pendent, blue-violet, rarely white or pink; sepals flared, coloured, petals elongated into curved spurs. Garden varieties of various colouring. Flowers from May to July. Grows in deciduous woods from lowlands to highlands. Much and long-cultivated in gardens, along with some Siberian and North-American species.

Family: **Buttercup** — *Ranunculaceae*

1 *Aconitum vulparia* (syn. *A. lycoctonum*). Poisonous, variable perennial herb with fibrous root system and widely branched stem, up to 1 metre high. Leaves palmately parted, segments 3—5 wedge-shaped, downy or smooth. Inflorescences of branched racemes, with well-spaced yellow, hairy flowers with long, cylindrical helmet-shaped spur. Flowers from June to August. Grows in deciduous woods and thickets from highlands to mountains. Sometimes cultivated.

2 Common Monkshood *Aconitum napellus*. A poisonous, perennial herb, with tuberous roots and erect, branched inflorescences. Leaves palmately divided, 3—5 lanceolate to widely linear segments. Dark violet flowers in dense racemes, the 'helmet' almost of same height and width. Flowers from June to August. Grows in moist woods and on banks of streams; also cultivated in gardens; occasionally becoming naturalized. Related lesser monkshood *(A. variegatum)* with 'helmet' much higher than wide, grows in similar places in mountains. Both strictly protected.

3 Wood Anemone *Anemone nemorosa*. Up to 25 cm. high herb with thin rhizome and solitary basal leaves. Stem simple, unbrached, with 3 petiolate leaves. Each leaf trifoliate, the segments bi- to trilobed. Flowers solitary, long-stalked, with usually six white tepals with pink flush outside. Hairy achenes with curved beak. Flowers from March to May. Grows in deciduous woods, thickets and damp meadows; almost common. Related yellow wood anemone *(A. ranunculoides)* has yellow flowers and almost sessile leaves.

4 Snowdrop Wind-flower *Anemone sylvestris*. Herb up to 35 cm. high with creeping rhizome and rosette of leaves. Leaves palmately 3—5 parted, segments toothed. Stem leaves divided into 5 oblong, lanceolate, deeply toothed segments. Flowers usually solitary, long-stalked, white, with five widely ovate tepals, hairy outside. Hairy achenes. Flowers from April to June. Grows on sunny, bushy slopes, in open woods, mostly on limestone soils, from lowlands to foothills, in milder regions. A protected plant.

5 *Anemone narcissiflora*. A variable tufted perennial. Stem up to 40 cm. high, hairy; basal leaves palmately 3—5 parted, each segment deeply toothed. Floral bracts usually in 3 to 5-lobed whorl. Flowers arranged in a several-stemmed umbel, erect; tepals white, sometimes flushed purple. Achenes hairless. Flowers from May to July. Grows in mountain meadows of Alps and other central-European mountains. Poisonous plant, strictly protected.

6 Larkspur *Consolida regalis* (syn. *Delphinium consolida*). Annual plant, with erect stem, up to 50 cm. high and branched only in upper half. Leaves much divided into linear segments; bracts linear, shorter than flower-stalks. Flowers in branched racemes, usually blue, spur reddish. Hairless follicles. Flowers from July to September. A field weed in southern Europe at lower altitudes; grown in gardens. This and the related species *C. ambigua* have given rise to the popular garden larkspurs.

Family: **Buttercup** — *Ranunculaceae*

1 *Delphinium elatum.* Perennial herb up to 150 cm. high, with simple stem, branched only at the inflorescence. Basal, long-petiolate leaves, smooth on the upper side, downy beneath, deeply palmately parted into widely wedge-shaped, deeply cut segments. Flowers dark blue to blue-violet, long-spurred, in dense raceme. Flowers in June and July, in original mountain habitats till September. Grows along mountain streams. Hybrids with this and two other species have given rise to the giant border delphiniums of gardens.

2 Alpine Anemone *Pulsatilla alpina.* Up to 30 cm. high herb with branched rhizome, rosette of basal leaves and several simple, hairy, single-flowered stems with whorl of bracts. Basal leaves long-petiolate, stem ones shortly petiolate, with deeply dissected segments. Flowers long-stalked, with 6 white tepals often flushed outside with pink or violet; sometimes yellow. Achenes have long, hairy awn to aid dispersal by wind. Flowers from May to August. Grows on rocky mountain slopes, in meadows and amongst knee-pine. Strictly protected, similar to other pulsatillas.

3 Pasque Flower *Pulsatilla vulgaris.* A variable species with large flowers in shades of purple and violet. Illustrated species has stem up to 50 cm. high. Basal leaves develop as the first flowers fade. They are long-petiolate, at first densely hairy, later thinly hairy, simply or twice pinnate, each leaflet deeply dissected; floral bracts divided into narrowly linear segments. Flowers with 6 tepals outside silky hairy, at first tulip-shaped, later opening wide, light to misty violet. Flowers from March to May. Grows on grassy slopes, on limestone soils. Also cultivated as rock-garden plant and occasionally escaping.

4 Fair Maids of France *Ranunculus aconitifolius.* Perennial, robust herb up to 1 metre high or more, with short rhizomes and a well-branched stem. Basal, long-petioled leaves are palmately five-parted, the segments lobed and deeply serrate; stem leaves similar to basal ones, mostly sessile. Flowers white, with 5 petals. Achenes shortly beaked. Flowers from May to August. Grows in mountain forests, along streams and in knee-pine. Poisonous.

5 Meadow Buttercup *Ranunculus acris.* A poisonous perennial herb, up to 1 metre high. Basal leaves long-petiolate, palmately five-parted, segments lanceolate, dissected and toothed. Stem sometimes with spreading hairs. Stem leaves similar to basal ones, upper leaves cleft into linear segments. Flowers with 5 glossy golden yellow petals. Achenes shortly beaked. Flowers from May to September. Grows abundantly in meadows and moist grassy places.

6 Creeping Buttercup *Ranunculus repens.* Perennial plant with erect flowering stems up to 50 cm. long, and creeping stems rooting at the nodes. Basal leaves trifoliate, each leaflet petiolate, lobed and toothed; stem leaves similar to basal ones, upper leaves sessile, cleft into lanceolate or linear segments. Flowers glossy golden yellow with 5 petals. Achenes smooth, with curved beak. Flowers from May to August. Grows abundantly in wet meadows, fields, along banks of streams and ponds; also a garden weed.

1

2

3

5

6

Familly: **Buttercup** — *Ranunculaceae*

1 Water Crowfoot *Batrachium aquatile* (syn. *Ranunculus aquatilis*). Perennial aquatic plant with floating, smooth, branched stem to 1 m. Submerged petiolate leaves much divided into linear, forked segments which collapse after being taken out of water. Leaves floating on water surface are long-petiolate, rounded to reniform, cordate, palmately three-to five-lobed. Long-stalked flowers above water surface, with 5 white petals. Achenes wrinkled, bristle tipped. Flowers from June to September. Grows in lakes and ponds at lower altitudes. Related river crowfoot *(B. fluitans)* has much longer segments to submerged leaves; segments of rigid-leaved crowfoot *(B. circinatum)* do not lose shape when taken out of water.

2 Noble Liverleaf *Hepatica nobilis* (syn. *H. triloba, Anemone hepatica*). Perennial herb with shortly creeping rhizome and single-flowered stems. Leaves trilobed, leathery, softly hairy on underside. A whorl of 3 calyx-like bracts immediately beneath the flower. Flower stalks hairy; flowers with 6—10 tepals, blue to light or dark violet, less frequently rosy or whitish. Achenes without appendages. Flowers in February to April. Grows in deciduous groves and bushy places from lowlands to foothills; locally abundant only. A protected plant.

3 Lesser Celandine *Ficaria verna* (syn. *Ranunculus ficaria*). Perennial herb with tubers among fibrous roots. Smooth stem up to 20 cm. high. Basal and stem leaves petiolate, cordate, rounded to reniform, scalloped to notched, smooth, glossy. Some forms have tiny tubers in axils of basal leaves. Flowers solitary, with 8—12 tepals of glossy yellow. Achenes small, ovoid. Flowers from March to May. Grows commonly in open woods, meadows, ditches and along banks.

4 French Meadow-rue *Thalicrum aquilegiifolium*. Robust herb up to 1 metre or more high with erect stem, branched in the upper part, grooved and hairless. Leaves bi- to tripinnate, leaflets obovate, lobed, smooth and grey-green, resembling those of columbine. Flowers in dense corymbose panicles; no petals and the small whitish sepals soon falling; stamen filaments violet, thickened. Ovaries and achenes long-stalked, pendent. Flowers from May to July. Grows in moist forests and thickets and by the waterside from foothills to mountains. Similar but much smaller lesser meadow-rue *(T. minus)* has yellow stamens and greenish sepals.

5 Spring Pheasant's Eye *Adonis vernalis*. Poisonous perennial plant, up to 40 cm. high, with thick rhizome. Erect stem scaly at base. Leaves sessile, up to four cleft into linear segments. Flowers solitary, large, of 10—20 narrowly elongated bright glossy yellow petals. Flowers in April and May. Grows on sunny slopes, bushy ravines and in pine-woods, as a rule on limestone soils. Occasionally cultivated for ornament. Strictly protected plant.

6 Summer Pheasant's Eye *Adonis aestivalis*. Annual herb up to 50 cm. high with erect, little branched stem. Basal leaves petiolate, upper ones sessile, as a rule cut into many linear segments. Flowers individual, smallish, petals red, rarely light yellow, at base usually with black spot. Achenes smooth, oblong-ovoid, beaked. Flowers from May to July. Grows as field weed at lower altitudes in milder regions.

1

2

5

3

6

4

Family: **Buttercup** — *Ranunculaceae*

1 Upright Clematis *Clematis recta*. Perennial herb up to 1.5 m. high, with erect, non-climbing stems. Basal stem leaves simple, upper ones odd-pinnate, leaflets ovate to lanceolate, entire, petiolate. Flowers arranged in terminal panicles; white, composed of 4 petal-like sepals. Achenes have long, hairy style. Flowers in June and July. Grows on bushy slopes, in open woods and meadows, at lower altitudes, mainly on limestone soils. The climbing, white to green-white flowered traveller's joy — *C. vitalba* of Europe (including Britain) and northern Africa is more abundant and flowers from July to September. Many exotic species and cultivated varieties and hybrids are grown in gardens.

Family: *Aristolochiaceae*

2 Asarabacca — *Asarum europaeum*. Perennial evergreen herb with branched, scaly rhizome. Stems prostrate, each lateral shoot usually with two long-petiolate, reniform, entire, glossy deep green leaves. Fleshy, bell-shaped flowers with 3 lobes brownish outside, dark violet within, are hidden by leaves. Flowers from March to May. Grows in humid groves and among bushes from lowlands to mountains.

3 Birthwort *Aristolochia clematitis*. Foetid perennial herb with erect, unbranched stems, up to 50 cm. or more high. Leaves alternate, long-petiolate, rounded cordate. Flowers in small groups in axils of leaves; at first erect, later drooping. Corolla tubular, slightly curved, swollen at base, dull yellow. Capsule pear-shaped. Flowers in May and June. Grows in thickets, in hedges and vineyards at lower altitudes, in temperate regions. Formerly cultivated as a medicinal plant and later becoming naturalized.

Family: **Poppy** — *Papaveraceae*

4 *Papaver alpinum*. Perennial tufted herb, with unbranched flowering stems up to 20 cm. high. Leaves petiolate, simply pinnate, segments linear to linear-lanceolate, deeply lobed, grey-green. Flowers white or yellow, calyx, with black bristles, falls off as flower expands; petals widely obovate. Seed-heads small, obovate with a flat top. Flowers in July and August. Grows on screes, and among rocks at high elevations of the Alps and Carpathians.

5 Field Poppy *Papaver rhoeas*. Annual herb with erect, simple or little branched stems, bristly, leafy, up to 1 metre high. Leaves pinnate, segments deeply lobed and toothed, lower ones petiolate, upper sessile and bristly. Solitary flowers on long stalks with bristles; drooping in bud, erect in bloom. Calyx green, bristly, falling as flower opens. Corolla of 4 bright red petals; stigma usually ten-lobed. Seed-heads obovate, flat topped. Flowers from May to September. Grows as weed in fields and gardens, on spoil heaps and wasteland, from lowlands to foothills in temperate regions; locally abundant, elsewhere missing.

6 Greater Celandine *Chelidonium majus*. Perennial herb releasing orange latex when cut. Stem up to 60 cm. high, erect and branched. Leaves somewhat hairy, lower ones petiolate, odd-pinnate, upper leaves sessile, deeply cut; segments lobed and toothed, underside grey-green. Flowers in umbels, yellow, petals soon falling. Capsule linear. Flowers from May to October. Grows in open woods, thickets and hedgerows, from lowlands to foothills.

Family: **Fumitory** — *Fumariaceae*

1 Common Fumitory *Fumaria officinalis*. Annual, grey-green herb, up to 30 cm. high, with erect or ascending stem, branched and leafy. Leaves petiolate, bipinnate; petiolate leaflets palmately parted into linear segments. Flowers in upright racemes, small and narrow, rosy red, dark purple at tip; tiny sepals persistent. Fruits globular, single-seeded. Flowers from May up to October. Grows commonly as weed in fields, gardens and on wasteland from lowlands to foothills.

2 *Corydalis cava*. Perennial herb up to 30 cm. high, with hollow-topped underground tuber and erect stem, as a rule with two leaves. Leaves cut into several lobed leaflets. Flowers in erect raceme, bracts under flowers entire; corollas rosy-purple, yellow-white, spurred. Capsules long and narrow, beaked. Flowers from March to May. Grows in woods and thickets, from lowlands to foothills. Related *Corydalis fabacea* has pendent, few-flowered raceme while *Corydalis solida* has palmately lobed bracts beneath the flowers.

Family: *Cruciferae* (syn. *Brassicaceae*)

3 Charlock or **Wild Mustard** *Sinapis arvensis*. Annual plant up to 50 cm. high with erect, little branched stem, irregularly hairy. Leaves mostly unparted, irregularly toothed, lower ones lyre-shaped, pinnatisect. Flowers have expanded, yellow-green sepals, corollas yolk-yellow, of four petals. Seed pod, either somewhat hairy or not at all, with short beak. Flowers from June up to October. Grows fairly abundantly as field weed in lower altitudes. Related *Sinapis alba*, cultivated for seeds, has stem leaves lyre-like, pinnatisect to pinnately parted.

4 Wild Radish *Raphanus raphanistrum*. Annual herb with erect, slender, bristly stem. Leaves petiolate, lower ones lyre-shaped to pinnately lobed, unequally dentated; top leaves often unparted and irregularly toothed. Petals sulphur yellow, violet-veined, sepals erect. Fruit is a pod or loment, dehiscent, with beaked last segment. Flowers from June to October. Grows fairly abundantly as weed in fields and on wasteland. Related radish *(R. sativus)* with flowers white or violet-tinted and non-dehiscent loment is cultivated as vegetable.

5 Hoary Cress *Cardaria draba*. Perennial, grey-downy herb, up to 50 cm. high. Basal leaves ovate, stem ones usually shallowly toothed, clasping, arrow-shaped. Flowers in branched, crowded racemes, corollas white. Siliqua (pod) heart-shaped with long, persistent style. Flowers from May to July. Grows as weed in fields, on wasteland and trenches. Native of eastern Mediterranean, today abundantly naturalized, especially in milder regions.

6 Field Pennycress *Thlaspi arvense*. Annual hairless herb, up to 30 cm. high, after bruising gives out a foetid smell. Stems slender, leaves distantly toothed, dentated, arrow-shaped, stem clasping. Flowers in erect racemes; calyx yellow-green, corolla white. Siliquas large, flat, ovately rounded, with wide rim, deeply dissected. Flowers from May to October. Commonly grows as weed in fields, fallows and on wasteland.

Family: *Cruciferae*

1 Shepherd's Purse *Capsella bursa-pastoris.* Annual to biennial herb, up to 50 cm. high, stem often branched. Basal leaves pinnatisect to almost entire, arranged in rosette, stem leaves clasping. Many-flowered inflorescences; flowers small, white, occasionally petal-less. Siliquas roughly triangular with many small seeds. Flowers from February to November, sometimes whole year round. Grows as common weed in fields, gardens, on wasteland and along paths from lowlands to mountains.

2 Perennial Honesty *Lunaria rediviva.* Perennial plant up to 140 cm. high, with creeping rhizome and erect, unbranched stem. Leaves petiolate, cordate, upper ones triangular, toothed. Flowers light violet, rarely whitish. Siliquas large, elliptical, tapering to both ends, with membraneous partition and stiff valves. Flowers from May to July. Scattered on screes, in open mountain forests and in ravines from foothills to mountains. Protected plant. Cultivated honesty *(L. annua)*, native of eastern Mediterranean, has sessile upper leaves and large, broad siliquas.

3 Golden Alison *Alyssum saxatile.* Evergreen sub-shrub with oblanceolate, grey-felted leaves. Stems up to 30 cm. high, upright, few-leaved. Inflorescence branched; flowers in dense corymbs; petals shallowly lobed, golden yellow, siliquas hairless. Flowers in April and May. Grows on sunny rocks. Also cultivated as rock-garden plant.

4 Mountain Alison *Alyssum montanum.* Perennial sub-shrub, 10—20 cm. high. Stems and grey-green leaves have grey hairs which are branched and distinctly star-shaped under lens. Lower leaves obovate or spatulate, upper ones oblanceolate. Flowers in simple racemes; sepals as well as petals soon fall, corollas golden yellow. Raceme during fruition much elongated, siliquas almost round. Flowers from April to June. Grows on rocks, dry and sunny slopes, sandy places and margins of pine-woods at lower altitudes, in warm regions.

5 Common Whitlow-grass *Erophila verna.* Tiny, annual, only 2 to 10 cm. high with basal rosette of leaves and simple, leafless, filamentous stem. Leaves elliptic or lanceolate, entire or toothed. Few-flowered inflorescences; upper side of sepals hairy, margins white or light violet, membraneous. Petals distinctly cleft, white; siliquas elliptic to almost rounded, without style. Flowers from March to May. Grows gregariously in places from lowlands to mountains, on slopes, in fields, meadows, fallows, and on walls.

6 Lady's Smock *Cardamine pratensis.* Perennial herb, 20—40 cm. high, with short rhizome and erect, hollow stem. Basal leaves in rosette, odd-pinnate, with up to 8 pairs of ovate leaflets, angularly toothed. Stem leaves pinnately divided, with linear, usually entire segments. Flowers often in dense racemes, lilac or violet-tinted, distinctly violet-veined. Anthers yellow; siliquas linear without beak. Flowers from April to June. Grows abundantly in damp meadows, from lowlands to mountains. Related bitter cress *(C. amara)* has rather weak, semi-decumbent stems and white flowers with violet anthers.

Family: *Cruciferae*

1 Common Winter-cress *Barbarea vulgaris*. Biennial, almost hairless herb up to 50 cm. high. Lower leaves lyre-shaped, pinnately lobed, terminal leaflet broadly ovate, somewhat lobed or toothed; base of leaf stem clasping. Racemes dense, branched; flowers golden yellow, petals almost double length of sepals. Siliquas erect on short stalks. Flowers from May to July. Grows in meadows, ditches, along streams, and also in fields and on wasteland, from lowlands to mountains.

2 *Hesperis matronalis*. Perennial, robust herb, up to over 1 metre high, hairy. Lower leaves oblong-ovate to lanceolate, upper ones smaller, almost sessile, all distantly toothed. Raceme long, sometimes branched; flowers large, fragrant, usually violet, rarely reddish or white, petals somewhat shallowly toothed. Siliquas cylindrical, up to 10 cm. long. Flowers from May to July. Grows wild in Mediterranean; often cultivated and becoming naturalized on waste ground, along hedges, in thickets and open woods.

3 Garlic Mustard or **Jack-by-the-Hedge** *Alliaria petiolata* (syn. *A. officinalis*). Biennial herb, smelling of garlic when bruised. Stems erect, often branched at the top. Lower leaves long-petiolate, cordate, irregularly sinuate toothed; stem leaves shortly petiolate, ovate to triangular, irregularly toothed. Flowers small, white; siliquas long, stalked, erect. Flowers from April to June. Grows in open woods, thickets, in hedgerows and on wasteland, abundant from lowlands to foothills.

Family: **Mignonette** — *Resedaceae*

4 Wild Mignonette *Reseda lutea*. Perennial herb with erect stems, little or not branched, up to 50 cm. high. Leaves once pinnately cut into linear segments, with wavy margins. Flowers in dense racemes, during fruition becoming elongated. Each floret yellow-green, with 6 narrow petals, the 4 upper ones lobed. Upright oblong capsules. Flowers from May to September. Grows on grassy slopes and waste ground and as weed of cultivated land at lower altitudes in milder regions. Garden mignonette *(R. odorata)*, a North-African species, is cultivated in gardens; it has almost undivided leaves, reddish anthers and pendent fruits.

Family: **Rockrose** — *Cistaceae*

5 *Helianthemum chamaecistus* (syn. *H. nummularium*). Procumbent, evergreen, hairy shrublet 10 to 20 cm. high. Leaves oval or oblong-ovate, densely white, hairy beneath. Inflorescence a few-flowered raceme, flowers large, 2—2.5 cm. in diameter. Two minute outside sepals linear, three inner ones larger, ovate. Corolla of five yellow, rarely yellowish white petals. Flowers from June to October. Grows on sunny grassy slopes, and in open scrub, from lowlands to mountains.

Family: *Silenaceae (Caryophyllaceae)*

6 Corn Cockle *Agrostemma githago* (syn. *Lychnis githago*). Annual plant with erect stem up to 1 metre high, grey hairy. Leaves opposite, linear-lanceolate, hairy. Long-stalked flowers solitary; calyx bell-shaped, with five slender lobes; corolla red-purple, petals obovate. Capsules ovoid with black, reniform, poisonous seeds. Grows as weed in cereal crops in lower altitudes; formerly more abundant. Native probably of eastern Mediterranean.

Family: *Silenaceae*

1 Ragged Robin *Lychnis flos-cuculi*. Perennial plant up to 80 cm. high. Stems of two sorts; decumbent and leafy and erect flowering. Opposite leaves narrowly to oblong lanceolate, entire. Open dichasial inflorescence; calyx bell-shaped, with 5 triangular teeth. Petals rose-red, cleft into four linear segments. Capsule broadly ovoid. Flowers from May to July. Grows in damp meadows, marshes, fens and open wet woods, from lowlands to mountains.

2 *Lychnis alba* (syn. *Silene alba, Melandrium album*). Annual to perennial herb, up to 1 metre high, softly downy, stems erect, branched. Lower leaves petiolate, oblanceolate, upper ones lanceolate to elliptic, sessile, all opposite. Flowers arranged in open dichasia. Flowers dioecious, stalked, opening in afternoon, slightly fragrant, calyx bell-shaped, inflated, with 5 pointed teeth; petals white, lobed. Capsule widely ovoid, enveloped in persistent calyx. Flowers from June to September. Grows in hedgerows, meadows, on waste and cultivated land, from lowlands to foothills. Related *Silene dioica* (syn. *Melandrium rubrum*) has red flowers and hairy stems.

3 Red German Catchfly *Lychnis viscaria* (syn. *Viscaria vulgaris*). Perennial plant up to 50 cm. high, with smooth stem, having sticky zones beneath each pair of the upper leaves. Bottom leaves oblong-lanceolate, upper ones linear-lanceolate, all opposite, often with red tint. Inflorescence an interrupted spike-like panicle of axillary cymes. Calyx tubular, reddish, corolla bright red; ovoid capsules. Flowers from May to July. Grows in pastures, on stony slopes and dry rocks, from lowlands to foothills; very rare in Britain.

4 Moss Campion *Silene acaulis*. Perennial plant, cushion-like, densely leafy with numerous stems, only 2—4 cm. high. Leaves spreading, linear, pointed, sessile. Flowers solitary, short-stalked. Calyx narrowly bell-shaped, petals bright to dark rose; capsules stalked, ovoid. Flowers from June to September. Grows on stony slopes and ledges, screes and among rocks above forest zone in mountains of western and central Europe.

5 Bladder Campion *Silene vulgaris* (syn. *S. cucubalus*). Herb up to 50 cm. high, perennial, grey-green and smooth. Leaves elliptic lanceolate, entire, lower ones almost, upper leaves distinctly sessile. Flowers arranged in corymbose cymes, lower ones with long stalks, upper flowers short-stalked. Calyx inflated, ovoid, strikingly net-veined, yellowish green or with tint of purple. Petals usually white, deeply bilobed. Capsules broadly ovoid. Flowers from June to September. Grows on grassy slopes, by the roadside, on margins of woods, and on cultivated land, from lowlands to mountains.

6 Nottingham Catchfly *Silene nutans*. Up to 50 cm. high, perennial, with erect and un-branched stems. Lower leaves spathulate, upper ones with short petioles, lanceolate to linear-lanceolate, with short hairs. Inflorescence a lax panicle of dichasial cymes, glandularly hairy; flowers long-stalked, more or less drooping. Calyx cylindrical, petals whitish, deeply bilobed. Capsules ovoid. Flowers from May to August. Grows on sunny slopes, among rocks, at outskirts of woods, and on shingle, from lowlands to foothills.

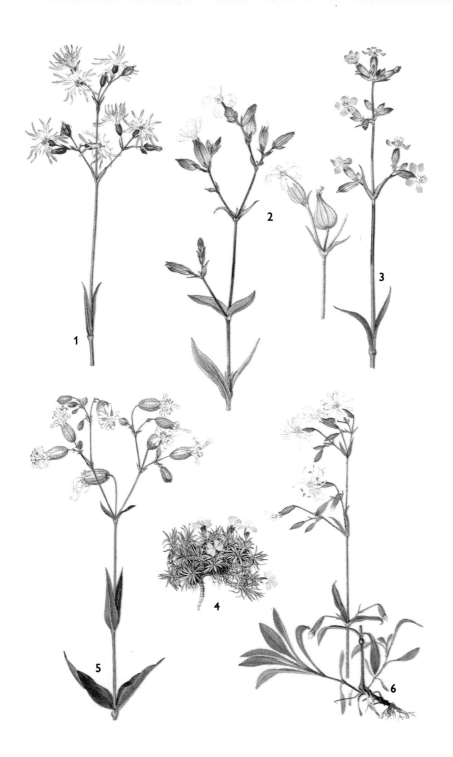

Family: *Silenaceae*

1 German Pink *Dianthus carthusianorum.* Perennial, tufted herb, over 25 cm. high, with slender flowering stems and short, leafy, non-flowering ones, little branched. Leaves linear, fused at the base into a short sheath, pointed, stiff, rough on margins. Inflorescence a dense corymbose head, flowers almost sessile, bracts under calyx leathery, brown to red-brown, bluntly obovate, with awn-like point. Calyx cylindrical, smooth with maroon tint; petals purple red, with toothed tip; capsules narrow oblong. Flowers from June to September. Grows on grassy, stony dry slopes and field boundaries.

2 Maiden Pink *Dianthus deltoides.* Perennial, sparsely tufted herb, with prostrate leafy stems and erect flowering ones. Leaves linear, pointed, opposite, roughly hairy on margins. Flowers long-stalked, solitary, bracts under calyx membraneous. Calyx cylindrical, sometimes reddish; petals carmine red, toothed at tip; conspicuously bristled and white-dotted at base. Flowers from June to September. Grows in dry pastures, banks and field boundaries, from lowland to foothill country. Some related species, e.g. carnation *(D. caryophyllus)* and China pink *(D. chinensis)*, are cultivated in gardens.

3 Soapwort *Saponaria officinalis.* Perennial robust plant, up to 75 cm. high, erect, usually with finely downy stem, branched only in upper part. Leaves ovate to elliptic, pointed, sessile, three to five-veined. Flowers pink, sometimes white, in terminal corymbs. Calyx usually light green, hairy; petals blunt or square tipped. Capsules oblong ovoid. Flowers from June to September. Grows in hedgerows, by streams and in open moist woods, from lowlands to foothills. A double-flowered form is sometimes cultivated and becomes naturalized on banks and wasteland.

4 Greater Stitchwort *Stellaria holostea.* Perennial, sparsely tufted plant with creeping rhizome and erect, square stems, up to 30 cm. high. Leaves spreading, narrowly lanceolate, pointed, opposite, underside and margins rough. Flowers in an open, terminal, few-flowered dichasia. Petals white, double the length of calyx, almost deeply bilobed. Flowers from May to September. Grows in hedgerows, on bushy slopes and in open woodland from lowlands to foothills. Related common chickweed *(S. media)* has much smaller flowers and petals of same length as calyx.

5 Field Mouse-ear *Cerastium arvense.* Perennial herb, sparsely tufted, up to 30 cm. high, with numerous stems creeping or ascending, with sterile leafy shoots. Leaves narrowly oblong to linear-lanceolate, pointed, hairy. Flowers in a lax dichasia. Sepals hairy, with whitish membraneous margins; petals double the calyx length, white, bilobed. Flowers from April to July. Grows in dry grassland and on banks, from lowlands to mountains.

6 *Cerastium holosteoides* (syn. *C. vulgatum*). Perennial tufted herb up to 30 cm. high, with ascending, flowering stems and semi-prostrate, leafy, sterile shoots. Leaves oblanceolate to elliptic, bluntly pointed, with short hairs. Flowers in an open dichasia. Petals slightly longer than calyx, small, white, bilobed. Flowers from May to October. Grows by the roadside, on dunes, in dry meadows and on grassy slopes, from lowlands to mountains.

Family: *Stellariaceae (Alsinaceae)*

1 Sand Spurrey *Spergularia rubra*. Annual or biennial plant, somewhat tufted, decumbent or ascending. Stems 5—25 cm. long; leaves narrowly linear, sharply pointed, shorter than stem internodes. Stipules ovate, fused around the node, silvery membraneous. Flowers in a small terminal cyme; flower stalks nodding, after fertilization again erect, and elongated when capsule is mature. Petals rose, usually shorter than sepals. Flowers from May to September. Grows in sandy or gravelly soils, from lowlands to foothills.

Family: **Violas** — *Violaceae*

2 Sweet Violet *Viola odorata*. Perennial herb with short, thick rhizomes and long prostrate stolons. Basal leaves ovate-orbicular, cordate, sparingly hairy. Stems up to 10 cm. high, with widely ovate stipules, entire or glandular fringed. Fragrant flowers blue-violet or white, rarely pink; petals whitish at base, the lowest one spurred; calyx has appendages which are much shorter than the spur. Flowers in March and April. Grows in woods, thickets and hedgebanks at lower altitudes; often cultivated in gardens. Related heath violet *(V. canina)* is distinctly hairy and has narrower leaves, and unscented flowers with a whitish spur.

3 Common Violet *Viola riviniana*. Perennial plant with short rhizome and basal rosette of leaves. Stems erect, usually 10—15 cm. high. Leaves long-petiolate, ovate-orbicular, deeply cordate, crenate; stipules lanceolate, deeply fringed. Flowers large, various shades of blue-violet, spur paler. Calyx with angularly rounded appendages. Flowers in April and May. Grows in open woods, hedgebanks, heaths, pastures and among rocks, from lowlands to mountains. A very variable species; the smaller forms distinguished as *V. riviniana* ssp. *minor*.

4 Heartsease or **Wild Pansy** *Viola tricolor*. Annual or perennial herb, usually tufted, up to 20 cm. high, with branched, erect or ascending stem. Leaves petiolate, ovate to lanceolate; stipules deeply lobed. Flowers on long stalks; lanceolate sepals have blunt to rounded appendages. Petals often double calyx length, two upper ones mostly violet, others light yellow, or entirely blue-violet or yellow; spur longer than calyx appendages. Flowers from May to September. Grows in fields and meadows, on wasteland, from lowlands to foothills. Related field violet *V. arvensis* has much smaller light yellow flowers, the calyx and corolla of equal length. *Viola × wittrockiana* is the cultivated hybrid garden pansy with large flowers of varied colouring.

Family: **Goosefoot** — *Chenopodiaceae*

5 Good King Henry *Chenopodium bonus-henricus*. Only perennial goosefoot; stem up to 50 cm. or more high, unbranched. Petiolate leaves triangular, with pointed basal lobes and a wavy margin. Globose clusters of flowers arranged in dense, terminal, leafy, pyramidal panicle. Flowers have minute five-lobed perianth which enfolds the base of the tiny ovoid capsule. Flowers from May to August. Grows abundantly near human dwellings and by roadsides from lowlands to foothills. Related sowbane *(C. hybridum)* and especially stinking goosefoot *(C. vulvaria)* are slightly poisonous and distinctly malodorous.

6 Shining Orache *Atriplex nitens*. Annual herb up to 150 cm. high, with branched stems. Leaves triangular, lobed, on upper surface glossy, dark green, on underside silvery grey with a mealy coating. Inflorescence drooping, especially during fruiting. Pair of enlarged bracts in which fruit is enclosed, is rhomboid, entire, longer than fruit stalks. Minute flowers are greenish. Flowers from July to September. Grows on wasteland and by roadsides at lower altitudes. Related common orache *(A. patula)* has rhomboid-lanceolate to linear-oblong leaves and floral bracts with one or two small teeth on each side.

Family: **Knotgrass** — *Polygonaceae*

1 Sheep's Sorrel *Rumex acetosella*. Perennial plant, often with red tint; stem up to 25 cm. high, decumbent or erect. Lower leaves long-petiolate, hastate, upper ones linear-lanceolate. Inflorescence a small branched raceme; flowers have small greenish perianth; during fruition this enlarges and more or less encloses the fruit. Flowers from May to August. Grows on heaths and pastures, and as a weed in fields and gardens from lowlands to foothills.

2 Common Sorrel *Rumex acetosa*. Over 50 cm. high, perennial. Lower stem leaves narrowly ovate, arrow-shaped, with pointed basal lobes. Stipules fused as a fringed sheath. Inflorescence a branched raceme; flowers have green perianth. Inner segments rounded cordate with tiny, round swelling, enlarging during fruit development; outer segments reflex back. Flowers from May to July. Grows in light woodland clearings, in damp meadows, and by roadsides, from lowlands to mountains. Eaten in salads and sauces. Related curled dock *(R. crispus)* has a triangularly ovate fruiting perianth and the lower leaves with waved and curled margins.

3 Bistort or **Easter-ledges** *Polygonum bistorta*. Perennial herb with thick rhizome and simple stems up to 1 metre high. Basal leaves long petiolate, ovate, pointed, entire, stem leaves triangular-ovate, sessile. Inflorescence a dense terminal spike, individual flowers rosy, rarely whitish. Flowers from May to July. Grows in damp meadows, pastures and by roadsides, often in dense colonies or clumps, from lowlands to mountains. *Polygonum persicaria* has leaves with large, horseshoe-shaped maroon blotch.

4 Knotgrass *Polygonum aviculare*. An annual, decumbent plant with branched stem, up to 50 cm. long, forming, often dense, mats. Leaves elliptic, spathulate, lanceolate or linear with membraneous stipules, fused into sheaths, usually lacerated. Flowers in clusters of one to six in leaf axils; perianth whitish, often pink tinted; enlarging during fruition and becoming red. Flowers from May to October. Grows in waste places, by roadsides, along paths and as farm and garden weed, from lowlands to hill-country.

5 *Polygonum convolvulus*. Annual, prostrate or twining, with angular stems up to 1 metre long. Leaves ovate-accuminate to triangular, arrow-shaped. Flowers in an interrupted, terminal raceme; perianth of 5 segments, the outer two somewhat keeled. Flowers from July to October. Grows as field and garden weed, and on wasteland at lower altitudes.

Family: **Nettle** — *Urticaceae*

6 Hop *Humulus lupulus*. Twinging, perennial, dioecious plant, with coarsely hairy stems, 2—6 metres long. Stipules triangular-ovate; leaves opposite, long-petiolate, lower ones palmately three- to five-lobed, cordate, upper leaves more shallowly lobed to ovate, all boldly toothed. Male flowers in axillary panicles, female ones in ovoid, cone-like spikes. Fruiting heads pendent, light greenish-yellow, their scales covered with golden yellow glands. Flowers from July to August. Grows in hedgerows, amongst scrub, and at edges of woodland at lower altitudes. Has been cultivated since 8th century in fields for flavouring beer.

Family: **Nettle** — *Urticaceae*

1 Small Nettle *Urtica urens.* Annual herb, 10—30 cm. high, with erect, little branched stems. Leaves ovate to elliptic, serrate. Erect inflorescences of same length as petioles or shorter; tiny flowers have light green perianth. Fruit a tiny ovoid nutlet. Whole plant covered with stinging hairs; sharply 'burns' on touch. Flowers from June to September. Grows abundantly as weed in fields and gardens, on wasteland and by rubbish tips at lower altitudes.

2 Stinging Nettle *Urtica dioica.* Robust, perennial, dioecious herb with a far-creeping rhizome. Stems erect, rarely branched, up to 150 cm. tall. Leaves petiolate, ovate, cordate, pointed, serrate. Male inflorescences spreading or pendent panicles, longer than leaf petioles; female always drooping and longer. Perianth greenish, nutlet ovoid. Whole plant covered with stinging hairs, but sometimes without. Flowers from June to October. Grows as a farm and garden weed on waste ground, in thickets, damp woods, ditches and in hedgerows, from lowlands to mountains.

Family: **Sundew** — *Droseraceae*

3 Common Sundew *Drosera rotundifolia.* Perennial herb, forming solitary or tufted rosettes. One to several erect stems, 10—20 cm. high, usually red tinted, bearing a few-flowered spike of tiny, white flowers. Leaves rounded and fleshy, long-petiolate, reddish, with long, glandular hairs; fruit is capsule. Flowers in July and August. Grows in bogs and wet peaty places, on moors and heaths, from lowlands to mountains. Grows in sites with soil poor in nitrogenous substances; acquires missing compounds from bodies of insects. Sensitive, glandular hairs exude sticky liquid which traps insects; special glands secrete substances for digesting soft parts of insect body.

Family: **Crassula** — *Crassulaceae*

4 Orpine or **Livelong** *Sedum telephium.* Perennial herb with thick rootstock and erect stems up to 50 cm. high. Leaves ovate to oblong-lanceolate or obovate, toothed, tapered to sessile base, alternate, opposite or in whorls of three, fleshy grey-green. Inflorescence flattened and compact, composed of numerous cymes; sepals 5, green, corollas reddish purple. Flowers from July to September. Grows among rocks, on hedgebanks, walls, and in light dry woods from lowlands to mountains.

5 Wall Pepper *Sedum acre.* Perennial, mat-forming plant, 5—10 cm. high, with prostrate, much branched stems. Leaves widely ovate to ovoid trigonous, blunt, sessile, thickly set and usually overlapping, having a sharply burning taste. Inflorescence a few-flowered cyme; flowers short-stalked, corollas bright yellow, starry. Flowers in June and July. Grows on sunny slopes, among rocks, in sandy places, on wasteland, walls and dunes, from lowlands to foothills.

6 *Sempervivum soboliferum.* Perennial herb with leaves arranged in a dense basal rosette. Leaves ovate, reddish brown at tip, margins shortly bristled. Flowering stems glandular-hairy, up to 20 cm. high, thickly leaved. Calyx also glandular, sepals red-tipped. Petals six, pointed, greenish yellow. Flowers in July and August. Grows on rocks, stony slopes and walls, from lowlands to mountains. Protected plant. Common houseleek *(S. tectorum)*, bearing rosy flowers, and other species are cultivated in gardens.

Family: **Saxifrage** — *Saxifragaceae*

1 Meadow Saxifrage *Saxifraga granulata*. Perennial, somewhat tufted plant, up to 40 cm. high, with basal rosettes and stems usually branched. Overwinters as a cluster of small bulbils from the axils of the basal leaves. These leaves are reniform, cordate, glandular-hairy, usually with large crenations. Stem leaves almost sessile, much smaller. Inflorescence a loose terminal cyme. Flowers shortly glandular, petals white, at least three times longer than calyx. Capsules ovoid or sub-globose. Flowers in May and June. Grows in well-drained grassland and on margins of woods at lower altitudes.

2 Livelong Saxifrage *Saxifraga paniculata* (syn. *S. aizoon*). Perennial herb with stiff, grey-green leaves in numerous basal rosettes. Basal leaves obovate to ligulate, serrate; the margins with small glands which secrete calcium carbonate. Stem up to 30 cm. tall, leaves small, ligulate, finely serrate. Inflorescence open, paniculate, corollas white, often red-dotted. Capsules globose. Flowers in June and July. Grows scattered on rocks, screes and stony barrens in mountains. Many related species grow in Alps, some of them cultivated in gardens.

3 Grass of Parnassus *Parnassia palustris*. Perennial herb with few-leaved basal rosette and stems 10—20 cm. high. Basal leaves long-petiolate, ovately cordate, smooth. Single-flowered stems with one sessile clasping leaf. Flowers of five white petals; five gland-fringed stami-nodes alternate with five stamens. Capsule ovoid. Flowers from June to September, in low-lands much later than in mountains. Grows in damp meadows and on heaths and moors from lowlands to foothills, in mountains, in peaty meadows and among wet rocks.

Family: **Rose** — *Rosaceae*

4 Wood Goatsbeard *Aruncus dioicus* (syn. *A. sylvester*). Perennial, clump-forming herb up to 2 metres high, with erect, smooth stems. Leaves long-petiolate, two or three times pinnate, the leaflets ovate to lanceolate, shortly petiolate to almost sessile, pointed and unequally toothed. Inflorescence a large, dense, terminal panicle, composed of numerous, minute, unisexual or dioecious cream-white flowers. Fruits are tiny brown follicles. Flowers in July. Grows in damp mountain forests and thickets and often naturalized by roadsides, from hilly country to mountains.

5 Meadowsweet *Filipendula ulmaria*. Perennial, clump-forming plant up to 150 cm. high, with short rhizomes and erect, stiff, seldom branched stems. Leaves odd-pinnate, with double-toothed ovate leaflets, terminal one larger, palmately three- to five-lobed. Flowers in large, dense, terminal cymes, creamy-white, fragrant. Flowers from June to September. Grows in swamps, marshes, fens, damp or wet woods, and in lowlands and foothills. Drop-wort *(F. vulgaris)* thrives in dry habitats, is smaller and has a tuberous rootstock.

6 Marsh Cinquefoil *Potentilla palustris* (syn. *Comarum palustre*). Perennial, woody-based herb up to 1 metre high. Leaves odd-pinnate with 5—7 oblong, toothed leaflets, dark green above, hairy on veins and grey-green beneath. Flowers in sparse terminal cymes, the five-lobed calyx outside green, inside red-purple. Petals smaller than calyx lobes, deep purple, stamens dark red; achenes ovoid. Flowers in June and July. Grows in fens, bogs, marshes, and by water, from lowlands to foothills.

Family: **Rose** — *Rosaceae*

1 Silverweed *Potentilla anserina*. Perennial herb with thick rhizome and creeping, rooting stems, up to 50 cm. long. Leaves odd-pinnate, with 7—12 pairs of main leaflets alternating with pairs of much smaller ones. The large leaflets oval, serrate, underside silky, white-felted. Golden yellow flowers solitary, on slender stalks; sepals 5, ovate. Flowers from May to August. Grows in waste places, in pastures, on paths, roadsides and banks, from lowlands to foothills. Related creeping cinquefoil *(P. reptans)* has palmate leaves with 3—7 obovate leaflets.

2 Golden Cinquefoil *Potentilla aurea*. Perennial herb with thick rhizome. Stems ascending, up to 25 cm. long, growing from axils of basal rosette leaves. Leaves palmate, with 5 oblong to obovate leaflets toothed at the top; margins and undersides silvery and silky hairy on veins; upper side smooth and glossy. Flower stalks long and hairy, flowers rich yellow with a darker base. Flowers from June to September. Grows in mountain meadows and on rocky slopes.

3 *Potentilla tabernaemontani* (syn. *P. verna*). Perennial mat-forming plant with much branched rhizome and numerous prostrate shoots, often rooting at the nodes. Leaves long-petiolate, palmate, with 5 somewhat hairy, toothed, wedge-shaped to obovate leaflets. Stalked flowers with shallowly notched yellow petals. Flowers from March to June. Grows on sunny, grassy slopes, in sandy places and among rocks from lowlands to foothills. Related hoary cinquefoil *(P. argentea)* has leaflet margins recurved and white-felted underside, similarly to stems.

4 Tormentil *Potentilla erecta*. Perennial herb with short, thick, branched rootstock and erect or ascending leafy stem, up to 30 cm. long. Basal leaves petiolate, stem ones almost sessile, usually trifoliate; leaflets wedge-shaped, obovate, toothed, lobed stipules large and conspicuous. Flowers slender, stalked, small, with 4 rounded, faintly notched yellow petals. Flowers from June to August. Grows on heaths, heather moors and in rocky and grassy places, from lowlands to mountains.

5 White Cinquefoil *Potentilla alba*. Perennial herb with much-branched rhizome and numerous flower stems, about 10 cm. high, from axils of basal leaves. Leaves palmate, with 5 lanceolate leaflets, finely toothed at tip; upperside dark green, underside silvery, silky-hairy. Flowers white; sepals of same length as epicalyx. Achenes hairy. Flowers from May to July. Grows in dry woods, meadows and on grassy slopes at lower altitudes, in milder regions.

6 Wild Strawberry *Fragaria vesca*. Perennial tufted herb with branched rhizome and creeping, rooting stolons. Stems up to 20 cm. high emerge from axils of leaves. Leaves trifoliate, leaflets obovate to ovate, toothed, lateral ones sessile. Flower stalks have appressed hairs; flowers are white; ripe strawberries sub-globose to bluntly conical, red. Flowers in May and June. Grows in woodland clearings, open woods, on bushy slopes, banks and hedgerows, from lowlands to mountains. Related *Fragaria moschata* is larger, has flower stalks with spreading and lateral leaflets shortly petiolate. Fruits whitish, on sunny side red flushed.

Family: **Rose** — *Rosaceae*

1 Mountain Avens *Dryas octopetala*. Plant with woody stems forming cushion-like tufts, several centimetres high. Leaves petiolate, ovate-oblong, with rounded teeth, leathery, on underside white, upper surface dark green, glossy. Flowers solitary on erect, up to 10 cm. long stalks; petals 7—10, white, obovate. Achenes have long, hairy appendages and resemble those of Pasque flower. Flowers from June to August. Grows on rocks, screes, and grassy slopes in mountains and by the sea, predominantly on limestone soils.

2 Common Avens *Geum urbanum*. Perennial tufted herb, up to 50 cm. high, with thick rhizome and basal rosette of leaves. These are petiolate, odd-pinnate, with lanceolate lateral and broadly ovate to orbicular terminal leaflets, irregularly double-toothed. Stem leaves trifoliate or trilobed. Flowers erect, calyx after flowering reflexing; petals yellow. Achenes bristly hairy with a sharp hook on the modified style. Flowers from May to August. Grows in open woods, thickets, along hedgerows and on wasteland, from lowlands to foothills.

3 Water Avens *Geum rivale*. Perennial plant up to 1 metre high, with thick rhizome. Stems erect, hairy, often red flushed. Basal leaves in rosette, long-petiolate, lyre-like, pinnate, terminal leaflet large, rounded, trilobed; lateral leaflets ovate, all hairy and toothed. Stem leaves are trifoliate. Flowers drooping; calyx purple, petals orange-pink; after fertilization flowering stem erect. Achenes hairy, with a stalked hook. Flowers in May and June. Grows in wet meadows, marshes, streamsides and damp woods, from hilly country to mountains.

4 Common Agrimony *Agrimonia eupatoria*. Perennial plant up to 1 metre high, hairy, with thick rhizome. Stem little branched. Basal leaves odd-pinnate, leaflets elliptic, toothed; stem leaves smaller, with few leaflets. Flowers short-stalked, arranged in simple, erect raceme; corollas small, yellow; calyx hairy, with numerous deep grooves and bearing hooked spines. Flowers from June to August. Grows on hedge banks, along field boundaries, by roadsides and on bushy and grassy hills, from lowlands to foothills.

5 Great Burnet *Sanguisorba officinalis* (syn. *Poterium officinale*). Perennial herb up to 1 metre high, with thick rhizome and erect, branched stems. Basal leaves odd-pinnate in basal tufts; leaflets shortly petiolate, oblong-ovate, toothed, upper side glossy dark green, under side blue-green, hairless. Floral heads oblong-ovoid, dull crimson; flowers very small, without petals. Flowers from July to September. Grows fairly abundantly in damp meadows, from lowlands to foothills. *Sanguisorba minor* grows in well-drained hill grassland, has globose, reddish green heads, and leaflets widely ovate with green undersides.

6 Common Lady's Mantle *Alchemilla vulgaris*. Perennial herb, with a thick, somewhat woody rhizome and tufts of basal leaves. Stems ascending or erect, 10—30 cm. high, hairy to smooth. Petiolate basal leaves rounded or reniform, palmately lobed and toothed. Flowers without petals, yellow-green, in open panicles; sepals either smooth or hairy. Flowers from May to September. Grows in meadows, pastures, along brooks and at outskirts of woods, from lowlands to mountains.

Family: *Fabaceae (Papilionaceae)*

1 Common Lupin *Lupinus polyphyllus.* Perennial plant up to 150 cm. high. Stems leafy, erect, unbranched. Leaves petiolate, palmate, with cuneate, elliptic, hairy leaflets. Pea-shaped flowers in dense, upright racemes; corollas blue or blue and white. Pods large, hairy and many-seeded. Flowers from June to August. Native of North America; at one time cultivated as forage for farm animals and for green manuring in gardens. Also grown for ornamental purposes and often going wild. South-European species are sometimes cultivated as forage, having white or yellow flowers.

2 Common Melilot *Melilotus officinalis.* Biennial herb with erect, branched stems up to 1 metre high, angular, usually smooth. Leaves petiolate, trifoliate, with oblong-elliptic, toothed leaflets, the central one distinctly petiolate; stipules lanceolate, entire. Dense axillary stalked racemes bearing tiny yellow drooping flowers. Pods ovoid, smooth and black. Flowers from June to September. Grows in fields, wasteland and by roadsides, from lowlands to hilly country. Related white melilot *(M. albus)* has white flowers.

3 Lucerne *Medicago sativa.* Perennial herb, up to 80 cm. high, with erect, smooth stems and trifoliate leaves; leaflets narrowly obovate, central one distinctly petiolate. Flowers purple, rarely whitish, in dense, short racemes. Pods spirally twisted, two to three turns. Flowers from June to September. Native of eastern Mediterranean and western Asia; long cultivated for forage and often well naturalized. Related sickle medick *(M. falcata)* is native of central Europe, has yellow flowers and sickle-shaped pods. Hybrid populations are often encountered.

4 White Clover *Trifolium repens.* Perennial herb with creeping, rooting stems, ascending at the tips, up to 30 cm. long. Leaves long-petiolate, trifoliate, leaflets sessile, obovate to obcordate, finely toothed at tip, with lighter angled band towards the base. Flower heads globose; florets white or pink; after flowering light brown. Flowers from May to September. Grows in meadows, lawns and ditches. Cultivated as a fodder crop.

5 Red Clover *Trifolium pratense.* Perennial herb almost 50 cm. high, with erect, little-branched stems. Leaves in basal tuft are trifoliate and long-petiolate; leaflets sessile, obovate to elliptic, entire, usually with a whitish or red-brown crescent-shaped spot on upper surface. Stem leaves smaller, sessile. Flower heads globose to ovoid, flowers purple-pink or pale red, rarely whitish. Flowers from June to September. Grows in meadows, by the roadside and in forest clearings, from lowlands to mountains. Often cultivated for forage. Cultivated *Trifolium incarnatum* has striking cylindrical heads. Tiny haresfoot trefoil *(T. arvense)* has small hairy heads and palest pink flowers.

6 Kidney Vetch *Anthyllis vulneraria.* Perennial herb with hairy stem, up to 30 cm. high, ascending to erect. Odd-pinnate basal leaves; 11—15 leaflets, elliptic to linear-oblong, terminal one much larger than lateral ones. Globose flower heads singly or in clusters. Flowers light yellow to reddish. Flowers from May to August. Grows on sunny grassy banks and slopes.

Family: *Fabaceae*

1 Common Birdsfoot Trefoil *Lotus corniculatus.* Perennial herb, well-branched rhizome, decumbent or ascending stems, up to 30 cm. long, distinctly angular. Leaves odd-pinnate, the 5 leaflets smooth, entire, broadly ovate to lanceolate, underside grey-green. Flowers short-stalked, in 3—10 flowered umbels, corollas intense yellow, outside usually reddish. Flowers from May to September. Grows in pastures and on grassy and bushy slopes from lowlands to mountains. Related marsh birdsfoot trefoil *(L. uliginosus)* has hollow, round stems, larger inflorescence and grows in moist habitat.

2 Common Crown Vetch *Coronilla varia.* Perennial, robust herb with numerous stems, decumbent or ascending, often climbing, branched, up to 1 metre long. Leaves odd-pinnate, the 9—17 leaflets shortly petiolate, oblong elliptic with a short point. Long-stalked inflorescence erect; white, pink or purple flowers in 10—20 flowered umbels. Pods slender, breaking up into one-seeded sections. Flowers from June to August. Grows on field boundaries, bushy slopes and by the roadside, from lowlands to foothills. Slightly poisonous.

3 Sainfoin *Onobrychis viciifolia.* Perennial, robust herb, scattered with hairs, up to 50 cm. high, with stiff, erect stem. Leaves odd-pinnate, the 11—25 leaflets obovate to linear-oblong. Racemes ovoid to cylindrical, flowers bright red or pink, the standard petal purple-striped. Pods short, flat, one-seeded. Flowers from May to July. Commonly cultivated forage since 16th century; often becomes locally naturalized. Found along field boundaries, by the roadside and on dry slopes at lower altitudes.

4 Bush Vetch *Vicia sepium.* Perennial herb with branched rhizome and erect or climbing stem up to 50 cm. high. Leaves pinnate, terminated in branched tendril; the 10—18 leaflets ovate to elliptic, mucronate, and pointed. Flowers in threes to sixes in axils of leaves; corollas pale purple, calyx teeth unequal, shorter than calyx tube. Flowers from May to August. Grows in hedgerows, thickets, open woods and meadows, from lowlands to mountains. Related common vetch *(V. sativa)* has larger flowers in groups of one to three in the leaf axils. Large forms cultivated as forage and well naturalized by roadsides and on waste ground.

5 Tufted Vetch *Vicia cracca.* Perennial herb with strong, creeping rhizome and angular, softly hairy stems, up to 1 metre or more high. Pinnate leaves terminate in branched tendril; the 12—30 leaflets oblong to linear-lanceolate, underside usually hairy. Inflorescence a 10 to 40-flowered, one-sided raceme, stalked, almost as long as leaves; corollas blue-violet, rarely whitish. Pods short-stalked. Flowers from June to August. Grows in hedgerows, thickets, along field boundaries and in grassy places, from lowlands to mountains.

6 Hairy Milk Vetch *Oxytropis pilosa.* Perennial herb 15—30 cm. high, densely hairy. Erect, ascending stems bear odd-pinnate leaves with narrowly lanceolate leaflets. Dense inflorescence an elongated raceme; flowers light yellow. Pods linear with white hairs. Flowers in June and July. Grows on sunny grassy slopes at lower altitudes, in milder areas.

Family: *Fabaceae*

1 Earth-nut Pea *Lathyrus tuberosus.* Perennial, hairless, grey-green herb with creeping rhizome and tuberous, thickened roots. Stems climbing, up to 1 metre long, square. Leaves with one pair of obovate leaflets and branched tendril. Long-stalked inflorescences bear a few-flowered raceme; flowers fragrant, light purple, standard crimson. Flowers from June to August. Naturalized in Britain in fields and hedgerows especially on calcareous soils, at lower altitudes. Related annual sweet pea *(L. odoratus)* with large flowers of various colours is native of southern Europe and cultivated in gardens.

2 Narrow-leaved Everlasting Pea *Lathyrus sylvestris.* Perennial, robust plant with long, creeping rhizome. Numerous stems are ascending or climbing, up to 3 metres long, keeled or winged. Leaves with branched tendril, the 2 leaflets linear-lanceolate, petioles widely winged. Axillary, long-stalked inflorescences, with 3—8 rose-pink flowers. Pods to 8 cm. long, winged. Flowers in July and August. Grows in open woods, on bushy slopes and in hedgerows from lowlands to foothills. Related meadow vetchling *(L. pratensis)* is much smaller, with yellow flowers.

3 *Lathyrus vernus* (syn. *Orobus vernus*). Perennial herb with erect, self-supporting stems up to 40 cm. high. Pinnate leaves bright green, without tendrils, the 2 or 3 pairs of leaflets ovate and long-pointed. Inflorescence a few-flowered raceme. Flowers red-violet, later blue-green, wings with blue tint. Flowers in April and May. Grows in open woods, from lowlands to foothills.

4 Milk Vetch *Astragalus glycyphyllos.* Perennial herb with decumbent or ascending, hairless stems, sometimes creeping, up to 1 metre long. Leaves odd-pinnate, the 11—21 leaflets oblong-elliptic. Axillary, stalked inflorescences in racemes, shorter than leaves; flowers creamy-white, tinged greenish. Pods linear, sickle-shaped. Flowers in June and July. Grows in open woods, thickets and rough grassy places, from lowlands to foothills. Related alpine milk vetch *(A. alpinum)* has light blue flowers and violet-red keel.

Family: **Geranium** — *Geraniaceae*

5 Bloody Cranesbill *Geranium sanguineum.* Perennial herb with thick, creeping rhizome. Stems ascending, up to 50 cm. long, hairy. Basal leaves die early; stem ones are opposite, petiolate, deeply palmately lobed into five to seven narrow segments, which are further cut or lobed. Solitary, axillary, long-stalked flowers have 5 purple-crimson petals. Flowers from June to August. Grows in open bushy places, on stony slopes and in grassland, at lower altitudes.

6 Herb Robert *Geranium robertianum.* Annual or biennial herb, red-tinted, hairy, somewhat foetid. Erect or decumbent stems up to 40 cm. long. Leaves palmately lobed, petiolate leaflets once or twice pinnately dissected, segments toothed. Rose-pink flowers in pairs; corollas less than 15 mm. in diameter. Flowers from May to October. Grows in open woods, on screes and walls, from lowlands to mountains. Wood cranesbill *(G. sylvaticum)* has purple flowers; meadow cranesbill *(G. pratense)* has violet-blue and *Geranium phaeum* brown or black-purple flowers. All have strikingly beaked fruits.

Family: **Geranium** — *Geraniaceae*

1 Common Storksbill *Erodium cicutarium*. Annual or biennial herb with erect or inclined stems, hairy, up to 25 cm. long. Basal, long-petiolate leaves in rosette, upper ones are shortly petiolate; all leaves odd-pinnate, segments pinnatisect, hairy. Inflorescence a several-flowered, stalked umbel with rose-violet corollas; downy, long-beaked fruits follow. Flowers from April to October. Grows in fields, waste places, dry grassland and downs, from lowlands to mountains.

Family: **Oxalis** — *Oxalidaceae*

2 Common Wood Sorrel *Oxalis acetosella*. Perennial tufted herb up to 10 cm. high. Leaves and long-stalked flowers grow directly from stiff, creeping rhizome. Leaves trifoliate, leaflets sessile, obcordate and entire, underside usually reddish. Flowers white, veined lilac or purple. Fruit an explosive capsule. Flowers in April or May. Grows in damp forests or thickets and among rocks from lowlands to mountains. Introduced, yellow-flowered species: upright yellow wood sorrel *(O. europaea)* with leaves in whorls and procumbent yellow wood sorrel *(O. corniculata)* with prostrate stems and alternate leaves often purple-flushed.

Family: *Linaceae*

3 Flax *Linum usitatissimum*. Annual herb, up to 50 cm. high with erect, leafy stems. Leaves linear-lanceolate to linear, pointed, three-veined, entire. Flowers in cymose inflorescences; corolla of 5 light blue petals. Fruit a globular capsule. Flowers in June and July. Long cultivated for linen fibre; native of Asia Minor; mainly cultivated in foothills. Purging flax *(L. catharticum)* is a small slender plant with tiny white flowers and forked stems with opposite, obovate leaves.

Family: **Rue** — *Rutaceae*

4 Burning Bush *Dictamnus albus*. Perennial, aromatic plant with whitish, branched rhizome. Erect stems up to 1 metre high, inflorescence reddish glandular. Odd-pinnate leaves, the 9—15 leaflets ovate or lanceolate, finely toothed, with translucent dots; dark green. Flowers in terminal racemes; calyx dark-veined, rarely whitish, petals purple or white, outside glandular hairy, similarly to capsules. Flowers from May to June. Grows only rarely on sunny slopes and forested steppes in temperate regions. Also often cultivated in gardens. Strictly protected plant.

Family: **Milkwort** — *Polygalaceae*

5 Common Milkwort *Polygala vulgaris*. Perennial, tufted herb. Ascending, erect or decumbent stems up to 25 cm. long, usually simple and hairless. Leaves linear-lanceolate, pointed; bracts shorter than flower buds. Flowers are blue, rarely rose or white, with two enlarged sepals. Flat, obcordate capsule. Flowers from May to August. Grows in dry meadows, on grassy slopes and on outskirts of forests. *Polygala amara* has basal leaves in rosette.

Family: **Spurge** — *Euphorbiaceae*

6 Dog's Mercury *Mercurialis perennis*. Perennial plant with far-creeping rhizome and usually erect, round, unbranched stems. Petiolate leaves dull green, lanceolate to elliptic-ovate, toothed, as a rule with spreading hairs. Unisexual, minute, greenish flowers; pistillate ones long-stalked, solitary or in twos, male flowers in small clusters forming sparse racemes. Capsules globular, bristly. Flowers in April and May. Grows in shady deciduous woods and among rocks from lowlands to mountains. Related annual mercury *(M. annua)* has pale green glossy leaves, square, branched stem and almost sessile pistillate flowers.

1

2

3

4

5

6

Family: **Spurge** — *Euphorbiaceae*

1 Cypress Spurge *Euphorbia cyparissias.* Perennial plant up to 30 cm. high, with woody, branched rhizome. Stems tufted, erect, soon leafless at bottom, with red tint; densely leaved above, especially the lateral, non-flowering twigs. Narrowly linear leaves; yellowish bracts, after flowering reddish. Inflorescence a branched umbel with petalless flowers bearing wax-yellow glands. Capsules finely warty. Flowers in April and May. Grows in dry grassland and scrub and by roadsides from lowlands to foothills. All species of spurge have a white milky sap (latex).

Family: *Impatientaceae*

2 Touch-me-not *Impatiens noli-tangere.* Annual up to 1 metre high with erect stem, thickened at the nodes. Leaves petioled, alternate, ovate-oblong, pointed, toothed, with glands at base. Flowers in axillary few-flowered racemes, bright yellow, the mouth red-dotted, drooping, with curved spur. Cylindrical to ovoid explosive capsule. Flowers in July and August. Grows in damp woods and on the banks of rivers and streams, from lowlands to mountains. Related *Impatiens parviflora* has small, erect flowers with straight spur; Siberian plant, introduced to central Europe and now naturalized.

Family: **Mallow** — *Malvaceae*

3 Common Mallow *Malva sylvestris.* Perennial herb with ascending or erect, tough stems, up to 1 metre long. Leaves palmate, petiolate, shallowly 5—7 lobed and toothed. Stalked flowers in small axillary clusters. Calyx flattened, with triangular lobes; corollas rose-purple, striped darker, petals spathulate, notched at tip. Stamen filaments fused into tube. Fruit a disc-shaped schizocarp, when ripe splitting into single-seeded, disc-shaped nutlets. Flowers from June to September. Grows by roadsides, in hedgerows, on wasteland, at lower altitudes of temperate regions.

4 Dwarf Mallow *Malva neglecta.* Annual to perennial with decumbent or ascending, branched stems, almost 50 cm. long. Long-petiolate leaves, shallowly palmately lobed and toothed, with hairy underside. Axillary, stalked flowers reflexed during fruiting; sepals flat, corollas double calyx length, pale lilac to whitish, darker-veined, notched at tip. Fruits smooth. Flowers from June to October. Grows on waste ground, by roadsides and in fields, from lowlands to mountains. Similar small mallow *(M. pusilla)* is smaller, lighter green and little branched, with the corollas same length as calyx; fruits wrinkled.

Family: *Hypericaceae* (syn. *Guttiferae*)

5 Common St. John's Wort *Hypericum perforatum.* Perennial herb with erect stems, 50 cm. or more high, with two longitudinal, narrow ridges and numerous lateral, non-flowering, leafy twigs. Leaves ovate-elliptic, hairless, with conspicuous translucent dots. Flowers arranged in terminal inflorescences; stalks usually dotted with black. Corollas golden yellow, sepals and petals black-dotted; stamens in three bundles. Capsule conical, glandular, dotted. Flowers in July and August. Grows abundantly in woodland clearings, on bushy slopes, by the roadside and in fields, from lowlands to mountains. Related mountain St. John's wort *(H. montanum)* has rounded, sparsely leaved stem and fringed glandular sepals.

Family: *Lythraceae*

6 Purple Loosestrife *Lythrum salicaria.* Robust woody-based perennial up to 1 metre or more high. Erect, hairy stems, sharply square in section. Leaves ovate to lanceolate, base rounded or cordate, sessile, almost hairless. Terminal, dense, spire-like inflorescence. Flowers small, purple, with 6 obovate, waved petals. Fruit a small ovoid capsule. Flowers from July to September. Grows by water, in fens, marshes, swamps and in damp meadows, from lowlands to foothills.

Family: *Onagraceae*

1 Rosebay Willowherb *Chamaenerion angustifolium* (syn. *Epilobium angustifolium*). Perennial herb up to 1 metre or more high. Erect stems usually smooth and unbranched. Leaves oblong-lanceolate to linear-lanceolate, entire, or with a few distant teeth. Flowers in long dense racemes; calyx dark purple, petals 4, obovate, rose-purple, rarely whitish. Long, slender, cylindrical, downy capsules. Minute seeds, with long white hairs. Flowers in July to September. Grows in woodland clearings, on margins of woods, and on wasteland, often gregariously.

2 Broad-leaved Willowherb *Epilobium montanum*. Perennial herb up to 80 cm. high; erect or shortly ascending stems, simple or sparingly branched in inflorescence, with appressed hairs in two rows, before flowering usually drooping. Opposite, shortly petiolate leaves, elliptical-ovate, pointed, toothed, usually downy. Flowers in leafy terminal raceme; corollas up to 1 cm., petals notched at tip, pink, dark-veined. Stigma four-lobed, capsules downy and glandular. Flowers from June to September. Grows in woods, on bushy slopes, in hedgerows, on walls and as a weed in gardens, from lowlands high up to mountains. Many related species, e.g. great hairy willowherb *(E. hirsutum)* with flowers up to 2 cm. across and softly hairy stem.

3 Common Evening Primrose *Oenothera biennis*. Biennial plant up to 1 metre high. Erect stems, as a rule unbranched. Leaves in basal rosette, lanceolate; stem leaves smaller, alternate, finely toothed. Flowers up to 2 cm. in diameter are arranged in terminal, leafy racemes. Lanceolate sepals reflexed, petals obcordate, light yellow. Capsules cylindrical, finely hairy. Flowers from June to August. Native of North America, introduced to Europe and much cultivated in gardens. Now well naturalized in waste places, by the roadside and on banks, from lowlands to foothills.

Family: *Trapaceae*

4 Water Chestnut *Trapa natans*. Annual herb with long, submerged stem. Leaves of two types: submerged ones pinnately divided, with linear segments; rosette leaves floating on water surface with rhomboid blades, sharply toothed at apex; petioles slightly inflated. Axillary, solitary flowers with 4 small white petals. Fruit is conspicuous small edible nut with oily seed surrounded by the enlarged, woody, spiky, four calyx lobes. Flowers in July and August. Grows in still waters of lower altitudes; formerly more frequent.

Family: *Umbelliferae* (syn. *Apiaceae*)

5 Field Eryngo *Eryngium campestre*. Perennial herb, robust, spreading, up to 50 cm. high, grey-green, with well-branched stem. Leaves with bipinnate, spire-tipped segments. Flowers in ovoid capitula, bracts and sepals spiny; corollas small, white or purplish. Flowers in July and August. Grows in dry grassy places in milder regions of lower altitudes.

6 Wood Sanicle *Sanicula europaea*. Perennial herb with short, creeping rhizome. Erect, angular stems, up to 40 cm. high. Basal leaves petiolate, palmately 3—5 lobed, cordate, the segments again divided and sharply toothed; one or two sessile on flowering stem. Flowers small, arranged in several umbels grouped together. Corolla tiny, white or pinkish with protruding stamens. Flowers in May and June. Grows in deciduous woods, particularly on chalk and limestone, from lowlands to mountains; locally frequent only.

Family: *Umbelliferae*

1 Masterwort *Astrantia major*. Perennial herb with a somewhat woody rhizome. Erect stems up to over 50 cm. high, each with one or two leaves. Basal leaves petiolate, palmate, deeply five- to seven-lobed, segments ovate, toothed; stem leaves more deeply dissected, segments wedge-shaped with trilobed tip. Bracts lanceolate, white or flushed pink. Flowers in simple umbels, corollas white, stamens protruding from flowers. Flowers from June to August. Naturalized in Britain, growing on margins of forests and in meadows in a few places from lowlands to mountains.

2 *Falcaria vulgaris*. A perennial, grey-green herb with erect, much-branched stems. Leaves stiff, doubly trifoliate (each lobe or leaflet again 3-lobed), segments linear-lanceolate, pointed, sharply serrate. Several small secondary umbels form sparse compound umbels; tiny, white flowers. Flowers from July to September. Grows on dry grassy slopes and on field and meadow margins. Only just naturalized in eastern England and Guernsey.

3 Burnet Saxifrage *Pimpinella saxifraga*. Perennial plant up to 50 cm. high, with finely grooved, branched stems. Bottom leaves odd-pinnate, long-petiolate; leaflets more or less deeply lobed, sessile; blades of stem leaves smaller and less or not lobed. Inflorescence of compound umbels without bracts. Very small flowers, corollas white, rose or yellowish. Fruit a double, ribbed schizocarp. Flowers from July to September. Grows on grassy slopes, field boundaries, in pastures, and by the roadside, from lowlands to mountains.

4 Goutweed *Aegopodium podagraria*. Robust perennial plant, almost 1 metre high, with hollow, angular stems and far-creeping rhizomes. Leaves have stem-sheathing petioles; bottom ones twice, upper leaves simply trifoliate; leaflets ovate, petiolate, lateral ones usually lobed, toothed. Inflorescence of compound umbels without bracts; small white or rose-tinted corollas. Schizocarp brown with paler ribs. Flowers in June and July. Grows on waste ground, in damp woods and ditches; also a common garden and farm weed.

5 Wild Angelica *Angelica sylvestris*. Perennial, robust plant, up to 150 cm. high, with thick rhizome. Petiolate leaves have shallowly grooved petioles and inflated sheaths; bottom leaves two to three times pinnate, upper ones smaller and simply lobed; leaflets ovate, almost sessile, toothed. Dense compound umbels without bracts; small white or rosy corollas; three-ribbed schizocarp, somewhat winged on margin. Flowers from July to September. Grows in damp woods, thickets and hedgerows, from lowlands to mountains.

6 Fine-leaved Water Dropwort *Oenanthe aquatica*. Perennial, well branched, robust herb, with erect stems, up to 1 metre or more high, hollow, at base up to 5 cm. in diameter. Leaves sheathed, petiolate, three times pinnate; segments lobed and toothed, lanceolate; submerged leaves filamentous. Numerous compound umbels, the secondary umbels with bracts; small corollas white. Schizocarp narrowly ovoid, ridged. Flowers from June to August. Grows near or in water at lower altitudes and in moist places in hilly country. Related fool's parsley *(Aethusa cynapium)* has glossy coarser leaves and long slender floral bracts. It is a weed of cultivation on the better drained soils.

Family: *Umbelliferae*

1 Wild Parsnip *Pastinaca sativa*.Robust biennial herb up to 1 metre high; stem with angular grooves, more or less hairy. Odd-pinnate leaves; the leaflets ovate, serrate, lobed to pinnately divided. Secondary umbels on angular stalks, without bracts; small yellow flowers. Schizocarps elliptical, over 0.5 cm. large, flattened and winged. Flowers from July to September. Grows on grassy slopes, in meadows and ditches, along roads, from lowlands to foothills, particularly on chalk and limestone. Caraway *(Carum carvi)*, grown as a culinary herb, has upper leaves divided into filamentous segments and white flowers. The cultivated parsnip, with a thick fleshy root, is derived from this species.

2 Wild Carrot *Daucus carota*. Biennial herb almost 1 metre high, with erect, branched, hairy stem. Leaves twice or three times pinnate; pinnatisect segments of upper leaves linear. Dense, compound umbels have numerous pinnate bracts with linear segments. Flowers white, sometimes rosy, central umbels usually red or violet. Schizocarp ovoid, with hooked bristles. Flowers from June to September. Grows in dry meadows, field boundaries and on slopes from lowlands to mountains. *Daucus carota* subspecies *sativus* is the cultivated carrot.

3 Hogweed *Heracleum sphondylium*. Robust perennial herb up to 150 cm., somewhat foetid. Erect, grooved stems bristled and hollow. Large leaves, lower ones having a grooved petiole, upper leaves sessile with inflated sheaths, pinnate; segments asymmetrically lobed to pinnatisect, toothed. Large compound umbels usually without bracts; corollas white or pinkish. Flowers from June to September. Grows in damp meadows, on waste ground, by roadsides, from lowlands to mountains.

4 *Anthriscus sylvestris*. Perennial, robust plant up to 150 cm. high. Grooved, hollow stems usually bare or bristly at bottom. Pinnate leaves with toothed segments; bottom leaves are petiolate, upper ones sheathing and sessile. Long-stalked compound umbels, secondary umbels having bracts. Small flowers with white corollas. Schizocarps glossy, black, oblong-ovoid, pointed. Flowers from April to June. Grows in meadows, hedgerows and by roadsides. Poisonous rough chervil *(Chaerophyllum temulentum)* differs from it by fruits which are distinctly ribbed.

Family: *Plumbaginaceae*

5 Thrift or **Sea Pink** *Armeria maritima*. Perennial plant, 10—50 cm high, with cushions of linear, single-veined leaves, usually with bristled margins. Stems solitary, erect, smooth, with a globular head of rose-pink, occasionally white flowers. Funnel-shaped, persistent, chaffy calyx acts as a wing when the fruit is ripe. Bracts beneath capitulum sometimes red tinted. Flowers from May to October. Grows in sandy places, dunes, on rocks and screes, in meadows and pine-woods, from lowlands to mountains.

Family: **Primrose** — *Primulaceae*

6 Mountain Tassel-flower *Soldanella montana*. Small perennial herb with creeping rhizome and basal rosette of long-petiolate, reniform, faintly toothed and somewhat leathery leaves. Stems 10—30 cm. high, bearing umbels of up to six pendent flowers on finely glandular stalks. Violet-blue flowers, calyx five-parted, corolla bell-shaped. Ovoid capsule, opening by ten blunt teeth. Flowers in May and June. Grows in mountain and foothill forests and mountain meadows.

Family: **Primrose** — *Primulaceae*

1 Cowslip *Primula veris.* Perennial plant, up to 30 cm. high. Leaves in basal rosette, wrinkled, hairy beneath, ovate-oblong, with winged petioles. Stem with umbel of several, shortly stalked, fragrant flowers. Bell-shaped calyx, corolla yolk-yellow, with an orange spot at the base of each lobe. Corolla tube slightly longer than five-toothed calyx. Flowers from April to June. Grows on banks, in meadows and pastures, from lowlands to foothills.

2 Oxlip *Primula elatior.* Similar to preceding species. Leaves of basal rosette less wrinkled, on underside grey-green, ovate, irregularly toothed. Flowers not scented, with longer stalks. Calyx tubular, corolla pale yellow, larger and flatter than in cowslip. Corolla tube double length of five-toothed calyx. Cylindrical capsules longer than calyx. Flowers from March to May. Grows in deciduous woods, thickets and damp meadows, from uplands to mountains.

3 Bear's-ear *Primula auricula.* Perennial herb up to over 20 cm. high, finely and shortly glandularly downy and often somewhat mealy. Basal rosette of almost fleshy leaves with cartilaginous margin, rounded to ovate-obovate, tapering to wide petiole, usually entire, grey-green. Stem bears umbel of yellow, fragrant flowers, having a whitish throat; widely funnel-shaped corollas with the lobes notched at the tip. Capsules ovoid. Flowers from April to June. Grows on limestone rocks in Alps, Carpathians and their foothills; also cultivated. Protected plant.

4 Purple Sowbread *Cyclamen purpurascens* (syn. *C. europaeum*). Perennial plant with underground, flatly globose tuber. Leaves in basal rosette are long-petiolate, cordate, rounded, somewhat leathery, shallowly toothed; on upper surface dark green with silvery white patterning, underside carmine. Pendent, pink to carmine, fragrant flowers, the corolla reflexed sharply back. Globose capsule. Flowers from July to September. Grows in deciduous woods and among bushes, usually on limestone soils, only in eastern Bavaria, scattered in neighbouring Austria and southern parts of Czechoslovakia. Protected plant.

5 Yellow Loosestrife *Lysimachia vulgaris.* Perennial herb up to 150 cm. high, with creeping rhizome and erect, leafy stems. Leaves opposite, or more frequently in whorls of three, downy, shortly petiolate, ovate-lanceolate, pointed, entire. Golden yellow flowers, calyx and petals sometimes bordered with red. Flowers from June to August. Grows in fens, beside water, and in damp forests from lowlands to foothills.

6 Creeping Jenny *Lysimachia nummularia.* Perennial, creeping herb with stem up to 50 cm. long, rooting. Leaves broadly ovate to sub-orbicular, entire. Flowers solitary or in twos in leaf axils; corollas rich yellow, inside dotted with dark red. Capsule globose but seldom forms. Flowers from May to July. Grows in damp meadows, open woods, and ditches. Related wood pimpernel *(L. nemorum)* has ovate, pointed leaves, flower stalks longer than leaves, with smaller, more starry flowers.

124

Family: **Wintergreen** — *Pyrolaceae*

1 Larger Wintergreen *Pyrola rotundifolia*. Evergreen perennial up to 30 cm. high. Ascending, triangular stems. Leaves in sparse basal rosette, widely ovate to rounded, petiolate, indistinctly toothed, leathery; stem leaves scale-like, clasping. White flowers in dense, short raceme. Bracts usually of same length as flower stalks. Open, broadly bell-shaped corolla, petals double the length of lanceolate sepals. Flowers in June and July. Grows in woods and on moors, from lowlands to mountains. Protected plant.

2 One-flowered Wintergreen *Moneses uniflora*. Evergreen perennial, up to 10 cm. high. Round, petiolate, finely toothed, leathery leaves in basal rosette. Solitary, drooping flowers are fragrant, on long stalks; yellowish calyx, white corolla. Five-lobed stigma, ovoid capsule. Flowers from May to July. Grows in mossy forests from hilly country to mountains. Protected plant.

Family: **Gentian** — *Gentianaceae*

3 Spring Gentian *Gentiana verna*. Small evergreen perennial plant, up to 10 cm. high. Rhizome bears numerous basal leaf rosettes. Leaves elliptic to oblong-ovate, pointed. Erect, short stems, with one to three pairs of smaller leaves, bear solitary erect flowers; corolla tubular with five brilliant deep blue lobes. Flowers from March to May, in high mountains till August. Grows in meadows and on rocks from hilly country to mountains. Protected. Very rare in Britain. Marsh gentian *(G. pneumonanthe)* has corollas green-spotted at the throat and slender erect, often branched stems.

4 Spotted Gentian *Gentiana punctata*. Perennial, up to 60 cm. high plant with thick, branched rhizome and erect, hollow stem. Ovate to broadly elliptic leaves, pointed and sessile. Flowers in axils of upper leaves, sessile, erect, bell-shaped. Corollas yellow, dotted with dark purple. Flowers in July and August. Grows on barrens, in meadows and mountain pastures of Alps and Carpathians. Great yellow gentian *(G. lutea)* is gathered for bitter roots, although it is protected; it has unspotted golden yellow petals not joined into a tube.

5 *Gentiana acaulis*. Evergreen perennial tufted to mat-forming, up to 10 cm. high, with basal rosette of almost leathery, ovate-lanceolate leaves. Short-stalked, large flowers, up to 6 cm. long, erect; corolla funnel-shaped, rich blue, of lighter shade at mouth, often dark green spotted within. Grows in Alps and on their foothills in alpine meadows, also on screes and rocks. *G. acaulis* is a group name, and is now discarded as a specific epithet. Three main species are now recognized: *G. clusii*, *G. kochiana* and *G. angustifolia*. Trumpet gentian *(G. clusii)* has stemless flowers; broad-leaved trumpet gentian *(G. kochiana)* has flowers on a short leafy stem and with a bell-shaped calyx; narrow-leaved gentian *(G. angustifolia)* is rather similar, but has markedly narrower leaves and deep sky-blue flowers. These species are strictly protected.

6 Willow Gentian *Gentiana asclepiadea*. Perennial herb, up to 80 cm. high, often in dense tufts, with erect stems arching at the top. Ovate-lanceolate leaves, long-pointed and sessile. Axillary short-stalked flowers are borne in the upper leaf axils. Corollas funnel-shaped, azure blue, spotted purple within; rarely white. Flowers from July to September. Grows in Alps and Carpathians in woods, and along banks of streams.

Family: **Gentian** — *Gentianaceae*

1 *Centaurium erythraea* (syn. *C. umbellatum*, *C. minus*). Annual herb up to 50 cm. high. Erect, square stems, forked above. Obovate to elliptic leaves in basal rosette; stem ones smaller and narrower, pointed, sessile, entire. Short-stalked to sessile flowers are pink, rarely whitish, with a five-lobed tubular corolla. Capsules cylindrical. Flowers from July to September. Grows on margins of forests and thickets, in dry meadows and on grassy slopes.

2 Marsh Felwort *Swertia perennis*. Perennial herb up to 50 cm. high. Erect stems, often with violet tint. Basal leaves elliptic, petiolate, stem leaves lanceolate, sessile to semi-clasping. Flowers on winged, square stalks, in panicles. Corollas have five lobes, violet to light blue, dotted black-purple, greenish within. Fruit a capsule. Flowers from June to August. Grows in mountains, in peaty meadows and by streams.

Family: *Menyanthaceae*

3 Bogbean *Menyanthes trifoliata*. Perennial herb up to 30 cm. high, with thick, creeping rhizome and erect, leafless flowering stems. Basal leaves, direct from rhizome, have long petioles, trifoliate leaflets almost sessile, obovate. Conspicuous flowers in dense raceme. Corollas broadly funnel-shaped, divided into five fringed lobes, white or pinkish; violet anthers. Capsule broadly ovoid. Flowers in May and June. Grows in marshes, bogs, fens, and in ditches, lakes and ponds, from lowlands to mountains.

Family: *Apocynaceae*

4 Lesser Periwinkle *Vinca minor*. Evergreen perennial with long, creeping, rooting stems. Non-flowering stems are creeping and rooting; flowering ones are short, not more than 20 cm. high, erect or ascending. Leathery leaves are opposite, lanceolate to elliptic, entire. Long-stalked flowers are axillary, tubular, with five angular lobes, light blue to blue-violet, rarely white or pink. Fruit formed of two slender, cylindrical follicles, fused at the base. Flowers in April and May. Grows in deciduous woods and thickets, from lowlands to foothills; also cultivated in gardens and becoming naturalized in hedgerows.

Family: **Milkweed** — *Asclepiadaceae*

5 Swallow-wort *Cynanchum vincetoxicum* (syn. *Vincetoxicum officinale*, *V. hirundinaria*). Perennial herb up to 1 metre high, poisonous, with rhizome and numerous thick roots. Erect, simple stems with opposite, ovate-lanceolate, entire leaves, hairy on veins beneath. Inflorescences in upper leaf axils, flowers bell-shaped, corollas white, greenish or yellowish, small. Fruit a slender pod-like follicle; seeds have white, silky plumes. Flowers from May to August. Grows on sunny slopes and among rocks, on margins of woods and thickets, more frequently on calcareous soils, from lowlands to foothills in milder regions.

Family: **Convolvulus** — *Convolvulaceae*

6 Field Bindweed *Convolvulus arvensis*. Perennial, prostrate or twining plant, up to 1 metre long. Rhizomes extensive, penetrating to depths of 5 cm. Stems climb by twisting counter-clockwise. Leaves arrow-shaped, entire. Axillary flowers usually solitary, on short stalks, with widely funnel-shaped corollas, white or pink. Flowers from June to September. Grows in fields, on waste ground, roadsides, dunes, and in gardens as a pernicious weed.

Family: **Borage** — *Boraginaceae*

1 Hound's Tongue *Cynoglossum officinale*. Biennial herb up to 80 cm. high, with erect, leafy, branched stems. Lanceolate, pointed leaves, basal ones petiolate, stem leaves sessile to clasping, all entire, softly densely grey hairy, especially on under surface. Inflorescence of dense cymes. Corollas small, red-purple, rarely whitish. Nutlets ovate, flattened, margins thickened and bearing short barbed spines. Flowers from May to July. Grows on grassy slopes, field boundaries and by roadsides in lower altitudes of milder regions.

2 Corn Cromwell *Lithospermum arvense*. Annual herb up to 50 cm. high, with erect stems simple or branched towards the top. Leaves lanceolate to obovate, sessile. Inflorescence a leafy cyme; corollas white to bluish, their tubes sometimes with violet tint. Brown, wrinkled nutlets not glossy. Flowers from April to July. Grows as field weed, by roadsides and on wasteland, at lower altitudes. Related *Lithospermum purpureocoeruleum* is perennial, with purple flowers, later turning blue.

3 Common Forgetmenot *Myosotis arvensis*. Annual herb, rarely biennial, up to 40 cm. high, with greyish hairs and erect or ascending stems. Oblanceolate, densely hairy leaves. Inflorescence a bractless, dense cyme; flower stalks spreading. Calyx deeply lobed into lanceolate sepals, hairy. Nutlets ovoid, keeled, dark shining brown. Flowers from August to October. Grows along paths and in meadows, on wasteland, in sandy places, and as weed in fields. Related yellow and blue forgetmenot (*M. discolor*, syn. *M. versicolor*) has fruit-stalks shorter than calyx and corollas coloured according to age of flower, from yellow through to blue.

4 Wood Forgetmenot *Myosotis sylvatica*. Perennial herb up to 50 cm. high, fresh green, softly, usually densely haired. Erect stems with obovate to lanceolate leaves. Inflorescence a dense cyme, calyx with thick, hooked hairs; shorter than stalks; during fruition closed. Small corollas are over 5 mm. in diameter, azure blue, with a yellow eye. Glossy, black-brown nutlets. Flowers in May and June. Grows in woods and meadows from lowlands to mountains; often cultivated in gardens and several forms known. Related water forgetmenot *Myosotis scorpioides* (syn. *M. palustris*) has calyx with appressed hairs, divided only to one third, and an angular stem.

5 Lesser Honeywort *Cerinthe minor*. Biennial, rarely perennial herb, up to 50 cm. high, with erect stems. Leaves grey-green, ovate, clasping, lower ones usually white-spotted and warted. Calyx bristly-hairy; sulphur yellow corollas deeply cut into pointed lobes and drooping. Nutlets two-seeded. Flowers from May to July. Grows scattered in pastures, on field boundaries, slopes and along paths in lower altitudes of temperate regions and Alpine foothills.

6 Viper's Bugloss *Echium vulgare*. Robust annual or biennial herb up to 1 metre high with spreading bristles. Erect, simple stems. Leaves linear-lanceolate, sessile. Inflorescence dense axillary cyme. Calyx bristly hairy; corolla obliquely funnel-shaped to almost bilabiate, with rounded lobes, at first rose, later blue; rarely white. Nutlets triangular, roughly warted. Flowers from May to October. Grows on sunny grassy slopes, field boundaries, by roadsides and on wasteland from lowlands to foothills; locally abundant.

Family: **Borage** — *Boraginaceae*

1 True Alkanet *Anchusa officinalis.* Biennial or perennial plant up to 80 cm. high, with spreading hairs, rough. Erect much-branched stems with oblong-lanceolate leaves, entire, sessile with rounded base. Dense, short, axillary cymes bear five-lobed flowers, at first reddish, later dark blue-violet, rarely white, dotted. Nutlets brown, flowers from May to September. Grows in pastures, fields, by roadsides, on field boundaries and wasteland, from lowlands to foothills in milder regions. Related Italian alkanet (*A. italica*, syn. *A. azurea*) has large, light blue corollas.

2 Wrinklenut *Nonea pulla.* Perennial, grey-haired herb up to 50 cm. high, with erect, stiff stems. Leaves oblong to lanceolate, top ones semiclasping, entire, bristled to glandular hairy. Inflorescence of several dense, axillary cymes bearing short-stalked flowers. Calyx bell-shaped, enlarging after fertilization. Corolla tubular, funnel-shaped, brown-violet, rarely yellowish or whitish, tube white. Nutlets ovoid. Flowers from May to August. Grows on field boundaries, by roadsides and on wasteland, often on limestone soils in lower altitudes of milder regions.

3 Common Lungwort *Pulmonaria officinalis.* Perennial herb, up to 30 cm. high. Bottom leaves ovate-cordate, abruptly narrowed into petiole, pointed, usually spotted silvery-white; stem ones almost sessile, ovate to lanceolate. Bracted cymes short and dense. Flowers short-stalked, calyx enlarging after fertilization. Corolla purple-rose to pink, later turning violet-blue. Dark brown nutlets. Flowers from March to May. Grows in light woodland and bushy places from lowlands to foothills.

4 Common Comfrey *Symphytum officinale.* Perennial herb with robust, bristly, hairy stems up to 1 metre high. Stems usually well-branched, and keeled or winged. Longly tapering, broadly lanceolate leaves with winged petioles. Inflorescence of dense, bracted cymes. Short-stalked flowers purple or rarely rose or whitish. Corolla tubular; calyx with long-pointed lobes. Nutlets brown-grey, glossy. Flowers from May to July. Grows abundantly in damp meadows, on banks and in ditches from lowlands to foothills.

5 *Symphytum tuberosum.* Perennial herb up to 50 cm. high, with short bristly hairs. Thickened, tuberous rhizome. Erect, almost unbranched, indistinctly angular stems. Shortly tapering leaves, widely lanceolate with winged petioles. Inflorescence of few-flowered cymes. Flowers yellowish white with short hairs. Corolla tubular, with recurved lobes; calyx deeply cleft. Nutlets cuneoid, brown, wrinkled. Flowers in April and May. Grows from lowlands to foothills in damp woods and thickets, rarely in meadows.

Family: *Labiatae* (syn. *Lamiaceae*)

6 Common Bugle *Ajuga reptans.* Perennial herb up to 30 cm. high, with creeping shoots and long-petioled, obovate basal leaves. Erect, simple, square leafy stems, bearing short-stalked flowers in the axils of leafy, purple-tinted bracts. Calyx bell-shaped with triangular-ovate teeth; corolla violet-blue, rarely pink or white; lower lip deeply three-lobed. Fruit of four smooth brown nutlets. Flowers from May to August. Grows in meadows, thickets and woods from lowlands to mountains. Related upright bugle *(A. genevensis)* has no creeping stems, but underground stolons; upper floral bracts are shorter and usually three-lobed, corollas bright blue.

Family: *Labiatae*

1 Ground Ivy *Glechoma hederacea* (syn. *Nepeta hederacea*). Perennial herb up to 30 cm. high, with long-creeping prostrate stems, rooting at the nodes. Leaves petiolate, reniform to broadly ovate-cordate, having rounded teeth. Axillary flowers usually in twos; calyx tubular, hairy, indistinctly bilabiate; corollas blue-violet with a bilobed upper and trilobed lower lip bearing dark purple pattern. Flowers from April to July. Grows in woods, bushy places, grassy slopes, on wasteland, and sometimes as weed in gardens, from lowlands to mountains.

2 Common Self-heal *Prunella vulgaris*. Perennial herb, somewhat hairy or glabrous, up to 30 cm. high, with short leafy rhizomes and ascending, often brown-violet stems. Petiolate, ovate to elliptic leaves, entire or irregularly toothed. Inflorescence of axillary, bracted flowers arranged in short, dense, oblong head. Corollas blue-violet, rarely pink or white; upper lip hooded and bristly-hairy. Glossy nutlets. Flowers from May to September. Grows in pastures, dry meadows, open woods and by the roadside. Related large-flowered self-heal *(P. grandiflora)* is more robust and has larger flowers. It is sometimes grown in garden.

3 *Melittis melissophyllum*. Perennial herb up to 50 cm. high, with erect stems and soft hairs. Erect, unbranched stems bear cordate-ovate, toothed and pointed leaves. Scented flowers are borne in axils of upper leaves. Corollas long-tubuled, white or pink, lower lip rosy, central lobe usually yellow and with dark rose spots. Triangular, smooth nutlets. Flowers in May and June. Grows in open woods and hedgerows especially on limestone soils, at lower altitudes in milder regions. Sometimes cultivated for its distinctive flowers.

4 Large Hemp-nettle *Galeopsis speciosa*. Robust annual herb, up to 1 metre high with branched stems swollen at nodes. Leaves petiolate, ovate, serrate, long-pointed. Flowers in whorls in the upper leaf and bract axils. Corolla longer than calyx, light yellow, central lobe of lower lip violet. Flowers from June to September. Grows in open woods, clearings, bushy places and on wasteland. Common hemp-nettle *(G. tetrahit)* has smaller flowers light purple or whitish with the lower lip purple-spotted.

5 Black Horehound *Ballota nigra*. Perennial herb up to 1 metre high, stems and leaves grey-hairy. Ovate to orbicular leaves wrinkled, pointed and toothed. Calyx bell-shaped; corolla purple, central lobe of lower lip mottled whitish. Flowers from June to September. Grows on wasteland, edges of fields, among bushes and along hedgerows, from lowlands to foothills.

6 Yellow Archangel *Galeobdolon luteum* (syn. *Lamium galeobdolon*). Perennial plant up to 50 cm. high, with far-creeping leafy stolons and erect. simple flowering stems. Leaves petiolate, ovate, pointed, toothed. Flowers in whorls in the upper leaf axils. Calyx bell-shaped with pointed triangular lobes. Corolla yellow with large, hooded upper lip. Nutlets smooth, trigonous. Flowers from April to July. Grows in damp woods and thickets from lowlands to mountains. Related white dead-nettle *(Lamium album)* does not have stolons and bears white flowers.

Family: *Labiatae*

1 Spotted Dead-nettle *Lamium maculatum*. Perennial herb up to 50 cm. high. Petiolate leaves ovate-cordate to toothed, pointed, usually with a central silvery-white zone. Flowers in whorls in the upper leaf axils. Corollas purple, lower lip dark violet-spotted; tube curved. Triangular-obovoid, black-green nutlets. Flowers from April to September. Grows in open woods, on wasteland and by roadsides. Only naturalized in Britain as an escape from gardens. Similar red dead-nettle *(L. purpureum)* with red-purple flowers, almost straight corolla tubes and plain green leaves is a common annual weed.

2 Hedge Woundwort *Stachys sylvatica*. Perennial herb up to 1 metre high, with creeping rhizomes and erect stems. Leaves long-petiolate, ovate-cordate, toothed and pointed. Flowers in bracted whorls, red-purple or crimson. Flowers from June to September. Grows in damp woods, among bushes and in hedgerows from lowlands to mountains. Related marsh woundwort *(S. palustris)* has almost sessile, lanceolate leaves with rounded teeth and light purple flowers.

3 Wood Betony *Betonica officinalis* (syn. *Stachys betonica*). Perennial herb up to 1 metre high, with erect stems, having long internodes. Leaves petiolate, ovate-oblong, cordate, with rounded teeth; upper ones almost sessile and smaller. Dense oblong inflorescence with linear bracts. Corolla purple-red, tube whitish. Flowers in July and August. Grows in open woods, on hedgebanks and on grassy slopes from lowlands to foothills.

4 Whorled Clary *Salvia verticillata*. Perennial herb up to 50 cm. high, hairy and foetid. Basal leaves ovate with rounded teeth, usually fading or dead at flowering time. Stem leaves petiolate, smaller, sometimes pinnately lobed. Inflorescences spike-like, composed of several bracted whorls. Corolla violet, rarely whitish or pink. Flowers from June to September. Grows by the roadside, on grassy slopes and rocky places in the mountains of central Europe, west to Spain; often naturalized elsewhere.

5 Meadow Clary *Salvia pratensis*. Perennial herb up to 50 cm. high, with erect stems. Leaves long-petiolate, ovate to oblong-cordate, shallowly lobed with irregular rounded teeth, wrinkled. Inflorescence a long-petiolate, ovate to oblong-cordate, shallowly lobed with irregular rounded teeth, wrinkled. Inflorescence formed of several whorls of blue, rarely pink or white flowers; upper lip of corolla hooded, lower one small and rounded. Flowers from May to August. Grows on dry slopes, in meadows, bushy places, hedge banks and on field boundaries, mainly in milder regions.

6 Pot Marjoram *Origanum vulgare*. Perennial aromatic herb up to 50 cm. high, with a woody rhizome. Stems erect, leafy. Short-petiolate leaves ovate, almost entire, glandular. Inflorescence a dense corymbose cyme. Flowers rose-purple, rarely white. Nutlets ovoid, smooth, brown. Flowers from July to September. Grows fairly abundantly on sunny grassy slopes, in bushy places, and on margins of forests, mainly in milder regions.

Family: *Labiatae*

1 *Thymus praecox.* Small mat-forming undershrub up to 7 cm. tall (in flower). Stems creeping, up to 50 cm. long, rooting. Ascending. Flowering stems four-angled, with two opposite sides densely hairy. Leaves subortucular to oblanceolate with marked venation on under surface. Inflorescences compact, rounded to ovoid. Flowers rose-purple to red, occasionally white. Flowers from May to June. Grows on sunny, grassy or rocky slopes at lower altitudes of milder regions, especially on limestone soils. True *T. serpyllum* has the stems sparsely and evenly hairy all round. It is one of many European species of thyme.

2 Corn Mint *Mentha arvensis.* Perennial herb up to 50 cm. high, often purple-tinted, aromatic, with underground rhizomes. Decumbent or ascending stems are densely leafy. Leaves narrowly to broadly ovate, toothed. Inflorescence of several axillary whorls. Calyx with triangular teeth. Corolla lilac to blue-purple. Flowers from June to October. Grows in moist fields, ditches, and in open wet woods from lowlands to foothills. Peppermint *(Mentha × piperita)*, a hybrid of water mint and spearmint *(M. aquatica × M. spicata)* is often cultivated for flavouring.

Family: *Solanaceae*

3 Deadly Nightshade *Atropa bella-donna.* Perennial herb, glandular-hairy, up to 150 cm. high with thick, erect, branched stems. Leaves alternate, or on the flowering stems in unequal pairs; ovate to elliptic, entire, with a winged petiole. Flowers drooping, solitary, seemingly axillary, having bell-shaped corollas, outside brown-purple, inside yellowish. Berries globose, black, subtended by the star-like enlarged calyx. All parts of this plant are poisonous. Flowers from June to August. Grows scattered in woodland clearings, on margins of forests and wasteland from lowlands to foothills.

4 Henbane *Hyoscyamus niger.* Annual to biennial herb, up to 80 cm. high, sticky glandular-hairy and foetid. Erect, densely leafy stems bear alternate oblong-ovate, somewhat irregularly lobed leaves, the lower ones petiolate, top ones semi-clasping. Flowers in axils of upper leaves. Calyx bell-shaped, glandular, hairy, prominently net-veined; corolla funnel-shaped dull yellow, violet-netted. Anthers violet. Capsules with lids contain black-brown seeds. Whole plant poisonous. Flowers from June to October. Grows on wasteland, by roadsides, and on sandy ground, often near the sea, in lowland areas, more frequently in milder regions.

5 Winter-cherry *Physalis alkekengi.* Perennial herb up to 60 cm. high, with creeping rhizome. Erect stems somewhat angular, upper part downy. Petiolate broad leaves ovate, usually entire, pointed. Flowers solitary, axillary, stalked; globular lantern-shaped inflated calyx; dull white or yellowish green corolla. Berries orange, enclosed in the enlarged inflated calyx, both red when ripe. Flowers from May to August. Grows in deciduous woods, bushy places and on waste ground, in central and southern Europe. Cultivated and escaping here and there.

6 Black Nightshade *Solanum nigrum.* Annual herb up to 60 cm. high. Erect or decumbent branched stems. Leaves widely ovate or rhomboid, shallowly lobed or with a sinuate margin. Flowers in small leafless cymes. Corollas white, with 5 spreading pointed lobes. Berries usually black, rarely greenish or yellowish. Flowers from June to October. Grows as weed in fields, gardens and on wasteland from lowlands to foothills. Related bittersweet or woody nightshade *(S. dulcamara)* is a semi-climbing shrub with violet flowers and yellow anthers fused into cone, protruding from reflexed corolla; berry translucent red. Both species poisonous.

Family: **Snapdragon** — *Scrophulariaceae*

1 Common Mullein *Verbascum thapsus*. Biennial herb up to 2 m. high, covered with dense whitish felted hair. Leaves, obovate to oblong in basal rosettes; stem ones lanceolate, with winged stalks that run down the stem. Light yellow flowers in a spire-like panicle; corollas up to 2 cm. in diameter. Filaments of two longer stamens smooth, those of three shorter ones hairy. Flowers from July to September. Grows on hedgebanks, sunny slopes and wasteland, from lowlands to foothills. Related large-flowered mullein *(V. thapsiforme)* has flowers up to 4 cm. in diameter, and filaments of bare stamens are double anther length.

2 White Mullein *Verbascum lychnitis*. Biennial herb up to 1.5 metre high, with short hairs. Oblong to lanceolate basal leaves have small rounded teeth or are entire; stem leaves almost sessile, ovate, pointed. Inflorescence a narrow stiff panicle; flowers white or yellow; stamen filaments of almost equal length, white-woolly. Flowers from June to August. Grows in waste places, on sunny slopes, forest margins and by roadsides, from lowlands to foothills. Related dark mullein *(V. nigrum)* has bottom leaves usually cordate and filaments of stamens violet-woolly.

3 Purple Mullein *Verbascum phoeniceum*. Biennial herb up to 1 m. high, with stem usually densely glandular. Leaves of basal rosette ovate, stem ones sparse, cordate and sessile. Flowers in terminal raceme; dark violet corollas up to 3 cm. in diameter. Flowers from May to July. Grows scattered at outskirts of forests, on bushy, sunny slopes and in sandy places at lower altitudes in milder regions. Cultivated in Britain and occasionally escaping.

4 Toadflax *Linaria vulgaris*. Perennial herb up to 40 cm. high, usually unbranched. Alternate, sessile leaves linear-lanceolate, entire, grey-green. Flowers in dense terminal raceme; corollas snapdragon-like, sulphur yellow, with palate of lower lip orange; corolla tube with long spur. Ovoid capsule. Flowers from June to October. Grows abundantly in fields, on wasteland, by roadsides and among rocks from lowlands to foothills. Sometimes a weed of gardens. Tiny alpine toadflax *(L. alpina)* is grey, decumbent, with leaves in whorls; violet flowers have lower lip with orange palate.

5 Field Cow-wheat *Melampyrum arvense*. Annual herb up to 40 cm. high, downy. Opposite, lanceolate leaves; bottom ones entire, upper leaves have several long, large teeth at the base. Flowers in dense spike, bracts purple. Corollas tubular bilabiate, pink, with yellow throat and deep pink lips. Flowers from May to September. Grows in fields, on slopes and margins of woods, mainly in the lowlands. Rare in Britain. Related crested cow-wheat *(M. cristatum)* has reddish crested bracts, smaller yellow and purple flowers and grows mainly in open woods.

6 Common Cow-wheat *Melampyrum pratense*. Annual herb up to 50 cm. high with spreading branches. Linear-lanceolate to narrowly ovate, entire leaves. Flowers arranged in a sparse, one-sided spike, the lower ones well spaced. Calyx lobes unequal, pointed; corollas whitish to lemon yellow, with a narrow mouth. Flowers from May to September. Grows in forests and in clearings, from lowlands to mountains. Wood cow-wheat *(M. sylvaticum)* has triangular-lanceolate sepals and yellow to orange-yellow flowers with wide open mouths.

Family: **Snapdragon** — *Scrophulariaceae*

1 Germander Speedwell *Veronica chamaedrys*. Perennial herb up to 25 cm. high, little branched. Prostrate or ascending stems have hairs in two rows. Leaves are opposite, ovate to elliptic, toothed. Sparse floral racemes in axils of upper leaves; corollas sky-blue with a white eye. Capsules obcordate, shorter than calyx. Flowers in May and June. Grows on field boundaries and grassy banks, in meadows, open woods and among bushes. Thyme-leaved speedwell *(V. serpyllifolia)* has white or pale blue flowers and rounded to oblong leaves.

2 Common Speedwell *Veronica officinalis*. Perennial herb with rooting prostrate stems up to 30 cm. long. Finely serrate leaves elliptic to ovate or obovate, shortly petiolate, toothed. Racemes arise in upper leaf axils. Flowers light violet to lilac. Capsules obcordate, glandular. Flowers from June to August. Grows in dry woods, clearings and on heaths and moors. Buxbaum's speedwell *(V. persica)* has stalks longer than ovate, toothed leaves and sky-blue and white flowers solitary in leaf axils.

3 Spiked Speedwell *Veronica spicata*. Perennial herb, up to 50 cm. high, downy, on top glandular. Leaves opposite, oval or ovate, blunt, toothed along the sides. Flowers in dense, terminal racemes; corollas violet-blue. Obcordate, glandular capsules. Flowers from June to August. Grows in rocky places, on sunny grassy slopes, in pastures and on field boundaries from lowlands to foothills, mainly in milder regions. Rare in Britain.

4 Yellow-rattle *Rhinanthus minor*. Annual herb with a simple or branched stem up to 60 cm. Leaves linear-lanceolate with rounded teeth. Inflorescence a terminal bracted raceme. Calyx inflated; corolla yellow, hooded, just protruding from calyx. Flattened capsules hidden in calyx. Flowers from May to July. Grows scattered as field weed, in meadows and heaths, from lowlands to mountains.

5 Lousewort *Pedicularis sylvatica*. Perennial herb with decumbent stems, only at tip ascending, up to 20 cm. high. Alternate, pinnately lobed leaves, the segments toothed. Inflorescence a few-flowered terminal raceme. Inflated, unequally five-toothed calyx; corollas pink. Flowers from May to July. Grows scattered in damp meadows and on moors and heaths from lowlands to mountains.

6 Yellow Foxglove *Digitalis grandiflora* (syn. *D. ambigua*). Perennial herb up to 1 metre high. Erect stems glandular hairy. Alternate leaves, bottom ones oblanceolate, upper leaves ovately lanceolate, sessile. Flowers in one-sided, dense raceme. Corollas tubular, bell-shaped, somewhat flattened and lobed, light yellow without, brown-netted within. Flowers in June and July. Grows in clearings, on overgrown rocky slopes, and in open woods from hilly country to mountains. Grown in gardens and very rarely escaping.

Family: *Orobanchaceae*

1 Toothwort *Lathraea squamaria*. Perennial whitish or pinkish parasitic herb, up to 25 cm. high. Stout branched rhizome with fleshy, white scale leaves. Erect stem is fleshy, unbranched, with a few scale leaves. Flowers in one-sided, dense raceme, at first drooping at tip. Corollas tubular, bilabiate, dull purple, lower lip reddish. Capsules explosive, with large seeds. Flowers from March to May. Grows in deciduous woods at lower altitudes; parasitic on roots of deciduous trees, especially hazel and elm.

2 Red Broomrape *Orobanche alba*. Perennial yellowish parasitic herb up to 30 cm. tall. Slender stems unbranched, thickened underground, glandular hairy. Stem bracts ovate-lanceolate; flowers in sparse raceme with reddish bracts. Calyx bilabiate. Corolla tubular, curved, labiate, upper lip dark glandular hairy with purple tint, rest of corolla whitish. In Britain flowers reddish throughout. Flowers in June and July. Grows on sunny grassy slopes, mainly in milder regions; parasitic on thyme and other members of the *Labiatae*.

Family: **Plantain** — *Plantaginaceae*

3 Ribwort *Plantago lanceolata*. Perennial herb up to 45 cm. high, with deep green leaves in basal rosette and simple, erect flowering stem. Leaves lanceolate, sometimes obscurely toothed. Grooved stem and dense ovoid to cylindrical spike. Corollas brownish with white anthers. Capsule with ovoid lid. Flowers from May to September. Grows as a weed in meadows, fields, pastures, by roadsides, on wasteland, from lowlands to mountains. Related hoary plantain *(P. media)* has elliptic to ovate hoary leaves, round stems and filaments of stamens light violet.

4 Great Plantain *Plantago major*. Perennial herb up to 30 cm. high. Broadly ovate to elliptic leaves in basal rosette narrow abruptly to a cordate base and winged petiole. Erect stems bear a long, dense, narrow spike of small yellowish white flowers; anthers lilac, turning to dull yellow, filaments whitish. Capsules broadly ovoid with lids. Flowers from June to October. Grows as a weed in pastures, fields, on wasteland and by roadsides, from lowlands to mountains.

Family: **Madder** — *Rubiaceae*

5 Field Madder *Sherardia arvensis*. Annual herb with slender, generally prostrate stems, up to 30 cm. long, branched and square. Leaves in whorls of 4—6, with tiny prickled hairs, lanceolate to elliptic, pointed, single-veined. Inflorescence a few-flowered umbel terminating the branches. Corollas with 4 narrow cross-like lobes. Fruit of 2 obovoid mericarps. Flowers from June to October. Grows as a weed in fields, on wasteland and by roadsides, from lowlands to foothills, more frequently on calcareous soils.

6 Woodruff *Galium odoratum* (syn. *Asperula odorata*). Perennial herb up to 40 cm. high, with far-creeping rhizomes and erect, square, smooth flowering stems. Leaves lanceolate to elliptic, with marginal prickles, tip usually with small hard point, in whorls of up to 6. Flowers in terminal, long-stalked cymes. Corollas small, white, funnel-shaped, with 4 blunt lobes. Double mericarp has hooked bristles. Flowers in May and June. Grows in deciduous woods and among bushes, from lowlands to mountains.

Family: **Madder** — *Rubiaceae*

1 Goosegrass or **Cleavers** *Galium aparine.* Annual herb with stems bearing hooked bristles, prostrate or climbing, square, up to 120 cm. long. Leaves in whorls of 6—8, linear, oblanceolate, margins with small, curved bristles. Flowers in stalked, axillary cymes; four-parted corollas very small, whitish, with spreading lobes. Double mericarps with small white hooks. Flowers from June to October. Grows in hedgerows, thickets, on wasteground and in fields, and at outskirts of forests, from lowlands to mountains.

2 Lady's Bedstraw *Galium verum.* Perennial herb with creeping rhizome and prostrate to erect, angled stems, up to 60 cm. long or more, branched at the top. Leaves narrowly linear, single-veined, in upwards of 8—12 whorls. Bright yellow cross-shaped flowers in dense terminal panicles. Flowers from May to September. Grows abundantly in meadows, on sunny grassy banks, field boundaries, in hedgerows and on dunes. Low-growing *Galium cruciata* has unbranched stems with spreading white hairs and three-veined ovate-elliptic, hairy leaves; flowers pale yellow.

3 Hedge Bedstraw *Galium mollugo.* Perennial herb up to 1 metre long with decumbent, ascending or erect stems, often climbing, square, smooth. Leaves linear to obovate, edge finely prickly, tip pointed. White cross-shaped flowers in long, terminal panicles. Corolla lobes prolonged into slender point. Double mericarps wrinkled. Flowers from May to September. Grows in meadows, on field boundaries, in hedgerows, at outskirts of forests and on dunes, from lowlands to mountains.

Family: *Loniceraceae*

4 Danewort *Sambucus ebulus.* Perennial herb, malodorous, poisonous, up to 150 cm. high with erect, grooved stems. Leaves petiolate, odd-pinnate, leaflets 7—13, sharply serrate, oblong-lanceolate. Dense flat-topped, panicle-like cymes bear small 5-petalled, white or pale pink flowers; anthers violet. Fruits are glossy black globose drupes. Flowers in June and July. Grows in woodland clearings, margins of forests, among bushes and in hedgerows, from lowlands to foothills. Related species are woody plants.

Family: **Valerian** — *Valerianaceae*

5 Smooth-fruited Cornsalad *Valerianella dentata.* Annual herb up to 30 cm. high, with erect, repeatedly forking stems, usually with single flower in forks of branches; further flowers in terminal heads. Tiny bluish white flowers; calyx margin with one tooth longer than others. Leaves spathulate, blunt, opposite, sometimes toothed at the base. Flowers from June to September. Grows in fields, wasteland, on rocky slopes and old walls, from lowlands to foothills. Related common cornsalad *(V. locusta)* has forked branches without flowers and entire leaves.

6 Common Valerian *Valeriana officinalis.* Perennial herb up to 1 metre high, with stout erect stems and shortly creeping rhizomes. Pinnately divided leaves, bottom ones petiolate, upper leaves sessile. Flowers in dense cymose head with usually two main branches. Corollas white or pink, tubular, with 5 lobes. Achenes conical with crown of pappus. Flowers from June to September. Grows in damp meadows, and in bushy places from lowlands to mountains. Smaller marsh valerian *(V. dioica)* has almost unparted, ovate spathulate basal leaves, stem ones pinnately lobed, and unisexual flowers.

Family: **Scabious** — *Dipsacaceae*

1 Teasel *Dipsacus fullonum* (syn.*D. sylvester*). Biennial herb up to 200 cm. high with robust, angled stems, prickly on the angles. Basal leaves in rosette, oblong to elliptic, stem ones lanceolate, opposite, fused at base, prickly on margins and central rib. Stalks of inflorescences densely prickly, flowers in a dense ovoid head, rose-purple, rarely whitish. Involucral bracts linear, pointed, prickly, longer than head. Flowers in July and August. Grows in open woods and thickets, on stream banks and wasteland, in ditches and by the roadside, usually at lower altitudes. *D. fullonum* subspecies *sativus* is cultivated for napping cloth. It has larger heads and stiff, spiny floral bracts.

2 Field Scabious *Knautia arvensis*. Perennial herb almost 1 metre high with spreading hairs and erect stems. Basal rosettes of somewhat grey-green leaves, oblanceolate to obovate, stem ones pinnately lobed, segments lanceolate. Long-stalked flowering heads; corollas bluish lilac to rarely pink, whitish or yellowish; outer florets with 2 enlarged petals. Achenes ovoid, hairy, with a crown of persistent calyx lobes. Flowers in July and August. Grows in meadows, on field boundaries, grassy slopes and margins of forests from lowlands to mountains.

3 Yellow Scabious *Scabiosa ochroleuca*. Perennial herb up to 50 cm. high, with erect stems. Leaves of basal rosettes obovate, lyre-shaped, pinnately lobed, terminal lobe toothed; stem leaves with linear, toothed segments. Long-stalked flower heads; outer florets with 2 enlarged petals. Light yellow corollas; calyx bristle, hairy, at first reddish. Flowers from July to October. Grows on sunny slopes, field boundaries, rocky slopes and margins of forests, in lower altitudes of milder regions. Sometimes grown in gardens.

Family: **Campanula** — *Campanulaceae*

4 Peach-leaved Bellflower *Campanula persicifolia*. Perennial plant up to 1 metre high, with shortly creeping rhizome and erect stems. Glossy, smooth leaves are shallowly toothed; basal ones lanceolate to oblanceolate, top ones narrowly lanceolate. Flowers up to 4 cm. long, in an open raceme. Corolla broadly bell-shaped, blue-violet to white, with 5 broad lobes. Erect capsules with three basal openings. Flowers from June to September. Grows in woods, thickets and on bushy slopes, from lowlands to mountains. Often cultivated in Britain and escaping; well naturalized in a few places.

5 Clustered Bellflower *Campanula glomerata*. Perennial herb up to 40 cm. or more high, usually with downy hairs and erect stems. Basal leaves petiolate, ovate-cordate, stem ones sessile, lanceolate, toothed. Sessile flowers in terminal and or axillary heads; corollas erect, bell-shaped, dark blue to blue-violet, less frequently white. Flowers from June to September. Grows on bushy or grassy slopes, in open woods and clearings from lowlands to mountains. Several forms are grown in gardens.

6 Alpine Bellflower *Campanula alpina*. A perennial herb up to 15 cm. high, with basal rosette of hairy, oval leaves, toothed at the tips. Stem leaves lanceolate, usually toothed, rarely entire. Drooping flowers on hairy stalks; corollas broadly bell-shaped, light blue, with recurved lobes, woolly hairy on margins. Flowers in July and August. Grows on screes and among rocks in mountains. In Alps is accompanied by bearded bellflower *(C. barbata)* with larger, light violet-blue flowers having prominently woolly hairy corolla lobes.

Family: **Campanula** — *Campanulaceae*

1 Spiked Rampion *Phyteuma spicatum.* Perennial herb up to 80 cm. high, with erect stems. Long-petioled bottom leaves are cordate-ovate, with rounded teeth; stem leaves lanceolate. Flowers in dense, cylindrical head; corollas whitish-yellow, tubular; linear petals. Capsule ovoid, with two openings. Flowers from May to July. Grows in deciduous woods and thickets, from lowlands to mountains. Rare in Britain. Related round-headed rampion *(P. orbiculare)* has dark blue flowers in globose head.

2 Common Sheepsbit *Jasione montana.* Biennial herb with erect hairy stems up to 50 cm. high. Basal leaves, linear to oblong, hairy, mostly withered at flowering time; stem ones smaller with wavy margins. Flowers in globose heads, bracts triangular-ovate, pointed. Corollas bright blue, rarely rosy or whitish; linear petals. Capsule ovoid. Flowers from June to August. Grows in grassy places, dunes, on rocky slopes and on cliffs, especially on non-calcareous soils, from lowlands to foothills.

Family: *Compositae* (syn. *Asteraceae*)

3 Chicory *Cichorium intybus.* Perennial herb, up to 150 cm. high, with a milky sap. Stiff, erect, branched stems. Basal leaves petiolate, in rosette, oblanceolate, irregularly lobed, bristle beneath; stem leaves sessile, upper ones lanceolate. Inflorescence a capitulum, involucral bracts in two rows. All florets strap-shaped, five-toothed at the tips, blue, rarely rose or whitish. Achenes without hairs, crowned with short scales. Flowers from July to October. Grows by roadsides on wasteground and in pastures, from lowlands to foothills. Much cultivated for roots (chicory) and as salad vegetable (chicons).

4 Mouse-ear Hawkweed *Hieracium pilosella.* Perennial herb with long, leafy stolons and leafless, single-headed flowering stems, up to 30 cm. high. Leaves in basal rosette linear to obovate-oblong, white hairy floccose beneath, sparingly so above. Linear involucral bracts grey-green, hairy on margins. All florets ligulate, five-toothed, yellow, outer ones reddish, striped. Achenes purple-black, with pappus. Flowers from May to October. Grows in meadows, on grassy slopes and banks, and by roadsides, from lowlands to mountains.

5 *Hieracium aurantiacum.* Perennial herb up to 50 cm. high, with creeping stolons and erect stems. Leaves of basal rosette oblong to lanceolate, hairy, glandular, woolly hairy beneath. Flower heads in a terminal cluster covered with black-based glandular hairs. Capitula have dark orange florets. Flowers from June to August. Grows in mountain meadows of central Europe. Sometimes grown in gardens and escaping; can become an aggressive weed.

6 Common Dandelion *Taraxacum officinale.* Perennial herb with a milky latex-like sap, 20—40 cm. high. Leaves of basal rosette are angularly, pinnately lobed, either deeply or shallowly. Leafless stems with single capitula; outer involucral bracts linear, spreading or reflexed; inner ones erect and longer; strap-shaped florets golden yellow. Achenes with pointed tubercles, beaked, crowned by parachute-like pappus. Flowers from April to September. Grows commonly in meadows, pastures, lawns, by roadsides and as field weed, from lowlands to mountains.

Family: *Compositae*

1 Prickly Lettuce *Lactuca serriola*. Biennial herb up to 150 cm. high, with a milky sap and prickly hairs. Bottom stem leaves pinnately lobed and toothed; upper leaves lanceolate, clasping. Leaf blades vertical, usually in a north-south plane (compass plant). Capitula in large panicles; all florets strap-shaped, yellow. Achenes with small points and stalked pappus. Flowers from July to September. Grows on wasteland, banks, dunes and walls at lower altitudes in milder regions. Related *Lactuca sativa* is cultivated as a salad vegetable.

2 Giant Cat's-ear *Hypochoeris uniflora*. Perennial herb up to 40 cm. high, with erect stems bearing a solitary capitulum, usually leafless. Leaves of basal rosette lanceolate, toothed, coarsely hairy. Large capitula up to 5 cm. in diameter, the involucre bearing soft blackish hairs; florets yellow. Achenes beaked, crowned with pappus. Flowers from July to September. Grows in mountain meadows, in rocky places and in clearings of knee-pine.

3 Greater Goatsbeard *Tragopogon dubius*. Biennial herb up to 50 cm. high, with erect, branched and leafy stem. Leaves linear-lanceolate, sharply pointed, usually grey-green. Stems thickened and hollow beneath capitula. Solitary capitula with yellow florets. Involucral bracts longer than outer florets. Achenes up to 4 cm. long, with spiny projections and stalked pappus. Flowers from May to July. Grows on sunny, grassy slopes, field boundaries and by roadsides at lower altitudes of milder regions.

4 Common Vipersgrass *Scorzonera humilis*. Perennial up to 40 cm. high, with brownish-black rhizome and erect, simple, almost leafless stems, usually with single capitulum. Basal leaves petiolate, linear-lanceolate, woolly hairy when young, later smooth. Capitula with a bell-shaped involucre and yellow florets. Achenes ribbed and crowned with pappus. Flowers in May to July. Grows in damp meadows, on moors and in open forests, from hilly country to mountains. Rare in Britain. Related purple vipersgrass *(S. purpurea)* has lilac flowers and linear leaves.

5 Hemp Agrimony *Eupatorium cannabinum*. Perennial, robust herb up to 150 cm. high with erect, leafy stems. Leaves short-petiolate, hairy, opposite, three- to five-lobed and toothed. Dense inflorescences, small, few-flowered capitula, narrowly cylindrical involucre. Florets pink or whitish tubular, with five corolla lobes. Achenes black, crowned with pappus. Flowers from July to September. Grows in damp open woods, on banks, in ditches and marshes, from lowlands to mountains.

6 Golden-rod *Solidago virgaurea*. Perennial herb up to 75 cm. high. Stems erect, simple, leafy. Basal leaves obovate to oblanceolate, petiolate, toothed; upper ones lanceolate, sessile. Small yellow capitula arranged in dense, erect raceme or panicle. Outer ligulate florets longer than involucre, inner florets tubular. Achenes downy, crowned with pappus. Flowers from July to October. Grows in open woods, among rocks, in hedgerows, on cliffs and dunes, from lowlands to mountains. A very variable plant with several distinct forms varying from 5 to 75 cm. in height.

Family: *Compositae*

1 Daisy *Bellis perennis*. Perennial herb up to 10 cm. high. Leaves in basal rosette, obovate to spathulate, widely toothed. Erect stems with single capitula. Conical receptacle hollow, involucral bracts lanceolate, blunt. Central florets tubular, yellow; outer ones ligulate, white, often red-tinted on the backs. Flowers from March to November. Grows in grassy places from lowlands to mountains. Large-flowered forms are cultivated, some with 'double' flower-heads (all florets ligulate).

2 Alpine Aster *Aster alpinus*. Perennial herb up to 20 cm. high. Erect, unbranched stems with single capitula, few-leaved. Three-veined, hairy, entire leaves; basal ones spathulate, stem leaves lanceolate, sessile. Capitula up to 4 cm. in diameter, involucral bracts lanceolate, hairy. Central florets yellow, tubular, outer ones strap-shaped, violet-blue, rarely rose. Flowers from June to August. Grows in rocky, stony places or on grassy slopes in mountains. Also grown in gardens.

3 *Erigeron canadense*. Annual or biennial plant, up to 1 metre high, with erect, densely leafy, simple stems and a large paniculate inflorescence. Leaves lanceolate; bottom ones petiolate, upper leaves sessile. Tiny capitula with membraneous bordered involucral bracts. Central florets yellowish white, tubular; outer one dirty white, slightly longer than involucral bracts. Achenes. Flowers from July to October. Native of North America but extensively naturalized on wasteland, by roadsides, on dunes and walls. Also a weed of farmland and gardens.

4 Blue Fleabane *Erigeron acer*. Biennial to perennial herb, up to 30 cm. high, with erect, reddish, leafy stems, all coarsely hairy. Leaves usually entire, bottom ones obovate-lanceolate, petiolate; upper leaves lanceolate, sessile. Capitula terminate upper lateral branches, 1 cm. in diameter; cylindrical involucre has linear bracts with grey hairs. Central florets whitish to yellow-green, tubular; outer ones short-ligulate, filamentous, slightly longer than central flowers, purple. Flowers from June to September. Grows particularly in limestone areas, on dry, grassy slopes, dunes, banks and walls, from lowlands to foothills.

5 Cat's-foot *Antennaria dioica*. Perennial evergreen plant with stolons up to 20 cm. high, with stems and leaves white-woolly beneath. Basal leaves spathulate, stem ones lanceolate to linear. Separate-sexed capitula in close terminal cluster, stalked; involucral bracts overlapping, chaffy in texture, whitish or pink; florets usually whitish. Flowers in May and June. Grows in hill pastures, rocky places, in open pine-woods and on heaths and moors, from foothills to mountains.

6 Edelweiss *Leontopodium alpinum*. Perennial herb up to 20 cm. high, thickly white woolly hairy. Erect simple stems sparsely leaved. Basal leaves in rosette, oblanceolate, petiolate, entire; stem ones alternate, smaller. Small hemispherical capitula grouped at end of stem into a dense cluster, surrounded by star-like unequal bracts which are lanceolate and white felted; florets tiny, yellowish white. Flowers from June to September. Grows in mountain pastures, on limestone rocks and screes in central and south-eastern Europe. Protected plant in some countries.

Family: *Compositae*

1 Wood Cudweed *Gnaphalium sylvaticum.* Perennial herb up to 50 cm. high, erect, simple leafy stems. Single-veined, entire leaves on upper surface downy or bare, underside grey felted; bottom ones lanceolate, upper leaves linear. Small capitula clustered in axils of upper leaves; involucral bracts bordered light brown. Tiny florets narrowly tubular, pale brown. Flowers from July to September. Grows in open woods, clearings and on heaths and moors, from lowlands to mountains.

2 *Inula britannica.* Perennial herb up to 60 cm. high, with appressed hairs and erect, leafy stems. Hairy basal leaves oblong-ovate to lanceolate, toothed or entire; upper ones sessile, cordate and clasping. Capitula solitary or in groups of up to four at end of branches. Widely ovoid involucre, bracts linear-lanceolate, glandular, hairy. Florets yellow, central ones tubular, outer ones long ligulate. Flowers from July to September. Grows scattered in damp meadows, ditches, streamsides and damp woods, from lowlands to hilly country. Probably now extinct in Britain.

3 Common Cocklebur *Xanthium strumarium.* Annual, grey-green herb, up to 75 cm. high, with a stout, sparsely leaved stem. Leaves cordate triangular, lobed and toothed. Axillary capitula single sexed; male ones with several flowers, greenish female capitula have two flowers tightly enclosed in spiny involucral bracts. Achenes enclosed in spiny, woody involucre. Flowers from July to October. Native of South America, introduced and established on wasteland, by roadsides and on tips, usually at lower altitudes in milder regions.

4 Tripartite Bur-marigold *Bidens tripartitus.* Annual herb up to 60 cm. high, with maroon-tinted, much branched stems. Opposite, petiolate stem leaves three- to five-lobed, segments lanceolate, toothed. Capitula solitary at ends of branches; outer involucral bracts enlarged and leafy, inner ones ovate, brownish. Florets yellow, ligulate ones missing. Achenes obovoid, flattened, edges barbed, with two to three straight barbed awns. Flowers from July to October. Grows in ditches, by ponds and rivers and in water meadows, from lowlands to foothills. Related nodding bur-marigold *(B. cernuus)* has larger nodding capitula.

5 Corn Chamomile *Anthemis arvensis.* Annual herb, up to 50 cm. high. Erect, well-branched stems. Twice or three times pinnately divided leaves, segments linear. Solitary, long-stalked capitula; receptacle conical, bearing lanceolate, pointed, chaffy awns. Yellow central tubular florets, outer ones white, ligulate. Achenes truncate ovoid, without pappus. Flowers from May to October. Grows in fields, on wasteground and by roadsides from lowlands to foothills.

6 Stinking Mayweed *Anthemis cotula.* Annual herb, foetid, up to 50 cm. high, with well-branched stems. Leaves twice to three times pinnately divided, with narrowly linear, toothed segments. Solitary stalked capitula, bracts of involucre with wide membraneous rim. Central, tubular florets yellow, outer ones ligulate, white. Achenes lop-sided, ovoid, ribbed, without pappus. Flowers from June to October. Grows in fields, on wasteland and by roadsides, from lowlands to foothills.

Family: *Compositae*

1 Gallant Soldier *Galinsoga parviflora.* Annual herb up to 70 cm. high, with erect, branched, leafy stems. Leaves opposite, ovate, pointed, sharply toothed. Small capitula in terminal, leafy clusters. Central tubular florets yellow, outer ones shortly ligulate, white. Achenes with scaly pappus. Flowers from May to October. Native of South America, introduced to Europe and now a familiar weed in fields, gardens and on wasteland, from lowlands to foothills. Related hairy galinsoga or shaggy soldier *(G. ciliata)* is similar, but more or less densely covered with long hairs.

2 Sneezewort *Achillea ptarmica.* Perennial up to 60 cm. high, with woody creeping rhizome and erect, leafy stems. Leaves linear-lanceolate, sessile, sharply toothed. Capitula in a loose terminal cluster, involucral bracts bordered with dark brown. Central florets whitish, surrounded by up to 12 ligulate flowers of same length as involucre. Flowers from July to September. Grows on heaths, in ditches and damp meadows from lowlands to foothills. Double-flowered forms are often cultivated in gardens.

3 Yarrow *Achillea millefolium.* Perennial up to 50 cm. high, with far-creeping stolons and erect flowering stems. Leaves twice to three times pinnate, segments linear-lanceolate, spreading. Small capitula in dense flattened corymbs. Central florets creamy, surrounded by up to five ligulate florets white, or sometimes pink, or cerise. Flowers from June to October. Grows in meadows, pastures, woodland clearings, among rocks and by the roadside from lowlands to mountains. Pink and cerise flowered forms are grown in gardens.

4 *Matricaria recutita* (syn. *M.chamomilla*). Annual herb, up to 50 cm. high, pleasingly aromatic with branched stems. Leaves alternate, sparse, up to three times pinnately divided into narrow, linear segments. Individual capitula at end of upper branches, long-stalked; central florets yellow and tubular, outer ones white and ligulate, soon reflexing backwards. Receptacles of capitula hollow, conical. Achenes ovoid, ribbed, without pappus. Flowers from March to August. Grows as a weed in fields, gardens and by roadsides, from lowlands to foothills, mainly in milder regions. Once much cultivated as a medicinal herb and still used as a substitute for true chamomile.

5 Pineapple Weed *Matricaria matricarioides.* Annual herb, up to 30 cm. high, sweetly aromatic, with branched, densely leafy stems. Sessile leaves up to three times pinnately divided into linear-lanceolate segments. Capitulum stalks short, thickened at top; involucral bracts with translucent membraneous rim. All florets yellow-green, tubular. Receptacles hollow, conical. Achenes ovoid, truncate, ribbed, pappus absent. Flowers from June to August. Native of north-eastern Asia, introduced and now a common weed of cultivated land, roadsides, wasteland and along paths, from lowlands to foothills.

6 Scentless Mayweed *Tripleurospermum maritimum* subspecies *inodorum.* Annual or biennial herb, up to 50 cm. high, with erect stems usually branched only on top. Leaves up to three times pinnately divided into narrowly linear segments. Long-stalked capitula. Central florets yellow, tubular; outer ones white, ligulate. Achenes ovoid, truncate, ribbed, without pappus. Flowers from June to October. Grows in fields, fallows, on wasteland and by roadsides, from lowlands to foothills. *T. maritimum* ssp. *maritimum* is perennial and more or less prostrate, growing only near the sea.

2

3

4

1

6

5

Family: *Compositae*

1 Tansy *Tanacetum vulgare* (syn. *Chrysanthemum vulgare*). Perennial, with creeping rhizomes and erect stems up to 1 metre high. Leaves twice pinnately divided, segments lanceolate, toothed; pleasingly aromatic when bruised. Numerous capitula in dense corymbs. All florets yellow, tubular, five-lobed. Achenes ovoid, crowned with a short membraneous cup. Flowers from July to September. Grows by the roadside, on wasteland, and in hedgerows, from lowlands to mountains. Formerly much grown as a medicinal and pot-herb.

2 Ox-eye Daisy *Chrysanthemum leucanthemum*. Perennial herb up to 70 cm. high, with erect, simple stems, occasionally sparsely branched. Bottom leaves simple, spathulate, petiolate, shallowly lobed and toothed; upper ones oblong-lanceolate, sessile, clasping. Long-stalked capitula; central florets yellow, tubular, outer ones white, ligulate. Achenes obovoid, grooved. Flowers from June to October. Grows in meadows, on grassy slopes, banks, and by the roadside.

3 Wood Chrysanthemum *Chrysanthemum corymbosum*. Perennial up to 1 m. high, with erect, densely leafy stems. Bottom leaves petiolate, stem ones sessile, all pinnately lobed, the segments doubly toothed. Capitula in corymbs. Central florets yellow, tubular, outer ones white, narrowly ligulate. Flowers from June to August. Grows in open woods and among bushes, on sunny slopes, from lowlands to mountains, mainly on limestone, in milder regions.

4 Mugwort *Artemisia vulgaris*. Perennial herb up to 120 cm. high, with erect, stiff, branched stems. Leaves pinnately lobed, underside thinly white felted, segments lanceolate to oblong, lobed, toothed, upper leaves simply pinnate with entire segments. Small capitula arranged in long, dense, pyramidal panicles. Minute, tubular flowers reddish-brown. Flowers from July to September. Grows on waste ground, by roadsides and in hedgerows, from lowlands to mountains.

5 Coltsfoot *Tussilago farfara*. Perennial herb, up to 25 cm. high, with creeping rhizome and erect, simple stem, bearing single capitulum. Basal tufts of leaves develop after flowering period. Leaves long-petiolate, rounded, polygonal, shallowly 5—12 lobed, cordate, shallowly black toothed, underside grey felted. Scale leaves on flowering stems ovate, numerous, yellowish. Capitula solitary; bracts linear, sometimes with red tint. Yellow florets, in centre tubular, linear-ligulate marginal ones. Achenes cylindrical, ribbed, with crown of pappus. Flowers in March and April. Grows in fields, on wasteland, on banks and in ditches, from lowlands to mountains.

6 Purple Coltsfoot *Homogyne alpina*. Perennial evergreen herb up to 15 cm. high, with thin creeping rhizome. Stems with thick, grey hairs are erect, bearing a single capitulum, usually with two ovate, claspingly sessile leaves. Long-petiolate leaves in basal tufts are almost leathery, cordate-orbicular or reniform, shallowly sinuate toothed. Capitula with linear bracts; florets pale violet, slightly longer than involucra. Achenes cylindrical, ribbed, crowned with pappus. Flowers from May to July. Grows in mountain forests, meadows and on barrens. Very rare in Great Britain, being found in Scotland only and even there not native.

Family: *Compositae*

1 Common Butterbur *Petasites hybridus* (syn. *P. officinalis*). Perennial herb up to 1 metre high, partly dioecious. Thick, branched rhizomes strikingly aromatic if bruised or cut. Erect, simple flowering stems often violet-tinted. Basal leaves long-petiolate, cordate angularly rounded to reniform, bluntly toothed. Lanceolate stem bracts clasping, bottom ones sheathed. Capitula in dense racemes, during fruition elongated; involucres flushed purple. Florets pink, seemingly bisexual, tubular, five-lobed, pistillate ones shortly tubular. Achenes cylindrical, with pappus. Flowers in April and May. Grows gregariously on river and canal banks, in ditches and damp meadows from lowlands to mountains.

2 White Butterbur *Petasites albus*. Perennial herb up to 80 cm. high, with long-creeping rhizome. Very similar to preceding species. Stem and scales light green. Leaves of basal rosette rounded, reniform, cordate, angularly lobed, sharply toothed, grey-felted to smooth on underside. Florets yellowish white, seemingly bisexual; five-lobed, pistillate ones shortly tubular. Flowers in April and May. Grows in open woods, along streams and on wasteland, from foothills to mountains; in higher altitudes more frequent and often gregarious.

3 Mountain Arnica *Arnica montana*. Perennial herb up to 50 cm. high, with long-creeping rhizome. Erect stems glandular hairy, usually with only one capitulum. Basal rosette leaves ovate, entire; stem ones opposite, oblong-lanceolate. Involucral bracts lanceolate; florets orange-yellow, central ones tubular, outer ones ligulate. Achenes with a crown of pappus. Flowers in June and July. Grows in meadows, forest glades and on margins of peat-bogs from foothills to mountains, mainly at higher altitudes. Protected plant in some countries.

4 Austrian Leopards-bane *Doronicum austriacum*. Perennial herb up to 150 cm. high, with short rhizome and angular, erect, hairy stems bearing several capitula. Basal leaves petiolate, ovate-cordate, toothed; stem ones elongated, cordate to auriculate, clasping. Long-stalked capitula with linear-lanceolate involucral bracts. Florets yellow, in centre tubular, marginal ones long-ligulate. Achenes of central flowers with pappus, outer ones without. Flowers in July and August. Grows in open woods and river banks, from foothills to mountains.

5 Common Ragwort *Senecio jacobaea*. Perennial up to 1 metre high, with erect, densely leafy stems branched in upper part. Basal leaves pinnately lobed, stem ones usually sessile, smaller. Capitula in flattened compound corymbs; florets yellow, central ones tubular, outer ones ligulate. Flowers from July to September. Grows on grassy slopes, in meadows, on margins of forests and by roadsides, from lowlands to foothills.

6 *Senecio nemorensis*. Perennial herb up to 150 cm. high, usually hairy. Stem leaves oblong-oval to lanceolate, stalkless, half clasping, toothed, underside downy. Capitula in flattish compound corymbs. Central florets tubular, surrounded by five outer ligulate ones; light yellow. Achenes with long pappus. Flowers from May to July. Grows in forests and clearings from foothills to mountains.

Family: *Compositae*

1 Lesser Burdock *Arctium minus.* Biennial herb up to 1.5 m. high, with erect, stout, well-branched stems, woolly hairy. Leaves petiolate, ovate-oblong, cordate, entire or shallowly toothed, on underside thinly grey-felted. Capitula in racemes, involucral bracts with sharply hooked tips. Tubular, red-violet florets. Achenes ovoid, without pappus. Flowers from July to September. Grows in light woodland, on wasteland and by roadsides from lowlands to foothills.

2 Musk Thistle *Carduus nutans.* Biennial herb up to 1 metre high, with winged, spiny stems. Leaves elliptic, cottony-hairy, pinnate-lobed, with a spiny toothed margin. Capitula solitary, nodding, long-stalked; involucral bracts spine-tipped, webbed with cottony hairs. Florets tubular, red-purple. Achenes grey, smooth, with a light globose pappus. Flowers from July to September. Grows on sunny grassy slopes, in pastures and by the roadside, from lowlands to foothills.

3 Welted Thistle *Carduus acanthoides.* Biennial plant up to 1 metre high, with winged, spiny stems. Leaves lanceolate, pinnate-lobed, the margins waved and set with spines. Capitula on short, erect, winged spiny stalks; involucral bracts spiny. Florets red-purple. Flowers from June to September. Grows in pastures, on wasteland and by roadsides, from lowlands to foothills, especially in milder regions.

4 Creeping Thistle *Cirsium arvense.* Biennial plant up to 1 metre high, or more, with erect, leafy stems and far-creeping rhizomes. Leaves oblong-lanceolate, pinnately lobed, spiny toothed, upper ones smaller and sessile. Capitula in terminal clusters, sometimes violet-tinted; bracts pointed or shortly spined. Imperfectly dioecious pale purple florets. Achenes ovoid with long white pappus. Flowers from July to September. Grows on wasteland, as field and garden weed, in forest clearings and by roadsides, from lowlands to mountains. Spear thistle *(C. vulgare)* is a biennial herb, with spiny-winged stems, and the leaves thinly grey felted beneath.

5 Marsh Thistle *Cirsium palustre.* Biennial herb up to 1.5 m. high, with little branched spiny winged stems. Basal leaves sometimes red-tinted, oblanceolate; stem leaves pinnate-lobed with winged bases, spiny-toothed. Capitula in crowded leafy clusters, somewhat cottony hairy and purple tinted; florets red-purple. Flowers from July to September. Grows in marshes, damp meadows, woodland clearings and in hedgerows from lowlands to mountains.

6 Cabbage Thistle *Cirsium oleraceum.* Perennial herb up to 120 cm. high with erect, distantly leaved, rarely branched stems. Softly spiny leaves, bottom ones deeply pinnately lobed with toothed segments, upper leaves smaller, cordate, sessile. Capitula in clusters subtended by enlarged yellowish bracts. Yellow-white florets. Flowers from June to September. Grows in damp meadows, marshes, open moist woods and by streams, from lowlands to foothills. Naturalized in a very few places in Britain.

Family: *Compositae*

1 Brown-headed Knapweed *Centaurea jacea*. Perennial herb up to 50 cm. high, with erect, branched stems, sparsely leaved. Upper leaves oblanceolate, sessile, with one or two large teeth. Capitula solitary at end of branches, bracts with distinct dry-membraneous, fan-shaped appendages. Florets red-purple. Achenes ovoid, grey, glossy, without pappus. Flowers from June to October. Grows in grassland and wasteplaces from lowlands to mountains. Only naturalized in a few places in southern Britain. Greater knapweed *(C. scabiosa)* has pinnate-lobed leaves and larger heads. It is found in grassy places and by roadsides throughout lowland Britain.

2 Cornflower *Centaurea cyanus*. Annual or overwintering herb up to 60 cm. high, with erect, branched stems. Leaves lanceolate, the basal ones often with narrow pinnate lobes. Capitula solitary at ends of branches, cottony hairy, central one with narrow-toothed appendages. Central florets violet, marginal ones much larger, spreading, bright blue, rarely whitish or rosy. Achenes with a brush-like crown of stiff hairs. Flowers from June to October. Grows in cornfields and waste places. Formerly a common weed of cornfields throughout Europe, but now on the decline where good farming practices prevail.

3 Mountain Cornflower *Centaurea montana*. Perennial herb up to 60 cm. high, with erect, little-branched stems. Leaves lanceolate, entire, underside cobwebby hairy, upper surface smooth, stem leaves sessile with winged bases. Stalked capitula often solitary, bracts with black, short-toothed border. Central flowers violet, outer ones larger, blue, sometimes rose or white. Flowers from May to October. Grows in mountain meadows and forest clearings, from foothills to mountains. Grown in gardens in Britain and sometimes escaping.

4 Stemless Carline-thistle *Carlina acaulis*. Perennial plant with usually very short flowering stems, only a few centimetres tall. Leaves in basal rosette pinnate-lobed and spiny toothed. Capitula solitary, over 15 cm. in diameter; outer involucral bracts leaf-like, inner ones linear, upper surface silvery glossy, underside yellowish, in sunshine widely expanded, in wet weather rolled tightly closed. Tubular, whitish or pinkish florets. Achenes. Flowers from July to September. Grows scattered in dry pastures and on stony slopes from lowlands to foothills.

5 Common Carline-thistle *Carlina vulgaris*. Biennial herb up to 50 cm. high, with erect, purplish, cottony hairy stems. Under surface of leaves cobwebby woolly, later bare, oblong-lanceolate, with undulate margins densely spiny toothed. Basal leaves in rosette, dying before flowering starts. Stem leaves cordate, sessile, the topmost ones transformed into bracts. Capitula terminate lateral branches; inner involucral bracts straw-yellow, spreading and resembling ray florets. Florets purple. Achenes with short hairs and crowned with pappus. Flowers from July to September. Grows on sunny grassy slopes and banks, particularly on limestone, from lowlands to mountains.

6 Great Globe-thistle *Echinops sphaerocephalus*. Perennial herb up to 2 m. high, with robust, woody, white-woolly stems. Bottom leaves petiolate, stem ones sessile, lanceolate, pinnate-lobed and spiny toothed. Single-flowered, narrow capitula aggregated into dense globose heads. Florets bluish or white, tubular. Achenes oblong-ovoid, with a cup-like crown of partly fused hairs. Flowers from June to August. Grows on forest margins, in vineyards, quarries, on river banks and wasteland, and by roadsides, in lower altitudes of milder regions. Grown in gardens in Britain and sometimes escaping.

Subclass: **Monocotyledones** — *Butomidae*

Family: **Flowering Rush** — *Butomaceae*

1 Flowering Rush *Butomus umbellatus*. Perennial herb up to 150 cm. high, with creeping rhizomes and erect flowering stems. Basal tufts of leaves are sheathed, triangular at base, expanding to a linear blade. Pink flowers in many-flowered terminal umbels. Six obovate tepals, 3 smaller than the rest, and 6—9 stamens. Fruits a cluster of small ovoid follicles. Flowers from June to August. Grows in ditches and on margins of ponds, lakes and rivers, from lowlands to foothills.

Family: **Water-plantain** — *Alismataceae*

2 Common Water-plantain *Alisma plantago-aquatica*. Perennial herb up to 1 metre high, with short, thickened rhizome and erect stems. Submerged leaves (when present) linear, those above the water are long-petiolate, prominently ribbed, broadly ovate, pointed. Flowers in well-branched, whorled panicle; both sepals and petals in threes; petals obovate, pale white, lilac or rarely pink. Fruits a doughnut-shaped schizocarp. Flowers from June to September. Grows in shallow water and on banks of ponds, lakes, canals, slow flowing rivers, and in ditches, from lowlands to foothills. Related arrowhead *(Sagittaria sagittifolia)* has arrowhead-shaped leaves, larger, fewer, white flowers and petals with black-violet spot at base.

Family: **Pondweed** — *Potamogetonaceae*

3 Broad-leaved Pondweed *Potamogeton natans*. Perennial submerged aquatic herb with stem up to 1 m. long or more in deep water. Floating leaves long-petiolate, elliptic, pointed, cordate. Submerged leaves linear. Tiny, greenish flowers, without petals, in erect, cylindrical spikes, emerging above water surface. Flowers from June to August. Grows in lakes, ponds, rivers and ditches, from lowlands to foothills.

Family: **Lily** — *Liliaceae*

4 White False Helleborine *Veratrum album*. Perennial herb, with stout erect leafy stems, up to 150 cm. high. Underside of leaves downy, pleated, widely elliptical, upper ones lanceolate, some in whorls of three. Flowers in dense, long panicles, greenish-white or yellowish, bottom ones bisexual, upper flowers mostly male. Capsular fruits many-seeded. Flowers from June to August. Grows in mountain meadows, pastures, and in rocky places, from foothills to mountains.

5 Meadow Saffron *Colchicum autumnale*. Perennial, poisonous herb with a large corm often deeply buried. Basal, oblong-lanceolate leaves develop in spring together with maturing capsule. Flowers pale-purple, long-tubular, with 6 oblong, spreading tepals. The three-celled ovary below ground; capsule ripens above ground in spring. Flowers from August to November. Grows in damp meadows and open woods, from lowlands to foothills.

6 Martagon or **Turk's Cap Lily** *Lilium martagon*. Perennial herb with robust erect stems up to 1 metre high, and a scaly bulb. Leaves obovate-lanceolate pointed, mostly in whorls of 5—10. Flowers in open racemes, stalked and nodding; tepals with reflexed tips, dull purple, brown-spotted, sometimes white. Fruit an ovoid ridged capsule. Flowers from June to August. Grows in deciduous woods, thickets and pastures, more frequently on limestone soils, in mountains. Protected plant in some countries. In Britain often grown in gardens, escaping, and now well naturalized in a number of wooded areas.

Family: **Lily** — *Liliaceae*

1 Ramsons *Allium ursinum*. Perennial herb up to 50 cm. high with a bulbous rootstock and leafless stems. Basal leaves, two to three only, elliptic to lanceolate, long-petiolate. Umbellate inflorescence ensheathed while immature in two or three bracts. Flowers up to 1 cm. across, star-shaped, with 6 pointed lobes, perianth white. Fruit a flattened, 3-lobed capsule. Flowers from April to June. Grows scattered in deciduous woods, from lowlands to mountains, often gregariously. Related crow garlic *(A. vineale)* has narrowly linear leaves and dense heads of bulbils and purple-red flowers; sometimes bulbils only.

2 *Allium flavum*. Perennial herb up to 50 cm. high, with ovoid bulbs. Hollow channelled leaves narrowly linear, grey-green. Spathe composed of two unequally long bracts. Stamens project from bell-shaped, yellow perianth. Capsules triangularly ovoid. Flowers from June to August. Grows on sunny slopes, among rocks, and in sandy places at lower altitudes of south-eastern Europe. Related *Allium suaveolens* with rosy flowers grows in the Alps.

3 May Lily *Maianthemum bifolium*. Perennial herb up to 15 cm. high with thin, creeping rhizome and erect stems, usually with two shortly petiolate, cordate-ovate, pointed leaves. Stalked racemose inflorescence bears small, white starry flowers with 4 perianth lobes. Fruit a small, red, globose berry. Flowers from May to July. Grows in woods and among bushes from lowlands to mountains. Very rare in Britain.

4 Common Solomon's Seal *Polygonatum multiflorum*. Perennial plant up to 80 cm. high, with thick, creeping rhizome and smooth, rounded stems arching at the top. Leaves alternate, ovate to elliptic, bare. Axillary flowers usually in clusters of 2 to 5, pendulous. Perianth of six fused tepals, narrowly tubular, greenish white. Fruits are globular, blue-black berries. Flowers in May and June. Grows in shady woods and among bushes, from lowlands to foot-hills. Related angular Solomon's seal *(P. odoratum)* has angular stems and flowers solitary or in twos. *Polygonatum verticillatum* has narrowly lanceolate leaves in whorls. All species poisonous.

5 Lily-of-the-Valley *Convallaria majalis*. Perennial, poisonous herb, up to 20 cm. high, with creeping rhizome. Usually two petiolate leaves with sheathing scales at base, elliptic-lanceolate, entire. Erect stem, flowers in one-sided raceme, short-stalked, drooping, very fragrant, white or occasionally pinkish. Perianth broadly bell-shaped, consists of six short tepals. Fruits are sub-globose red berries. Flowers in May and June. Grows in open deciduous woods, and among bushes, from lowlands to mountains. Protected plant in some countries.

6 Herb Paris *Paris quadrifolia*. Perennial herb up to 30 cm. high, with creeping rhizomes and erect stems. Obovate-lanceolate leaves in one whorl of four. Flowers stalked, solitary, the perianth in whorls of four. Outer tepals lanceolate, green; inner ones narrowly linear, yellow-green. Eight stamens with anther connective awl-like. Fruits black globose berries. Flowers from May to August. Grows in deciduous and mixed forests and glades, from lowlands to mountains.

Family: **Iris** — *Iridaceae*

1 Yellow Flag *Iris pseudacorus*. Perennial herb up to 1.5 m. high with thick, shortly creeping, branched rhizome and erect flowering stems branched at the top only. Leaves sword-shaped. Long-stalked flowers; perianth segments in two whorls of 3; outer tepals ovate, recurved, yellow, with violet-brown veining; inner tepals erect, obovate, yellow, shorter than crown-shaped stigma arms. Capsule bluntly triangular ovoid. Flowers in May and June. Grows in or close to water, rivers, ponds, lakes and ditches, mainly at lower altitudes. Related Siberian iris *(I. sibirica)* has blue-violet flowers and linear leaves. Not native to Britain, but much cultivated in gardens and occasionally escaping.

Family: *Amaryllidaceae*

2 Snowdrop *Galanthus nivalis*. Perennial herb up to 20 cm. high with brown-scaly bulb. Two basal leaves linear, grey-green, blunt, scale-sheathed at base. Erect stem with solitary pendent flower in axil of membraneous bract. Outer perianth whorl consists of three obovate-oblong, white tepals, inner three are shorter, blunt and shallowly notched, with green spot near tip. Flowers in February and March. Grows in woods and hedgerows from lowlands to mountains. Much cultivated in gardens and escaping.

3 Spring Snowflake *Leucojum vernum*. Perennial herb up to 30 cm. high, with globose bulbs and 3 or 4 linear, dark green basal leaves. Drooping flowers solitary or in twos. All 6 tepals are equally long, white, with yellowish green spot at the tip. Flowers from February to April. Grows in shady deciduous woods, forest glades and damp meadows from lowlands to mountains. Often cultivated in gardens but rarely escaping.

Family: **Rush** — *Juncaceae*

4 Field Woodrush *Luzula campestris*. Perennial, tufted herb, up to 15 cm. high, with erect stems and shortly creeping rhizomes. Linear leaves have sparse but long white hairs. Tiny flowers in few-flowered panicle, usually nodding. Tepals six, brown, equally long, lanceolate, pointed, with a membraneous border. Flowers from March to June. Grows in meadows, open woods and on grassy banks and lawns from lowlands to mountains. The similar hairy woodrush *(L. pilosa)* is larger, with distinctly stalked flowers in a lax cyme and rather more hairy leaves. It is usually found in woods and hedgerows only.

5 Soft Rush *Juncus effusus*. Perennial herb almost 1 metre high, densely tufted. Erect stems filled with spongy pith. Leaves direct from rhizome, cylindrical, resembling stems. Inflorescences apparently lateral, emerging below the top of the stem. The apparent stem tip is, in fact, a cylindrical bract. Small, six-lobed flowers are brownish. Flowers from June to August. Grows in damp meadows and near water from lowlands to mountains. *Juncus conglomeratus* is similar, but inflorescence is a dense, rounded head. Jointed rush *(J. articulatus)* has distinct stem leaves and a terminal, open inflorescence. Toad rush *(J. bufonius)* has very slender branched stems, and filamentous leaves.

Family: **Sedge** — *Cyperaceae*

6 Common Cottongrass *Eriophorum angustifolium*. Perennial grassy herb, sparsely tufted, up to 50 cm. high, with erect stems. Leaves grooved, narrowly linear, slender pointed. Stalked ovate spikelets in pendant clusters of 3 to 5; tiny lanceolate bracts with white membraneous border. Perianth of numerous fine bristles which elongate and become white and cottony after flowering. Flowers in April and May. Grows in bog pools on heaths and moorland and in acid fens, from lowlands to mountains.

Family: **Sedge** — *Cyperaceae*

1 Bulrush *Schoenoplectus lacustris*. Perennial herb 1—3 metres high, with thick, creeping rhizomes and rounded stems. Sheathed leaves with linear triangular blades. Spikelets in large terminal clusters; glumes broadly ovate, often fringed. Fruit a triangular ovoid nut. Flowers from May to July. Grows in wet soil and near or in water at lower altitudes, often gregariously.

2 Wood Club-rush *Scirpus sylvaticus*. Perennial herb up to 1 metre high, sparsely tufted, with short rhizomes and usually erect stems. Leaves widely linear, flat, rough on margins. Dense, large, well-branched inflorescence of sessile spikelets in clusters. Glumes ovate, entire, greenish-brown. Nuts broadly ovoid. Flowers from June to August. Grows in damp meadows, ditches, and on river or lake banks from lowlands to mountains.

3 Common Sedge *Carex nigra*. Perennial herb up to 70 cm. high, with creeping rhizomes and triangular stems, rough textured in upper part. Flat, linear, grey-green leaves often rolled when dry. Spikelets in terminal raceme, the topmost ones male, lower ones female. Black-brown glumes obovate, with a pale mid-rib. Female flowers with two stigmata each. Flowers in May to July. Grows in wet meadows and near water, from lowlands to mountains.

4 Spring Sedge *Carex caryophyllea*. Perennial herb 20—40 cm. high, with branched rhizome and slender, bluntly triangular stems. Leaves flat, keeled, stiff, rough textured. Spikelets close together, sessile; sometimes lowest one distant and short-stalked; male spikelet terminal; others female. Glumes rusty brown, glossy with green mid-rib. Nut ovoid, triangular, brownish. Flowers in April and May. Grows in dry grassland and margins of woods, particularly on limestone, from lowlands to foothills. At least 100 species of sedges grow in central Europe.

Family: **Grasses** — *Gramineae* (syn. *Poaceae*)

5 Feather-grass *Stipa capillata*. Perennial herb, densely tufted, up to 80 cm. high, with erect stems. Bristly leaves grey-green, rough on margin. Panicles greenish, spikelets with shortly awned glumes, lemma with wavy awns, up to 15 cm. long. Flowers in July and August. Grows on sunny, grassy and stony slopes in lower altitudes of milder regions. Common feather-grass *(S. pennata)* has straight awns and silvery white hairs. It is sometimes grown in gardens but not recorded as a genuine escape in Britain.

6 Meadow Fescue *Festuca pratensis*. Perennial tufted herb, up to 80 cm. high, with erect stems. Leaves narrowly linear, upper side rough, underside smooth. Panicles sparse and open; spikelets up to 10-flowered. Flowers have three stamens with pendulous anthers on long slender filaments; two stigmata; lanceolate glumes, lemma usually awnless. Flowers in June and July. Grows in meadows and other grassy places from lowlands to mountains.

Family: **Grasses** — *Gramineae*

1 Annual Meadow-grass *Poa annua*. Annual or short-lived perennial herb, up to 30 cm. high, branched. Ascending or erect stalks, rooting at lower nodes. Blades slightly rough on margins. Open, often one-sided panicle with few-flowered spikelets. Bottom glume single-veined, upper one three-veined, both smooth, lemma has dry-membraneous margin similar to palea. Flowers almost all year round. Grows in lawns, pastures, on wasteland, and as a weed of farms and gardens, almost everywhere.

2 Common Meadow-grass *Poa pratensis*. Perennial, tufted herb, up to 80 cm. high, with shortly ascending or erect, smooth, rounded stalks and creeping stolons. Blades flat or rolled, stem leaves usually erect and stiff. Open erect panicles of 3—5 flowered spikelets. Glumes equal, lemmas five-veined, hairy at base. Flowers in May to July. Grows in meadows and other grassy places, and on dunes, from lowlands to mountains.

3 Quaking-grass *Briza media*. Perennial, tufted herb, up to 50 cm. high, with short, branched rhizome. Slender, smooth, erect stalks. Flat blades, stem ones short, rough on margin. Open sparse panicles of drooping, quaking spikelets often of purplish hue, broadly ovoid. Glumes asymmetrically obovate, keeled, lemma inflated, with a paler border. Flowers in May and June. Grows in all kinds of grassy places, from lowlands to mountains.

4 Cock's-foot *Dactylis glomerata*. Perennial, densely tufted herb, up to 1 metre high with stout rough stalks. Broad flat blades rough on margins and veins. Spikelets in dense, often one-sided panicles. Glumes unequal, lemmas keeled, pointed. Flowers from May to August. Grows in most grassy places and in open woods, from lowlands to mountains.

5 Crested Dog's-tail *Cynosurus cristatus*. Perennial, tufted herb up to 60 cm. high with erect, smooth stalks. Narrowly linear leaf blades, rough at tip. Panicles dense and spike-like, one-sided. Almost sessile spikelets arranged in two rows; sterile spikelets, formed only of lemmas, have a comb-like arrangement; fertile ones are three- to four-flowered, with short awns. Flowers in June and July. Grows in meadows and other grassy places, from lowlands to mountains.

6 Blue Mountain-grass *Sesleria albicans* (syn. *S. caerulea* and *S. calcarea*). Perennial, tufted herb up to 40 cm. high with stalks leafy only in lower part. Blades with distinctly cartilaginous border, rough, flat. Two scaly bracts beneath short spike-like inflorescence. Spikelets glistening blue-grey, rarely yellowish, usually with two flowers. Shortly awned glumes, toothed tipped lemmas, paleas with two terminal teeth. Flowers from March to June. Grows in hill pastures and on stony slopes, usually on limestone, in foothills and mountains.

Family: **Grasses** — *Gramineae*

1 Perennial Rye-grass *Lolium perenne*. Perennial, densely tufted herb, with erect stalks, up to 50 cm. high. Smooth, flat linear leaves. Spikelets arranged in an open two-ranked spike. Each spikelet flattened, with 8—11 florets. Single glume longer than half of spikelet, lemmas shortly pointed. Flowers from May to September. Grows in most grassy places, from lowlands to foothills. Much sown as a fodder crop and for rough lawns.

2 Common Couch *Agropyron repens*. Perennial herb with far-creeping, stiff rhizomes and erect stalks, up to 150 cm. high. Leaf blades sparsely veined. Slender spike two-ranked, rhachis rough. Spikelets compressed, three- to five-flowered, with equal, veined glumes and shortly awned lemmas. Flowers from June to September. Pernicious weed of farms and gardens; grows in fields, on wasteland and in hedgerows, from lowlands to mountains.

3 Barren Brome *Bromus sterilis* (syn. *Anisantha sterilis*). Annual herb, somewhat tufted, up to 90 cm. high, with stiff stalks. Flat leaf blades rough on margins. Large, open, spreading panicles, with pendulous, narrowly wedge-shaped spikelets. Each spikelet up to six-flowered, often flushed dull purple; awn-like pointed glumes and lemma with awn up to 3 cm. long. Flowers in May and June. Grows on wasteland, by roadsides and as a farm and garden weed, at lower altitudes.

4 Tufted Hair-grass *Deschampsia cespitosa*. Perennial, densely tufted herb, up to 2 m. high, with rough stalks. Leaf blades flat, rough on upper surface, smooth beneath, with sharp ribs. Large, open panicles with arching or lax branches. Spikelets two- or three-flowered, short-stalked, usually violet-tinted; blunt, membraneously bordered glumes and shortly awned, toothed lemmas. Flowers from June to August. Grows in damp meadows and open woods from lowlands to mountains. Wavy hair-grass *(D. flexuosa)* has bristly leaves and distinct lemmas.

5 Yorkshire Fog *Holcus lanatus*. Perennial herb of tufted habit, up to 1 metre high, softly short-hairy, with erect or ascending stems. Leaves flat, sheaths somewhat inflated. Panicles spreading only during flowering; two- to three-flowered stalked spikelets with coarse bristly glumes and tiny lemmas with awns not projecting beyond the upper glume. Flowers from June to September. Grows in meadows, open woods and waste places, from lowlands to mountains.

6 Sweet Vernal-grass *Anthoxanthum odoratum*. Perennial herb, densely tufted and sweetly aromatic, with erect, smooth stalks, up to 50 cm. high. Leaves with flat, usually hairy blades. Panicles spike-like compressed. Spikelets yellow-green, very shortly stalked, bearing 2 sterile and one hermaphrodite florets; lanceolate glumes, lemmas awned, hairy; two stamens only. Flowers in May and June. Grows in dry meadows, pastures, open woods, heaths and moors, from lowlands to mountains. Contains coumarin, which provides the new-mown hay smell.

Family: **Grasses** — *Gramineae*

1 Wood Small-reed *Calamagrostis epigeios*. Perennial herb, tufted and robust, up to 2 m. high, with erect, reedy, grey-green stalks. Leaf sheaths and blades rough. Dense, well-branched panicles. Spikelets stalked, greenish or brownish with violet tint. Awl-pointed glumes, lemmas three-veined, membraneous, awned and a basal tuft of hairs. Flowers in July and August. Grows in damp open woods, ditches and fens, mainly in lowlands.

2 Meadow Foxtail *Alopecurus pratensis*. Perennial herb up to 1 metre high, loosely or compactly tufted, with short rhizomes and erect, smooth stalks. Leaf blades flat, rough, the sheaths somewhat inflated. Dense, cylindrical, spike-like inflorescence. Spikelets very shortly stalked; pointed glumes fused together at their bases, the keeled back silky-hairy, lemma almost of same length as glumes, with protruding awn. Flowers in May and June. Grows in damp meadows and other grassy places, from lowlands to mountains. Related *Alopecurus aequalis* is much smaller, with whitish anthers, turning orange.

3 Timothy *Phleum pratense*. Perennial herb up to 1 metre high, densely tufted, with erect stalks. Leaf blades very rough. Dense grey-green, spike-like inflorescence, with almost sessile spikelets. Glumes whitish dry-membraneous, on greenish keel bristly hairy and shortly awned; white-membraneous lemma, violet anthers. Flowers from June to August. Grows in meadows and other grassy places from lowlands to foothills, more frequent in lower altitudes. Extensively sown hay and forage.

4 Mat-grass *Nardus stricta*. Perennial, densely tufted herb, up to 30 cm. high, with short rhizomes and erect slender stems. Grey-green leaves, filiform, prickle pointed, with conspicuous basal sheaths. Flowering spike sparse, one-sided, spikelets single-flowered. Glumes missing, lemma with short rough awn; three stamens, one stigma. Flowers in May and June. Grows on heaths and moors, sometimes locally abundant, from lowlands high up in mountains, usually on acid soils.

5 Common Reed *Phragmites communis*. Perennial robust herb up to 3 metres high, with tough, long-creeping rhizome and erect, grey-green stems. Conspicuously double-ranked leaves of sterile shoots; blades flat, rough beneath, gradually tapering to point. Large, dense, panicles; spikelets grey, sometimes purple-tinted with long silky hairs. Unequal glumes, lemmas long-pointed, awnless. Flowers from July to September. Grows in marshes, swamps and shallow water, often gregariously, forming extensive colonies.

Family: **Orchid** — *Orchidaceae*

6 Lady's Slipper *Cypripedium calceolus*. Perennial downy herb up to 50 cm. high, with shortly creeping rhizome and erect stems, scaly at base. Only three or four leaves, alternate, ovate, prominently ribbed. Flowers solitary, or less frequently two, in axil of upper leaf. Lip light yellow, red-dotted, tepals maroon; three-lobed stigma. Flowers in May and June. Grows scattered in deciduous woods on calcareous grounds from lowlands to mountains. Probably now extinct in Britain. Protected plant in some countries.

1

3

6

2

4

5

Family: **Orchid** — *Orchidaceae*

1 Large White Helleborine *Cephalanthera damasonium*. Perennial herb up to 45 cm. high with slender leafy stem, scaly at bottom. Leaves ovate to lanceolate. Flowers 3—12 in a loose spike. Cream-white tepals, bracts usually longer than ovary. Flowers in May and June. Grows scattered in deciduous woods, from lowlands to foothills. Related red helleborine *(C. rubra)* has rose to purple flowers and stem glandularly downy above.

2 Common Helleborine *Epipactis helleborine* (syn. *E. latifolia*). Perennial herb up to 60 cm. high, with erect stems, downy above. Broadly ovate green leaves mostly spreading, sessile, clasping, on under surface downy. Raceme one-sided, elongated, many-flowered. Each flower at first drooping, straightening up while flowering. Inner tepals greenish and dull purple-brown. Flowers from July to September. Grows in forests from lowlands to mountains. Related dark-red helleborine *(E. atrorubens)* has ovaries densely glandular downy, flowers dark purple, fragrant, and whole plant is purple-tinted; protected in some countries.

3 Lesser Butterfly Orchid *Platanthera bifolia*. Perennial herb almost 30 cm. high, with tuberous rootstock and erect, hollow stems. Basal leaves, two opposite widely elliptic; stem bears up to three small, leafy bracts. Open spike of white, spurred, fragrant flowers. Flowers in June and July. Grows in open woods, among bushes and sometimes on heaths, from lowlands to mountains.

4 Fragrant Orchid *Gymnadenia conopsea* (syn. *Habanaria conopsea*). Perennial herb up to 40 cm. high, with lobed tubers and erect stems. Leaves grey-green, narrowly oblong-lanceolate, bottom ones close to each other. Floral spike has lanceolate bracts, often with purple margins. Purple, rarely whitish tepals; spurs of double length. Conspicuously twisted ovary. Flowers from May to July. Grows scattered in open woods, meadows and on grassy slopes from lowlands to mountains, usually on limestone.

5 Green-winged Orchid *Orchis morio*. Perennial herb up to 25 cm. high with undivided, globose tubers and green stem. Leaves grey-green, lower ones lanceolate, upper ones smaller and narrow. Flowers in short terminal raceme, purple, rarely whitish, green-veined. Helmet-like perianth, lip red-purple, dark-spotted; spur thick, cylindrical. Flowers from April to June. Grows in dry meadows and on grassy slopes, from lowlands to foothills. Related species of *Ophrys* have lip without spur but with striking design, simulating bee, bumblebee or other insect body.

6 Fen Orchid *Dactylorchis majalis* (syn. *Dactylorhyza majalis*). Very variable perennial herb up to 40 cm. high, with finger-like divided tubers and erect, hollow stems. Leaves oblong-lanceolate, shortly sheathed, dark green, sometimes black-brown spotted. Dense floral spike; flowers reddish to purple, with spotted outer tepals, lip purple-red, three-lobed, spur shorter than ovary. Flowers from May to July. Grows in damp meadows, fens, marshes, dune hollows, from lowlands to foothills. Several forms are now given specific rank, *D. praetermissa* and *D. purpurella* being the most noteworthy.

Family: **Arum** — *Araceae*

1 Sweet Flag *Acorus calamus.* Perennial iris-like herb up to 1 metre high, with thick, fragrant rhizomes. Sword-shaped leaves arranged in two ranks. Triangular stems with a bract similar to leaf continuing in stem direction. Minute flowers in apparently lateral spadix, with 6-lobed, green-yellow perianth. Fruits do not mature in northern Europe. Flowers from June to August. Grows near and in water, from lowlands to foothills. Native of southern Asia and northwestern U.S.A., introduced about 400 years ago and naturalized in Europe.

2 Bog Arum *Calla palustris.* Perennial aquatic herb, up to 30 cm., with hollow, green rhizome. Leaves broadly ovate-cordate. Axillary stems bear short, cylindrical, short-stalked spadix. Minute yellow-green flowers without a perianth. Fruits are red berries. Flowers from May to August. Grows in pools, arms of rivers and peat-bogs from lowlands to foothills, rarely at higher altitudes, in central and northern Europe. Naturalized only in Britain.

3 Lords-and-Ladies or **Cuckoo-pint** *Arum maculatum.* Perennial plant, almost 50 cm. high, with short tuberous rhizome and erect stem. Leaves long-petiolate, triangular ovate to arrow-shaped. Spathe cyathiform, whitish or greenish, rarely red-tinted inside, with violet blotches. On spadix, lowest are female flowers, above them male ones; above these ring of sterile, bulb-like thickened 'flowers' modified into thick bristles; spadix tip violet-brown or yellowish. Fruits are red, poisonous berries. Flowers in April and May. Grows in open deciduous woods, in hedgerows and on hedgebanks, from lowlands to foothills.

Family: **Bur-reed** — *Sparganiaceae*

4 Branched Bur-reed *Sparganium erectum* (syn. *S. ramosum*). Perennial aquatic herb up to 50 cm. high with thick, spreading rhizomes. Stiff, erect leaves, triangular in section. Erect robust stems, with terminal stiff panicle. Flowers in globose heads, unisexual, bottom ones female, upper ones male; perianth much reduced, 3-lobed. Fruit ellipsoidal, shouldered yellow-brown nut. Flowers from June to August. Grows in shallow water and on mud or wet soil from lowlands to foothills. Related unbranched bur-reed *(S. emersum)* has simple stems, racemose inflorescences and long-beaked fruits.

Family: **Reedmace** — *Typhaceae*

5 Lesser Reedmace *Typha angustifolia.* Perennial herb up to 3 metres high, with extensively creeping rhizome and rigid erect, round stems. Erect, linear leaves not more than 1 cm. wide. Inflorescence composed of two separate cylindrical spadices, one above the other; bottom one has female flowers, upper one male florets. Bottom spadix is narrow, red-brown. Unisexual flowers without any perianth. Fruits stalked with long pappus-like hairs. Flowers in June-July. Grows in water and wet soil, from lowlands to foothills. Related great reedmace *(T. latifolia)* has leaves up to 2 cm. wide and spadices united one above other, bottom one dark brown and thick. This is much more common in Britain than *T. angustifolia.*

Family: *Lemnaceae*

6 Ivy Duckweed *Lemna trisulca* (a). Tiny perennial, aquatic herb, floating just beneath water surface. Leaf-like thalli ovate lanceolate, petiolate, branching from the middle. Flowering plants rare, smaller and floating. Grows in stagnant waters at lower altitudes. **Common duckweed** *(L. minor)* (b) has floating thalli round to broadly ovate, usually growing gregariously. **Great duckweed** *(L. polyrhiza)* (c) has roundly ovate thalli with reddish underside, each with bundle of rootlets.

CHARACTERISTICS OF INDIVIDUAL GROUPS OF ANIMALS

CLASS: GASTROPODS — *Gastropoda*

The majority of gastropods are characterized by a spiral shell, the shape of which varies with the species. The shell may also be glossy, dull, transparent, finely grooved, etc., and is often brightly coloured. We find flat, spherical and tall shells with the most diverse forms. In some species the shell is reduced; all that is left are chalky granules lying below the epidermis of the mantle. In others, a horny dorsal plate is formed. The body of gastropods with a shell consists of a foot, a head, and a *visceral hump*, which is asymmetrical and spiral and fits into the shell. The foot — the part of the body extruded from the shell — has strong muscles and terminates anteriorly in the head, which has a mouth and sensory organs. The head carries one or two pairs of tentacles, usually retractile. Simple eyes are present on the tip or at the base of the

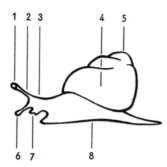

tentacles. On the floor of the gullet there is a tongue-like strip, known as the *radula*, covered with minute teeth, which the animal uses as a food-grater. Many species of gastropods are hermaphrodites, i.e. the individual possesses both male and female sex organs.

1 Snail with shell
1 *Eye; 2 first pair of tentacles; 3 head; 4 shell; 5 tip of shell; 6 second pair of tentacles; 7 mouth; 8 foot.*

CLASS: BIVALVES — *Bivalvia*

Bivalve shells are composed of two, usually symmetrical, concave valves connected to each other by a muscular ligament. In some species the inner wall of the valves is covered with a deep pearly lining. Some species are hermaphroditic, while in others the sexes are separate. Both fresh- and salt-water species exist; some marine species may weigh as much as 200 kg. Bivalves have a flat-sided foot and the only signs of a head are flaps on either side of the mouth, which does not have a radula like that of the gastropods. Neither do bivalves possess tentacles and most of them do not even have eyes, although parts of their body are sensitive to light.

2 Bivalve
1 *Connecting ligament; 2 shell; 3 foot; 4 connecting ligament; 5 right valve; 6 left valve; 7 excretory siphon; 8 inhalant siphon.*

CLASS: ARACHNIDS — *Arachnoidea*

The body of these terrestrial arthropods has two parts. The anterior part, known as the *prosoma* or *cephalothorax* (i.e. head and thorax combined), is formed by six original segments and is covered with a dorsal plate. It carries six pairs of appendages, the first two of which have usually been converted to mouth parts, while the other four are ambulatory limbs. (In mites, some or all of the legs may be suppressed.) The posterior part of the body *(opisthosoma)* is the abdomen. In some groups, e.g. scorpions, the abdomen is segmented, while in others (spiders) it is non-segmented. The organ of vision is composed of a various number of simple eyes, usually grouped on the anterior margin of the cephalothorax. The first pair of appendages are jaws *(chelicerae)*, which generally terminate in pincers, and the second pair are the pedipalps, which can have different forms. Arachnids, particularly spiders, possess spinning glands which open through special eminences on the abdomen.

3 Spider
1 *First pair of legs;* 2 *second pair of legs;*
3 *third pair of legs;* 4 *fourth pair of legs;*
5 *pedipalps;* 6 *jaws;* 7 *eyes;* 8 *cephalothorax;*
9 *abdomen (episthosoma).*

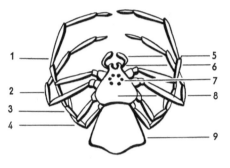

CLASS: CENTIPEDES — *Chilopoda*

Centipedes have an extremely elongate, flat-backed and distinctly segmented body. The head is divided off from the body and carries a pair of long antennae. The number of body segments varies from 15 to over 100 and from each segment grows one pair of sturdy limbs terminating in claws. The mouth part consists of one pair of mandibles and two pairs of weak maxillae. The appendages of the first body segment have evolved into strikingly large, hard, pincer-like organs containing a poison gland.

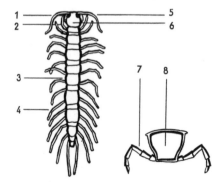

4 Centipede
1 *Eye;* 2 *jaw appendages;* 3 *body segments;*
4 *legs;* 5 *antennae;* 6 *head;* 7 *leg;* 8 *cross-section of body.*

187

CLASS: MILLIPEDES — *Diplopoda*

In these arthropods the body segments are fused in pairs, so that each such double segment carries two pairs of limbs. The body is usually cylindrical or vaulted and has a chitinous covering. Short antennae and a few simple eyes are present on the head. The mouth part consists of a pair of mandibles and a curious formation *(gnathochilarium)* produced by fusion of the maxillae.

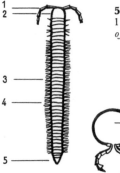

5 Millipede
1 *Antennae;* 2 *head;* 3 *body segments;* 4 *legs;* 5 *'tail';* 6 *cross-section of body;* 7 *leg.*

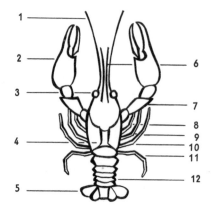

6 Crayfish
1 *First pair of antennae;* 2 *'nipper' (chela), termination of first pair of thoracic appendages;* 3 *eye;* 4 *shell (carapace);* 5 *telson;* 6 *second pair of antennae;* 7-11 *first to fifth pair of thoracic appendages;* 12 *abdominal appendages (5 pairs).*

CLASS: CRUSTACEANS — *Crustacea*

Crustaceans are mostly aquatic arthropods with two pairs of antennae, the first of which are simple, while those of the second, shorter pair are forked. The form of the body segments varies. In most cases, the head and a few thoracic segments have fused to form a cephalothorax, which is followed by the abdomen and then by the last segment, known as the *telson*. There are never less than five pairs of limbs which are initially biramous. Crustaceans breathe by means of gills, which are situated at the base of their thoracic and sometimes also abdominal appendages. Some species have no gills, however, and the animal breathes with the whole of its body surface. The body is generally covered with a chitinous shell, frequently reinforced with calcium carbonate. From time to time the shell is shed, together with the outer organs, such as the antennae. The three pairs of jaws include one pair of mandibles and two pairs of maxillae. The sexes are usually separate. In most cases swimming larvae hatch out from the eggs and in some species they pass through a whole series of stages before they metamorphose to the adult individual.

188

CLASS: INSECTS — *Insecta*

The body of the members of this class of arthropods is divided into three main parts — a head, a thorax and an abdomen. Extremely mobile antennae, with a varying number of segments, are attached to the front sides of the head. The antennae, which have different shapes, are sensory organs with mainly olfactory and tactile function. On the sides of the head there are usually large compound eyes, made up of many small prismatic eyes *(facets)*. An insect's mouth can be adapted for biting, sucking, or licking. It is covered by an upper lip *(labrum)* and a lower lip *(labium)* with small palps. The actual oral apparatus is composed of a pair of mandibles and a pair of maxillae, which carry maxillary palps. A small tongue-like formation *(hypopharynx)* protrudes from the mouth. The thorax is composed of three main segments, each with one pair of legs. Two pairs of wings usually grow from the dorsal aspect of the second and third segment, but some insects are wingless, or, as in the case of flies, only one pair is properly developed, while the other pair is rudimentary and acts as an organ of balance. In certain insects, such as beetles, the forewings are very tough and form a protective case for the delicate hindwings.

7 Beetle
1 *Antenna;* 2 *eye;* 3 *head;* 4 *first thoracic segment;* 5 *second thoracic segment;* 6 *wing-case(elytron);* 7 *third thoracic segment;* 8 *wings;* 9 *femur;* 10 *tarsus;* 11 *foot;* 12 *abdomen.*

8 Butterfly
1 *Antenna;* 2 *palp;* 3 *forewings;* 4 *thorax;* 5 *hindwings;* 6 *abdomen.*

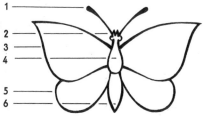

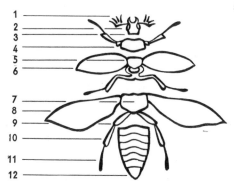

9 Butterfly's head
1 *Antennae;* 2 *palps;* 3 *compound eye;* 4 *proboscis.*

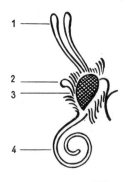

The abdomen is formed by a varying number of segments, looking like rings. In some species of insects, the female has an egg-laying organ, or *ovipositor*, on its abdomen. The sexes are usually separate and the male and female of some species are very different from each other in appearance. Some groups of insects develop by complete metamorphosis, others by incomplete metamorphosis. In complete metamorphosis, the larvae (or caterpillars in butterflies) which emerge from the eggs bear no resemblance whatsoever to the adult insect.

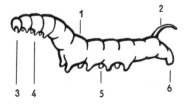

10 Caterpillar
1 *Body rings;* 2 *'horn';* 3 *mandibles;* 4 *three pairs of limbs;* 5 *prolegs;* 6 *anal appendages.*

The larvae undergo several moults and lastly turn into chrysalises *(pupae)*, from which, after a time, the adult insects emerge. In incomplete metamorphosis, the newly hatched larvae already resemble their parents, but are wingless. These larvae, which are known as *nymphs,* moult several times and become steadily more and more like the adult insect. This is the basic scheme, but the development of some species or groups of insects is rather more complicated.

11 Butterfly pupa
showing contours of butterfly's body.

CLASS: LAMPREYS — *Cyclostomata*

Lampreys have neither an upper nor a lower jaw, and their cylindrical body is covered with scaleless skin. They have no paired appendages, but the hind part of their body is bordered by a single continuous fin. They likewise have only one nostril and a round, suctorial mouth. Behind their eyes, 6—14 pairs of gill apertures can be seen on the sides of their body.

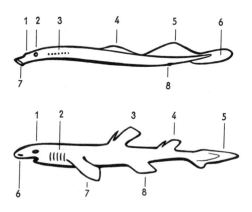

12 Lamprey
1 *Single nostril;* 2 *eye;* 3 *gill-slits;* 4, 5, 6 *continuous fin border;* 7 *mouth;* 8 *anus.*

13 Shark
1 *Eye;* 2 *gill-slits;* 3, 4 *dorsal fins;* 5 *caudal fin;* 6 *nostril;* 7 *pectoral fin;* 8 *abdominal fin.*

CLASS: CARTILAGINOUS FISHES — *Chondrichthyes*

Primitive fishes possess proper jaws, the lower one of which is movable. Their body can be either bare, or covered with placoid scales, and they have a cartilaginous skeleton. The upper lobe of their caudal fin is larger than the lower lobe and contains the end of the spine. They usually have 5—7 gill-slits on the sides of the body.

CLASS: BONY FISHES — *Osteichthyes*

Fishes have either a cartilaginous or a bony skeleton. Their body is usually covered with scales and is only occasionally scaleless. In some fishes the scales have fused to form a breastplate composed of bony plates. Practically all true fishes possess proper fins. The paired fins *(pectoral* and *pelvic)* correspond to fore- and hind-limbs, while of the other, unpaired fins, there may be one or more dorsal fins, a caudal fin and one or more anal fins. The jaws are armed with teeth or toothless. Most fishes have a lateral line along the sides of their body, which contains sensory cells enabling them to perceive vibrations produced in the water by commotion, sound, etc.; it is thus a kind of radar apparatus.

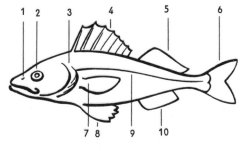

14 Fish
1 *Nostril;* 2 *eye;* 3 *gill-cover (operculum);* 4 *first dorsal fin;* 5 *second dorsal fin;* 6 *caudal fin;* 7 *pectoral fin;* 8 *abdominal fin;* 9 *lateral line;* 10 *anal fin.*

CLASS: AMPHIBIANS — *Amphibia*

These four-footed vertebrates develop by metamorphosis. The larva (tadpole) lives in water and breathes by means of gills, while the adult animal possesses lungs and can live in water or on dry land. Only a few species are viviparous, i.e. produce larvae or young by eggs hatched within the female's body. Their scaleless, glandulous skin secretes poison. Frogs are tailless and their powerful hind legs have webbed feet. The eye has a nictitating membrane. Newts and salamanders have a well developed tail and their legs are relatively short and puny. Amphibian larvae first of all possess gills, but during metamorphosis the gills (and in the case of frogs the tail also) are absorbed.

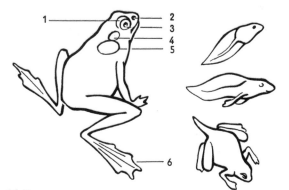

15 Frog
1 *Upper eyelid;* 2 *nostril;* 3 *nictitating membrane;* 4 *vocal membrane;* 5 *vocal sac;* 6 *interdigital webbing.*

16 Development of tadpole

CLASS: REPTILES — *Reptilia*

Reptiles are higher vertebrates and no longer require an aquatic environment for their development. They reproduce usually by laying eggs on land. Their skin has a horny epidermis and is covered with horny scales to prevent their body from becoming too dry. In testudinates, bony plates are formed and these, fused with some of the bones, give rise to a carapace consisting of dorsal and abdominal parts.

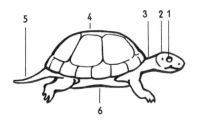

Reptiles cannot regulate their body temperature gaining heat or cold from the environment around them, and during the cold season they hibernate. Their four limbs may all be well developed, or the front pair, sometimes both pairs, may be reduced or absent altogether. Their jaws are generally armed with teeth, although in some groups, e.g. the testudinates, the jaws may resemble a bird's beak. The lizards have usually well developed eyelids. In snakes they are always fused together and transparent.

17 Tortoise
1 *Eye;* 2 *head;* 3 *neck;* 4 *dorsal shell (carapace);* 5 *tail;* 6 *abdominal shell (plastron).*

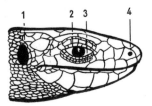

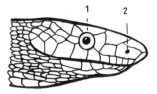

18 Lizard's head
1 *Ear-drum (auricular orifice);* 2 *eyelid;* 3 *lower eyelid;* 4 *nostril.*

19 Head of snake
1 *Eye;* 2 *nostril.*

CLASS: BIRDS — *Aves*

Birds are vertebrates with a constant body temperature and their body is covered with feathers to insulate the bird's warm body. Their forelimbs have been converted

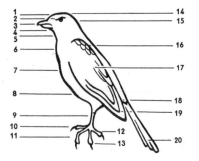

to wings. Apart from a few exceptions, all birds can fly. The shape of the beak is adapted to suit the kind of food they catch and eat. The beak is covered with a layer

20 Bird's body
1 *Forehead;* 2 *eye;* 3 *beak;* 4 *chin;* 5 *throat;* 6 *crop;* 7 *breast;* 8 *belly;* 9 *tarsus;* 10 *inner toe;* 11 *middle toe;* 12 *hind toe;* 13 *outer toe;* 14 *crown;* 15 *nape;* 16 *wing coverts;* 17 *secondaries;* 18 *upper tail coverts;* 19 *primaries;* 20 *tail feathers.*

of a horny substance, while the shanks and toes are covered with scales. Birds moult regularly and some species assume special nuptial plumage when preparing to mate. Each species builds its own, typical form of nest. Birds are oviparous and their eggs have a hard shell. The parents incubate their eggs by sitting on them and keeping them warm with their own bodies. The young hack their way out of the egg-shell by means of an 'egg-tooth' at the tip of their beak, which grows specifically for this purpose. Some 600 species of birds occur in Europe and about 300 of them nest there regularly.

CLASS: MAMMALS — *Mammalia*

Mammals are quadruped vertebrates and, apart from a few exceptions, have a constant body temperature. Their body is covered with hair, in some species the hairs are fused together and form spines. Many mammals have whiskers (special tactile hairs). Except for the egg-laying monotremes, mammals are viviparous. The young develop in the female's uterus and are at first fed on the mother's milk. Large species give birth to only a few young (usually only one), while small species produce large litters. Some mammals wear horns mounted on an abnormal growth of the frontal bone; horns are permanent fixtures. Other species wear bony antlers, which every year are shed and grow again. Mammals have characteristic dentition, with several types of teeth. In the various groups, the limbs are adapted to the animals' mode of life. The senses of smell, sight and hearing are very well developed. Some mammals regularly migrate, like birds. In some cases (e.g. in bats) the forelimbs have been transformed to a flying apparatus, so that the animal is capable of active flight. Mammals can be terrestrial, arboreal or aquatic.

 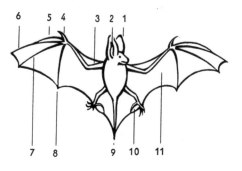

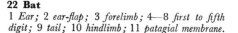

21 Roe Deer
1 *Tine;* 2 *antler;* 3 *pedicle;* 4 *ear;*
5 *tail;* 6 *hoof (third and fourth digit).*

22 Bat
1 *Ear;* 2 *ear-flap;* 3 *forelimb;* 4—8 *first to fifth digit;* 9 *tail;* 10 *hindlimb;* 11 *patagial membrane.*

193

Class: **Gastropods** — *Gastropoda*

Subclass: **Pulmonates, Lung Snails** — *Pulmonata* (p. 196). Gastropods with no operculum on dorsal side of foot. Have lungs and are hermaphroditic. Mainly terrestrial.

Order: **Land Pulmonates** — *Stylommatophora* (p. 196). Two long retractile tentacles with eyes. Another pair of shorter retractile tentacles. Terrestrial animals, but require moisture. Include types with and without a shell.

Family: **Amber Snails** — *Succineidae* (p. 196). Conically ovoid, usually amber yellow, shells. Most species live near water or in swamps.

Family: *Pupillidae* (p. 196). Small to minute gastropods living on plants, rocks, under moss, wood, etc. Long, ovoid shells with conical tip.

Family: *Enidae* (p. 196). Gastropods with tapering, finely grooved shell over 8 mm. high. Tip blunt. Walls relatively thick and strong.

Family: *Clausiliidae* (p. 196). Gastropods with tall, slender, fusiform shell. Irregular folds at orifice, often extending deep into shell. Identifiable mainly from the structure of the shell orifice.

Family: **Slugs** — *Arionidae* (p. 196). Robust shell-less gastropods. Anteriorly situated dorsal scutellate mantle. Respiratory aperture at right lower margin of anterior half of scutellum. Rounded, blunt-tipped body. Rudiment of shell present as chalky granules below scutellum.

Family: **Keeled Slugs** — *Limacidae* (p. 198). Slim-bodied gastropods with ridge along whole or caudal part of back. Tip of body pointed. Rudiment of shell as chalky plate below wrinkled scutellate mantle. Respiratory aperture situated in posterior half of scutellum.

Family: *Helicidae* (p. 198). Terrestrial gastropods with flattened to spherical shell. Their sexual organs possess calcareous 'dart', used in reciprocal pairing.

Order: **Aquatic Pulmonates** — *Basommatophora* (p. 200). Mainly freshwater gastropods with shells. Some species live beside water. Eyes at base of single pair of non-retractile tentacles.

Family: **Pond Snails** — *Lymnaeidae* (p. 200). Aquatic animals living in fresh or brackish water, mainly on aquatic plants. Very diverse shells. Have wide foot and short head. Crawl on under side of thin layer of slime on surface of water and appear to be swimming. They feed on algae, rotting and fresh vegetation, microorganisms. Eggs laid in capsules attached to aquatic plants. In times of drought form a protective 'trap-door'.

Family: *Planorbidae* (p. 200). Aquatic gastropods with discoid shell, small head and foot and long, thin tentacles. Only freshwater molluscs with red blood.

Subclass: *Prosobranchiata* (p. 200). Gastropods with operculum on dorsal aspect of foot, which acts as a door when the animal retires into its shell. One pair of non-retractile tentacles with eyes at base.

Order: *Ctenobranchia* (p. 200). Smaller gastropods with diversely shaped shells and protrusible mouth. Terrestrial and aquatic.

Family: *Pomatiasidae* (p. 200). Gastropods with shell of circular shape. Terrestrial.

Family: **River Snails** — *Viviparidae* (p. 200). Large gastropods with short, robust body and wide foot. Head tapers off into club-like snout. Long tentacles. In males, the right tentacle is thicker than the left and is used as an organ of copulation. Viviparous.

194

Class: **Bivalves** — *Bivalvia*

Their shells formed of two, usually symmetrical, convex valves. Some species hermaphroditic, in others the sexes are separate. Fertilization effected in water.

Order: *Eulamellibranchia* (p. 202). Minute to huge species inhabiting fresh and salt water. Two-layered gills, gill filaments usually joined by cross-fibres.

Family: **Freshwater Mussels** — *Unionidae* (p. 202). Large bivalves inhabiting mud at bottom of rivers and ponds. The larva (glochidium) has a barbed shell for attachment to the gills or skin of fishes (usually near the fins). It lives on its host until its metamorphosis is completed and then drops to the bottom, where it goes on growing.

Family: **Freshwater Pearl Oysters** — *Margaritanidae* (p. 202). Bivalves with a large, strong, heavy shell locked by two catches on the left valve and one on the right.

Family: **Orb Cockles** — *Sphaeriidae* (p. 202). Small to minute, thin-walled, heart-shaped or rounded shells. Viviparous hermaphrodites. Found in slow-flowing or stagnant water.

Family: **True Oysters** — *Ostreidae* (p. 202). Shells of unequal size and irregular shape. The deeper and thicker right valve is firmly attached to a stable object, while the smaller left valve usually acts as a lid. No locking device on shell. Degenerate foot. Hermaphroditic, but no self-fertilization, as the male and female reproductive cells develop at different times.

Family: **Cockles** — *Cardiidae* (p. 202). Heart-shaped shells. Mantle covered by long tactile flaps. Very large, finger-like foot with knee. Burrows in sea, sand or ooze.

Family: **Piddocks** — *Pholadidae* (p. 202). Strikingly elongated, whitish or yellowish shell. The valves, which are open at both ends, are armed with file-like rows of teeth.

Order: *Filibranchia* (p. 202). Interlocking valves with numerous teeth. Gills composed of two rows of long gill filaments.

Family: **Scallops** — *Pectinidae* (p. 202). Valves usually asymmetrical and deeply fluted. Characterized by 'auricles' — extensions of valves on either side of toothless locking device. Most scallops swim by snapping the two valves together and quickly expelling the water, on the rocket propulsion principle. Adults of many species anchored to base by byssus — viscid threads secreted by a gland (byssus pit) which harden on contact with water. Mantle edged with tentacles and bright, stalked eyes. Colouring of different individuals of same species often very variable.

Family: **Mussels** — *Mytilidae* (p. 202). Symmetrical, often elongate, valves covered with thick skin. Well developed byssus pit. Live anchored to firm base, e.g. a rock, wooden structure, etc. In some places collected on large scale as delicacy. Greatest producer and consumer France, round whose coasts some 50,000 tons are gathered every year (half of these are exported).

Class: **Gastropods** — *Gastropoda*

Family: **Amber Snails** — *Succineidae*

1 *Succinea putris*. Distributed in Europe, western and northern Asia. Common mainly in lowlands. Frequents lake- and pond-sides, ditches and marshes. Height 16 —22 mm. (in Danube basin up to 27 mm. high and 13 mm. wide). Life span up to 3 years. Lives on fresh and decaying vegetation. In pairing, one partner plays male and other female role. Each individual lays 50—100 eggs on damp ground. Spends winter and dry part of summer in crevices or among rotting leaves.

2 *Succinea pfeifferi*. Distributed in Europe and cool parts of Asia and northwest Africa. Occurs in low-lying country, lives on reeds and in waterside mud. Often found in large numbers on floating plants. Height 12—15 mm., width about 7 mm. Transparent shell. Similar biology to preceding species.

Family: *Pupillidae*

3 *Abida frumentum*. Inhabits southern Europe and warm parts of central Europe. Frequents dry, grassy slopes. Height 6—10 mm., width 3 mm. Likes damp rocks, trees and other plants.

Family: *Enidae*

4 *Zebrina detrita*. Distributed over central, western and southern Europe, and south-western Asia. Common in limestone regions. Frequents warm spots. Plain-coloured or brown-striped shell. Height 18—25 mm., width 9—10 mm. Life span from 4 to 5 years. Shell often covered with dried slime and hardened soil.

Family: *Clausiliidae*

5 *Laciniaria biplicata*. Distributed in central Europe, southern England, north-eastern France, Belgium; northern limit Sweden. Several subspecies. Very variable. Height 17—19 mm., width 4 mm. Inhabits forests, gardens, parks and hillsides, lives on tree-trunks, rocks, walls, etc. Usually produces live young, which take 5—10 months to develop. Life span about $3\frac{1}{2}$ years.

6 *Laciniaria turgida*. Inhabits eastern part of central Europe (chiefly the Carpathians), but exact distribution not known. Very variable. Height 12—17 mm. Fusiform, transparent, glossy shell. Smaller shells at higher altitudes. Lives mainly in damp mountain forests; is especially abundant in thickly overgrown valleys, but also encountered in drier places. Several very similar species distributed all over Europe.

7 *Clausilia dubia*. Distributed in central, western and northern Europe as far as Sweden. Mainly inhabits mountains and rocky hills. Frequents rocks, ruins, walls, etc. Height 11 to 16 mm., width about 3 mm. Variably grooved. In winter hides under moss or fallen leaves.

Family: **Slugs** — *Arionidae*

8 Red Slug *Arion rufus*. Inhabits central and western Europe. Found in damp woods and meadows. Length 12—15 cm. Very large respiratory aperture. Variable colouring, from all shades of orange and brown to black. Black forms in colder areas, abundant local incidence of red forms in places. Border of foot usually red. Omnivorous. Often found on dead animals or excreta. Lays 300—500 eggs in piles, under stones, in moss, etc. Self-fertilization also observed.

9 Forest Slug *Arion subfuscus*. Distributed over whole of Europe. Chiefly inhabits lowland and mountain forests. Length 4—7 cm. Variable colouring. Basic colour yellow to reddish yellow; back brown, sides often striped. Foot yellowish white. Produces yellow or orange slime. Most frequently found on mushrooms, behind bark of tree-stumps, etc. Also eats fruit and parts of plants.

196

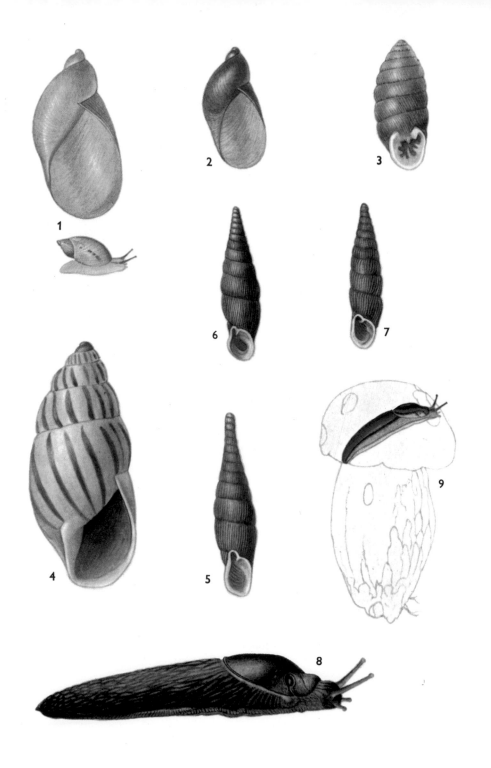

Family: **Keeled Slugs** — *Limacidae*

1 Great Greyslug *Limax maximus*. Distributed in southern and central Europe; extends to England and south of Scandinavia. Found in gardens, parks, cellars, etc. Variable colouring, often in association with differences in temperature. Length up to 15 cm. Frequently raids vegetable stocks in cellars, etc., but also eats other gastropods. When pairing, both partners hang twisted round a rope of slime attached to a twig. Active mainly at night and in damp weather.

2 Ash-blackslug *Limax cinereoniger*. Inhabits almost whole of Europe. Found mainly in deciduous woods in hilly and mountainous regions. Lives near trees, behind bark, under stones, etc. Colouring very variable (some specimens white), but mantle and foot always dark. Life span 3 years. Partners intertwine during pairing. Self-fertilization also known.

Family: *Helicidae*

3 *Helicodonta obvoluta*. Distributed in southern and central Europe and south-eastern England. Inhabits forests on warm limestone slopes. Lives under stones, leaves, etc. Forms white, parchment-like operculum in dry weather. Height 6 mm., width 13 mm. Thin-walled, discoid shell, hairy in young specimens.

4 *Helicigona lapicida*. Inhabits central and western Europe. Lives on damp rocks and tree-trunks in beechwoods. Often found on walls of ruins. Height 8.5 mm., width 17 mm. Shell partly transparent.

5 *Helicigona rossmässleri*. Inhabits the Carpathians. Lives on rocks and tree-trunks in damp forests. Commonest at altitudes of 800—1,400 metres above sea level. Attains 10—13 mm. Several tens of similar species occur in the Alps and mountains of central Europe.

6 White-lipped Slug *Cepaea hortensis*. Distributed over central and western Europe. Frequents damp spots in open woods, in gardens and at foot of rocks, etc. Shells of variable colouring; some specimens plain yellow or reddish, others striped. Width 15—25 mm., height 16 mm.

7 *Cepaea nemoralis*. Distributed in central and western Europe and Baltic coast. Lives in open woods and gardens and near human communities. Height 17—18 mm., width 20—24 mm. Basic colouring: different shades of yellow or red; usually striped with rich dark brown bands.

8 *Cepaea vindobonensis*. Inhabits eastern and south-eastern Europe; extends to the Alps and Danube and Vltava basins. Found primarily on limestone slopes, on outskirts of forests, etc., secondarily in vineyards and on banks. Width 19—25 mm., height 17—18 mm. Basic colour whitish to yellow; always striped.

9 Roman or **Edible Snail** *Helix pomatia*. Distribution area from south-eastern England across central Europe to Balkans. Is found today in places where it did not live originally. Inhabits open deciduous woods and thickets, chiefly in warm, low-lying country or hills. Frequents chalky regions. Often found on walls of ruins, etc. Height and width 40 mm.; it is the largest European snail. Mean life span up to 6 years. Vegetarian. Pairing time May to August. After 6—8 weeks, each individual lays 20—60 eggs 5—6 mm. in diameter in pits in the soil. In dry weather the shell is closed with a slimy secretion which looks like parchment when dry and ensures several months' survival. In winter a chalky operculum is added. Hibernates from October to April.

Family: *Helicidae*

1 *Isognomostoma personatum.* Distributed over central Europe, mainly the Alps, Pyrenees, Carpathians and German uplands. Does not occur in lowlands. Usually frequents rubble, hides under fallen trees and often under stones. Height about 6 mm., width 9—10 mm. Easily identified by three teeth on narrow aperture of rough, hairy shell.

2 *Zenobiella umbrosa.* Inhabits eastern Alps, German uplands, western Bohemia and Slovakia. Inhabits damp forest valleys, bogs and dense vegetation at foot of rocks, etc. Likes to climb tall plants where it can be found on leaves. Width of shell 9—13 mm., height 6—7 mm. Thicker shells in limestone areas.

Family: **Pond Snails** — *Lymnaeidae*

3 Great Pond Snail *Lymnaea stagnalis.* Its range of distribution includes whole of Europe, Morocco, northern Asia, North America. Lives in stagnant water at low altitudes. Has elongate, ovoid, pointed shell 45—60 mm. high and 22—34 mm. wide. Feeds on algae and parts of rotting vegetation. Eggs laid in capsules attached to aquatic plants. Life span 3 years.

4 Marsh Snail *Galba palustris.* Distributed over whole of Europe, Algeria, northern Asia and North America. Found in low-lying country in stagnant water, creeks and ditches. Has elongate, ovoid shell with dull lustre and finely grooved surface. Size very variable. Height 20—30 mm., width 10—18 mm. Colouring dark, inner surface usually deep violet.

Family: *Planorbidae*

5 Ram's Horn *Planorbis planorbis.* Distributed over almost whole of Europe. Found at low altitudes in stagnant and brackish water. Discoid shell about 3.5 mm. high and 15—17 mm. wide. Red blood. Frequents aquatic plants. Often seen surfacing for air. Feeds on algae, etc. Life span 2—3 years.

6 Great Ram's Horn *Planorbarius corneus.* Distributed over most of Europe except northern regions. Inhabits stagnant or slow-flowing, thickly overgrown water at low altitudes. Width of shell 25—37 mm., height 10—17 mm. Specimens in swamps and ponds small. Shells of young snails covered with bristles.

Family: *Pomatiasidae*

7 Round-mouthed Snail *Pomatias elegans.* Inhabits warm regions of Europe, particularly southerly areas. Lives under stones, fallen trees, on rocks and walls. Height 10—17 mm., width 8—13 mm.

Family: **River Snails** — *Viviparidae*

8 Common River Snail *Viviparus viviparus.* Distributed over large part of central Europe. Occurs in pools, ponds, creeks, etc. Lives at bottom in mud. Height 30—45 mm., width 25—35 mm. Specimens with shell of up to 50 mm. are known. Has operculum with accretion grooves. Gives birth to live young with small shell. Feeds mainly on algae and organic debris.

9 *Viviparus fasciatus.* Distributed over whole of Europe except most northerly parts. Inhabits large rivers or river-fed reservoirs. Found between stones. Height 28—32 mm., width 22 to 24 mm. Likewise produces live young. Feeds on algae, organic debris in mud and occasionally plankton.

Class: **Bivalves** — *Bivalvia*

Family: **Freshwater Mussels** — *Unionidae*

1 *Unio tumidus*. Distributed over practically whole of Europe. Found in slow-flowing lowland rivers, lakes and ponds. Length of shell 70—90 mm. Annually lays up to over 200,000 eggs, incubated 4—6 weeks in female's gills. The hatched larvae (glochidia) hook themselves to fish gills, but after a few weeks drop to the bottom and live in the mud like adult animals. The adult mussel lives on microorganisms and debris.

2 *Anodonta cygnea*. Distributed over almost whole of Europe. Commonest in stagnant lowland waters. Length 170—260 mm. Hermaphroditic, lays up to 400,000 eggs a year. The eggs, produced in the winter, remain several months in the mussel's gills. The hatched larvae attach themselves to fish skin. When fully developed they leave their host and settle in the mud at the bottom. The adult animal lives on microorganisms.

Family: **Freshwater Pearl Oysters** — *Margaritanidae*

3 Pearl Mussel *Margaritana margaritifera*. Inhabits western, northern and occasionally central Europe. Scattered incidence. Inhabits small, cold rivers and clear streams. Length up to 150 mm., width 70 mm. Thick-walled valves. The small glochidia live as parasites in fish gills. Pearls may be formed in the mantle. Grows very slowly (only a few mm. a year), but has life span of up to 80 years. Feeds on microorganisms and debris on bed of streams and rivers.

Family: **Orb Cockles** — *Sphaeriidae*

4 *Musculium lacustre*. Distributed over practically whole of Europe. Lives in rivers, streams, ponds and swamps. Common in lowlands. Length 8—14 mm., width 6—8 mm.; 3—4 mm. thick. Has thin-walled, transparent valves. Hermaphroditic and viviparous. Tolerates long droughts.

Family: **True Oysters** — *Ostreidae*

5 Edible Oyster *Ostrea edulis*. Distributed over European coasts from North Africa to Arctic Circle. Hermaphroditic, alternation of sexes in same individual. Free-swimming larvae hatch from the eggs. Up to 3 million eggs laid yearly by one oyster. Diet consists of plankton and debris. Collected as delicacy.

Family: **Cockles** — *Cardiidae*

6 Edible Cockle *Cardium edule*. Its area of distribution includes Atlantic, North, Baltic, Mediterranean and Black Seas. Diameter 3—4 cm. Lives in sand or mud in tidal zone, to depths of 10 metres. Can 'leap' distances of over 50 cm. with long, bent foot. Lives on plankton.

Family: **Piddocks** — *Pholadidae*

7 Common Piddock *Pholas dactylus*. Distributed from Mediterranean to Norway. Tunnels in soft rocks and wood. Length up to 9 cm., width 3.5 cm. Secretes phosphorescent slime. Damages ships, but not seriously.

Family: **Scallops** — *Pectinidae*

8 *Pecten varius*. Its range of distribution includes Atlantic Ocean from Spain to western Norway and North Sea. Shell 3—7 cm. in diameter. Colouring very variable. Adult sessile, young swim by snapping valves together.

Family: **Mussels** — *Mytilidae*

9 Blue Edible Mussel *Mytilus edulis*. Distributed in Arctic Ocean to North Africa, North and Baltic Seas. Forms large colonies, anchored to base by byssus. Settles in places with strong tides. Length 6—10 cm. One individual can lay up to 12 million eggs a year. Feeds on algae, debris and protozoans. Collected and sold as delicacy. Flesh rich in vitamins A, B, C and D. In many places piles are driven into the sea bed to provide the mussels with a ready-made base.

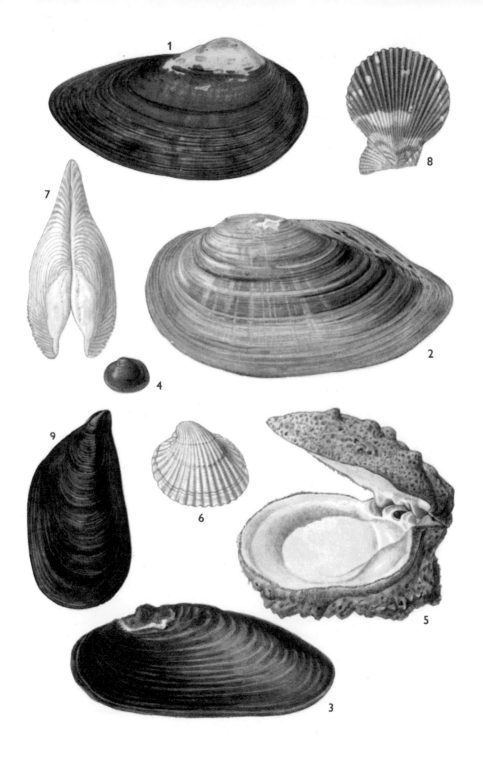

The arachnids are a very large class of arthropods comprising in all about 30,000 species. They have a segmented body, but the segments are often fused to form larger units. Of their six pairs of appendages, the first two pairs are usually converted to mouth parts.

Order: **Spiders** — *Araneae* (p. 206). Very abundant animals, with 6—8 eyes, dorsal scutellum covering anterior part of body (prosoma) and soft abdomen. Jaws connected to poison gland. European species harmless to man. Males generally smaller than females. Abdomen terminates in spinneret producing fine, but strong, quickly hardening filaments. Predacious animals, live on other, small animals which they catch in webs or by pouncing on them.

Family: **True Spiders** — *Araneidae* (p. 206). Small to moderately large spiders weaving striking net-like webs in which to catch prey. Females usually spend all their life in one place. Young spread by broadcasting on floating gossamer. Powerfully developed mandibles. About 50 species in central Europe.

Family: *Tetragnathidae* (p. 206). Spiders with strikingly long mandibles up to the same length as their cephalothorax. First two pairs of ambulatory appendages also very long. Over 10 species in central Europe.

Family: *Agelenidae* (p. 206). Spiders weaving strong, thick, more or less horizontal webs. Lie in wait for prey in funnel-shaped 'parlour' at base of web. One species, which lives under water, weaves bell-like web and fills it with air.

Family: **Wolf Spiders** — *Lycosidae* (p. 206). Robust spiders which build no web, but pounce on their prey. Run well and quickly. Special non-wetting bristles on their feet enable them also to run over water. Female carries egg cocoon firmly attached to its abdomen. About 70 species in central Europe.

Family: *Pisauridae* (p. 206). Robust spiders which do not weave web, but pounce on prey. Female carries egg cocoon in mandibles.

Family: **Crab Spiders** — *Thomisidae* (p. 206). Possess spinnerets, but do not actually weave webs. Lie in wait on flowers and other parts of plants for prey, which they usually catch with their fore limbs (the first two pairs are extremely long). Over 40 species in central Europe.

Family: **Jumping Spiders** — *Salticidae* (p. 208). Small spiders 2—12 mm. long, with stocky body and short, strong legs and large, central primary eyes. Males have much longer mandibles than females. Diurnal hunters, pounce on prey. Can jump long distances with great agility. Over 70 species in central Europe.

Family: *Eresidae* (p. 208). Robust spiders inhabiting warm, sandy or stony regions. Dig burrows in ground.

Order: **Pseudoscorpions** — *Pseudoscorpionidea* (p. 208). Small, extremely flattened arachnids 1—6 mm. long, with broad abdomen attached to cephalothorax across full width. Four pairs of ambulatory appendages. Palps terminate in claws. Harmless animals living in moss, humus and often in vicinity of man (e.g. in old books, etc.).

Order: **Harvestmen** — *Opilionidea* (p. 208). Small to large arachnids with segmented abdomen and nipper-like pedipalps. Four pairs of very long ambulatory appendages, which are easily snapped off and are capable of spasmodic movement for some time afterwards.

Order: **Mites and Ticks** — *Acari* (p. 208). Minute (sometimes microscopic) arachnids. Non-segmented cephalothorax fused with abdomen to form single unit. Mostly terrestrial, but some species aquatic. Mouth parts adapted for sucking or stabbing. Six-legged larvae transformed to nymphs of different types. Many species parasitic. Over 2,000 species in central Europe. Some species very abundant.

Class: **Centipedes** — *Chilopoda*
Body flat and distinctly segmented. One pair of limbs on each segment of trunk.

Order: *Lithobiomorpha* (p. 208). Long body and long antennae. Adults have 15 pairs of limbs, young individuals only seven.

Class: **Millipedes** — *Diplopoda*
Cylindrical body. Usually two pairs of limbs on each segment, but only one pair on 2nd to 4th.

Order: *Oniscomorpha* (p. 208). Body short, wide and vaulted, with 12—13 segments in trunk. Curl up when in danger.

Order: *Opisthospermophora* (p. 208). Body long and cylindrical, with over 30 segments in trunk. Legs short and weak.

Class: **Spiders and Scorpions** — *Arachnoidea*

Order: **Spiders** — *Araneae*

Family: **True Spiders** — *Araneidae*

1 Garden or **Diadem Spider** *Araneus diadematus*. Abundant in central Europe. Female over 15 mm. long. Basic colour variable. Adult specimens from August to October. Builds large, vertical webs. Female lays 45—600 eggs, wrapped in yellow cocoon. Young hatch following spring but do not mature for another year. Male woos female by shaking its web. Catches insects in the web.

2 *Argyope bruennichi*. Abundant in sunny meadows from July to September. Female 10 mm., male 3 mm. Cocoon, containing up to 400 eggs, hung between blades of grass. Young hibernate in cocoon. After pairing the female devours the male.

3 *Singa nitidula*. Abundant in central Europe. Female about 6 mm., male 3 mm. Elongated ovoid, glossy abdomen. Found from May to July on shrubs and tall plants in meadows near rivers or streams.

Family: *Tetragnathidae*

4 *Tetragnatha extensa*. Found all over central Europe. Up to 11 mm. long. Strikingly elongated body. Builds web in damp spots between grasses and rushes. Attaches egg cocoon to rushes, etc.

Family: *Agelenidae*

5 House Spider *Tegenaria derhami*. Widespread all over Europe. Length 6—11 mm. Looks much larger because of its long legs. Frequents houses, cattle-sheds, etc. Builds dense, horizontal webs in corners. Can be found whole year round. Lives several years. Catches insects. Female suspends spherical egg cocoon from several webs disguising it with fragments of mortar, etc.

6 Water Spider *Argyroneta aquatica*. Inhabits whole of central and northern Europe. Body length 8—15 mm. (male larger than female). The only subaquatic spider. Lives in clean pools. Weaves 'diving-bell' between aquatic plants and fills it with air. Bell also used as receptacle for eggs. Found whole year round. Life span two years.

Family: **Wolf Spiders** — *Lycosidae*

7 *Xerolycosa nemoralis*. Distributed over whole of central Europe. Length 5—7 mm. Common in woods, especially coniferous. Does not build web. Runs about among stones, pine needles, etc., catching small insects. Found from May to August. Egg cocoon carried attached to tip of female's abdomen. Female also carries young on its body for short time.

Family: *Pisauridae*

8 *Pisaura mirabilis*. Abundant in low-lying country. Length up to 13 mm. Elongated abdomen, long legs. Found on ground or leaves. Hunts prey. Male woos female with gift of fly; takes advantage of situation while female eats fly. Does not build web. Female carries egg cocoon in jaws.

Family: **Crab Spiders** — *Thomisidae*

9 *Diaea dorsata*. Common everywhere in central Europe. Length 5—7 mm. Found on bushes in both coniferous and deciduous forests. Lies in wait for insects, with two pairs of long legs in typical splayed position. Walks sideways. Seen mainly in May and June.

10 *Misumena vatia*. Common in central Europe. Female 10 mm., male only 4 mm. Frequents tall plants and bushes, chiefly in May. Lies in wait for insects in flowers.

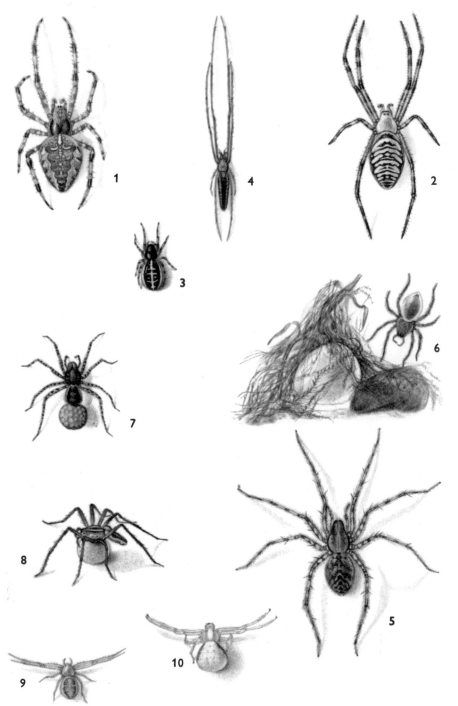

Family: **Jumping Spiders** — *Salticidae*

1 Zebra Spider *Salticus zebraneus.* Inhabits warm parts of Europe. Length up to 6 mm. Short legs. Appears in sunny spots early in spring. Male performs nuptial 'dance' in front of female. Female weaves nest and then lays eggs in it and guards them.

Family: *Eresidae*

2 *Eresus niger.* Inhabits warmer parts of Europe. Length 8—16 mm. Female velvety black. Male has red abdomen with 4 black spots. Found in sandy areas, lives in colonies. Scrapes holes 10 cm. deep, lined with cobwebs. Erects porch over entrance and builds web traps in vicinity. Hunts tiger beetles. Female lives 3 years, male only one.

Order: **Pseudoscorpions** — *Pseudoscorpionidea*

3 Book Scorpion *Chelifer cancroides.* Very common. Length 3—4 mm. Lives among leaves, behind bark, in old books, etc. Catches small insects and mites. Spread by flies. Nuptial 'dances'. Female lays 5—18 eggs in pouch on underside of body. Able to spin cocoons.

Order: **Harvestmen** — *Opilionidea*

4 Common Harvester *Opilio parietinus.* Abounds in damp, shady spots. Hunts flies and ants. Males fight at pairing time. Female lays small piles of eggs in damp soil or cracked ground. Young hatch early in spring.

Order: **Mites and Ticks** — *Acari*

5 Sheep or **Castor-bean Tick** *Ixodes ricinus.* Inhabits almost whole of Europe. Male 1 to 2 mm., female up to 4 mm. (several times larger when engorged). After fertilization and engorgement with vertebrate blood female lays up to 3,000 reddish eggs on ground or between stones. After sucking blood, the 6-legged larvae turn into nymphs, find fresh hosts and moult again to become adult males and females. Total time of development 178 to 274 days.

6 *Trombidium holosericum.* Very common. Length about 2.5 mm. Found on bushes, grass, ground, etc., from spring until autumn. Larvae 6-legged and bright red. Lives mainly on insects' eggs.

7 Common Beetle Mite *Parasitus coleoptratorum.* Occurs over most of Europe. Often found on dung beetles, used by adult female as means of transport to new dwelling-place, manure, compost, etc. Initial diet mouldy or rotting matter, later flies' eggs. Eggs usually unfertilized, but sometimes produce males.

Class: **Centipedes** — *Chilopoda*

Order: *Lithobiomorpha*

8 *Lithobius forficatus.* Common all over central Europe. Length 20—30 mm. Lives under stones, behind bark, etc., in woods and gardens. Solitary species. Can crawl both forwards and backwards. Bite harmless. Moults as it grows. Lives on insects, spiders, etc. Life span several years.

Class: **Millipedes** — *Diplopoda*

Order: *Oniscomorpha*

9 *Glomeris pustulata.* Widespread in central Europe. Length 4.5—14 mm. Resembles wood-louse, also able to curl up. Lives under stones, tree trunks, etc. in open country. Diet rotting leaves. Crawls very slowly. Eggs laid singly, in special nest made by female from damp clay. Life span 7 years.

Order: *Opisthospermophora*

10 *Julus terrestris.* Very common in central Europe. Length 20—50 mm. Coils itself up when disturbed. Lives under stones and leaves, behind bark, etc. Staple diet decomposing matter. Nocturnal animal. Female lays eggs in piles encased in capsule made of soil and secretion and fitted with ventilating shaft.

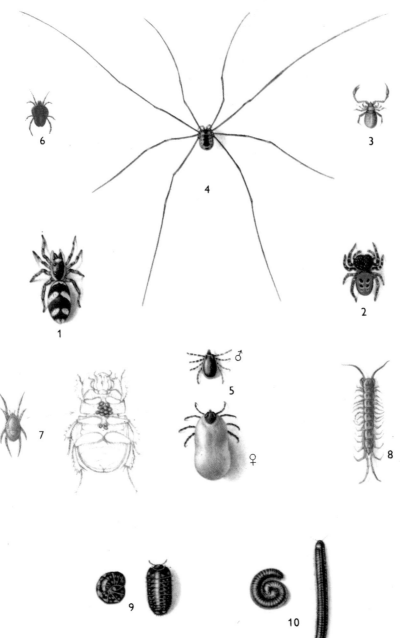

Class: **Crustaceans** — *Crustacea*

Mostly aquatic arthropods living in salt and fresh water, but include some terrestrial species. Some species parasitic. Size varies from minute or microscopic to several decimeters. Body and limbs segmented, but segmentation often invisible, especially in parasitic types. Body usually covered with hard shell, which is shed several times during animal's life. New covering is at first soft, but in a few days is reinforced with calcium salt deposits and hardens to a strong shell again. Two pairs of antennae are a characteristic feature.

Subclass: **Low Crustaceans** — *Phyllopoda* (p. 212). Mostly minute crustaceans measuring only 0.25 mm., although some species measure 1—10 cm. Body segmented, but number of segments varies considerably with species. Thoracic appendages (up to 40 pairs) are leaf-shaped or lobular and have gill pouches at base. Appendages used for swimming and for gathering food. Eyes well developed. Sexes separate, although incidence of males in some species is very small. Eggs, which can be, but do not need to be, fertilized, give rise to quickly maturing larvae. Phyllopoda live in stagnant fresh water, sometimes only at given time of year. Some species occur in salt water.

Order: **Branchiopods** — *Anostraca* (p. 212). Small freshwater crustaceans (only Artemis lives in salt water). Usually occur in small, seasonal tracts of water. Eleven pairs of thoracic swimming appendages.

Order: **Water Fleas** — *Cladocera* (p. 212). Small crustaceans usually found in fresh water. Head free, body encased in bivalvular, transparent shell. Second pair of antennae branched, unusually large and employed for swimming. Occur in large numbers.

Subclass: **Barnacles** — *Cirripedia* (p. 212). Adults sessile, attached to various bases. Usually occur in groups. Live only in sea, found on rocks, ships and flotsam, but also on mollusc shells and even crabs' claws, etc. Usually hermaphroditic, i.e. one individual possesses both male and female sex glands, but small males occur in some species. Free-swimming larvae known as nauplii hatched from eggs. Some species parasitic.

Order: *Thoracica* (p. 212). Marine crustaceans anchored from dorsal aspect. Body encased in shell. Six pairs of waving, lash-like, biramous thoracic appendages.

Subclass: **Higher Crustaceans** — *Malacostraca* (p. 212). Constant number of body segments (20 — head 6, thorax 8, abdomen 6, including fan-shaped telson). First pairs of thoracic appendages converted to nippers in some species. Body protected by very thick shell. Two pairs of appendages and three pairs of mouth parts on head. Sometimes great differences in body structure between individual species. Live mostly in salt and fresh water. Terrestrial species frequent damp spots.

Order: **Sea Lice and Allies** — *Isopoda* (p. 212). Shell-less crustaceans with flat-backed, segmented body. Uniramous ambulatory thoracic appendages of equal length. Found in water and in damp spots on land.

Family: **Water Lice** — *Asellidae* (p. 212). Abdominal segments fused to form wide scutellum. Abdominal appendages transformed to gills. Occur in salt and fresh water.

Family: **Sea Woodlice** — *Ligiidae* (p. 212). Swift-footed animals found on seashore or in damp places.

Family: **Land Woodlice** — *Porcellionidae* (p. 212). Small species with no eyes and with vaulted body. Occur in damp spots.

Order: **Flea Shrimps** — *Amphipoda* (p. 212). Shell-less crustaceans with extremely flat-sided body. Uniramous thoracic appendages with gill plates, biramous abdominal appendages.

Family: **Freshwater Shrimps** — *Gammaridae* (p. 212). Extremely flat-sided body.

Family: *Caprellidae* (p. 212). Small marine crustaceans with truncated abdomen, rod-like body and multi-segmented limbs. Live among aquatic plants in sea.

Order: **Decapods** — *Decapoda* (p. 214). Characterized by ten pairs of ambulatory appendages, the first three pairs of which terminate in nippers (chelae). Nippers on first pair of limbs usually huge; used for catching prey and for defence. Three more pairs of appendages act as accessory jaws. Shell strong and thick. Include mostly large species, but some members measure only a few millimetres.

Sub-order: **Long-tailed Decapods** — *Macrura* (p. 214). Decapods with long, tapering abdomen.

Family: **Crayfishes** — *Astacidae* (p. 214). Wide rostrum between eyes. Symmetrical nippers on first pair of ambulatory limbs. Inhabit fresh water.

Family: **Lobsters** — *Homaridae* (p. 214). Long, narrow rostrum. Nippers on first pair of ambulatory limbs asymmetrical. Marine animals.

Family: **Prawns** — *Palaemonidae* (p. 214). Flat-sided body, large abdomen curving down at tip. Thin thoracic limbs. Toothed rostrum.

Family: **Shrimps** — *Crangonidae* (p. 214). Short, toothless rostrum. First pair of thoracic limbs large.

Family: **Hermit Crabs** — *Paguridae* (p. 214). Nipper on right first ambulatory limb larger than on left. Inhabit shells of marine gastropods.

Sub-order: **True Crabs** — *Brachyura* (p. 214). Short, flat abdomen worn tucked under cephalothorax. Very well developed chelae, sometimes asymmetrical.

Family: **Velvet Crabs** — *Portunidae* (p. 214). Oval shell, wider at front than at back. Short antennae. Fifth pair of ambulatory appendages can be used for swimming.

Family: **Sea Spiders** — *Majidae* (p. 214). Triangular shell, length greater than width. Long rostrum with two points.

Family: **Woolly Crabs** — *Grapsidae* (p. 214). Wide, almost square body. Wide, hairy nippers.

Class: **Crustaceans** — *Crustacea*

Order: **Branchiopods** — *Anostraca*

1 *Branchipus stagnalis*. Common all over central Europe. Length up to 23 mm. Found in wet ditches and pools. Occurs from April to September. Swims upside down. Lives on micro-organisms. Female lays eggs in a special pouch on its abdominal segments, carries them a short time and then drops them into the mud. The eggs can survive five years of drought.

Order: **Water Fleas** — *Cladocera*

2 Common Water Flea *Daphnia pulex*. Abounds in stagnant water. Length about 2 mm. Fertilized hibernated eggs produce only females which reproduce further by unfertilized eggs. Eggs laid by the last generation also give rise to males and the females again lay fertilized eggs.

Order: *Thoracica*

3 Goose Barnacle *Lepas anatifera*. Lives off coasts from North to Mediterranean Sea. Length 3—4 cm. Locally abundant. Usually occurs in deep water but often found on floating objects. Anchored to base by thick, flexible stalk. Lives on plankton gathered by the gyrating movements of its six pairs of lash-like limbs. Hermaphroditic. Larvae hatch from eggs.

4 Acorn Barnacle *Balanus crenatus*. Inhabits tidal zone of North Sea and western Baltic. Very abundant. Lives in colonies. Attached to base over wide area of body surface. Often found on crabs' claws. Individuals in colonies stranded by tide enclose themselves in their shell, compound of 6 parts, by means of a leathery 'lid'. Size 10—20 mm.

Order: **Sea Lice and Allies** — *Isopoda*

Family: **Water Lice** — *Asellidae*

5 Hog-slater *Asellus aquaticus*. Plentiful in central and northern Europe. Length up to 13 mm. Lives at bottom of stagnant or slow-flowing water. Female carries the eggs or embryos in a brood pouch on the underside of its thorax. Lives on rotting vegetable debris. If water dries up, burrows in mud.

Family: **Sea Woodlice** — *Ligiidae*

6 Sea Woodlouse *Ligia oceanica*. Common on coasts from central Norway to Spain. Length up to 28 mm. Found under stones or among seaweed on rocky shores. Runs very quickly and dashes for water if in danger. Leads amphibian existence.

Family: **Land Woodlice** — *Porcellionidae*

7 Common Woodlouse *Porcellio scaber*. Abundant all over central Europe but has been carried to all parts of world. Length up to 16 mm. Colouring rather variable, but usually marbled. Lives in damp buildings, cellars, cracked walls, behind bark, etc. Large communities common. Breathes by means of gill plates on underside of abdomen. Lives on decomposing matter.

Order: **Flea Shrimps** — *Amphipoda*

Family: **Freshwater Shrimps** — *Gammaridae*

8 Common Freshwater Shrimp *Gammarus pulex*. Very common in central Europe. Length up to 24 mm. Inhabits shallow lakes, ponds and streams. Found under stones or among plants. Good swimmer. Mainly vegetarian. Usually winters on sandy bottoms, but often under stones. Sexes separate. Female lays eggs in brood pouch on legs where they are then fertilized. Young remain a short time with female.

Family: *Caprellidae*

9 *Caprella linearis*. Found off coasts of North and Baltic Seas as far as Kiel. Length up to 20 mm. Flat-sided, thread-like body. Legs terminate in prehensile claws. Frequents algae, seaweed, etc. Crawls swiftly over sea bed in search of prey. Predacious, catches small crustaceans, worms, polyps, etc. Deep red with light red eyes.

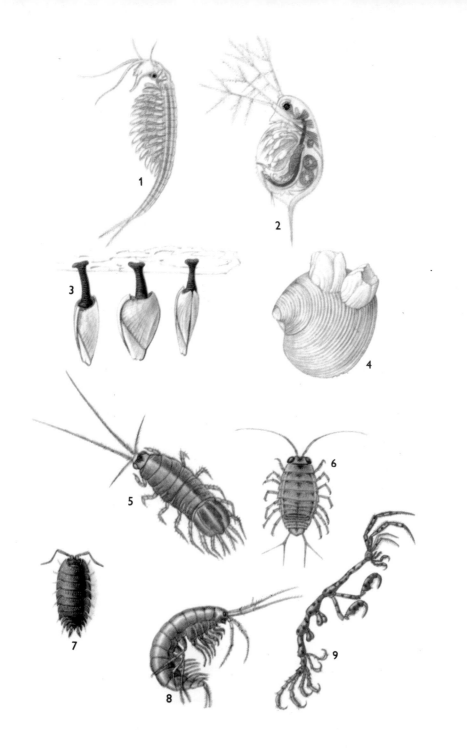

Order: **Decapods** — *Decapoda*

Sub-order: **Long-tailed Decapods** — *Macrura*

Family: **Crayfishes** — *Astacidae*

1 Common Crayfish *Astacus astacus*. Distributed in central Europe and southern Scandinavia. Length up to 22 cm. Occurs at low altitudes. Likes clean flowing water, but also found in ponds and lakes. Digs holes in banks to hide in during day. Hunts at night. Catches insects, gastropods, tadpoles and small fish. Also likes carrion. Occasionally eats green stuff. Eggs laid from October to December, attached in clumps to female's abdominal limbs. One female lays 6—150 eggs. Young hatched between May and July. They resemble the adult animals and remain attached to female's body for about 14 days. The young moult five times a year, adult specimens twice and old female only once.

Family: **Lobsters** — *Homaridae*

2 Lobster *Homarus gammarus*. Distributed from North Sea to Mediterranean and Black Sea. Length 35 cm., occasionally up to 50 cm. Takes 7—10 years to reach 20 cm. Inhabits rocks on sea bed. Nocturnal animal. Every two years, in July and August, lays up to 3,000 eggs which are carried on the underside of female's abdomen. Larvae hatch after 11 months. After four moults they resemble the adults. Life span 30 years. Caught in lobster-pots as delicacy.

Family: **Prawns** — *Palaemonidae*

3 Common Prawn *Palaemon squilla*. Lives in North and Baltic Seas. Length 5—6 cm. Frequents seaweed near shore in summer, deeper water in winter. Lives on algae, debris, small crustaceans, etc. Eggs laid in summer. Almost transparent when alive, turns pinky-red when boiled. Delicacy.

Family: **Shrimps** — *Crangonidae*

4 Common Shrimp *Crangon crangon*. Distributed from North Sea to Mediterranean. Length 4—5 cm. Frequents coastal zone, enters brackish water in summer. Lives on small molluscs, fish roes, etc. Eggs laid April-June and October-November. Delicacy. Does not change colour when boiled.

Family: **Hermit Crabs** — *Paguridae*

5 Common Hermit Crab *Eupagurus bernhardus*. Distributed from Mediterranean to North Sea where it is very abundant. Length about 3.5 cm. Frequents shore but also found at depths of 450 m. on sandy or rocky bottom. Wears marine gastropod shells to protect its soft abdomen. Closes aperture of shell with claw. Lives on small animals and debris. Large numbers of young may be found in shallow water.

Sub-order: **True Crabs** — *Brachyura*

6 Common Shore Crab *Carcinus maenas*. Its distribution area ranges from Mediterranean to Iceland. Abundant in North Sea, rare in Baltic. Length 5—6 cm., width up to 8 cm. Large well-developed nippers. Can swim short distances. Runs rapidly sideways on sea bed and on land. If stranded by tide, hides under large pebbles or burrows in sand. Lives on remains of different animals and plants.

7 Spider Crab *Macropodia rostrata*. Plentiful in North Sea and Baltic bays as far as Kiel. Also occurs in Mediterranean. Frequents coastal zone to depth of 100 m. Hides in rocks or sand. Length up to 18 mm. Rostrum formed of two long, joined spines. Eats small molluscs, crustaceans, algae, etc.

8 Mitten Crab *Eriocheir sinensis*. Native of rivers of northern China and shores of Yellow Sea. Brought to Europe, now lives in Elbe, Weser and other rivers. Locally abundant. Length up to 7.5 cm. Very wide chelae thickly covered with fine hairs. Travels long distances upstream. Attains adulthood after 4 years and then returns to sea where female lays eggs. Larvae can hatch only in salt water.

Class: **Insects** — *Insecta*

Largest group of animals comprising over one million known species. Body consists of three parts — head, thorax and abdomen. Thorax carries three pairs of legs and usually 1 or 2 pairs of wings. Body generally encased in chitin. Development by complete metamorphosis (egg — larva — pupa — imago) or by incomplete metamorphosis (larva gradually acquires adult form by successive moults). In some cases development more complicated.

Order: **Springtails** — *Collembola* (p. 224). Small, wingless insects with short body. Forked caudal appendage used for jumping. Many species.

Order: **Fish Moths**— *Thysanura* (p. 224). Wingless insects with small, spindle-shaped body covered with fine scales. Long, thread-like feelers on head. Nocturnal animals.

Order: **Mayflies** — *Ephemeroptera* (p. 224). Delicate, soft-bodied insects. Adults have degenerate mouth parts. Forewings large, hindwings very small. Adults live only short time, predacious larvae live up to 3 years in water. Incomplete metamorphosis.

Order: **Stone-flies** — *Plecoptera* (p. 224). Small, flat-backed insects with long, thread-like feelers. Both pairs of wings folded against body when resting. Larvae live in water. Incomplete metamorphosis.

Order: **Earwigs** — *Dermaptera* (p. 224). Moderately large, flat-bodied insects with short forewings. Conspicuous pincers at end of abdomen are larger in males. Incomplete metamorphosis.

Order: **Alderflies** — *Megaloptera* (p. 224). Moderately large insects with large head and thread-like antennae. Large, wide wings folded roof-wise over back when resting. Larvae live in water. Complete metamorphosis.

Order: **Snoutflies** — *Mecoptera* (p. 224). Small to moderately large insects with tip of head forming an elongated snout. Long, thickly veined wings. Tip of male's abdomen curves upwards in many species. Larvae live in damp soil. Complete metamorphosis.

Order: **Fleas** — *Aphaniptera* (p. 224). Small, wingless insects with flat-sided body. Hindlimbs adapted for jumping. Parasitic. Complete metamorphosis.

Order: **Bird Lice** or **Biting Lice** — *Mallophaga* (p. 224). Small, wingless, flat-bodied insects. Parasites living in plumage and fur. Over 300 species known in Europe. Incomplete metamorphosis.

Order: **Snakeflies** — *Raphidioptera* (p. 226). Moderately large insects with long neck-like prethorax. Membraneous wings folded roof-wise when resting. Predacious larvae live behind bark. Complete metamorphosis.

Order: **Nerve-winged Insects** — *Neuroptera* (p. 226). Small to moderately large insects with two pairs of membraneous wings of almost equal length folded roof-wise when resting. Complete metamorphosis.

216

Order: **Cockroaches** — *Blattodea* (p. 226). Flat-bodied insects with long, thread-like feelers. First pair of wings more chitinized. Wings sometimes absent. Larvae live in the same way as adults. Incomplete metamorphosis.

Order: **Mantids** — *Mantodea* (p. 226). Large insects with long body and neck-like elongated prethorax. First pair of limbs powerfully developed for seizing prey. Larvae live like adults. Incomplete metamorphosis.

Order: **Caddis-flies** — *Trichoptera* (p. 226). Moderately large insects with semi-transparent wings. Found near water, larvae in water. Complete metamorphosis. Over 300 species in Europe.

Order: **Dragonflies** — *Odonata* (p. 228). Large insects with long abdomen. Large, prominent eyes, small feelers. Long, narrow, veined wings. Predacious. Larvae (nymphs) live in water. Incomplete metamorphosis.

Sub-order: **Damsel-flies** — *Zygoptera* (p. 228). Both pairs of wings of almost equal size, folded vertically when resting. Fly relatively slowly.

Sub-order: **Giant Dragonflies** — *Anisoptera* (p. 228). Wings held spread when resting, second pair wider than first. Very large eyes. Swift fliers.

Order: **Straight-winged Insects** — *Orthoptera* (p. 230). Moderately large or large insects with powerful mouth parts adapted for biting. Forewings rigid, hindwings tucked beneath them. Hind limbs usually adapted for jumping. Females have ovipositor. Larvae resemble adults but wingless. Incomplete metamorphosis.

Family: **Green Grasshoppers** — *Tettigoniidae* (p. 230). Large species with flat-sided body. Long, thread-like feelers. Males 'chirp' by rubbing bases of forewings together.

Family: **Crickets** — *Gryllidae* (p. 230). Small to large species with stout body and large head. Thread-like feelers. Males have 'chirping' apparatus on forewings.

Family: **Mole Crickets** — *Gryllotalpidae* (p. 230). Large species with conspicuously strong, wide forelimbs like mole's. Males 'chirp'. Fly clumsily.

Family: **Field Grasshoppers** — *Acrididae* (p. 230). Small to large species with large, vertically held head. Short feelers. Flat-sided body. Underwings often brightly coloured. 'Chirp' by rubbing hind femora against edges of upper wings.

Order: **Bugs** — *Heteroptera* (p. 232). Small to moderately large species with flat-backed body. Forewings partly chitinous, hindwings membraneous — wings occasionally absent. Stabbing or sucking proboscis. Larvae resemble adults but wingless. Incomplete metamorphosis.

Family: **Water-boatmen** — *Corixidae* (p. 232). Slim, long-bodied aquatic bugs. Suck plant juices. Fly at night.

Family: **Back-swimmers** — *Notonectidae* (p. 232). Aquatic species with large head and carinate body. Long hindlimbs with swimming hairs. Swim upside down. Predacious.

Family: **Water-scorpions** — *Nepidae* (p. 232). Large aquatic species with very flat or slim, elongated body. Forelimbs adapted for catching prey. Have breathing tube. Predacious.

Family: **Pond Skaters** — *Gerridae* (p. 232). Very slim, long-legged species living on surface of water. Predacious.

Family: **Soldier-bugs**— *Reduviidae* (p. 232). Long feelers and legs. Robust proboscis. Stab.

Family: **Fire-bugs** — *Pyrrhocoridae* (p. 232). Brightly coloured bugs living in communities on walls, etc.

Family: **Marginated Bugs** — *Coreidae* (p. 232). Herbivorous species with feelers on top of head. Sides widened to form border.

Family: **Stink-bugs** — *Pentatomidae* (p. 232). Larger species with ovoid body, wide scutum and very large scutellum. Often brightly coloured. Suck plant and insect juices.

Order: **Plant-bugs** — *Homoptera* (p. 234). Usually small insects with two pairs of membraneous wings, often folded roof-wise when resting. Mouth parts adapted for stabbing and sucking. Suck plant juices.

Sub-order: **Cicadas** — *Cicadoidea* (p. 234). Small to huge species. Large head with short feelers. Sclerous wings, in some species transparent. Larvae usually resemble adults.

Sub-order: **Plant-lice** — *Aphidoidea* (p. 234). Small species, either wingless or with four delicate wings. Long proboscis. Development often complicated. Frequently gregarious. About 900 species in Europe.

Sub-order: **Scale-insects** — *Coccoidea* (p. 234). Small insects, males have wings but no proboscis. Wingless, scutate-bodied females often sit immobile on plants and suck juice with proboscis. Over 500 species in Europe.

Order: **Ants, Wasps and Bees** — *Hymenoptera* (p. 236). Mostly perfectly developed insects. Free head with biting mouth parts. Two pairs of membraneous wings. Females have ovipositor. Complete metamorphosis.

Family: **Sawflies** — *Tenthredinidae* (p. 236). Smallish, stout-bodied species with thread-like antennae. Larvae resemble caterpillars and have 6—7 pairs of prolegs and one pair of claspers.

Family: **Cimbicid Sawflies** — *Cimbicidae* (p. 236). Small species with widened, club-like antennae.

Family: **Wood Wasps** — *Siricidae* (p. 236). Small to large species with elongated cylindrical body. Fairly long, thread-like antennae. Females have strikingly long ovipositor.

Family: **Ichneumon Flies** — *Ichneumonidae* (p. 236). Moderately large species with very long, thin abdomen. Long, thread-like feelers. Female's ovipositor conspicuously long.

Family: **Braconids** — *Braconidae* (p. 236). Small to minute species. Legless larvae live as parasites on caterpillars etc.

Family: **Aphid Wasps** — *Aphidiidae* (p. 236). Tiny species developing solely in plant-lice.

Family: **Gall-wasps** — *Cynipidae* (p. 236). Smallish species with flat abdomen and well-developed thorax. Legless larvae form galls on plants.

Family: **Beetle-wasps** — *Scoliidae* (p. 238). Large wasps with brightly coloured body. Develop in beetle larvae.

Family: **Mutillids** or **Velvet Ants** — *Mutillidae* (p. 238). Brightly coloured wasps frequenting flowers. Females often wingless.

Family: **True Wasps** — *Vespidae* (p. 238). Moderately large to large, usually black-yellow in colouring. Generally form communities. Live on insects and plant juices.

Family: **Potter Wasps** — *Eumenidae* (p. 238). Moderately large, solitary wasps. Form stocks of paralysed insects for offspring.

Family: **Digger Wasps** — *Psammocharidae* (p. 238). Moderately large wasps with very long legs. Wide wings. Solitary. Dig burrows for larvae which are fed on spiders.

Family: **Ants** — *Formicidae* (p. 240). Usually small insects with bent feelers. Live in organized communities. Males and females have long wings, workers are wingless.

Family: **Thread-waisted Wasps** — *Sphegidae* (p. 240). Moderately large wasps with base of abdomen stalk-like elongated. Short feelers. Catch and paralyse insects as food for offspring.

Family: **Cuckoo Wasps** — *Chrysididae* (p. 240). Small wasps with shimmering metallic colours. Parasites of other wasps.

Family: **Bees** — *Apidae* (p. 242). Moderately large to large species with hairy body. Both solitary and sociable types. Bee community consists of queen, workers and males — drones.

Order: **Beetles** — *Coleoptera* (p. 244). Large order. Over 6,000 species in central Europe. Highly chitinized body. In most species membraneous wings folded under thick sheaths (wing case). Mouth parts adapted for biting. Complete metamorphosis.

Family: **Tiger Beetles** — *Cicindelidae* (p. 244). Moderately large beetles with large head and conspicuous eyes. Large, sharp, curved mandibles. Oval wing sheaths. Slim legs.

Family: **Ground Beetles** — *Carabidae* (p. 244). Moderately large to large beetles with strong mandibles, long legs and elongated body. Wings degenerated in many species. Predacious.

Family: **Water Beetles** — *Dytiscidae* (p. 246). Small to large beetles with ovoid body. Adapted for aquatic existence. 'Row' with long hind legs. Predacious. Able to fly.

Family: **Whirligig Beetles** — *Gyrinidae* (p. 246). Small beetles describing circles on water surface.

Family: **Water Scavenger Beetles** — *Hydrophilidae* (p. 246). Small to large beetles with ovoid body. Short antennae. Herbivorous. Larvae predacious.

Family: **Rover Beetles** — *Staphylinidae* (p. 248). Small to moderately large, with very long body and short wing sheaths.

Family: **Sexton and Carrion Beetles** — *Silphidae* (p. 248). Varying sizes. Club-like antennae. Usually develop in decomposing body of animals.

Family: **Steel** or **Hister Beetles** — *Histeridae* (p. 248). Small species with flat, gleaming body. Chase insects.

Family: **Carpet Beetles** — *Dermestidae* (p. 248). Small species with cylindrical body and bowed head.

Family: **Stag Beetles** — *Lucanidae* (p. 250). Moderately large to large beetles. Males' mandibles often enormously elongated. Fan-shaped antennae.

Family: **Chafers** — *Scarabaeidae* (p. 250). Well-developed beetles with strong legs. Bent antennae with fan-shaped, fronded tip. Over 700 species in Europe.

Family: **Metallic** or **Flat-headed Wood-borers** — *Buprestidae* (p. 252). Small to large, long-bodied beetles, mostly brightly coloured with metallic sheen. Blind, legless larvae usually found in wood.

Family: **Click Beetles** — *Elateridae* (p. 254). Small to moderately large beetles with elongated body. Able to spring into air from supine position.

Family: **Leather-winged Beetles** — *Cantharidae* (p. 254). Smallish, elongate, soft-bodied beetles. Both wing sheaths and wings reduced in some species. Predacious.

Family: **Chequered Beetles** — *Cleridae* (p. 254). Small to moderately large beetles with gaily coloured wing cases. Predacious.

Family: **Death Watch Beetles** — *Anobiidae* (p. 254). Minute beetles with hard cylindrical body. Head covered by plate. Bore in dry wood.

Family: **Darkling** or **Pineate Beetles** — *Tenebrionidae* (p. 256). Small to moderately large, with beaded antennae. Colouring usually dark. Some species occur in houses.

Family: **Blister** or **Oil Beetles** — *Meloidae* (p. 256). Moderately large to large insects with leathery-soft wing sheaths. Some species have short wing case. Herbivorous. Secrete acrid repellents.

Family: **Snout Beetles** or **Weevils** — *Curculionidae* (p. 256). Small beetles with head produced to typical 'snout'.

Family: **Bark Beetles** — *Scolytidae* (p. 256). Small, stout-bodied, with very hard covering. Rounded head protected by plate. Bore behind bark.

Family: **Longicorn Beetles** — *Cerambycidae* (p. 258). Small to large with elongated body and exceptionally long antennae. Long, sturdy legs. Powerful jaws. Over 500 species in Europe.

Family: **Leaf Beetles** — *Chrysomelidae* (p. 264). Smallish beetles with arched, oval body. Thread-like antennae. Often have metallic lustre. Eat leaves.

Family: **Ladybirds** — *Coccinellidae* (p. 264). Small beetles with ovoid body. Short, club-like antennae. Adult beetles and larvae both predacious.

Order: **Moths and Butterflies** — *Lepidoptera* (p. 266). Insects with four wings usually covered with fine scales. Jaws converted to coiled proboscis. Long antennae, thin legs. Larvae (caterpillars) have three pairs of thoracic legs and usually four pairs of prolegs and one pair of claspers. Over 4,000 species in central Europe.

Family: **Ghost Moths** — *Hepialidae* (p. 266). Large moths with long, very narrow wings folded roof-wise when resting. Very short antennae. Zigzag flight. Seen in evening.

Family: **Carpenter Moths** — *Cossidae* (p. 266). Comparatively large moths with robust body. Very short antennae. Wings folded roof-wise when at rest. Caterpillars live in wood.

Family: **Bear Moths** — *Syntomidae* (p. 266). Smallish species with large forewings. Resemble burnet moths.

Family: **Burnet Moths** or **Foresters** — *Zygaenidae* (p. 266). Smallish with stocky body. Club-like antennae. Narrow forewings. Ungainly in flight. Sit motionless on plants.

Family: **Bagworm Moths** — *Psychidae* (p. 266). Small, with few scales on wings. Wingless females live in bag-like case in which they have pupated.

Family: **Clearwings** — *Sesiidae* (p. 268). Smallish, with narrow, partly scaleless forewings and transparent hindwings. Resemble bees or wasps.

Family: **Puss Moths** — *Notodontidae* (p. 268). Moderately large, stout-bodied moths. Triangular forewings, much smaller hindwings. Wings folded roof-wise.

Family: **Procession Moths** — *Thaumetopoeidae* (p. 268). Small moths with sturdy body. Caterpillars live in large nests.

Family: **Silk Moths** or **Saturnids** — *Saturniidae* (p. 268). Large, thick-bodied nocturnal moths. Large wings. Conspicuous colourful eye spots on forewings.

Family: **Meadow Moths** — *Lemoniidae* (p. 270). Moderately large nocturnal moths with stout, hairy body. Pectinate antennae, long in males, short in females.

Family: **Birch Moths** — *Endromiidae* (p. 270). Moderately large nocturnal moths. Hairy abdomen. Pectinate antennae. Caterpillars have wart-like excrescence at end of body.

Family: **Tent Caterpillar Moths** — *Lasiocampidae* (p. 270). Small to large nocturnal moths with strong, hairy body. Large and triangular forewings, rounded hindwings. Degenerated proboscis. Males have doubly pectinate antennae.

Family: **Tussock Moths** — *Lymantriidae* (p. 272). Moderately large nocturnal moths with stocky, hairy body. Wide wings. Short antennae, doubly pectinate in males.

Family: **Owlet Moths** — *Phalaenidae* (p. 272). Moderately large to large nocturnal moths. Robust body. Wings folded roof-wise when at rest. Very long, thread-like antennae.

Family: **Tiger Moths** — *Arctiidae* (p. 274). Moderately large to large nocturnal moths with strong body and short antennae. Wide wings, often very brightly coloured, folded roof-wise when resting. Shaggy, warty caterpillars.

Family: **Geometers** or **Emeralds** — *Geometridae* (p. 274). Small to moderately large nocturnal moths with slim body and large wings, held flat when at rest. 'Looper' caterpillars.

Family: **Hawk Moths** — *Sphingidae* (p. 276). Moderately large to large, with streamlined body. Narrow, powerful wings. Hindwings much smaller. Club-shaped antennae. Very long proboscis. Swift, skilful fliers. Caterpillars have long spine at tip of abdomen.

Family: **Skipper Butterflies** — *Hesperiidae* (p. 278). Small, stocky, wide-headed butterflies with short antennae.

Family: **Satyrs** or **Meadow Browns** — *Satyridae* (p. 280). Moderately large butterflies marked with eye spots.

221

Family: **Fritillaries** — *Nymphalidae* (p. 280). Moderately large, gaily coloured butterflies. Wide, often indentated wings. Large eyes. Caterpillars frequently wear spines. Angular chrysalis.

Family: **Blues, Coppers** or **Hairstreaks** — *Lycaenidae* (p. 284). Small butterflies. Males usually blue or fiery red, females usually dark brown. Short forelimbs. Very common.

Family: **Swallowtails** — *Papilionidae* (p. 284). Large, usually brightly coloured butterflies. Hindwings sometimes 'spurred'. Short, club-tipped antennae.

Family: **Whites** — *Pieridae* (p. 286). Moderately large butterflies, mostly white, yellow or orange. Well developed forelimbs.

Order: **Two-winged Flies** — *Diptera* (p. 288). Small insects with body clearly divided into head, thorax and abdomen. Head very mobile. Conspicuously large compound eyes with metallic sheen in many species. Usually also three simple eyes on top of head. Feelers short or long. Only one pair of wings — second pair used for balance. Complete metamorphosis. Worm-like larvae. Mouth parts adapted for stabbing, sucking or licking. Sexes separate.

Family: **Crane-flies** — *Tipulidae* (p. 288). Relatively large species with very long, brittle legs. Often attracted by light. Larvae gnaw roots. About 60 species in central Europe.

Family: **Gall-gnats** — *Cecidomyidae* (p. 288). Small mosquito-like species with long legs. Females have elongated ovipositor. Larvae live mostly in plant galls. Many species, each specific for particular plant.

Family: **Hair-gnats** — *Bibionidae* (p. 288). Robust species with silky body. Males have large eyes. Black, red or yellow in colouring. Seen on warm days in April and May. Fly slowly. Occur in woods, often in great numbers. Larvae live in soil. Many species.

Family: **Gadflies** — *Tabanidae* (p. 288). Moderately large to large stout-bodied insects. Projecting, strong proboscis with 4—6 sharp bristles. Extremely large, gleaming eyes. Long, powerful wings. After sucking blood, fertilized females lay eggs, often in water. Males live on plant juices, females on blood of mammals. Over 50 species in central Europe.

Family: **Bee-flies** — *Bombyliidae* (p. 288). Moderately large insects, usually with hairy body. Good fliers. Proboscis generally very long and thin. Adults suck sweet plant juices. Larvae hyperparasitic, i.e. live as parasites on parasitic larvae. About 50 species in central Europe.

Family: **Soldier-flies** — *Stratiomyidae* (p. 288). Smallish flies with flat, wide, often brightly coloured body. Flutter on flowers and suck nectar. Larvae live in water or soil.

Family: **Hover-flies** — *Syrphidae* (p. 290). Usually brightly coloured, moderately large flies. Some 'imitate' bees and wasps. Darting flight. Able to hover. Larvae either flat (live on greenflies), or oval with 'tail' (live in liquid manure). Very many species.

Family: **Fruit-flies** — *Drosophilidae* (p. 290). Minute flies often found in houses. Most develop in fermenting fruit juice, vinegar, wine, etc. Larvae of some species live as parasites on insects.

Family: **Horse-ticks** or **Forest-flies** — *Hippoboscidae* (p. 290). Tiny flies greatly altered by parasitism. Very flat body with tough skin. Long proboscis. Very long legs with claws and suctorial pads. Wings developed, but in some species break off or degenerate. Female lays well-developed larvae.

222

Family: **True Flies** — *Muscidae* (p. 290). Fairly slender flies. Develop in fresh mammalian excreta, garbage, etc. Some parasitic. Many species attack humans.

Family: **Blow-flies** — *Calliphoridae* (p. 290). Smallish flies, often with metallic violet to green body. Larvae develop in excreta and decomposing flesh. Some species parasitic. Flesh-flies also lay eggs or maggots on freshly killed animals or meat. Buzz loudly while flying.

Family: **Caterpillar-flies** —*Larvaevoridae* (p. 290). Flies with stout, bristly body. Females lay eggs on skin of caterpillars or other insect larvae. Larvae burrow into host's body and devour it from within. Useful for combating pests.

Class: **Insects** — *Insecta*

Order: **Springtails** — *Collembola*

1 Black Water Springtail *Podura aquatica*. Common in Europe. Length 1 mm. Wingless. Found in vast numbers on aquatic plants or directly on surface of streams, puddles, pools, etc. Scaly body. Jumps by means of forked caudal appendage. Female lays up to over 1,300 eggs. Larvae hatch in 12 days. Several generations a year. Lives on rotting vegetable debris.

Order: **Fish Moths** — *Thysanura*

2 Silverfish *Lepisma saccharina*. Very common. Length about 10 mm. Often frequents buildings. Nocturnal insect. Comes out after dark and looks for scraps. Found in bathrooms and lavatories, behind wallpaper, etc.

Order: **Mayflies** — *Ephemeroptera*

3 Common Mayfly *Ephemera vulgata*. Widespread in central Europe. Length 14—22 mm. Black-spotted wings. Larvae live in slow-flowing water, bent drainpipes, etc. Development takes 2 years. Swarming time May to August. Attracted by light.

4 White Mayfly *Polymitarcis virgo*. Common in central Europe. Length 10—18 mm. Snow-white. Larvae live in large rivers. Develops 2 years. Swarming time August to September. Mass incidence. Adults live only 1—3 days. Female lays eggs on surface of water. Larvae resemble adult insects and live on small animals. Fully developed nymphs leave water and moult (subimago). Next moult produces adult insect capable of further reproduction.

Order: **Stone-flies** — *Plecoptera*

5 *Perla abdominalis*. Common in central Europe. Length 17—28 mm. Found near large ponds and rivers. From April to June, adult insects cling to underside of leaves. Predacious larvae hide under stones on water bed. Mature larvae climb tree trunks, its dorsal skin splits and winged insects emerge. Female lays eggs on surface of water in the evening time.

Order: **Earwigs** — *Dermaptera*

6 Common Earwig *Forficula auricularia*. Distributed all over Europe. Length 9—16 mm. Pincers at tip of abdomen used for defence or for unfolding membraneous wings. Appears from April to October. Female lays piles of eggs in spaces under stones and guards both eggs and wingless larvae. Eats eggs of other insects and parts of plants.

Order: **Alderflies** — *Megaloptera*

7 Luteous Alderfly *Sialis flavilatera*. Lives all over Europe. Length 19—38 mm. Found near water in May and June. Larvae live in water, eat other insects and their larvae. Pupate in damp soil on bank. Adult insects live only few days. Female lays up to 2,000 eggs on rushes, hatched larvae drop into water. Development takes 2 years.

Order: **Snoutflies** — *Mecoptera*

8 Scorpion-fly *Panorpa communis*. Found all over Europe. Length about 20 mm. Male has tapering abdomen like scorpion's. Female lays up to 75 eggs in hollows in ground. Caterpillar-like larvae live in moss, etc. Eats vegetable and animal matter. Sometimes sucks wounded insects dry.

Order: **Fleas** — *Aphaniptera*

9 Human Flea *Pulex irritans*. Lives all over the world. Length about 4 mm. Wingless. Adults parasitic on man. After sucking blood, female lays eggs in crevices etc. Legless larvae live on organic debris in which they also pupate. Female lays 4—8 eggs daily for 3 months. Flea-bites turn red and swell.

Order: **Bird Lice** or **Biting Lice** — *Mallophaga*

10 Fowl-louse *Menopon gallinae*. Very common in Europe. Length 1—1.5 mm. Wingless. Lives in plumage of fowls, eats feathers, bites skin and sucks their blood. Female attaches eggs to feathers. Occasionally, but not for long, can live as parasite on man.

224

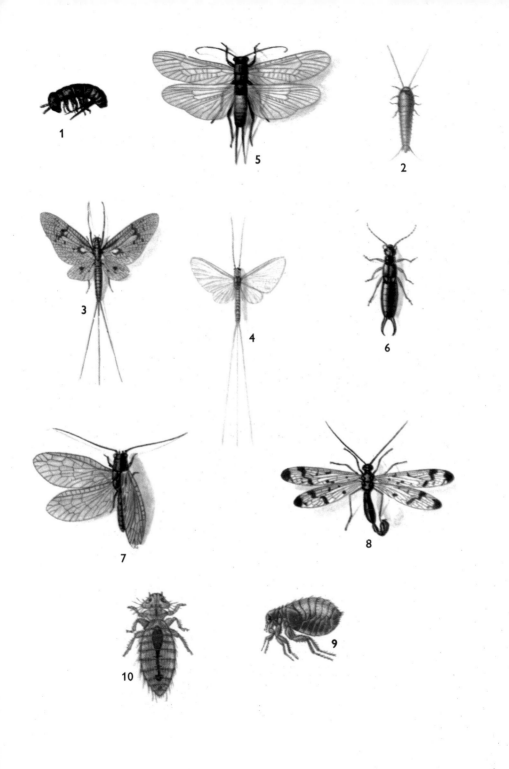

Order: **Snakeflies** — *Raphidioptera*

1 Snakefly *Raphidia notata*. Distributed all over Europe. Length up to 30 mm. Inhabits woods, especially sunny outskirts. Appears during summer, from April. Female has long ovipositor. Catches insects and spiders. Flat larvae live behind bark and catch insects. Female lays up to 50 eggs on wood.

Order: **Nerve-winged Insects** — *Neuroptera*

2 Owl-fly *Ascalaphus macaronius*. Lives in warm regions, including central Europe. Length up to 30 mm. Found on sunny slopes, etc. Appears in June. Catches small animals on wing. Larvae live on ground, in grass, and catch other insects, especially ants. Pupate in soil.

3 Ant Lion *Myrmeleon formicarius*. Abundant in central Europe. Wing span up to 75 mm. Adult insects live only from June to August. Female lays single eggs in sand. Larvae make funnel-shaped pits, in which they mainly trap ants, sucking them dry with their strong hollow jaws. Pupate in soil in sandy cocoon.

4 Green Lacewing *Chrysopa vulgaris*. Very common. Length about 20 mm. Flies mainly in evening. In autumn often seen at windows. Hunts plant lice. Female lays eggs on long stems near plant lice, on which larvae live 10—24 days before pupating. Two generations a year. Adults of second generation hibernate and are brownish, in spring greenish.

Order: **Cockroaches** — *Blattodea*

5 Croton Bug or **German Cockroach** *Blatella germanica*. Today distributed over whole of the world. Length 11—15 mm. Runs well but flies badly. Hides during day in buildings. Comes out after dark to look for food. Eats vegetable and animal matter, paper, leather, etc. Likes warmth. Reproduces whole year round. Female lays about 30 eggs in special capsule carried on its abdomen. Capsule shed after 14 days. After hibernating, larvae moult 6 times before maturing to adult insects.

6 Black-beetle or **Oriental Cockroach** *Blatta orientalis*. Found all over Europe. Length 19—30 mm. Inhabits old houses, bakeries, etc. Likes warmth. Occurs whole year round. Nocturnal insect. Lives on both vegetable and animal matter. Female lays eggs in capsules (ootheca). Life span up to 6 years.

Order: **Mantids** — *Mantodea*

7 Praying Mantis *Mantis religiosa*. Inhabits only warmest parts of central Europe. Length of male 60 mm., female 75 mm. Lives on bushes. Slow-moving. Appears from June to September. Waits motionless for prey, seizes it with long forelimbs. Lives mainly on insects. In autumn, after pairing, female often devours male. Female lays eggs in capsules attached to twigs. Predacious larvae hatch in spring, mature in August.

Order: **Caddis-flies** — *Trichoptera*

8 Macro-caddisfly *Phrygaena grandis*. Abundant throughout central Europe. Wing span up to 70 mm. Appears near water from April to August. Female lays piles of eggs on underside of leaves near water surface. Larvae form cases from fragments of plants and pupate in these under water. Imagos emerge en masse, flutter over water and pair.

9 Rhomboid Caddis-fly *Limnophilus rhombicus*. Abundant in central Europe. Length 17 to 44 mm. Appears from May to September. Larvae make case of criss-cross fragments of bark, wood and leaves. Pupates under water. Imago-like pupa bites through cocoon envelope, floats to surface and immediately splits open, releasing adult insect. Adults pair in evening over water. Common fish food.

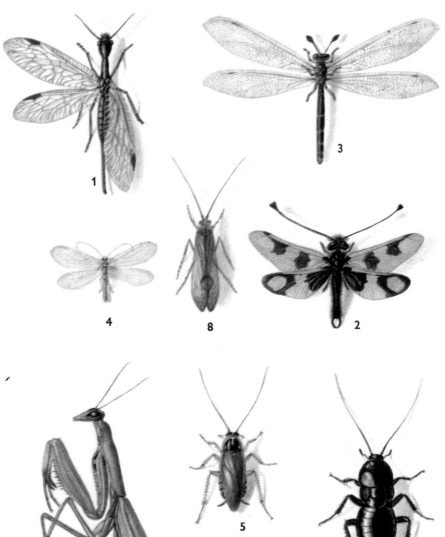

Order: **Dragonflies** — *Odonata*

Sub-order: **Damselflies** — *Zygoptera*

1 Blue Damselfly *Calopteryx virgo*. Abundant all over central Europe. Length 34—39 mm. Male has blue wings, female brownish. Frequents flowing water and ponds. Appears from May to August. Female lays eggs in plants under water, often submerging completely to do so. Slim larvae, which take 2 years to develop, have three leaf-like caudal appendages. When fully developed, they crawl out, grip a reed and wait until dorsal skin splits, releasing adult insect.

2 *Calopteryx splendens*. Very common beside both stagnant and flowing water from May to September. Length 33—40 mm. Male has broad bluish band on wings. Larvae live in water. Develop in same way as preceding species.

3 *Coenagrion puella*. Found everywhere in central Europe. Length 23—30 mm. Male has slim blue body, female greenish. Appears from May to end of September. Flies among reeds and tall grass beside water. Female lays eggs in plants, often submerging completely. Larvae live in stagnant or slow-flowing water. Develop one year. Mature nymph crawls out of water and after one more moult is transformed to adult insect, whose wings and abdomen soon grow to full length.

Sub-order: **Giant Dragonflies** — *Anisoptera*

4 Giant Dragonfly *Anax imperator*. Scattered over whole of Europe. Length up to 60 mm. Appears from June to August, often far from water. Swift, skilful flier. Catches insects on wing. Larvae live at bottom of stagnant water, are exceptionally predacious and even hunt small fish. Female lays eggs in plants, but does not submerge completely. Development takes one year.

5 Brown Dragonfly *Aeschna grandis*. Widely distributed in Europe. Length 49—60 mm. Green-blue with black spots. Appears from end of June to end of September. Frequents forest clearings, footpaths near ponds and rivers, etc. Develops 2—3 years. Predacious larvae live among aquatic plants at bottom of stagnant water. Often catch small fish or tadpoles.

6 *Gomphus vulgatissimus*. Abundant everywhere in central Europe. Length 33—37 mm. Appears from May to end of July. Flies quickly, catches insects on wing. Female lays eggs in water while flying. Relatively thick-bodied larvae breathe with intestinal gills. Predacious, catch chiefly insect larvae, small tadpoles and newt larvae. Usually take 3 years to develop.

7 *Libellula quadrimaculata*. Widely distributed in Europe. Length 27—32 mm. Appears from May to middle of August. Rapid, apparently aimless, zigzag flight. Catches insects on wing. Female lays eggs in water while flying. Stout, fat larvae live mainly at bottom of small ponds and pools. Development takes 2 years. Form of migration in large numbers over considerable distances observed.

8 *Libellula depressa*. Abundant local incidence in Europe. Length 22—28 mm. Flat abdomen, sky-blue in male, brownish in female. Appears from May to beginning of August. Found near ponds and rivers but also far from water. Female lays eggs on surface of stagnant water. Larva short, fat and grey-brown. Development takes 2 years. This species also often migrates in large numbers.

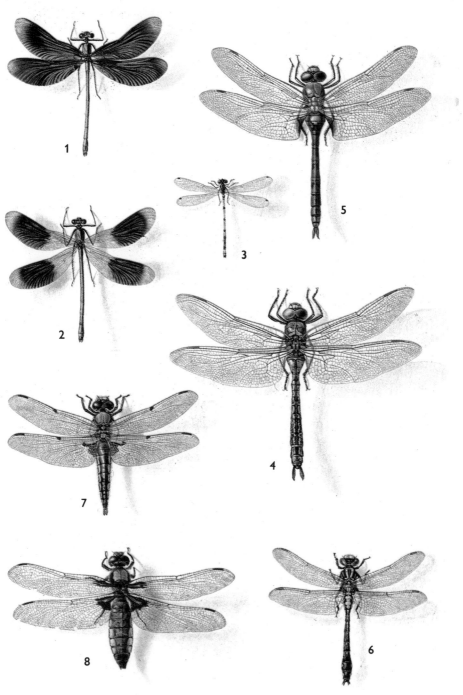

Order: **Straight-winged Insects** — *Orthoptera*

Family: **Green Grasshoppers** — *Tettigoniidae*

1 Katydid or **Green Grasshopper** *Tettigonia viridissima*. Common all over central Europe. Length 28—35 mm. Long antennae. Adult specimens can fly. Female has long ovipositor. Appears from July to October in lowlands and uplands. Males can often be heard chirping loudly in evening from tall trees, but often also during daytime. Female lays 70—100 eggs in soil. Nymphs live in meadows. Last moult before complete maturation end of July. Larvae and adult insects largely predacious. Catch different insects, occasionally also eat plants.

2 *Decticus verrucivorus*. Abundant in places. Length 22—35 mm. Spotted wings. Lives in grass or clover fields. Appears from June to September. Carnivorous. Nymphs often gregarious.

Family: **Crickets** — *Gryllidae*

3 Old World Field Cricket *Gryllus campestris*. Distributed over most of Europe. Length 20—25 mm. Lives in dry meadows and slopes in lowlands. Appears from May to July. Digs burrows as hideaways. Solitary, except at pairing time, when male chirps loudly to attract female. Female lays up to 300 eggs in ground with ovipositor. Nymphs hibernate, mature following spring. Lives on vegetable and flesh diet.

4 House Cricket *Acheta domestica*. Originally from Mediterranean region, brought to Europe for laboratory purposes. Length 15—25 mm. Frequents warm places, requires at least 10°C. Diverse diet. Female lays eggs in damp soil, etc., up to 4,000 during its 2 months' life span. According to temperature, nymphs are hatched in 8—30 days and moult 9—11 times before turning into adults. Male chirps. Does not fly very well but spreads easily.

Family: **Mole Crickets** — *Gryllotalpidae*

5 Common Mole Cricket *Gryllotalpa gryllotalpa*. Locally abundant over whole of Europe. Length 35—50 mm. Forelimbs resemble mole's. Flies clumsily. Adults found from May to September. Lives in earth and digs burrows. Male chirps on warm days. Female lays up to 300 eggs in underground chamber lined with saliva. Nymphs hibernate, mature following spring. Lives on vegetable and flesh diet. Garden pest in some places. Tries to get quickly under ground as it is awkward above it.

Family: **Field Grasshoppers** — *Acrididae*

6 *Stenobothrus lineatus*. Very common in central Europe. Length 16—23 mm. Lives in dry meadows and steppes. Appears from July to September. Males chirp by drawing teeth on inner aspect of femora over ridges on wing case. Female has ovipositor and lays eggs in ground. Eats plants, but does not do much damage.

7 *Omocestus viridulus*. Very common in central Europe. Length 13—24 mm. Particularly abundant in uplands. Found in dry places on hillsides and in meadows from July to September. Female greenish, male grey-brown. Lives on parts of plants, but does little damage. Eggs laid in ground.

8 *Psophus stridulus*. Abundant local incidence. Length 20—34 mm. Red underwings, seen only when it soars into air. Appears from July to October in dry, sunny, often rocky places, in forest clearings and on hillsides. Male flies with creaking sound. Female lays eggs in piles in ground, wrapping them, like other grasshoppers, in frothy secretion. Eggs hibernate. Larvae, hatched in spring, have huge appetite. Adult form attained after 5 moults. Vegetarian.

9 *Oedipoda coerulescens*. Abundant in places. Length 16—24 mm. Bluish underwings. Seen from July to September.

Order: **Bugs** — *Heteroptera*

Family: **Water-boatmen** — *Corixidae*

1 Water-boatman *Corixa punctata*. Common all over central Europe. Length about 10 mm. Found in every larger pool or pond. Occurs often in winter, below ice. Flies on summer evenings, frequently enters open windows. Produces creaking sounds under water.

Family: **Back-swimmers** — *Notonectidae*

2 *Notonecta glauca*. Distributed over whole of central Europe. Length about 20 mm, spindle-shaped body. Inhabits stagnant water. Rows with long hindlegs, usually upside down. Predacious. Hunts other insects, stabs them with proboscis and sucks them dry. Its prick can be felt. Flies on summer nights.

Family: **Water-scorpions** — *Nepidae*

3 Water-scorpion *Nepa cinerea*. Very common in fishpond regions. Length 20—25 mm. Pincer-like forelimbs for catching prey, e.g. insects and fish fry. Long breathing tube at end of body. Lives at bottom of stagnant or slow-flowing water. Sucks prey dry.

4 Water Stick-insect *Ranatra linearis*. Occurs in fishpond regions, at bottom of stagnant water. Long, stick-like body with long legs. Length 30—40 mm. Breathing tube at end of body. Predacious. Catches aquatic insects and larvae with forelimbs and sucks them dry. Stabs painfully.

Family: **Pond Skaters** — *Gerridae*

5 Common Water-strider *Gerris lacustris*. Common European insect. Length about 20 mm. Found on surface of stagnant water or creeks. End of body and legs covered with non-wetting hairs allowing it to run swiftly over water surface. Predacious, catches insects on surface. Reproduces on land.

Family: **Soldier-bugs** — *Reduviidae*

6 Red Assassin-bug *Rhynocoris iracundus*. Widespread in central Europe. Length up to 15 mm. Slim body, long legs. Lives on sunny grassy slopes, frequents umbelliferous flowers and other plants. Predacious. Catches insects and sucks their body juices. Lies motionless in wait for prey. Stabs painfully.

Family: **Fire-bugs** — *Pyrrhocoridae*

7 Common Fire-bug *Pyrrhocoris apterus*. Abundant everywhere in central Europe. Length about 10 mm. Found most often at foot of lime- and chestnut-trees, behind loose bark and on walls. Appears from early spring until late autumn. Occurs in masses, together with nymphs. Lives on juices of dead insects, fruit and seeds.

Family: **Marginated Bugs** — *Coreidae*

8 Marginated Bug *Coreus marginatus*. Very widely distributed. Length about 15 mm. Has almost square head. Flies on warm days. Lives on bushes and plants. Emits characteristic acrid odour. Vegetarian.

Family: **Stink-bugs** — *Pentatomidae*

9 Cabbage-bug *Eurydema oleraceum*. Common all over Europe. Length 5.5—7 mm. Metallic lustre, somewhat variable colouring. Occurs on outskirts of fields, etc. Sucks plant juices and in large numbers causes great damage. Mainly attacks brassicaceous plants. Important pest.

10 Striped Bug *Graphosoma lineatum*. Inhabits southern Europe and warm parts of central Europe. Length about 10 mm. Found in gardens on carrot plants, in forests on flowers, raspberry canes, etc. Summer insects. In south does damage to cereals.

11 Red-legged Stink-bug *Pentatoma rufipes*. Very common. Length 13—16 mm. Appears in summer in gardens and woods, especially on oaks and alders. Hunts, stabs and sucks caterpillars, but lives mainly on plant juices. Damages berry-bearing plants, cherry-trees, etc. Nymphs hibernate behind scales of bark.

1

3

2

6

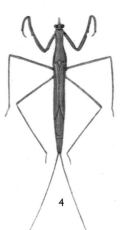

7

8

4

9

10

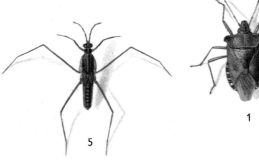

5

1

Order: **Plant-bugs** — *Homoptera*

Sub-order: **Cicadas** — *Cicadoidea*

1 Mountain Cicada *Cicadetta montana*. Inhabits only warm parts of central Europe, e.g. Danube basin. Length about 25 mm. Males have special chirping apparatus between thorax and abdomen. Punctures bark and twigs. Ground-dwelling larvae suck roots of trees. Development takes several years.

2 Blood-red Spittle-bug *Cercopis sanguinolenta*. Very common in some parts of central Europe. Length about 10 mm. Lives on plants in lowland meadows. Appears from June to August. Female lays eggs in grass. Larvae hatch in spring and suck plant juices. Larvae secrete liquid into which they pump air, turning it into protective froth.

3 Froth-bug *Philaenus spumarius*. Occurs over whole of Europe. Length about 10 mm. Frequents meadows and margins of forests. Female lays eggs chiefly in willow twigs. Hatched larvae suck these twigs. Greenish larva lives in protective froth. Matures after 5 moults. Adult insect can fly and hop well.

4 Green Leaf-hopper *Empoasca decipiens*. Abundant all over Europe. Length about 3 mm. Small and inconspicuous. Appears from June to September in deciduous woods and gardens. In large numbers does damage by sucking trees. Over 200 similar species in Europe, many of which are injurious to cereals and other crops.

Sub-order: **Plant-lice** — *Aphidoidea*

5 Black Bean Aphid *Aphis fabae*. Very common in Europe. Small and black. Spends winter on spindle-trees, from which winged females fly to poppies, sugar-beet plants, etc. and suck their juices. In large numbers causes plants to wither and die.

6 *Acyrthosiphon onobrychis*. Abundant in central Europe. Summer insect, occurs mainly on peas but also on other plants. Sucks juice in stems. Like other plant-lice, unfertilized females produce live young (parthenogenesis), fertilized females lay autumn eggs. Males, which are smaller than females, hatch from fertilized eggs. Colony is founded by wingless female hatched from fertilized egg.

7 *Megoura vicia*. Common summer insect, forms colonies on vetches, etc. Biology similar to preceding species.

8 Woolly Aphid *Eriosoma lanigerum*. Widespread over most of Europe, but originally from America. Chiefly attacks apple-trees. Lives in colonies which look like white tufts of cotton-wool. Actual body brown, contains blood-red fluid. Larva hibernates behind bark or in ground. During summer reproduces without fertilization. Males and egg-laying females hatch in autumn. One of most dangerous fruit pests.

9 Yellow Fig Gall-louse *Sacchiphantes abietis*. Widely distributed in Europe. Length about 1.5 mm. Lives permanently on firs. By sucking twigs induces formation of scaly galls. All generations, fertilized and unfertilized, lay only eggs. Fertilized female of last generation lays single egg, larva of which hibernates.

Sub-order: **Scale-insects** — *Coccoidea*

10 *Eulecanium corni*. Abundant in Europe. Length of female about 5 mm., male 2.5 mm. Lives mainly on plum-trees, ashes, hazels, etc. Wingless female firmly sessile on bark. Lays eggs under its pustulate body. Winged male eats no food. Larvae, after hibernating on roots of trees, suck twigs and females acquire pustulate, sessile form.

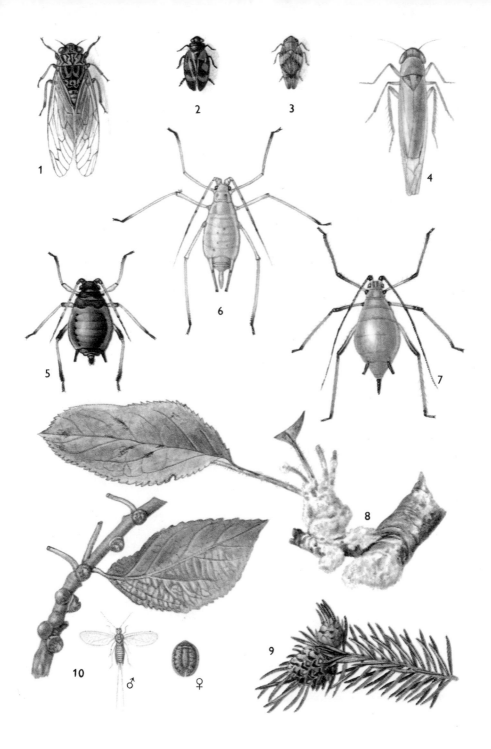

Order: **Wasps, Ants and Bees** — *Hymenoptera*

Family: **Sawflies** — *Tenthredinidae*

1 *Pontania viminalis.* Small sawfly, very common round water. Female lays eggs on underside of blade of willow leaves. This induces formation of reddish galls, harmless to trees

2 Lesser Fir Sawfly *Lygaeonematus abietinus.* Length 4.5—6 mm. Appears at end of April. Males hatched first. Female lays up to 100 eggs in young fir needles. Greenish larvae, hatched in 4 days devour needles. In June pupate in mould, in cocoon. Pest.

Family: **Cimbicid Sawflies** — *Cimbicidae*

3 Cimbicid Sawfly *Cimbex femorata.* Resembles large wasp but has club-tipped antennae. Bright green larva with red-striped back nibbles birch leaves, hibernates on branch in tough, parchment-like brown cocoon and pupates in it following spring. Does no damage.

Family: **Wood Wasps** — *Siricidae*

4 Horse-tail *Urocerus gigas.* Common, very striking over 40 mm. long, with cylindrical body. Female bores holes up to 1 5 cm. deep in healthy fir wood with its long ovipositor. In each hole lays 4 eggs — total up to 350. Appears from June to August. Larvae gnaw tunnels in wood, plug them with debris. Pupate after 2–3 years. Adult insect bites way out, often after wood has been processed. Pest.

Family: **Ichneumon Flies** — *Ichneumonidae*

5 Giant Ichneumon Fly *Rhyssa persuasoria.* Distributed over large part of Europe and Asia. Length up to over 40 mm. Inhabits large pine-woods. Female looks specifically for wood wasp larvae, pushes ovipositor into tunnel, stabs larva and lays egg in its body. Hatched larva then devours wood wasp larva. Very useful insect.

6 Sickle Wasp *Ophion luteus.* Striking appearance, common in Europe. Length about 30 mm. Curved, flat-sided abdomen. Occurs in clearings, in evening often attracted into houses by light. Parasite of large moth caterpillars. Female stabs caterpillar, lays eggs in its body and larvae devour caterpillar.

Family: **Braconids** — *Braconidae*

7 Vipionid *Apanteles glomeratus.* Tiny summer insect occurring in woods, gardens and meadows. Female lays eggs en masse in butterfly caterpillars, e.g. whites, fritillaries, etc. Minute larvae first of all live on host's adipose bodies. Later bore way out, immediately spin yellow cocoon and pupate. Caterpillar often surrounded by cluster of cocoons.

Family: **Aphid Wasps** — *Aphidiidae*

8 Aphid Wasp *Diaeretus rapae.* Very small and very common. Female lays egg in abdomen of plant-louse. Hatched larva devours contents of host's body and pupates inside it. Adult insect leaves dead host through hole which can often be seen on shrivelled plant-lice. Very useful species.

Family: **Gall-wasps** — *Cynipidae*

9 Oak Gall-fly *Cynips quercusfolii.* Abundant everywhere. Adult insect inconspicuous, but eggs give rise to galls, housing larvae, on underside of oak leaves ('oak-apples'). Larva pupates in autumn and insect often hatch early in winter. Females emerging at end of February lay unfertilized eggs in buds and these develop into gall-wasps of both sexes. Males measure only about 2 mm. Fertilized females lay eggs on leaves and cycle is repeated.

10 Robin's Pin Cushion or **Bedeguar Gall** *Diplolepis rosae.* Most widely distributed gall-wasp. Length 4—5 mm. Adult insect seldom noticed, but known from moss-like reddish or greenish galls containing larvae on rose-bushes and dog-roses. Only one generation known — females reproducing by parthenogenesis.

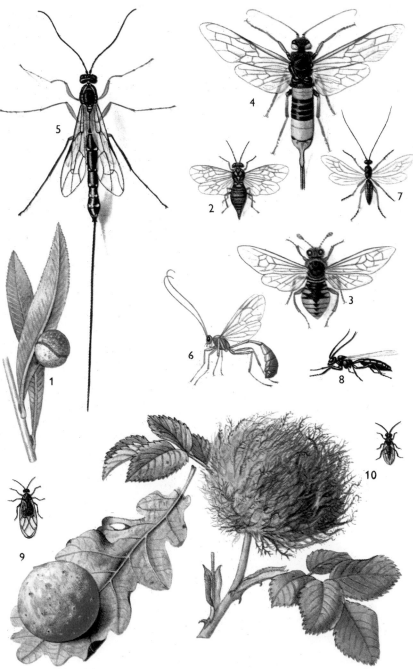

Family: **Beetle-wasps** — *Scoliidae*

1 Yellow-headed Beetle-wasp *Scolia flavifrons*. Huge wasp living in warm parts of Europe — in central Europe in south-east and south. Length about 50 mm. On sunny days can be seen on flowers. Female lays eggs on larvae of rhinoceros beetle. Hatched larva devours host's body from within and pupates beside its remains.

Family: **Mutillids** or **Velvet Ants** — *Mutillidae*

2 Velvet Ant *Mutilla europaea*. Common in central Europe. Slight resemblance to ant. Brightly coloured. Female wingless. Male visits flowers, female crawls on ground looking for bumble-bee nests. Lays eggs in body of bumble-bee larvae.

Family: **True Wasps** — *Vespidae*

3 Hornet *Vespa crabro*. Large wasp, abundant in places. Mainly inhabits old forests. Builds large, yellow-brown, papery nest in tree hollows, nesting-boxes, etc. Fertilized female hibernates in hiding-place. In spring lays foundations of nest by scratching away rotting wood and sticking it together with saliva, and sets up first comb. First larvae develop into workers which continue in building nest. Males and females hatch in autumn. After females have been fertilized, whole community except females dies. Hornets are predacious, attack other insects. Their sting is dangerous.

4 Pollistes Wasp *Polistes gallica*. Moderately large wasp, abundant in sunny places. Forms simple papery comb with several cells. Nest attached by stalk to base, usually wall, rock, etc., often also bush. Larvae develop into workers which lay eggs giving rise to males —drones. In the Alps and further north often builds nest in enclosed space, holes, nesting-boxes, etc.

5 Common Wasp *Paravespula vulgaris*. Commonest ground-dwelling wasp. Lives in large colonies founded by female. Builds first cells on stalk in hole in ground and lays eggs. Feeds hatched larvae for 20 days. Workers hatched 20 days after pupating. They extend nest, add storeys separated by stalk-like supports. Carry away grains of sand, etc., to widen hole. Workers can number up to 2,000. Nest has 5—14 combs. Life in community expires in autumn. Females — queens — hibernate in tree hollows, rooms in houses, etc.

6 German Wasp *Paravespula germanica*. Common all over Europe. Builds underground nests in fields. In south huge nests with about 60,000 members. In September nest contains average of 1,600 workers, 1,600 males and 700 females. Likes warmth, does not fly in cold weather. Diurnal insect. Lives on sweet fruit juice, nectar, etc. Offspring fed mainly on insects. Very aggressive if disturbed, attacks all intruders.

Family: **Potter Wasps** — *Eumenidae*

7 Potter Wasp *Eumenes coarctatus*. Inhabits whole of Europe. Solitary wasp. Length 11 to 15 mm. Builds fat-bellied, short-necked nest of clay and saliva on forest bushes or heather. Feeds larvae on small, hairless caterpillars, especially of geometers. Larvae frequently parasitised by other wasps (fire wasps).

Family: **Digger Wasps** — *Psammocharidae*

8 Brown Spider Wasp *Psammocharus fuscus*. Common in warm places all over Europe. Length 10—14 mm. Seen early in spring on flowering sallows. In sandy spots digs holes ending in chamber for larva, for which it brings spiders. Paralyses even large spiders with sting, when helpless drags them to nest. Though paralyzed, spider sometimes lives over month and larva feeds on its body.

Family: **Ants** — *Formicidae*

1 Red Wood Ant *Formica rufa*. Abundant in Europe. Several races with different biology. In one, only one female in nest, in another up to 5,000 females and annual production of up to 2 million individuals. Builds large, domed nest of conifer needles, leaves, etc. Winged males and females hold nuptial flight in summer. Omnivorous. Catch any form of life they can. Useful, destroy all insects within distance of 20 m. from nest. Length of workers 4 to 9 mm., females 9—11 mm.

2—4 Black or **Garden Ant** *Lasius niger*. Very widespread. Worker (4) 3—5 mm., male (2) and female (3) much larger. Underground nest with superstructure above ground. Pairing on warm summer days. After nuptial flight return to ground, females shed wings and males mostly die. Female founds new community and as soon as first workers are hatched confines itself only to egg-laying. After a time new males and females are hatched and cycle is repeated. Omnivorous. Partiality for secretions of plant-lice.

Family: **Thread-waisted Wasps** — *Sphegidae*

5 Red-bearded Fan Wasp *Ammophila sabulosa*. In Europe abundant in dry, sandy places. Length 18—20 mm. Digs burrows about 3 cm. long with chamber at end for larva. On leaving covers hole with small stone. Brings paralyzed pine hawk caterpillars for larva. Sits astride caterpillar and tugs it with jaws. Drags it into nest and attaches egg to its body. Firmly fills in entrance to nest and then builds another.

6 Bee-killer Wasp *Philanthus triangulum*. Inhabits warm parts of Europe. Length 12 to 16 mm. Occurs chiefly on sandy slopes, digs nests. Pounces on bees, falls with them to ground, quickly paralyses them and takes them to larvae. In large numbers damaging to honeybee population.

7 Sand Wasp *Bembex rostrata*. In central Europe common in warm, sandy places. Robust body. Prolongated upper lip. Digs tunnels up to 40 cm. long in sandy slopes or moors. Usually lives in colonies. Closes entrance with sand but finds nest unerringly. Catches flies, paralyses them with sting and takes them to larva. Also catches large gadflies and hover-flies. Larvae have huge appetite. Although well concealed, nest is found by scorpion-fly which rakes it open and lays egg on sand wasp larva.

Family: **Cuckoo Wasps** — *Chrysididae*

8 Fire Wasp *Chrysis ignita*. Very common in southern and central Europe. Length about 5 mm. Has concave abdomen and can curl up if in danger. Female has protrusible ovipositor. Frequents sunny walls, fences, etc. Looks for nests of solitary wasps, especially mason wasps of the genus *Odynerus*. Female forces way into nest, places egg on larva and quickly leaves. Fire wasp larva has large, hard head and jaws and lives on host's body juices. On maturing it pupates and adult insect emerges in spring. Adult fire wasp lives on nectar. Flies during summer.

9 Blue Cuckoo Wasp *Chrysis cyanea*. Abundant in central and southern Europe. Length about 4 mm. Most frequently found on old wooden fences. Biology similar to that of preceding species.

10 Copper-red Cuckoo Wasp *Chrysis cuprea*. Abundant local incidence in central Europe. Length 5—6 mm. Biology similar to that of fire wasp. On invading foreign nests, many cuckoo wasps are caught in act by very strong occupant. Cuckoo wasp folds feelers under head and curls up, leaving only its hard chitinous armour exposed so that water usually simply throws cuckoo wasp out without harming it.

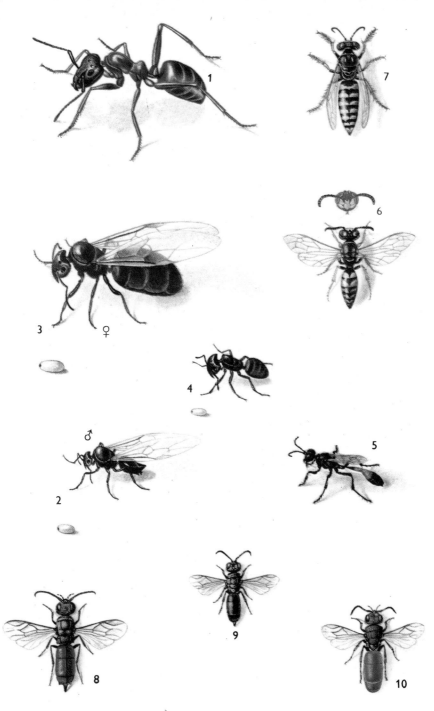

Family: **Bees** — *Apidae*

1 Blue Carpenter Bee *Xylocopa violacea*. Inhabits southern Europe and warm parts of central Europe. Resembles large bumble-bee. Has black-brown wings with violet sheen. Female bores vertical shafts up to 30 cm. deep in old wood, dividing them into chambers with partitions made of wood debris and saliva. Usually 12 chambers in each of which bee places stock of food and lays one egg.

2 Leaf-cutter Bee *Megachile centuncularis*. Distributed over warm parts of Europe. Length 10—12 mm. Female gnaws tunnels in old wood, lines them with fragments of leaves cut from bushes, chiefly dog-roses and garden roses. Places first cell on floor of tunnel, fills it with pollen, lays egg and closes cell with leaf. 'Cylinder' with 8—10 cells formed in tunnel.

3 Potter Bee *Anthidium manicatum*. Lives in warmer parts of Europe. With partly hairless, yellow-striped abdomen resembles wasp. Male has 'notched' abdomen and is larger than female. Lines nest with plant fluff.

4 Horned Bee *Eucera longicornis*. Lives in southern Europe and warm parts of central Europe. Length 10—12 mm. Locally abundant. Male has extremely long antennae. Appears in spring on sunny slopes and hillsides. Favours plants with composite flowers. Has very long mouth parts and can suck nectar from deep flowers.

5 Black Burrowing Bee *Andrena carbonaria*. Abundant all over Europe except for extreme north. Solitary bee. Length 10- 12 mm. Appears early in spring. Likes dandelions. Digs nest in ground, often in colonies. Long, slanting passages branch off into several side-chambers, each containing pollen and one egg.

6 Hairy-legged Mining Bee *Dasypoda hirtipes*. Fairly common in central Europe. Collects so much pollen on long hairs on hindlimbs that appears to be wearing trousers. Builds underground nest like preceding species.

7 Mourner Bee or **Armed Melecta** *Melecta armata*. Abundant in central Europe. Length 10—12 mm. Appears early in spring. Female stays near burrowing bees, enters their nests and lays egg before occupant can close chamber. Hatched larva consumes food stocks and burrowing bee larva starves to death.

8 Digger Bumble-bee *Bombus terrestris*. Very common all over Europe. After hibernating female lays foundations of nest in mouse-holes, etc., up to 1.5 m. underground. Lines nest with leaves, moss, etc., found in hole. Builds waxy chambers and fills them with pollen and nectar. Larvae also receive additional food. Up to 150 workers and over 100 young females hatch in 20 days. Workers die in autumn, males, old and young females go into hiding and hibernate.

9 Rock Bumble-bee *Bombus lapidarius*. Widely distributed in central Europe. Black with red-tipped abdomen. Nests underground, in piles of stones, rock crevices, etc. Not more than 300 individuals in nest.

10 Honeybee *Apis mellifica*. Universal insect, probably originally from India. Forms permanent community, always with one female — queen. In summer large number of males (drones) and up to 70,000 workers. Only queen lays eggs, in cells in waxy comb. Three types of cells, for workers, males and females. Queen lays up to 1,000 eggs daily in summer — total for one season up to 80,000. If queen is lost, workers rear new one. Development rapid, for workers 20 days. Queen lives 3—4 years. Swarm once or several times a year, after queen has prepared eggs for new queens. Old queen leaves hive and, accompanied by some workers, forms new community.

1

2

10

3

4

5

6

7

10

8

9

Order: **Beetles** — *Coleoptera*

Family: **Tiger Beetles** — *Cicindelidae*

1 *Cicindela campestris.* Locally abundant in Europe. Length 12—16 mm. Very large, striking mandibles. Appears from April to June. Frequents sunny, sandy places, paths, deserted quarries, etc. Runs about swiftly looking for prey, spots it reliably at distance of up to 15 cm. Catches mainly insect larvae, spiders and worms. If disturbed, immediately flies away but does not fly in cold weather. Larvae live in burrows up to 2 m. deep in clay or sandy soil. Larva has strongly sclerotized head. Waits at entrance to hole for prey (chiefly various insects), seizes it and devours it in burrow. Holds itself fast in passage by means of boss on abdomen. Development of larva takes 2—3 years. Pupates in July, beetles are hatched 4 weeks later and reproduce further following spring.

2 *Cicindela hybrida.* Lives mainly in forested regions. Length 12—14 mm. Beetles found in May and June on sandy forest paths and moors. Biology similar to that of preceding species.

3 *Cicindela silvatica.* Common in places. Length 14—16 mm. Appears in June on forest paths, in clearings, etc., mainly in pine-woods. Biology as for *Cicindela campestris.*

Family: **Ground Beetles** — *Carabidae*

4 *Carabus hortensis.* Locally abundant in central Europe. Length 24—30 mm. Found in forests and gardens, on bushy slopes, etc. Nocturnal predator. Catches insects, insect larvae, worms and small molluscs. Hides during day behind bark, under stones, etc. Like all ground beetles likes damp environment. In dry, waterless places dies in a few days. Long-bodied, large-jawed larvae also predacious. Catches other insect larvae, worms, etc.

5 Goldsmith *Carabus auratus.* Abundant in parts of central Europe, particularly Germany, but absent east of Oder. Length 22—26 mm. Seen mainly in May and June, in meadows, fields and gardens. Prefers clayey soil. Also found at higher altitudes. Often hunts in day-time. Eats worms, molluscs and soft parts of insects. Attacks cockchafers when laying eggs. All members of *Carabus* genus spray chewed parts of prey with gastric juice which quickly decomposes connective tissue and organs, making them easy to imbibe. Several beetles may attack a large worm. In spring and summer female lays single eggs in holes in ground — total about 50. Larvae, hatched in 8—10 days, are very predacious. Pupate in chamber in ground. Newly emerged beetles hibernate from end of August, majority of adult beetles die. Development from egg to young beetle takes 78 days.

6 *Carabus coriaceus.* Largest central-European ground beetle. Length up to 40 mm. Occurs in forests mainly in July and August. Nocturnal insect. Hides during day under stones, fallen trees, etc. In rainy weather crawls on to paths. Beetle and larva are both predacious.

7 Violet Ground Beetle *Carabus violaceus.* Very common in central Europe. Length 25—35 mm. Appears mainly in June and July near human dwellings, often found in sheds, cellars, etc. If handled ejects acrid fluid.

8 *Carabus cancellatus.* Very common everywhere in central Europe. Length 17—26 mm. Appears chiefly in May in woods, fields and gardens. Runs very quickly, 1 metre in 5—7 sec. Hides during day under stones, behind bark, etc. Very useful, destroys Colorado beetles. One specimen devours 9 Colorado beetle larvae daily, i.e. more than its own weight. Average time of development from egg to beetle takes 71 days under artificial breeding conditions.

Family: **Ground Beetles** — *Carabidae*

1 Searcher or **Caterpillar Hunter** *Calosoma sycophanta*. Distributed over practically whole of Europe. Length 24—30 mm. Very handsome beetle. Predacious. Climbs trees in search of prey, chiefly caterpillars. Female after hibernating lays 100—600 eggs. Larvae, hatched in 3—10 days, are likewise highly predacious. In 14 days one beetle (and also one larva) consumes about 40 large caterpillars. In June larva pupates in ground. Adult beetle hatched in September, does not emerge into open until following year in May. Early in July beetles leave trees and again burrow up to depth of 50 cm. in ground and hibernate. Beetle lives 2—3 years. Inhabits both deciduous and conifer woods at low and high altitudes.

2 Lesser Searcher *Calosoma inquisitor*. Found everywhere in central Europe. Length 15 to 18 mm. Lives primarily in oak-woods in lowlands. In years with a high incidence of caterpillars appears in great numbers already at end of April or beginning of May. Frequents tree tops, catches mainly caterpillars of geometers and other harmful moths. Retires to burrow in ground at beginning of July and hibernates. Larvae likewise predacious.

3 Bombardier Beetle *Brachynus crepitans*. Common in central Europe. Length 6—9 mm. Several individuals always live in company under stones in warm, sunny spots. When in danger, discharges from anal gland volatile fluid which turns to blue smoke with audible bang. Such 'salvoes' reliably frighten small foes away. The secretion burns and slightly resembles nitric acid.

4 *Pterostichus vulgaris*. Very widely distributed. Length 14—20 mm. Hides during day under flat stones etc. in damp, shady places. Runs quickly. Abundant everywhere, especially in central Europe.

5 *Zabrus gibbus*. Very common everywhere in central Europe. Length 14—16 mm. Adult beetles cling to cereal plants and devour grains. Larvae nibble young spring shoots or grass. In daytime both larvae and beetles hide in holes dug in ground.

Family: **Water Beetles** — *Dytiscidae*

6 Tiger Water Beetle *Dytiscus marginalis*. Common all over Europe. Length 30—35 mm. Male has widened tarsi. Inhabits ponds and pools etc. with abundant aquatic vegetation. Female makes slits in plant stems and into each pushes one egg. Larva has three-sided head with powerful, hooked mandibles, used for sucking tadpoles, small fish, etc. Beetles also predacious. Larva pupates beside water. Beetles fly in evening.

7 *Acilius sulcatus*. Distributed over whole of Europe. Length about 18 mm. Inhabits stagnant water with at least a little vegetation. Flies at night and sometimes visits man-made pools. Does damage to fish roes. Larvae, likewise predacious, lie in wait for prey among tangled aquatic plants.

Family: **Whirligig Beetles** — *Gyrinidae*

8 Common Whirligig Beetle *Gyrinus natator*. Common in places. Length 5—7 mm. Small but conspicuous for its gyrating movements on surface of still water. Dives like lightning when in danger. Predacious, catches small insects. Flies well. Larvae have hollow, hooked mandibles. Beetles usually gregarious.

Family: **Water Scavenger Beetles** — *Hydrophilidae*

9 Great Black Water Beetle *Hydrous piceus*. Locally common in central Europe. Length 35—45 mm. Inhabits stagnant water with plenty of vegetation. Beetle partly vegetarian but eats also fish roes. Female lays eggs in special capsule made of secretory substance and containing about 50 eggs. Larvae, hatched in 16 days, are predacious.

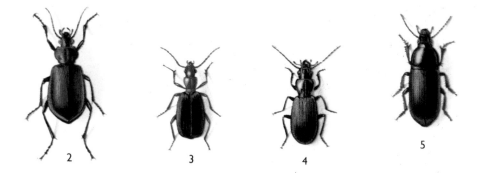

2   3   4   5

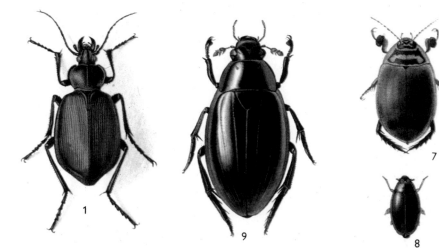

1   9   7

8

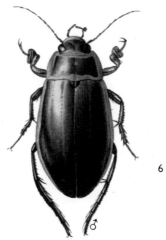

6 ♂   ♀

Family: **Rover Beetles** — *Staphylinidae*

1 *Staphylinus caesareus.* Widely distributed all over central Europe. Length 15—20 mm. Summer insect. Adult beetles found on putrefying flesh, rotting matter, etc. Beetles and larvae live on decaying matter but also attack insects, worms and molluscs. Larvae resemble adult beetles but have no wings or wing sheaths.

2 *Oxyporus rufus.* Distributed all over central Europe. Length 7—11 mm. Abounds in different mushrooms starting to decompose. Larvae also live in large numbers in mushrooms. One of the causes of 'wormy' mushrooms.

Family: **Sexton and Carrion Beetles** — *Silphidae*

3 Common Sexton or **Gravedigger Beetle** *Necrophorus vespillo.* Common European beetle. Length 12—22 mm. In evening and at night beetles look for animal carcass and scrape away earth under body until animal is burried. Female then lays eggs on body and larvae live on putrefying flesh. Larvae pupate in chamber in ground. Beetles often infested by mites of *Gamasus* genus.

4 German Gravedigger Beetle *Necrophorus germanicus.* Locally and sporadically found in Europe. Length 20—30 mm. Found under carcasses of larger animals, e.g. hares, rabbits, etc. Very retiring. Flies only at night. One of the largest but rarest members of this family.

5 Black Carrion Beetle *Phosphuga atrata.* Widespread in central Europe. Length 12 to 16 mm. Wing sheaths have three longitudinal ridges. Found from May under stones, paper, etc., in fields and on paths. Often crawls in open. Lives on dead snails and worms but sometimes attacks even live ones. In danger releases malodorous substance.

6 Four-spot Carrion Beetle *Xylodrepa quadripunctata.* Very common in central Europe. Length 12—14 mm. Inhabits oak-woods. Appears in spring. Lives on trees, attacks and eats caterpillars. Beetles disappear in June and are replaced by flat, predacious, caterpillar-eating larvae. At end of summer larvae pupate in ground. Beetles hatch in autumn, hibernate in ground and emerge following spring.

Family: **Steel** or **Hister Beetles** — *Histeridae*

7 Steel Beetle *Hister unicolor.* Distributed all over central Europe. Length 7—9 mm. Very hard body. Beetles frequently live in cow dung, horse manure, etc. Catch and eat small insects. Many other species in Europe, some with black, red-spotted wing sheaths.

Family: **Carpet Beetles** — *Dermestidae*

8 Larder Beetle *Dermestes lardarius.* Carried with furs all over world. Length 6—9 mm. Found in stores, households and open country. Larva's back thickly covered with long hairs. In open larvae live on remnants of skin of dead animals, on feathers, etc. Also found in collections of hides, stuffed birds, etc. Development often takes only 6 weeks. Beetles and larvae frequently found on food remnants, e.g. cheese, meat, etc.

9 Tallow Beetle *Anthrenus museorum.* Distributed all over Europe. Length 2—3 mm. Spherical body. Common pest in natural history collections. Damage done by both beetle and larva. Larvae 5 mm. long and hairy. Beetles often seen in flowers.

10 Carpet Beetle *Attagenus pellio.* Occurs everywhere. Length 4—7 mm. Very dangerous to furs, stuffed animals, carpets, upholstery, etc. Often found trying to get out of window. Hairy larva about 5 mm. long. Adults often seen also on flowers. In the illustration the rare species *A. punctatus.*

1

2

3

4

5

7

9

10

6

8

Family: **Stag Beetles** — *Lucanidae*

1 Common Stag Beetle *Lucanus cervus*. Inhabits whole of central Europe, from south of northern Europe as far west as Portugal. Length of male 37—75 mm., female 30—45 mm. Inhabits oak-woods and mixed forests. Female lays eggs in rotting oak stumps and trunks. Blind larvae develop 3—5 years and attain length of up to 10 cm. Future beetle's sex already discernible in pupa. Beetles hatch in autumn but do not leave hiding place until spring. By day frequent tree trunks with flowing sap. Fly in evening.

2 Balkan Stag Beetle *Dorcus parallelopipedus*. Distributed over large part of Europe. Length 20—32 mm. Abundant in places with sufficient old wood for development of larvae. Beetles rest on branches during day, fly only in late afternoon and evening. Appear at end of April and are still found in September. Larvae develop in rotting wood.

Family: **Chafers** — *Scarabaeidae*

3 Horned Dung Beetle *Copris lunaris*. Found in warmer parts of central Europe. Length 15—23 mm. Male has pointed horn on head. Mainly frequents cow dung. Makes chamber below dung from which female prepares food stocks for larvae.

4 Dung Beetle *Aphodius fimetarius*. Widely distributed over whole of Europe, Asia and North America. Length 5—8 mm. Female lays eggs in cow or horse dung which provides food for larvae. Some individuals hibernate and can often already be seen on sunny days at beginning of March.

5 Great Dor Beetle *Geotrupes stercorosus*. Inhabits whole of Europe. Length 12— 19 mm. Exclusively forest-dweller, usually found on carcasses, mushrooms, etc. In May and June digs vertical shaft up to 60 cm. deep, with side-arms, below excreta. Female fills passages wi.h dung and lays eggs. Larvae live on dung, hibernate and do not pupate until following year.

6 Common Cockchafer or **May-bug** *Melolontha melolontha*. Native of Europe. Length 20 to 30 mm. From May to June female lays 3 clutches of 15—30 eggs in ground. Larvae (grubs) develop 2—3 years and then pupate. Hatched beetle spends winter in ground and emerges following spring. Grubs eat small roots. Beetles nibble leaves of trees. Fly in evening. Usually swarm in middle of June. Incidence of cockchafers correlated to whether population development takes 3 or 4 years.

7 June-bug *Rhizotrogus solstitialis*. Distributed all over Europe. Length 14—18 mm. Very abundant. Flies after dusk, in some years in large numbers. Appears from June to beginning of August. Female lays eggs in July, in soft soil. Larvae, hatched about one month later, eat grass and cereal roots, etc. Pupate in spring of third year. Adults eat leaves of fruit trees. Important pest.

8 Walker *Polyphylla fullo*. Occurs in central Europe and southern England. Length 25 to 36 mm. Inhabits sandy lowlands. Female lays 25—40 eggs in sandy soil from June to August. Larvae eat grass roots. Pupate after 3 years. Three weeks later, in June, adult beetles fly out after dusk. Larvae sometimes hibernate fourth year and beetles do not appear until fifth. Larvae sometimes do damage to vines.

9 Garden Chafer *Phyllopertha horticola*. Inhabits most of Europe and extends east as far as Mongolia. Length 8.5—11 mm. Appears from May to July, often in immense numbers. Frequents gardens, orchards, margins of woods, etc. Beetles nibble flowers. Female lays eggs in ground. Larvae, hatched in 2 weeks, gnaw roots. Development takes 2—3 years.

Family: **Chafers** — *Scarabaeidae*

1 European Rhinoceros Beetle *Oryctes nasicornis*. Inhabits practically whole of Europe. Length 25—40 mm. Very variable over vast area of distribution. Larvae develop in rotting stumps and trunks of deciduous trees, mainly oaks and beeches, but also in old compost heaps. Larvae very fat, with dilated abdomen, very hard, large head and huge mandibles. Development of larva takes several years according to conditions. Before pupating larva forms cocoon of soil and sawdust in which mature beetle also remains for up to 2 months. Adult beetle appears from June to August. Nocturnal insect.

2 Goldsmith Beetle *Cetonia aurata*. Inhabits most of Europe. Length 14—20 mm. Beetles found from middle of May well into summer on flowering dog-roses, etc. Female lays eggs in rotting tree stumps, etc. and occasionally in ant-hills. Development usually takes one year. Mature larva forms cocoon of sawdust and soil, stuck together with special secretion. Larvae moult twice and attain length of 4—5 cm.

3 Hermit Beetle *Osmoderma eremita*. Inhabits practically all Europe but occurs only locally. Not very abundant. Length 24—30 mm. Beetles appear from end of May to July. Fly well. Female lays eggs in hollows in old deciduous trees, e.g. limes, beeches, oaks. Larvae develop several years (not less than 3) and grow to length of up to 10 cm. Before pupating larva forms sawdust cocoon. Beetle gives off curious odour.

4 *Trichius fasciatus*. Occurs over practically whole of Europe. Length 9—12 mm. Wing case designs very variable. Beetles frequent flowers and flowering bushes on warm, sunny days in summer. Female lays eggs in rotting wood of deciduous trees, especially beeches. Larvae develop 2 years. Particularly abundant in wooded uplands.

Family: **Metallic** or **Flat-headed Wood-borers** — *Buprestidae*

5 Pine-borer *Chalcophora mariana*. Found in central Europe, only in warm places. Length 25—30 mm. Copper-coloured back, burnished gold underside. Inhabits pine-woods. Fond of warmth like all members of this family. Beetles appear during hottest hours of sunny days. Found on tree trunks. Larvae develop in pine tree stumps and dry trunks. Bore characteristic flat winding tunnels. Flat larva has segmented body and wide head. Does not do serious damage.

6 Lime-borer *Poecilonota rutilans*. Occurs in warm places in central Europe. Abundant in some regions. Length 10—14 mm. Shows jewel-like metallic-blue back when flying. Appears in June and July in lime tree avenues or on limes on outskirts of forests. Female lays eggs in cracks in bark on sunny side of lime trunk. Larvae, which develop 2 years, devour wood. Repeated attacks of lime-borers cause tree to wither. Dangerous pest in large numbers.

7 Common Wood-borer *Buprestis rustica*. Fairly abundant in parts of central Europe. Length 13—18 mm. Tips of wing sheaths straight-edged. Inhabits conifer woods. Larvae live behind bark or in wood of stumps and freshly felled trees, particularly spruces. Development takes 2 years.

8 Metallic Wood-borer *Anthaxia nitidula*. Inhabits warm places in central Europe. Length 5—7 mm. Beetle appears in June and July. Locally abundant, found on roses, dandelions, ox-eyes, etc. Larvae live on blackthorns.

9 Two-spot Wood-borer *Agrilus biguttatus*. Widely distributed over central Europe. Length 12 mm. Tip of wing sheaths rounded. Appears on sunny days at end of May on tree stumps and flowers. Larvae live in oak stumps.

Family: **Click Beetles** — *Elateridae*

1 Blood-red Click Beetle *Elater sanguineus*. Occurs over practically whole of Europe. Length 13—18 mm. Inhabits foothill forests. Often appears by end of March. Larvae live behind bark or in pine stumps, often gregariously. Larva measures up to 2 cm.

2 Grey Click Beetle *Adelócera murina*. Distributed all over Europe. Length 11—17 mm. Found at both low and high altitudes. Lives in meadows, fields, clearings and gardens. Larva is field and forest pest, gnaws roots and other parts of all crops and young trees. Also carnivorous. Adult beetle appears from spring to autumn and nibbles beech and oak buds. Often found on ears of corn.

3 Wheat Wire-worm *Agriotes lineatus*. Lives in whole paleoarctic region. Length 8—9 mm. Found at both low and high altitudes. Beetles appear in meadows in May and June. Larvae eat any plants, do damage to tree nurseries and in south to vineyards, etc. Pupate in soil. Development takes 3—4 years.

Family: **Leather-winged Beetles** — *Cantharidae*

4 Soldier Beetle *Cantharis fusca*. Widely distributed in Europe. Length 12 mm. Appears from spring to summer on plants, bushes and ground. Catches and eats small insects, occasionally eats also young shoots. Hairy larvae have strong mandibles and are predacious. Live under leaves, etc., look for insects and small molluscs. Larvae hibernate in ground but on sunny days often found in snow. Pupate in early spring after hibernating.

5 *Phausis splendidula*. Very common all over central Europe. Length 9—11 mm. Mainly inhabits outskirts of damp deciduous woods. Nocturnal insect. Males fly in large numbers on warm evenings at end of June and in July. Females wingless, with vestigial wing case, crawl on ground. Has brightly luminescent light organ on underside of abdomen. Females and carnivorous larvae also luminescent. Adult beetle lives only shortly. Light organ probably used to attract partner.

6 *Malachius aeneus*. Very common everywhere in central Europe. Length 7—8 mm. Soft wing case. Appears in spring on almost all flowers. Larva frequents tunnels of bark beetles and other wood beetles.

Family: **Chequered Beetles** — *Cleridae*

7 Ant Beetle *Thanasimus formicarius*. Abundant all over central Europe. Length 7—10 mm. Female lays up to 30 eggs in groups of 2—4 behind bark scales. Larvae crawl into tunnels of bark beetles and other wood beetles and attack their larvae. Larva seizes prey in first two pairs of legs, turns it on to back, bites through its body at base of abdomen and devours it from within. Larva very active. Both larva and adult beetle can hibernate.

8 Bee-eating Beetle *Trichodes apiarius*. Lives in warm places in central Europe. Length 9—15 mm. Adult beetle frequents flowers and eats other insects. Seen from May to July. Larvae mainly develop in nests of solitary bees and eat their larvae or pupae.

Family: **Death Watch Beetles** — *Anobiidae*

9 Death Watch *Anobium pertinax*. Common European beetle. Length 5—7 mm. Lives in wood or in houses in old furniture where it devours tunnels. Bangs head on walls of tunnel to attract members of opposite sex. Knocking superstitiously supposed to portend death. Female lays eggs in opening of tunnel. If repeatedly attacked, old furniture may fall to pieces. Beetle 'plays possum' if handled.

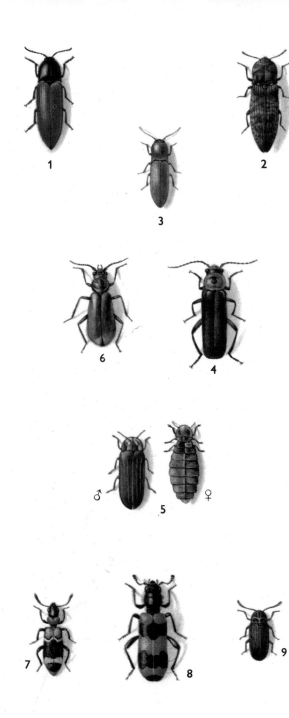

Family: **Darkling** or **Pineate Beetles** — *Tenebrionidae*

1 Cellar or **Churchyard Beetle** *Blaps mortisaga*. Widely distributed in central Europe. Length 22—28 mm. Appears from April to autumn. Often lives in houses. Hides during day under floor-boards, in cellars, etc., where larvae also live. Does no damage.

2 Meal-worm *Tenebrio molitor*. Today very common everywhere. Bred artificially. Larvae used to feed birds and lizards. Length 14—17 mm. Beetle often lives in houses, refuse, hen-houses and dove-cotes. Larvae also eat flesh, e.g. meat left on bones, dead bodies of small birds and mammals etc., otherwise found in meal stores, etc.

Family: **Blister** or **Oil Beetles** — *Meloidae*

3 Oil Beetle or **May-worm** *Meloe proscarabaeus*. Widely distributed. Length 12—35 mm. Female has large abdomen. Wingless with short wing sheaths. Appears in grass early in spring. Female lays eggs in small pits. Hatched larvae grasp different bees, including honey-bees, with claw-like legs and carry them to their nests, get into cells and devour host's egg and food stores. After complicated metamorphosis — firstly pseudopupa, then again larva — they pupate.

4 Spanish Fly *Lytta vesicatoria*. Lives in southern Europe and warmer parts of central Europe. Length 11—22 mm. Winged beetles appear en masse in June, mainly on ash trees. Eat leaves. Beetle produces potent poison, cantharidin. Female lays groups of 40—50 eggs in ground. Larvae attach themselves to bodies of solitary bees of *Osmia* genus and develop in similar way as preceding species.

Family: **Snout Beetles** or **Weevils** — *Curculionidae*

5 Pine Weevil *Hylobius abietis*. Abundant on all conifers. Length 8—14 mm. Beetle appears from May to September. Female lays 50—100 eggs in roots, bark of fresh pine, fir and larch stumps. Larvae eat bast and sap-wood. Before pupating form 'cradle'. Beetle lives several years.

6 White Pine Beetle *Pissodes piceae*. Locally common in central Europe. Length 7—12 mm. Appears on firs and is very serious pest. Sometimes multiplies to such a degree that tree is attacked from roots to crown. Female lays eggs on bark.

7 Nut Weevil *Curculio nucum*. Common in central Europe. Length 7—8 mm. Characterized by very long 'snout'. Appears from May to July. Female lays eggs in holes she has made with her 'snout' in young nuts. Larvae eat kernels.

8 *Cionus scrophulariae*. Fairly abundant. Length 4—6 mm. Can fold cylindrical 'snout' on underside of thorax. Lives gregariously on fig-wort and mullein. Legless larvae, wrapped in slimy envelope, nibble leaves and perianths. On pupation mucus hardens and protects pupa.

9 Granary Weevil *Calandra granaria*. Original home probably in southern Asia. Carried to all parts of world. Most dreaded grain pest. Length 3—4 mm. Beetle unable to fly and is spread only by carrying. Lives in badly ventilated granaries. Female lays eggs on grains of wheat, rye, etc.

Family: **Bark Beetles** — *Scolytidae*

10 *Ips typographus*. Inhabits cooler parts of Europe. Length about 4 mm. Dreaded spruce pest. Larvae devour tunnels perpendicular to maternal shaft.

11 *Dendroctonus micans*. Distributed all over central Europe. Length 6—9 mm. Inhabits spruce woods. Larvae form common widening tunnel. Beetles emerge at end of July. Attacks weakened trees.

12 *Myelophilus piniperda*. Widely distributed in Europe. Length 3.5—5 mm. Inhabits large pine-woods. Attacks mainly trunks of felled trees.

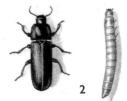

1

3

2

4

5

6

8

7

9

10

12

11

Family: **Longicorn Beetles** — *Cerambycidae*

1 *Prionus coriarius.* Inhabits whole of Europe, extends even to North Africa, Asia Minor and western Siberia. Length 19—45 mm. Male has saw-like antennae with 12 joints, female antennae with smaller teeth and 11 joints. Inhabits old deciduous, mixed and conifer woods. Very abundant in places. Larva develops in rotting trunks and oak, beech, fir, pine stumps, etc., often also in roots. Beetles swarm in July and August, often in daytime.

2 *Ergates faber.* Only locally found in Europe. Length 23—60 mm. Male's antennae longer than body, female's much shorter. Favours old pine-woods. Female lays up to over 300 single eggs usually on rotting wood which provides firm hold. Larvae often develop in old pine stumps, less often in spruce stumps. Occasionally attacks beams in wooden constructions combined with bricks, which keep wood damp. Also attacks telegraph poles, wooden fences, etc. Larvae measure up to 6.5 cm. Development takes several years. Beetles swarm at night from July to September. Adult beetle lives 3 weeks.

3 *Spondylis buprestoides.* Lives all over Europe and extends as far as Japan. Very plentiful in places. Length 12—22 mm. Larvae develop in old pine and occasionally spruce stumps. Beetles fly after dusk from June to September. Hide during day under logs, etc.

4, 5 *Cerambyx cerdo.* Inhabits Europe. Length 24—53 mm. Male's antennae much longer than body, female's same length as body or slightly shorter. Larvae develop mainly in oaks, occasionally in chestnuts, sycamores, beeches or ash trees. Female lays eggs usually in twos or threes in cracks in bark, preferably in old standing oaks. Larvae, hatched in 12—14 days, start to gnaw bark and hibernate there first year. In spring continue to eat bark and in June—July reach sap-wood and bast where they cause exudation visible as dark patch on trunk. After second hibernation larva bores to depth of 15—50 cm. in wood and forms chamber in which it pupates. Adult beetle emerges in same year after 5—6 weeks but does not leave chamber until following year. In living wood beetle's development takes 3 years, in felled trees up to 5 years. Small infestation does no damage but large-scale repeated infestation can cause even large trees to die, while larvae's tunnels depreciate wood. This species has been known to destroy whole oak avenues but is growing steadily rarer because of lack of old oaks. Beetles swarm in June and July, during evening and at night. One of the largest and handsomest European beetles. Can be bred from larvae in captivity.

6 Musk Beetle *Aromia moschata.* Widely distributed in Europe, extends to western Siberia. Length 13—34 mm. Adult beetle found mainly on willows but also on flowers of tall plants. Chiefly attacks old willows and in case of large-scale repeated invasion larvae completely destroy tree in few years. Musk beetle can also develop in poplars or alders. Adult beetle secretes strongly smelling substance. Swarm from June to August. Very beautifully coloured species.

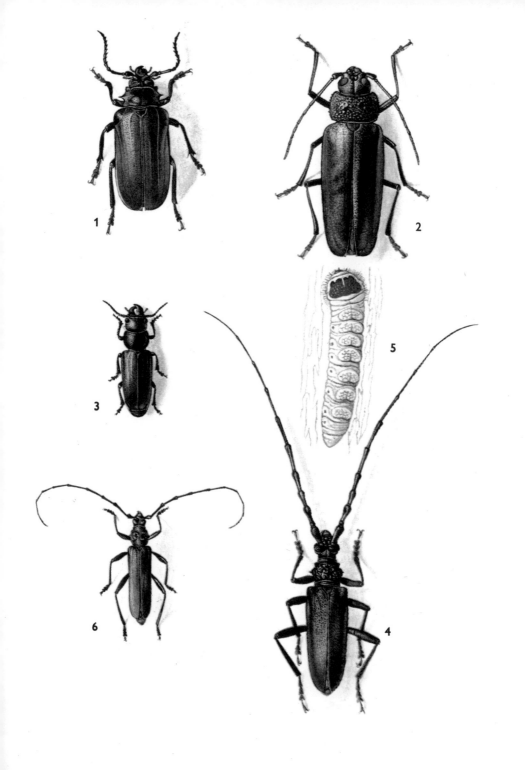

Family: **Longicorn Beetles** — *Cerambycidae*

1 *Necydalis major*. Distributed over Europe, extends up to Siberia. Length 21—32 mm. Incidence localized but abundant, especially in low-lying country. Very short wing sheaths. Larva develops in deciduous trees (e.g. poplars, limes, birches), fruit-trees and conifers (e.g. firs). Beetles fly in June and July and often sit on tree trunks or stacks of logs.

2 *Rosalia alpina*. Inhabits southern and central Europe, extends north up to south of Sweden. Length 15—38 mm. Colouring very variable. Incidence diminishing because of decreasing number of beeches but still quite abundant in places. Larvae develop in old beeches, occasionally in sycamores. Inhabits mountains above altitude of 600 m.; found chiefly on warm slopes. Flies in sunny weather from June to beginning of September. Does practically no damage. Numerous enemies, including woodpeckers, lizards, but especially beetle-collectors attracted by its striking colouring.

3 *Lamia textor*. Abundant in Europe and whole of Asia as far as Japan. Length 15—30 mm. Larvae develop in willows and aspens, mainly in old wood, also in roots. Unimportant pest. In summer adult beetles sit motionless on willow branches and are active only in evening.

4 *Callidium aeneum*. Lives in southern, central and northern Europe, extends east up to Siberia. Length 9—15 mm. Principally mountain-dweller but also often found in lowlands. Very rare in some places. Larvae develop in deciduous trees and conifers, chiefly oaks, beeches and pines. Eat surface of wood. Adult beetles appear from end of May to July.

5 *Callidium violaceum*. Inhabits Europe and whole of Asia as far as Japan. Length 8–16 mm. Abundant everywhere in central Europe, especially in conifer woods both at low and high altitudes. Larva lives in dry conifer woods, rarely in beeches, sycamores and fruit-trees. Eats wood from surface, after pupating bores deeper in wood. Female also lays eggs on felled trees, larvae develop even after wood has been processed and can damage rafters if wood is not divested of bark. Adult beetles appear from May to August.

6 *Leptura rubra*. Widely distributed all over Europe. Length 10—19 mm. Somewhat variable colouring, males usually yellowish, females reddish. Larvae live in spruce and pine stumps or trunks, occasionally found on telegraph poles. Adult beetle appears from June to September on flowering plants and bushes. Occurs at both low and high altitudes.

7 *Rhagium bifasciatum*. Distributed over whole of Europe. Length 12—22 mm. Larva develops in wood of old oaks and conifers. Most abundant on pines, spruces and oaks. Found high up in mountains. Adult beetles sit on flowers and flowering bushes, also on tree trunks. Appear from May to August. Relatively common everywhere in central Europe.

8 *Rhagium inquisitor*. Widely distributed in Europe. Occurs at both high and low altitudes. Length 10—21 mm. Very often seen in dwellings, brought on wood from forest. Larva lives behind bark of pines, spruces and firs. Beetles hatch in autumn but hibernate and appear from following April to beginning of September. Often encountered on stacks of logs, also on flowers and bushes.

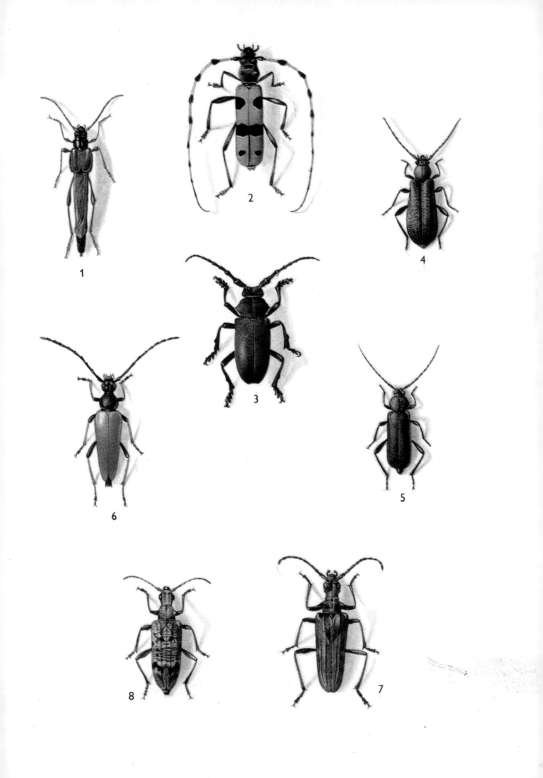

Family: **Longicorn Beetles** — *Cerambycidae*

1 *Dorcadion pedestre*. Occurs in eastern part of central Europe up to Balkans. Mainly inhabits lowlands but occasionally found at higher altitudes. Length 11—17 mm. Very abundant in spring from April to June. Unlike all other longicorn beetles larva develops underground, on grass roots. In steppe country beetles often found in large numbers on grasses.

2 *Acanthocinus aedilis*. Inhabits Europe and Asia. In central Europe common in pine-woods. Length 12—20 mm. Male has extremely long antennae. Larva develops in pines but is most often found in stumps in which it gnaws winding tunnels behind bark. Less frequently found on felled trees or standing trees weakened by other pests. Pupates in bark. Two generations a year — in March and August. Adult beetle appears from March to September. Beetle also sometimes develops in processed wood, e.g. furniture.

3 *Saperda carcharias*. Extends from Europe up to Siberia. Length 20—30 mm. Larvae develop in poplars or aspens and often do considerable damage. Female lays eggs in bark, preferably of young trees. Larvae bore into wood and form oval tunnels. Development takes 2 years. Beetles fly on warm evenings in June and July, nibble leaves or young bark of twigs. Bite rounded holes in leaves. In large numbers do great damage and can destroy young trees.

4 *Saperda populnea*. Inhabits Europe, North America and Africa. Length 9—15 mm. Abundant everywhere in central Europe. Female lays eggs on shoots or in hole bitten in bark, causing swellings on trunk. Larvae develop in aspens, also in poplars and sallows. Larva first of all lives on swelling and then bores into wood. Pupates at end of tunnel about 5 cm. long. Beetles fly from end of May to middle of July. In places does serious damage to young cultures.

5 *Oberea oculata*. Very common in Europe at both low and high altitudes. Length 15 to 21 mm. Larvae found in willows and sallows. Female lays eggs singly in holes bitten in twigs. Larva gnaws tunnel up to 30 cm. long. Development takes one year. Hatched beetles bite way out through round opening. Swarm in June and July but still encountered at beginning of September. Dozens of beetles often found sitting on willow twigs making grating sounds.

6 *Stenopterus rufus*. Abundant in southern and central Europe. Length 8—16 mm. Found in warm places. Larvae develop in deciduous trees, most frequently oaks. Adult beetles often encountered on flowers from May to August.

7 *Pachyta quadrimaculata*. Distributed over Europe and Asia as far as Mongolia. In central Europe very common in mountainous regions but rare in lowlands. Length 11—20 mm. Strong, robust body. Larvae develop in wood of spruces but often also in other conifers. Adult beetles appear on various flowers from June to August.

8 *Toxotus cursor*. Distributed over Europe and western Asia. In central Europe common in mountains and foothills. Length 25—32 mm. Several races are known, somewhat variable. Larvae develop in spruce, pine and fir stumps. Adult beetles often sit on stacked logs in forest or frequent forest plants in clearings etc. Beetles found from May to August.

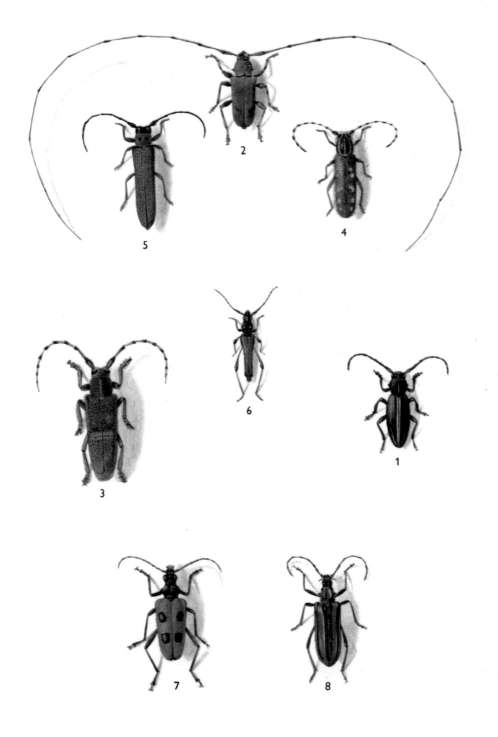

Family: **Leaf Beetles** — *Chrysomelidae*

1 *Donacia crassipes*. In central Europe common in places with water-lilies. Length 9—11 mm. Beetles sit on floating water-lily leaves. Female bites holes in leaves and through it lays eggs on underside. Larvae migrate further into depth and make slits in plant's air passages to obtain oxygen. Pupate under water in cocoon, likewise attached to air canal. In summer beetles also sit on other plants.

2 *Clytra quadripunctata*. Very abundant in central Europe. Length 8—11 mm. Adult beetles found in large numbers on willows, alders and limes. Larvae develop in anthills where they form bag-like covering from own excreta in which they hide and later pupate.

3 Poplar Leaf Beetle *Melasoma populi*. Inhabits whole of Europe. Length 6—12 mm. Frequents mainly poplars but also willows. Adult beetles and larvae nibble leaves often leaving only skeleton. If in danger, larvae emit pungent fluid from special warts.

4 Colorado Potato Beetle *Leptinotarsa decemlineata*. Originally from Mexico, has been carried to all parts of Europe. Female hibernates deep in soil, in spring gnaws germinating potatoes. Lays piles of up to 90 eggs on leaves of potato plants. Larvae gnaw leaves. After 20 days larvae pupate in ground, beetle emerges after 2—3 weeks and in 10 more days can again lay eggs. One female lays up to 700 eggs so that third generation can number 80 million. This prolific beetle has caused great damage in many parts of Europe.

5 Alder Leaf Beetle *Agelastica alni*. Very common in central Europe. Length 5—6 mm. Occurs in large numbers. Fertilized female has large abdomen and lays groups of 50 eggs on underside of alder leaves in May and June — total up to 900. Larvae eat leaves and pupate in ground. Beetles emerge in August, eat leaves and hibernate in foliage.

6 *Phyllotreta nemorum*. Widely distributed in central Europe. Minute, only 2 mm. long. Gnaws holes in leaves of cruciferous plants. Beetles gregarious. If approached, jump in all directions by means of strong last pair of legs. Larvae have developed legs and warty body. Devour inner portions of leaves often leaving only skeleton, so that plant withers. Most abundant in dry summers.

7 *Cassida viridis*. Widespread in central Europe. Length 7—10 mm. Head covered by plate. Occurs chiefly on labiate plants. Larva flattened with spiny sides and abdominal process on which it carries excreta remnants to disguise itself.

Family: **Ladybirds** — *Coccinellidae*

8 Seven-spot Ladybird *Coccinella septempunctata*. Very common. Length 5—8 mm. Found in most diverse places. Staple diet plant-lice. Female lays total up to 700 eggs in piles, near plant-lice. Larvae also eat aphids.

9 Two-spot Ladybird *Adalia bipunctata*. Very common in central Europe. Length 4 to 6 mm. In April and May female lays groups of 6—20 yellowish eggs near plant-lice. Larvae live on plant-lice or scale-insects. One larva consumes 15 aphids daily. Larva pupates after 20—35 days. Most of hatched beetles hibernate. Adult ladybird consumes 10 plant-lice daily.

10 Eyed Ladybird *Anatis ocellata*. Widely distributed in central Europe. Length 8—9 mm. Usually found in large numbers on conifers. In July female lays eggs on underside of needles and on bark. Larvae mainly eat eggs and larvae of yellow fig gall-louse. Very useful insect.

11 Four-spot Ladybird *Exochomus quadripustulatus*. Common all over central Europe. Length 3—5 mm. Occurs mainly on spruces and pines. Eats scale-insects. Pupates in larval skin.

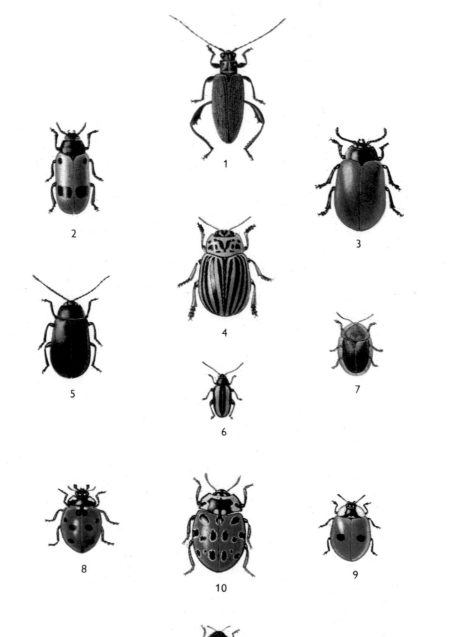

Order: **Moths and Butterflies** — *Lepidoptera*

Family: **Ghost Moths** — *Hepialidae*

1 White-winged Hop Moth *Hepialus humuli*. Common in parts of central Europe. Wing span 45—70 mm. Moth appears from May to August. Flies in evening in low zigzags. Caterpillar yellowish with sparse black hairs. Lives from April to May on hop roots, also on dandelions, sorrel and carrots. Pupates in chambers in ground. Female lays eggs on ground. Development takes 2 years. Male white, female brown-yellow.

Family: **Carpenter Moths** — *Cossidae*

2 Goat Moth *Cossus cossus*. Widely distributed in Europe. Wing span up to 90 mm. Appears in June and July. Nocturnal. During day sits on tree trunks. Female has ovipositor, lays eggs in cracks of bark. Caterpillar lives in trunks of oaks, willows, poplars and fruit-trees, gnaws long tunnels in wood. Hibernates twice, pupates in cocoon in May of third year. Perfect moth emerges 4—6 weeks later. In large numbers caterpillars completely ruin wood.

3 *Zeuzera pyrina*. Occurs in Europe, not very common. Wing span of males about 50 mm., of females up to 70 mm. Appears from May to beginning of August. Female lays single eggs on tree trunks. Caterpillar tunnels in wood. Lives in deciduous trees, chiefly ashes, elms and horse-chestnuts, also in many fruit-trees. Development takes 2 years. In large numbers damages wood. Caterpillar reddish, up to 5 cm. long.

Family: **Bear Moths** — *Syntomidae*

4 *Syntomis phegea*. Common everywhere in central Europe. Wing span about 40 mm. Appears in June and July. In flight resembles burnet moth. Grey to black hairy caterpillar lives on various herbaceous plants, chiefly dandelions. Hibernates and pupates following year in May.

Family: **Burnet Moths** or **Foresters** — *Zygaenidae*

5 Common Blood-drop Burnet Moth — *Zygaena filipendulae*. Common in Europe. Wing span about 35 mm. Appears in large numbers in meadows from beginning of June to end of August. Flies by day, ungainly and clumsily. Sits in sun on thistles etc. Caterpillar fat and yellowish with sparse hairs. Found mainly on birdfoot-trefoil but also on other plants. Pupates in brimstone-yellow, parchment-like cocoon. Moth releases repellent liquid if caught.

6 *Zygaena carniolica*. Very common in warm spots in central Europe. Wing span about 30 mm. Flies in June and July, slowly and clumsily. Caterpillar light green with white stripes and row of black spots. Lives in sainfoin and birdfoot-trefoil. Pupates in cocoon.

7 *Zygaena ephialtes*. Inhabits warm places in central Europe. Wing span about 30 mm. Seen on sunny grassy slopes in July and August. Caterpillar very variably coloured — yellowish to greenish with row of black (sometimes red) spots on sides and sparse hairs. Lives on bird's tare. Chrysalis black, in gleaming silvery cocoon.

Family: **Bagworm Moths** — *Psychidae*

8 Bagworm Moth *Pachytelia unicolor*. Widely distributed in central Europe. Wing span of male up to 28 mm. Appears in June and July in sparse conifer and deciduous woods. Adults live only two days. Female wingless with vestigial legs and antennae. After completing metamorphosis remains in bag and lays eggs in it. Caterpillar found on grasses, in bag formed of leaf and grass-blade fragments etc. Bags containing chrysalises often found on milestones etc. Male leaves chrysalis which is first expelled from bag.

Family: **Clearwings** — *Sesiidae*

1 Hornet Clearwing *Sesia apiformis*. Fairly common in central Europe. Wing span about 40 mm. Closely resembles hornet. Wings transparent. Appears from June to end of July. Sits on poplar trunks. Flies swiftly with humming sound. Female lays eggs singly, mainly on poplars, but also on birches, willows and limes (over 1,000 eggs altogether). Caterpillars bore through bark, hibernate, following year tunnel into wood and hibernate again. Pupate in sawdust cocoon. Before moth emerges chrysalis is expelled from opening.

Family: **Puss Moths** — *Notodontidae*

2 Great Puss Moth *Cerura vinula*. Widely distributed in Europe. Wing span up to about 70 mm. Flies after dusk from May to beginning of July. Striking, humped caterpillar with typical 'prongs' at tip of abdomen. Found on willows and poplars from July to September. Prongs are claspers converted to tubular appendages from which caterpillar extrudes pink filaments to scare foes. Caterpillar pupates in crack in bark, in cocoon made of wood debris and fragments of bark. Can do serious damage to tree nurseries.

3 Puss Moth *Phalera bucephala*. Very common in Europe. Wing span about 50 mm. Appears in May and June. Flies in evening, prefers lime and poplar avenues. Fine-haired, black-brown, yellow-striped caterpillar found from June to October on willows, limes, poplars and birches. Large number often crowd on single twig. Disperse when older. Pupate in ground. Dark, glossy chrysalis capable of motion.

Family: **Procession Moths** — *Thaumetopoeidae*

4 Oak Procession Moth *Thaumetopoea processionea*. Very common in central Europe, especially in southern parts. Wing span about 30 mm. Moths frequent only tops of oaks. Fly in August and September. Easily attracted by light. Female lays piles of 200—300 eggs and covers them with hairs from own body. Caterpillars, hatched in May, remain in common nests. Search for food at night crawling in head-to-tail procession. Pupate in July in cocoons, again in common nest.

Family: **Silk Moths** or **Saturnids** — *Saturniidae*

5 *Saturnia pyri*. Abundant in south of central Europe. Largest European moth. Wing span up to over 120 mm. Appears in May, flies on warm evenings in orchards, at margins of woods, etc. Caterpillar found from end of May to August on pear- and other fruit-trees. Has striking light blue tubercles with stiff bristles. Pupates in brown cocoon on bark between branches. Caterpillar makes squeaking sounds.

6 Emperor Moth *Eudia pavonia*. Occurs over large part of Europe. Wing span of male about 60 mm, female up to 75 mm. Flies in May and June. Seen in sparse deciduous woods and at margins of forests. Mature caterpillar bright green with black cross-stripes and yellow tubercles. Found from May to August on deciduous trees or shrubs, e.g. brambles. Chrysalis black-brown in whitish or yellowish-brown, very strong, pear-shaped cocoon.

7 *Aglia tau*. Very common in parts of central Europe. Wing span about 65 mm. Appears in April and May, chiefly in open beech-woods. Male flies in abrupt zigzags, female usually sits on tree trunk close to ground. Caterpillar greenish with white-yellow cross-stripes and one longitudinal stripe on sides. Found mainly on beeches from May to July. Pupates in loose cocoon.

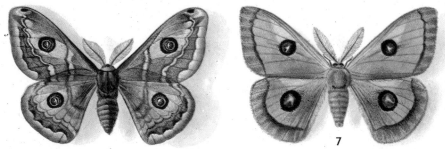

Family: **Meadow Moths** — *Lemoniidae*

1 *Lemonia dumi*. Distributed all over central Europe. Wing span up to 50 mm. Flies in evening from September to October, sometimes to November. Caterpillar found from May to July on marsh-marigold, lung-wort, garden lettuce and dandelions. Pupates in ground.

Family: **Birch Moths** — *Endromiidae*

2 Kentish Glory *Endromis versicolor*. Common in central Europe. Wing span about 50 mm. Moth often appears as soon as end of February, flies until May. Caterpillar lives on birches, sometimes on sycamores, seldom on other trees. Young caterpillars gregarious. Caterpillar green with whitish back and cross-stripes on sides. Chrysalis red, in cocoon.

Family: **Tent Caterpillar Moths** — *Lasiocampidae*

3 Pine Moth *Dendrolimus pini*. Abundant over whole of central Europe. Wing span of male about 55 mm., female up to 80 mm. Moth appears in July. Female lays 150—250 large eggs, in piles on pine twigs or needles. Caterpillars, hatched in 3 weeks, eat needles, moult 3 times, descend to ground at end of October and hibernate in loose top-soil. Crawl back to top of trees in spring, grow to 7—10 cm. and pupate in June. Some caterpillars hibernate once more. Chrysalis in cocoon attached to nibbled pine shoots or fixed in cracks in bark. Caterpillar brownish and hairy with light stripe on side.

4 Bramble Moth *Macrothylacia rubi*. Widely distributed in Europe. Wing span about 50 mm. Flies on summer evenings, often appears also during day, flies swiftly and jerkily. Female lays eggs mainly on brambles but also on roses and young oaks. Caterpillar velvety black and hairy with narrow orange cross-stripes. Found chiefly in autumn on grassy slopes and in meadows, parks, etc., crawling on ground. Often still seen in November looking for hideout in ground to hibernate. Pupates in spring of following year in soft, greyish cocoon. Many hibernating caterpillars die in ground.

5 Lappet Moth *Gastropacha quercifolia*. Abundant in practically whole of Europe. Wing span up to about 80 mm. Edge of wings indented. Flies from June to August. Caterpillar greyish brown, sparsely haired, with reddish tubercles on sides of back; grows up to 10 cm. Lives on fruit-trees, other deciduous trees and blackthorns. Pupates in soft hairy cocoon. In large numbers damages fruit-tree nurseries.

6 Lackey Moth *Malacosoma neustrium*. Widely distributed over practically whole of Europe. Wing span up to 40 mm. Flies from end of June to August. Female lays eggs ring-wise round young fruit-tree, blackthorn, poplar, oak and birch twigs — 200—400 eggs in one ring. Caterpillars not hatched until following May, after eggs have hibernated. Caterpillar thinly haired, with blue head and often blue, white and red stripes down body. Caterpillars gregarious. Weave whitish nests, crawl out in search of food. Disperse after third moult and in second half of June pupate in white or yellowish cocoon on bark or between leaves of trees.

7 *Lasiocampa quercus*. Abundant in temperate zone of Europe. Wing span up to 70 mm. Moth appears in woods and avenues from June to August. Caterpillar mainly brownish yellow with yellowish hairs, grows to 7 cm. Lives on various deciduous trees, also on conifers. Hibernates and pupates following May in firm, brown cocoon. In mountains and more northerly regions hibernates second time as chrysalis. Does little damage.

Family: **Tussock Moths** — *Lymantriidae*

1 Pale Tussock Moth *Dasychira pudibunda*. Abundant in whole of central Europe. Wing span about 45 mm. Appears in May and June, sometimes second generation in October. Inhabits sparse woods, orchards, etc. Caterpillar very variably coloured — yellow, pink or reddish, with hairs of same colour and with yellow or orange bristles on back. Lives on deciduous trees and pupates in yellow, extremely hairy cocoon.

2 Gold-tipped Tussock Moth *Euproctis phaeorrhoea*. Widely distributed in central Europe. Wing span about 35 mm. Flies from end of June to end of July. Female lays piles of eggs on underside of oak leaves and covers them with hairs. Caterpillars hatch in August. Gregarious, hibernate in nests and disperse in spring. Pupate at end of June in cocoon which is hidden in rolled leaf. Do damage in large numbers.

3 Nun or **Black Archer** *Lymantria monacha*. Very common in Europe. Wing span of male up to 45 mm., female up to 55 mm. Colouring very variable, including black aberrations. Appears in July and August. Female lays eggs behind scales of bark on conifers, occasionally also on deciduous trees. Caterpillars do not hatch until following year, usually in April. Disperse into tree crowns and eat needles or leaves. Pupate in cracks in bark after about 9 weeks. Very variably coloured. Have few hairs.

4 Gypsy Moth *Lymantria dispar*. Distributed over almost whole of Europe. Wing span of male 35—40 mm., female 55—70 mm. Flies from end of July to September, lives only 7—8 days. Female lays eggs in piles. Caterpillars do not hatch until following April or May; found on deciduous trees, mainly oaks, limes, etc. Caterpillar brownish and hairy, with blue and red tubercles. Pupates in loose cocoon on south side of tree trunks, often in groups.

Family: **Owlet Moths** — *Phalaenidae*

5 *Agrotis segetum*. Common European moth. Wing span about 40 mm. Moth appears in May—June and August—September in fields, meadows and gardens. Caterpillars eat turnips, cereals, grass, etc. Caterpillar smooth and greyish with light lines down back and sides and black spots. Hides during day, comes out to feed at night.

6 *Scoliopteryx libatrix*. Very common in Europe. Wing span about 40 mm. Forewings indented. Moth appears in August and September, hibernates in holes, cellars, etc., and flies again in March and April. Caterpillars found on poplars and willows from May to September. Caterpillar green with yellow band on sides. Chrysalis black.

7 Blue Underwing *Catocala fraxini*. Distributed over all central Europe. Wing span up to about 90 mm. Appears from end of July to September. Sits on tree trunks during day, flies in evening and at night. Caterpillar up to 10 cm. long; greyish or greenish, black-speckled, on back with light spot in black band on 8th segment. Found on ashes, poplars and elms.

8 Red Poplar Underwing *Catocala elocata*. Distributed over most of Europe. Wing span about 75 mm. Occurs from July to October. Clings to tree trunks during day. If disturbed, abruptly unfolds forewings, displaying red hindwings to frighten enemy. Caterpillar grey with dark dorsal and lateral stripes. Found mainly on poplars, also on willows, from May to June. Chrysalis reddish brown, dusted with blue.

9 Red Willow Underwing *Catocala electa*. Widely distributed in central Europe. Wing span about 70 mm. Flies in July and August. Caterpillar yellowish grey to brown with small black dots; over 7 cm. long. Found on willows in May and June.

Family: **Tiger Moths** — *Arctiidae*

1 White Tiger Moth *Spilosoma menthastri*. Widely distributed in central Europe. Wing span about 40 mm. Flies in evening in May and June. During day can be seen sitting on plants in forest clearings and in gardens. Caterpillar hairy, dark brown with orange-yellow line down back. Found through summer on various plants, chiefly stinging-nettles and mint. Pupates on ground. Chrysalis black in grey cocoon.

2 *Utetheisa pulchella*. Lives in southern part of central Europe but often strays far north. Wing span about 40 mm. Flies in June and September—October in damp meadows near woods, in clearings, etc. Caterpillar white and soft-haired, with black dots and red spots. Found on forget-me-not, viper's bugloss, rib-wort and other herbaceous plants in May—June and September—October.

3 *Phragmatobia fuliginosa*. Common over practically whole of Europe. Wing span 30—35 mm. Many colour varieties. Moth in April and May, second generation in August. Flies after dark, often enters open windows. Caterpillar grey to reddish brown, with tubercles surmounted by tufts of hairs. Found on forget-me-not, sorrel, bedstraw, wild lettuce, etc. Pupates in greyish white felty cocoon.

4 *Rhyparia purpurata*. Abundant in central Europe. Wing span about 45 mm. Several colour varieties. Flies after dark, in June and July. Caterpillar somewhat variable; usually black with dark red hairs and yellow lateral hairs. Has yellow, red and black spots on sides. Found on milfoil, rib-wort, bedstraw, etc. from autumn to spring.

5 Garden Tiger Moth *Arctia caja*. Distributed over most of Europe. Wing span up to 70 mm. Often very variably coloured. Moth abundant everywhere during summer. In daytime hides under leaves of plants or bushes. Caterpillar long-haired with black and white tubercles; dorsal hairs black, lateral hairs russet. Found on various plants from August to September and, after hibernating, from May to June.

6 *Panaxia quadripunctaria*. Fairly common in central Europe on sunny, and especially limestone, slopes. Wing span about 55 mm. Several colour varieties. Moth appears on grassy slopes in July. Caterpillar found on rib-wort, clover and willowherb, also beeches and oaks in April and May. Grey-brown to black with yellow dorsal and lateral stripes and orange-spotted sides. Pupates in loose cocoon.

7 *Panaxia dominula*. Fairly abundant in central and northern Europe. Wing span about 55 mm. Several colour varieties. Moth seen in June and July among bushes, on outskirts of woods, in avenues, etc. Caterpillar found in autumn and again in spring on stinging-nettle, deadnettle, wild strawberry, forget-me-not and willow, poplar and other trees.

Family: **Geometers** or **Emeralds** — *Geometridae*

8 Emerald *Geometra papilionaria*. Occurs in central and northern Europe. Wing span about 45 mm. Flies from June to August in sparse woods. Sits on tree trunks. Caterpillar green with yellow stripe along sides and five protuberances on back. Found on birch, alder, beech and hazel in May. Chrysalis yellow-green with reddish brown back.

9 Magpie Moth *Abraxas grossulariata*. Distributed over whole of Europe. Wing span up to 40 mm. Moth appears from June to August; common in gardens and in woods with wild gooseberry bushes. Caterpillar whitish with wide black spots on back and orange stripe along sides. Found on gooseberry bushes.

Family: **Hawk Moths** — *Sphingidae*

1 Death's Head Moth *Acherontia atropos*. Inhabits southern Europe, regularly flies to central and northern Europe. Wing span up to about 110 mm. Flies late in evening and at night. Excellent flier; comes in summer from Mediterranean region. In central Europe female usually lays eggs on potato plants, also on henbane. Caterpillars, which by end of summer measure 10 cm., are yellow-green with black, blue and yellow stripes and spots; large spine at tip of abdomen. Pupate in ground in hard clay capsule. In colder parts of central Europe chrysalis dies.

2 Convolvulus or **Morning Glory Hawk** *Herse convolvuli*. Abundant from Atlantic coast as far as Australia. Wing span about 105 mm. Flies after dark in May and June, second generation in August and September. Flies from south to extreme north of Europe. Female lays eggs on bindweed. Mature caterpillar, which measures 9 cm., is usually light brown or greenish with light oblique stripes on sides and dark stripe down back. Caterpillar found mainly on bindweed from June until autumn. Hides during day, often in holes in ground; comes out to feed towards evening. Chrysalis has curved proboscis sheath.

3 Privet Hawk *Sphinx ligustri*. Common in central Europe. Wing span about 90 mm. Appears in May and June, sometimes until August. Flies after dark; often attracted indoors by light. Caterpillar light green with oblique violet stripes, bordered with white on underside, on sides; yellow tip of abdomen. Found on elder, privet and other shrubs from end of June to September. Chrysalis reddish brown.

4 Pine Hawk *Sphinx pinastri*. Common all over central Europe. Wing span up to about 80 mm. Moth appears in conifer forests from April to September. Sits on tree trunks, blends with surroundings. Female lays eggs on pines and spruces. Caterpillars eat needles. Because of numerous parasites has never multiplied dangerously in central Europe. Caterpillar light green with brownish line on back, narrow white and yellow stripes on sides and red spots. Found on conifers from June to October. Chrysalis hibernates, sometimes twice.

5 Willow Hawk *Smerinthus ocellatus*. Common in central Europe. Wing span about 85 mm. Moth appears from May to August, mainly near water with groups of willows or poplars. Caterpillar green with blue cross-stripes on sides, whitish spots and a blue spine. Found from June to September on willow, poplar and young fruit-trees. Moth often attracted indoors by light.

6 Oak Hawk *Marumba quercus*. Inhabits southern Europe, rarely visits central Europe. Wing span up to about 100 mm. Appears in southern Europe from May to August, in central Europe usually in July. Inhabits oak-woods. Caterpillar green with oblique yellow stripes and orange spots on sides. Found from June to October chiefly on young oaks. Chrysalis brown with metallic lustre.

7 Poplar Hawk *Laothoe populi*. Locally abundant in central Europe. Wing span up to about 75 mm. Moth appears in May and June and sometimes in August and early September. Sits on poplar trunks. Caterpillar yellow-green with yellow spots and with oblique yellow stripes on sides. Found from June to September mainly on poplars, but also on willows. Pupates in ground. Chrysalis dark brown.

Family: **Hawk Moths** — *Sphingidae*

1 Spurge Hawk *Celerio euphorbiae.* Very common in central Europe. Wing span about 70 mm. Moth appears from May to September in clearings and pastures, by rivers and anywhere where spurge grows. Flies after dusk, visits flowers, sucks nectar with long proboscis. Caterpillar found on spurge in July and August. Strikingly coloured; basic colour black, red stripe down back and yellow spots and stripes on sides. Pupates in ground. Moth sometimes does not emerge for several years after several hibernating stages of pupa.

2 Bedstraw Hawk *Celerio gallii.* Common in central Europe. Wing span about 70 mm. Moth appears from May to July, sometimes to September. Flies swiftly after dark. Caterpillar usually dark green with yellow dorsal line and large, yellow, black-ringed spots on sides. Found from July to August on bedstraw, willowherb and spurge. Mainly frequents open sunny places. Chrysalis yellow-brown with dark lines.

3 Vine Hawk *Deilephila elpenor.* Very common in central Europe. Wing span about 65 mm. Moth appears mostly in May and June, rarely from July to September. Fast flier. Mainly frequents places with willows, e.g. streams, clearings, etc. Caterpillar found from June to end of August on willowherb, bedstraw, vines and other plants. Up to 8 cm. long. Three colour types — green, brown and blackish. Brown and white eye-spots on fourth and fifth segment. Chrysalis yellowish brown with black spots. Moth often attracted indoors by light.

4 Oleander Hawk *Daphnis nerii.* Inhabits North Africa and southern Europe. Wing span about 100 mm. In summer visits central Europe where female sometimes lays eggs and caterpillars can be found. Caterpillar up to over 9 cm. long; bright green with white lateral stripe from fourth segment and two white, blue-ringed eye-spots on either side of third segment. Found on oleanders and occasionally on winter-green from April to June, second generation in August and September. Chrysalis slim, brown-yellow, marked with black dots.

5 *Proserpinis proserpina.* Distributed over central and southern Europe. Wing span about 40 mm. Ragged-edged wings. Moth appears in May, flies after dusk. Caterpillar green or brownish with black marbling and with yellow, blue-rimmed spots on sides. Found in July and August on willowherb and evening primrose. Chrysalis reddish brown.

6 *Macroglossum stellatarum.* Common in central Europe. Wing span about 45 mm. Moth flies from June to October, mainly during day, in clearings, forest meadows, etc. Has very long proboscis, sucks nectar from trumpet flowers. Flies very abruptly, hovers like hummingbird when sucking nectar. Caterpillar green with white stripe along sides. First generation of caterpillars appears in June and July, second in August to September. Found on bedstraw and woodruff. Caterpillar hides by day, comes out in search of food at night. Chrysalis grey-brown or blue-green.

Family: **Skipper Butterflies** — *Hesperiidae*

7 Silver-spotted Skipper *Hesperia comma.* Widely distributed all over Europe. Wing span about 30 mm. Flies very quickly during daytime. Seen from June to August in clearings, on hillsides and in meadows, also in mountainous regions. Caterpillar dark grey with double black line on sides. Found in autumn on various meadow grasses, hibernates and reappears following spring. Makes itself tube from grass leaves. Chrysalis brownish, dusted with blue.

Family: **Meadow Browns** or **Satyrs** — *Satyridae*

1 Marbled White *Melanargia galathea*. Occurs in central and southern Europe. Wing span about 50 mm. Butterfly abundant from June to August in forest meadows and clearings, on slopes, etc., also at high altitudes. Flies during daytime. Caterpillar yellowish with dark dorsal and reddish lateral line. Hides by day, eats various grasses at night.

2 *Hipparchia circe*. Distributed over whole of central and southern Europe. Wing span up to about 80 mm. Flies from June to August in open woods. Caterpillar has dark brown, white-lined back and yellow-brown sides with russet, white and black lines. Found on different grasses from May to June.

3 *Hipparchia briseis*. Widespread in central Europe. Wing span about 55 mm. Flies from July to September. Frequents sunny rocky slopes, likes to settle on warm rocks or stones. Caterpillar yellowish grey. Dark line on back; one dark and two light lines along sides. Found mainly on sesleria but also on other grasses in autumn and, after hibernating, again until June.

4 *Pararge achine*. Occurs in central and northern Europe. Wing span about 50 mm. Flies in shady woods in June and July. Caterpillar light green with one black and two white lines on back. Found in August and September and, after hibernating, again in May on rye-grass and other grasses, also on wheat. Pupates in May. Chrysalis green with white stripes.

Family: **Fritillaries** — *Nymphalidae*

5 Peacock Butterfly *Nymphalis io*. Common all over Europe. Wing span up to about 60 mm. Butterfly occurs from March until autumn, sometimes in three generations. Hibernates often inside windows, in cellars and caves, etc. Caterpillar black with white dots and black spines. Caterpillars gregarious, live mainly on stinging-nettle, also on hops and brambles from April to September. Chrysalis light brown with golden spots, hangs head downwards. Butterfly emerges in 1—2 weeks but third generation pupa hibernates.

6 Camberwell Beauty *Nymphalis antiopa*. Common in central Europe. Wing span up to over 70 mm. Flies from June until autumn, hibernates and reappears from end of April. Mainly frequents birch groves. Sits on trunk and sucks sap from injured wood, also drinks nectar. Caterpillar black with striking, red-spotted back and black spines all over body. Gregarious, lives from May to June on birches, also on poplars, willows and elms.

7 Small Tortoiseshell *Aglais urticae*. Common European butterfly. Wing span about 50 mm. Two or three generations of butterflies appear from end of June until October. Hibernating males and females appear early in spring. Several varieties. Frequents hillsides, clearings, fields and gardens. Often found inside windows, in cellars, etc. Caterpillar black with yellow-green stripes down body and spines. Found from May until autumn on great and small nettle and occasionally on hops.

8 Comma Butterfly *Polygonia c-album*. Abundant in central Europe. Wing span about 50 mm. Several colour varieties. Butterfly in 2—3 generations from May to October, hibernates and reappears in early spring. Flies on outskirts of forests, in glades and in gardens. First third of caterpillar's body russet, remainder white, underside reddish. Armed with spines. Caterpillar found on nettle, gooseberry, hop, elm and hazel leaves. Chrysalis hangs head downwards.

Family: **Fritillaries** — *Nymphalidae*

1 Red Admiral *Vanessa atalanta*. Common in central Europe. Wing span about 60 mm. Butterfly in two generations, from June until autumn. Found almost anywhere in open places. Second generation butterflies hibernate and appear early in spring. Caterpillars variably coloured, most often black with yellow line on sides and with spines. Found in May—June and August—September in rolled leaves, chiefly of stinging-nettle.

2 Painted Lady *Vanessa cardui*. Distributed over practically whole of world. Very common in central Europe. Wing span about 55 mm. Butterfly appears in sunny places from end of May until autumn, in 2—3 generations. Likes to settle on flowers. Caterpillar brownish and spiny, with yellow stripes and dots. Found from May to September on leaves of stinging-nettle, colt's foot, burdock and other plants. Chrysalis grey with golden spots.

3 *Araschnia levana*. Abundant in central Europe. Wing span about 35—40 mm. Butterfly has spring and summer generation. Spring generation (March—April) yellowish red with black spots, summer generation (July—August) blackish brown with yellow spots. Caterpillars, gregarious when young, found in June and August—September on stinging-nettle. Resemble peacock butterfly caterpillars but have two long spines on head.

4 Purple Emperor *Apatura iris*. Occurs all over central Europe. Wing span about 60 mm. Upper surface of wings metallic-opalescent. Butterfly from June to August in sparse deciduous woods. Flies low, early in morning, sucks dung, carrion, etc. Caterpillar green with yellow stripes and dots and two long blue horns on head. Found from August on sallow, aspen and willow, hibernates and again eats leaves from April to June.

5 White Admiral *Limenitis camilla*. Occurs in central, southern and south-western Europe. Wing span about 50—55 mm. Butterfly seen from May to July in open deciduous woods. Favours damp places. Settles on blackberry flowers. Green, red-spined caterpillar found on honeysuckle. Hibernates.

6 Great White Admiral *Limenitis populi*. Locally abundant in central Europe. Wing span up to about 80 mm. Butterfly in July and August. Female has broad white bands on wings. Settles on damp ground, excreta, etc. Gliding flight. Caterpillar green with hairy excrescences. Hibernates in curled leaf and in spring, up to May, eats poplar leaves, mainly that of young trees. Also found on aspens. Butterfly leaves chrysalis in 3—4 weeks.

7 European Sailer *Neptis hylasaceris*. Occurs in warm parts of central Europe. Wing span up to about 55 mm. First generation of butterflies appears in May and June, second in July to August, in open deciduous woods. Local incidence only. Caterpillar yellow-brown with small tubercles. Found on lady's finger.

8 Silver-washed Fritillary *Argynnis paphia*. Very abundant in central Europe. Wing span up to about 70 mm. Butterfly seen from beginning of July to middle of September. Appears mainly in damp forest meadows, clearings, etc. Settles on thistles and sucks nectar. Female lays eggs on violets usually in August. Caterpillars, hatched in 14 days, hibernate until May and then gnaw young violet roots, mainly at night. Pupate at end of June. Caterpillar brownish with yellow dorsal stripe, dark lateral stripes and long yellow spines. Chrysalis found on tree trunks.

9 Queen of Spain Fritillary *Issoria lathonia*. Very common in central Europe. Wing span 40—45 mm. Butterfly in 2—3 generations from early spring until autumn. Flies in meadows and fields, on hillsides, etc. Caterpillars live on violets and sainfoin and hibernate. Caterpillar brownish with whitish back, brown-yellow lines on sides and short reddish spines.

1

2

3

6

5

7

4

8

9

Family: **Blues, Coppers** or **Hairstreaks** — *Lycaenidae*

1 *Lycaena virgaureae*. Abundant in central Europe. Wing span up to about 35 mm. Male has golden orange wings, female brown-spotted wings. Frequents clearings, meadows, etc. in open woods. Caterpillar dark green with yellowish stripes on back and bosses on body. Lives on sorrel from April to June. Pupates on stem or in ground.

2 Adonis Blue *Polyommatus bellargus*. Occurs in central and southern Europe. Wing span about 33 mm. Butterfly in two generations, May—June and July—September. Flies in fields, on hillsides, etc. Sucks nectar from clover and lucerne flowers etc. Caterpillar blue-green with dark dorsal stripes and often reddish yellow spots. Found from April to July on clover and other papilionaceous plants. Usually pupates in ground. Chrysalis greenish.

3 Large Blue *Maculinea arion*. Occurs in central Europe in several forms. Wing span about 25 mm. Butterfly appears from June to August on sunny slopes and meadows. Likes to settle on betony flowers. Caterpillar blue-green with dark dorsal line. Found on betony from autumn. Hibernates and pupates in anthills. Before pupating lives on ant larvae and pupae. Ants like its secretion.

Family: **Swallowtails** — *Papilionidae*

4 Swallowtail *Papilio machaon*. Distributed over whole of Europe. In central Europe generally two generations, April—May and July—August, in south up to October. Wing span up to about 80 mm. Good, enduring flier. Prefers dry hilly regions. Likes to settle on flowers and sucks nectar. Female lays eggs singly on umbelliferous plants, e.g. pimpernel, cummin, carrots, etc. Young caterpillar blackish, mature caterpillar light green with black cross-stripes and bright red spots. Chrysalis fixed to stems by fibres, head upwards. Some chrysalises hibernate twice.

5 Scarce Swallowtail *Papilio podalirius*. Very common in central Europe. Wing span up to about 75 mm. Spring and summer generation. Occurs mainly on sunny slopes. Female lays eggs singly on fruit-trees or blackthorn. Caterpillars hatch in 10 days. Caterpillar green with yellow dorsal stripe branching into oblique yellow cross-bands on sides. Pupates head upwards, held by fibrous loop round chrysalis. Surface of chrysalis uneven.

6 *Zerynthia hypsipyle*. Inhabits southern Europe and southern parts of central Europe. Wing span about 50 mm. Butterfly appears in April and May, abundant in places. Flies in open sunny spots where birthwort grows. Caterpillar found on birthwort from June to August. Caterpillar russet, reddish or grey with red excrescences. Chrysalis yellow-grey.

7 Black Apollo Butterfly *Parnassius mnemosyne*. Abundant in places in central Europe. Wing span up to about 60 mm. Butterfly appears in June mainly in mountainous regions, but also at lower altitudes. Caterpillar black with rows of red spots. Hides by day, comes out to eat late in evening. Found on fumitory in April and May. Chrysalis fat and yellowish, dusted with white.

8 Red Apollo Butterfly *Parnassius apollo*. Locally common in mountainous regions of central Europe. Wing span up to about 70 mm. Dark form known in the Alps. Butterfly from June to August on sunny slopes. Likes to settle on thistle flowers. Caterpillar black with two rows of large red spots and bluish tubercles. Found in May and June on stone-crop. Pupates in ground in loose cocoon. Chrysalis bluish.

♂

1

2

3

♀

6

5

8

7

4

Family: **Whites** — *Pieridae*

1 Large White *Pieris brassicae*. Common all over Europe. Wing span about 55 mm. Butterfly occurs from April until autumn in 2—3 generations. Flies practically everywhere. Female lays small piles of yellow eggs on underside of cabbage leaves and similar plants. Caterpillars devour leaves right down to stalk. Found from May to June and from August to September. Caterpillar yellow-green with black dots and yellow stripes on back and sides. Before pupating climbs on to higher object, e.g. wall or tree. Chrysalis yellow-green with black blotches and spots. Important pest. Caterpillars often attacked by ichneumon flies.

2 Small White, Cabbage or **Turnip Butterfly** *Pieris rapae*. Abundant all over Europe. Wing span about 45 mm. First generation of butterflies appear in April—May, second in July, sometimes third in autumn. Appears in fields, meadows and gardens. Caterpillar greenish with yellow stripes on back and sides. Found in June and again in August and September on cruciferous plants, mainly turnip leaves.

3 Black-veined White *Aporia crataegi*. Distributed over whole of Europe. Once important pest, now plentiful only in places. Wing span about 60 mm. Butterfly flies in June and July. Female lays eggs on underside of fruit-tree leaves (mainly apple-trees). Caterpillars appear from September, wrap themselves in leaves and hibernate. Early in spring form large nests round buds and eat them. Pupate at end of May on tree trunks etc. Caterpillar blue-grey with black and rusty brown stripes.

4 Orange-tip *Anthocharis cardamines*. Abundant in central Europe. Wing span about 40 mm. Male's forewings tipped with orange. Butterfly appears from beginning of April to June. Male very striking in flight. Flies close to ground in gardens, sunken lanes and forest paths. Caterpillar blue-green with white-striped sides. Found mainly on cress from June to August.

5 Pale Clouded Yellow *Colias hyale*. Very common in central Europe. Wing span about 40 mm. Butterfly appears from May to June and again from August to September. Flies on sunny, grassy slopes and over clover fields, stubble fields, etc. Caterpillar dark green with four yellow stripes down body. Found on vetches and clover in June—July and August—September. Chrysalis grey-green with yellow stripes.

6 Alpine Clouded Yellow *Colias palaenoeuropomene*. Found in central Europe in peat-bogs. Wing span about 50 mm. Butterfly seen from June to July or August over peat-bogs with plenty of crowberry plants on which caterpillars live. Caterpillar green with yellow stripe, edged below with black, along sides. Chrysalis yellow-green.

7 *Colias edusa*. Inhabits practically whole of Europe. Wing span about 50 mm. Basic colouring of male orange to yellowish red, female whitish to orange and yellow. Two butterfly generations, May—June and July—August. Seen on sunny slopes and in fields and clearings, etc. Caterpillar green with white, yellow-spotted stripe along sides. Found on papilionaceous plants.

8 Brimstone Yellow or **Yellow-bird** *Gonopteryx rhamni*. Common everywhere in central Europe. Wing span about 55 mm. Butterfly seen from July to autumn. Hibernates and reappears on sunny days at end of March. Flies in gardens, fields and meadows, etc. Caterpillar dark green with white stripe on sides. Found from July mainly on buckthorn, in mountainous regions also on bilberries. Chrysalis green with two white stripes on sides.

Order: **Two-winged Flies** — *Diptera*

Famliy: **Crane-flies** — *Tipulidae*

1 Crane-fly or **Daddy-longlegs** *Tipula oleracea*. Plentiful everywhere from April to June. Female lays up to 500 black eggs in ground. Larvae hatch in 2—3 weeks. Live on humus, later nibble roots of crops. Adult insect measures 15—23 mm. Often attracted indoors by light.

Family: **Gall-gnats** — *Cecidomyidae*

2 Hessian-fly *Mayetiola destructor*. Common over whole of Europe. Length 2.5—4 mm. Flies from April to May and again in September. Female lays eggs singly or in twos on underside of rye, wheat or barley leaves. Larvae, hatched in 8 days, suck blades. Second larval generation penetrates to roots of winter seedlings and causes swellings on plants which usually die.

3 Beech Gall-gnat *Mikiola fagi*. Abundant in beech-woods. Small and inconspicuous. Female lays eggs singly on upperside of beech leaves. Larvae form striking red galls, sometimes several on one leaf. Larvae of related species form similar galls on leaves of other trees.

Family: **Hair-gnats** — *Bibionidae*

4 March-fly or **St. Mark's Fly** *Bibio marci*. Very common in woods from March to May. Length 10—13 mm. Black, with extremely long legs. Flies slowly. Larvae found in humus, live on vegetable matter. In large numbers does damage to tree nurseries.

Family: **Gadflies** — *Tabanidae*

5 Gadfly *Tabanus bovinus*. Distributed over practically whole of Europe, mainly near ponds, lakes and rivers. Length 20—24 mm. Flies during summer. Female attacks warm-blooded animals and man and sucks their blood, needed for development of its eggs. Bite smarts and swells. Female lays eggs on aquatic plants. Larvae crawl down into water and live predaciously in mud. Development slow. After 7—8 moults larva transformed to immobile pupa. Gadflies have numerous enemies, for instance birds and spiders.

6 Horse-fly or **Cleg** *Haematopoda pluvialis*. Abundant near rivers and ponds. Length 10 mm. Male's eyes hairy; female's are hairless and beautifully green. Flies in summer. Bites viciously, especially before storms. Predacious larvae live in mud.

7 Greenhead *Chrysops caecutiens*. Very common near water. Length 8—9 mm. Female has golden green eyes. Appears from May to September. Female attacks large mammals and man and sucks their blood. Lays glossy black eggs on aquatic plants. Round-bodied, predacious larvae live in mud. Pupate in sand and soil.

Family: **Bee-flies** — *Bombyliidae*

8 *Hemipenthes morio*. Striking fly frequenting dry clearings. Length 5—12 mm. Found in summer. Female flies over bare ground looking for caterpillars attacked by caterpillar-fly or ichneumon fly larvae. Lays eggs on these and larvae parasitize parasites. Adult insects fly swiftly about in sunny parts of woods, settle on flowers and drink nectar.

Family: **Soldier-flies** — *Stratiomyidae*

9 Soldier-fly *Stratiomys chamaeleon*. Common, striking fly with flat abdomen. Length 12 to 14 mm. Appears mainly in summer. Flutters on flowers and bushes near water and drinks nectar. Not shy. Female lays eggs on leaves above water surface. Hatched larvae slip into water and live in tangled aquatic plants in shallows. Have long breathing tube. Predacious. Before pupating crawl out of water. Pupate in ground.

10 Green Soldier-fly *Eulalia viridula*. Abundant on leaves of bushes near water. Length 6—7 mm. On rainy days hides on underside of leaves.

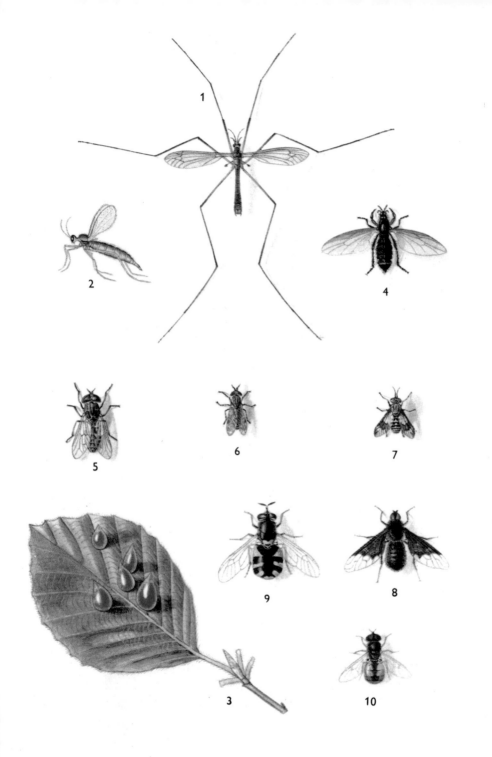

Family: **Hover-flies** — *Syrphidae*

1 Currant-fly *Syrphus ribesii*. Occurs in central Europe. Length 10—11 mm. In summer and autumn appears on flowers and sucks nectar. Darting flight. In sunny spots often flies in circles. Female lays eggs on leaves. Greenish larvae catch aphids, mainly on currant bushes but also on vegetables. One larva consumes about 300 plant-lice during development.

2 *Eristalis arbustorum*. Common in central Europe. Found mainly in clearings from summer until late autumn. Length 10—12 mm. Larva lives in mud, cesspools and manure. Larva cylindrical and whitish with tail-like breathing tube. Pupates on tree trunks etc.

Family: **Fruit-flies** — *Drosophilidae*

3 *Drosophila melanogaster*. Abundant in summer and autumn. Length only 3.5—4 mm. Appears in flocks on soft windfall fruit, in houses and on any fermenting material. Develops very quickly. In some places nuisance as carrier of undesirable yeast cells.

Family: **Horse-ticks** or **Forest-flies** — *Hippoboscidae*

4 Forest-fly *Ornithomyia avicularia*. Very common, especially in woods. Length 5—6 mm. Wings permanent. Parasite of various birds, lives in plumage and sucks blood. Females produce developed larvae which immediately pupate and drop to ground. Perfect insect capable of reproduction in 3 days. Normal life span 4—6 months.

Family: **True Flies** — *Muscidae*

5 Common House-fly *Musca domestica*. Occurs in human dwellings all over world. Length 7—8 mm. Female lays eggs in dung, manure and rotting refuse. Development takes only 14 days, several generations may occur in a year. Hibernates as larva or as pupa. Since fly alights on excrements and then on food and human skin, can transmit many dangerous infections.

6 Common Stable-fly *Stomoxys calcitrans*. Very common in cattle country. Length 6 to 7 mm. Female lays eggs in cow dung. Adult insect also flies into homes and bites man. Bites itch. Can transmit different diseases, e.g. anthrax and in south cholera, etc.

Family: **Blow-flies** — *Calliphoridae*

7 Gold Blow-fly *Lucilia caesar*. Very common everywhere. Settles on tall plants and leaves of bushes. Length 7—10 mm. Brightly gleaming body. Looks for putrefying animal carcasses and human excreta in which female lays eggs and maggots develop.

8 Bluebottle *Calliphora vicina*. Very common in dwellings. Robust body 8—12 mm. long. Appears from spring until autumn, betrayed by loud buzz. Female lays eggs in animal carcasses, excrements, cheese and meat. Maggots hatch in 24 hours, develop 4 weeks and pupate in ground.

9 Common Flesh-fly *Sarcophaga carnaria*. Very common everywhere. Length 10—16 mm. Found on flowers, walls, tree trunks and in dwellings. Female lays live, legless maggots on fresh vertebrate carcasses or meat in which maggots develop. Maggots pupate as brown, barrel-shaped pupae. Contaminates food.

Family: **Caterpillar-flies** — *Larvaevoridae*

10 Caterpillar-fly *Exorista larvarum*. Occurs everywhere in sunny grassy places. Length 6—15 mm. Female lays eggs on caterpillars. Larva penetrates caterpillar's body and devours it from within. Burnet moth caterpillars most frequent hosts but other species also. Mature larvae leave host's body and pupate in ground. Very useful insect as not more than 5 per cent of attacked caterpillars develop into moths.

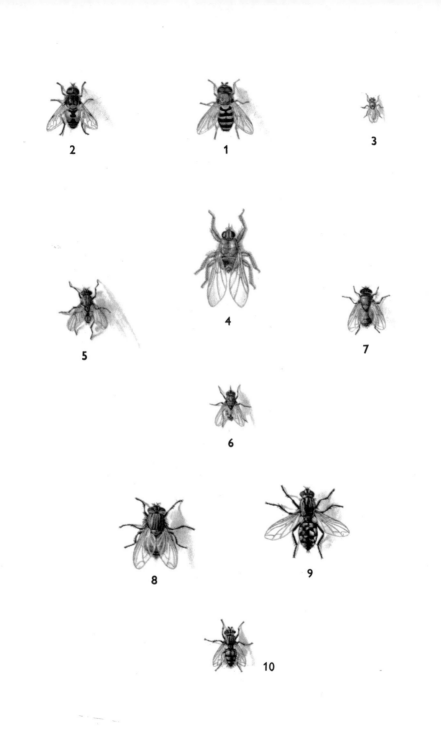

Subphylum: **Jawless Fishes** — *Agnatha*

Primitive, cartilaginous skull, no upper or lower jaw. Paired fins not developed.

Class: **Lamprey and Hag Fishes** — *Cyclostomata*

Order: **Lampreys** — *Petromyzoniformes* (p. 294). Vertebrates with elongated body and primitive cartilaginous skeleton. Round, jawless mouth. Only one nasal cavity closed at far end. Eel-like form with unpaired fin border along hind part of body. Seven gill-slits on either side of body, behind eyes. Larvae hatched from eggs transform to adult lampreys after 2—4 years. Larva's eyes covered with skin. Lampreys inhabit both salt and fresh water.

Subphylum: **Jawed Fishes** — *Gnathostomata* (p. 294). Skull with jaws. Lower jaw movable.

Class: **Cartilaginous Fishes** — *Chondrichthyes* (p. 294). Cartilaginous skeleton. Marine animals.

Order: **Sharks and Allies** — *Selachiformes* (p. 294). Elongated body covered with spiny scales. On either side 5—7 exposed gill-slits.

Order: **Rays and Allies** — *Rajiformes* (p. 294). Flat-backed body with extremely widened pectoral fins meeting on inner margin. Five pairs of gill-slits on underside. Tail often whip-like. Bottom-dwellers.

Class: **Bony Fishes** — *Osteichthyes*

Subclass: **Ray-finned Fishes** — *Actinopterygii* (p. 294). Breathe whole life by means of operculum-covered gills. Limbs in form of fins. Skeleton cartilaginous or bony. Body usually covered with scales.

Superorder: **Soft-boned Fishes** or **Chondrosteans** — *Chondrostei* (p. 294). Five rows of large bony plates down length of body. Cartilaginous skeleton. Teeth usually absent, otherwise minute. Tactile appendages (barbels) on underside of mouth.

Order: **Sturgeons and Allies** — *Acipenseriformes* (p. 294). Head produced to snout. Mouth toothless in adult life.

Superorder: **True Bony Fishes** — *Teleostei* (p. 294). Bony skeleton. Skull formed of flat bony plates. Body usually covered with dermal scales. Possess mucus-secreting skin glands. Pectinate gills. Economically important fishes.

Order: **Herrings and Allies** — *Clupeiformes* (p. 294). Marine and freshwater fishes with soft-rayed fins.

Family: **Herrings** — *Clupeidae* (p. 294). Flat-sided, mainly marine fishes. Migrate in large shoals to spawning sites in shallow water. Popular food.

Family: **Salmonids** — *Salmonidae* (p. 296). Predacious, swift fishes with small, rayless adipose fin between dorsal and caudal fin. Like cold, clean water. Live in salt and fresh water. Inhabit northern hemisphere. Spawn in winter.

Order: **Pikes and Allies** — *Esociformes* (p. 298). Predacious fishes with long, wide jaws with numerous teeth.

Family: **Pikes** — *Esocidae* (p. 298). Freshwater fishes with long, robust body. Tapering jaws with teeth. Dorsal and anal fins situated close to caudal fin.

Order: **Carps and Allies** — *Cypriniformes* (p. 298). Freshwater fishes with toothless jaws but with oesophageal teeth on last gill arch. Fleshy barbels usually present at edge of mouth.

Family: **Carps and Minnows** — *Cyprinidae* (p. 298). Most abundant European fishes inhabiting both flowing and stagnant water. Many bred artificially. Economically important.

Family: **Loaches** — *Cobitidae* (p. 304). Small freshwater fishes with long cylindrical body and 6—12 fleshy barbels on lips. Bottom-dwellers.

292

Family: **Catfishes** — *Siluridae* (p. 304). Freshwater fishes with naked, scaleless skin. Six long barbels round mouth; 2 on upper lip, 4 smaller ones on lower lip. Inhabit deep water.

Family: **North American Catfishes** — *Ictaluridae* (p. 304). Smaller fishes with 8 barbels; 2 behind nostrils, 2 on upper and 5 on lower lip.

Order: **Eels and Allies** — *Anguilliformes* (p. 306). No abdominal fins. Dorsal, anal and caudal fins joined. Small gill-slits.

Family: **Eels** — *Anguillidae* (p. 306). Predacious fishes with snake-shaped body. Mainly marine, some species found in rivers.

Order: **Gar Pikes and Allies** — *Beloniformes* (p. 306). Long-bodied fishes with blunt-rayed fins.

Family: **Gar Pikes** — *Belonidae* (p. 306). Mostly marine fishes. Dorsal and anal fins situated at end of body.

Order: **Lophobranchiate Fishes** — *Syngnathiformes* (p. 306). Body very long and thin, covered with bony plates. Jaws produced to snout terminating in suctorial mouth.

Family: **Pipe Fishes** — *Syngnathidae* (p. 306). Small marine fishes with bizarre forms. Males carry eggs and offspring in abdominal brood pouch.

Order: **Perches and Allies** — *Perciformes* (p. 306). Marine and freshwater fishes with hard rays in anterior part of double dorsal fin. Abdominal fins are moved to front so that they are situated below pectoral fins.

Family: **Sea Basses** — *Serranidae* (p. 306). Large, solidly-built marine and freshwater fishes. Anal fin has 3 spines.

Family: **Perches** — *Percidae* (p. 306). Predacious freshwater fishes of northern hemisphere with toothed or spiked gill-covers. Economically important.

Family: **Mackerels** — *Scombridae* (p. 308). Predacious marine fishes with spindle-shaped body tapering off sharply towards tail. Posterior part of dorsal and anal fin divided into several small fins.

Family: **Sculpins** — *Cottidae* (p. 308). Small, predacious fishes with large flat head and wide snout. Two dorsal fins, first small and spiny, second soft. Inhabit coastal waters, rivers and lakes.

Order: **Cods and Allies** — *Gadiformes* (p. 308). Mostly marine, occasionally freshwater fishes with soft-rayed fins. Abdominal fins in front of pectoral fins.

Family: **Cods** — *Gadidae* (p. 308). Single barbel on lower lip.

Order: **Flounders** — *Pleuronectiformes* (p. 308). Flattened, strikingly asymmetrical body. Upper aspect slightly arched and pigmented. Economically important marine fishes.

Family: **Soles** — *Soleidae* (p. 308). Adults have eyes on one side. Young have symmetrical body but one eye later migrates to other side. Young swim, adults lie flat on sandy bottom of sea.

Order: **Anglers and Allies** — *Lophiiformes* (p. 308). Skin naked or tuberculated. Abdominal fins on throat.

Family: **Anglers** or **Fishing Frogs** — *Lophiidae* (p. 308). Small, round gill apertures behind arm-like pectoral fin. Dermal appendages on mouth and underside of body. Marine fishes, frequently caught.

Order: **Sticklebacks and Allies** — *Gasterosteiformes* (p. 308). Isolated sharp spines on back, in front of dorsal fin. Scales reduced and sometimes replaced by bony plates. Marine and freshwater fishes.

Family: **Sticklebacks** — *Gasterosteidae* (p. 308). Small predacious fishes with sharply tapering hind part of body.

293

Class: **Lamprey and Hag Fishes** — *Cyclostomata*

Order: **Lampreys** — *Petromyzoniformes*

1 Brook Lamprey *Lampetra planeri*. Distributed over whole of Europe. Lives permanently in rivers and streams. Length up to 16 cm. In spring female lays 500—2,000 eggs. Larvae transform to adult individuals after 2—4 years. In spring, after completing metamorphosis, lampreys spawn in upper reaches where larvae also live. Adults die after spawning.

2 River Lamprey *Lampetra fluviatilis*. Lives in sea off coasts of northern Europe. Length up to 50 cm. In autumn migrates up rivers and in April or May spawns near source in places with sandy bed. Male builds nest — depression up to 50 cm. in diameter — in which female lays 5,000—40,000 eggs. Male and female then die of exhaustion. Larvae, hatched in 14—21 days, live on small organisms. Grow to 18 cm., undergo metamorphosis at end of summer of third year. Toothless mouth acquires teeth and eyes emerge onto surface of head. On completing metamorphosis which takes 6—8 weeks, young lampreys migrate to sea where they live predaciously on different fishes. Tear food to pieces with teeth and suck it in. Grow quickly. When adult, return to spawning sites in rivers and streams. Swim 15—25 km. daily against current. Lamprey has savoury flesh.

Class: **Cartilaginous Fishes** — *Chondrichthyes*

Order: **Sharks and Allies** — *Selachiformes*

3 Lesser Spotted Dog-fish *Scyliorhinus caniculus*. Lives off European coasts, including Mediterranean. Common round England. Length 1 m. Not dangerous to man. Hunts food (molluscs and crustaceans) on sea bed. Nocturnal animal. Female lays up to 20 eggs in hard capsules, with tendrils or corners for attachment to plants. Embryo takes about 6—7 months to develop. Fish's flesh edible but liver supposed to be poisonous.

Order: **Rays and Allies** — *Rajiformes*

4 Thorn-back Ray *Raja clavata*. Commonest European ray, also found in North Sea. Male attains 70 cm., female up to 125 cm. in length. Wide pectoral fins give body rhomboid form. Dorsal skin covered with sharp spines. Ray mainly frequents ooze in shallows. Lives on crabs, shrimps, plaice, etc. Hard egg capsules have process at each of four corners. Eggs laid individually in sand. Embryo takes 4.5—5.5 months to develop. Ray's flesh very tasty.

Class: **Bony Fishes** — *Osteichthyes*

Subclass: **Ray-finned Fishes** — *Actinopterygii*

Order: **Sturgeons and Allies** — *Acipenseriformes*

5 Common Sturgeon *Acipenser sturio*. Abundant off coasts of northern parts of Atlantic and in North Sea, Baltic, Mediterranean and Black Sea. Length about 2 m. (maximum given as 3 m.). Migrates in spring to large rivers to spawn and then returns to sea. Eggs, which resemble frog-spawn, are laid on stony bed. One female lays 800,000—2,500,000 eggs. Fry hatch in a few days. Young migrate to sea within 2 years. Sturgeon looks mainly on sea bed for food (molluscs, crustaceans, worms, small fish) using tactile barbels, seizes it in protrusible mouth. Has now practically vanished from European rivers.

6 Sterlet *Acipenser ruthenus*. Lives in rivers emptying into Black and Caspian Seas. In central Europe occasionally appears in Danube as far as Linz. Long snout. Length 50 cm. Spawning season May—June. Catches food in same manner as preceding species. Has excellent flesh. Caviare is eggs or roe of female.

Order: **Herrings and Allies** — *Clupeiformes*

Family: **Herrings** — *Clupeidae*

7 European Shad *Alosa alosa*. Inhabits North Sea. Length up to 70 cm. In spring swims upstream to spawn. Female lays up to 200,000 eggs on river bed. Feeds on small animals. Likes clear water.

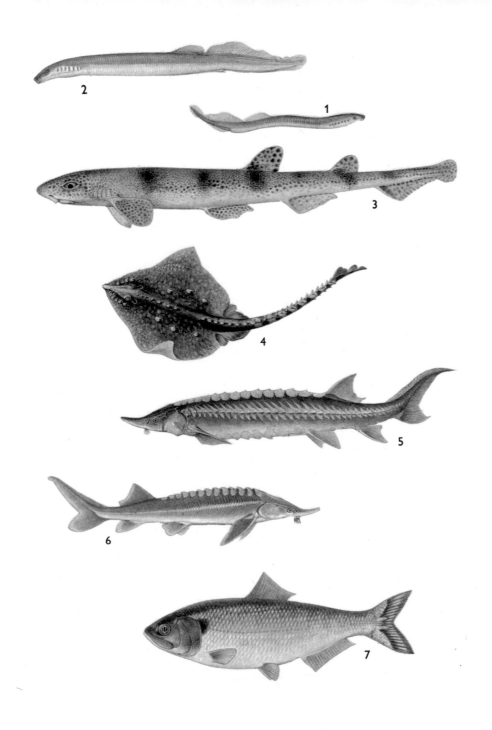

Family: **Salmonids** — *Salmonidae*

1 Salmon *Salmo salar*. Lives in sea off coasts of Europe, Asia and America. In autumn migrates en masse to source of rivers where it spawns in winter. The young (parrs) remain in river 3—5 years and then migrate to sea. Attain adulthood several years later. At spawning site, in cold water about 1 m. deep, female makes depression by slapping tail, lays eggs in it and covers them with sand. Unlike other migratory fishes, salmon spawn several times, although many die of exhaustion or are killed by predators. One female lays up to 40,000 eggs. Survivors return to sea in early spring. Adult salmon measures up to 1.5 m. and weighs 50 kg. Belongs to disappearing fauna of European rivers, although until fairly recent times hundreds of thousands still migrated inland to spawn every year. In time of migration and spawning does not eat. In sea lives on herrings, sprats, crustaceans, etc. Young salmon eat insect larvae and later small fish.

2 Trout *Salmo trutta*. Several species formerly differentiated, now races. Sea trout *(S.t. trutta)* lives off coasts from France as far as Baltic. Length 1.3 m. Migrates up rivers only at spawning time. Lake trout *(S.t.morpha lacustris)* inhabits Alpine and near-Alpine lakes and spawns in their inflowing streams. Female measures up to 80 cm., lays about 30,000 eggs. Most familiar form, brown trout *(S.t.morpha fario)* inhabits 'trout zone' of fast mountain streams. Distributed over whole of western, central and northern Europe as far as Finland and south to Italy and Morocco. Length up to 30 cm. Spawns in winter at age of 2—3 years, female lays up to 1,500 eggs. Likes clear water. Lives on insects, molluscs, worms, etc. One of the most popular fishes. Often bred artificially by collecting eggs and separating and cultivating viable ones. Rainbow trout *(Salmo gairdneri irideus)*, originally from North America, also bred in many parts of Europe. Tolerates warmer water, spawns in spring.

3 Huchen *Hucho hucho*. Lives in clean tributaries of Danube. Never migrates to sea. Measures up to 150 cm., weighs 15 kg. (occasionally up to 30 kg.). Highly predacious, catches fish and other aquatic vertebrates. In March—April swims short distances upstream and spawns on stony beds. Fully grown female lays up to 25,000 eggs. Sometimes bred artificially. Flesh excellent.

4 Alpine Charr *Salvelinus salvelinus*. Resembles trout. Inhabits cold Alpine lakes. Variable colouring and size (in lakes with poor food supply only up to 40 cm.). Dark, normal and large form measuring up to 80 cm. and weighing up to 10 kg. distinguished. First two live on plankton, third on fish. Spawns from November to January near shore or in July on bed, at depth of 20—80 m.

5 Freshwater Houting *Coregonus lavaretus*. Inhabits cold lower reaches of rivers, brackish water and deep lakes in northern part of central and northern Europe. Very variable. Four basic forms, each with own local variability, distinguished. Lives on plankton. Some forms successfully bred in ponds.

6 Grayling *Thymallus thymallus*. Distributed over most of Europe. High dorsal fin. Length up to 48 cm., weight about 1 kg. Inhabits clean rivers and larger streams but likes warmer water than trout. Males larger than females, brightly coloured in spawning season (March—April). Lives on insect larvae, small animals, etc. Valued by anglers for its tasty flesh.

Order: **Pikes and Allies** — *Esociformes*

Family: **Pikes** — *Esocidae*

1 Pike *Esox lucius.* Inhabits rivers and stagnant water over whole northern hemisphere. Length up to 1.5 m., weight 40 kg. and more. In Europe spawns in March and April. Female lays up to 1,000,000 eggs in shallow water. Fry sink to bottom. After 2—3 hours attach themselves to aquatic plants or stones by means of special gland at end of head. Mouth and gills do not open for 8 days. Young pike then surface to fill bladder with air. Pike lives on fish, amphibians, etc.

Order: **Carps and Allies** — *Cypriniformes*

Family: **Carps and Minnows** — *Cyprinidae*

2 Carp *Cyprinus carpio.* Originally from south-eastern European and Asian rivers (China, Japan), has now been introduced into all European rivers. Bred artificially in ponds. Occasionally can measure up to 1.5 m. and weigh 35 kg. River carp (wild form) has low body. Carp have been bred in Europe since 13th century. Many local breeds exist. Fully grown in 3—4 years. Spawning time May—June, at temperature of 15° to 20°C. Female lays 100,000—1,000,000 eggs, fry hatch in 3—6 days. In winter carp retires to deeper, muddy spots and hibernates. Lives on small animals and aquatic plants. Life span up to 50 years.

3 Crucian Carp *Carassius carassius.* Inhabits central and eastern Europe, also distributed in Asia and North America. Lives in stagnant and slow-flowing water. High body, no barbels. Length only 20—30 cm., weight about 1 kg. Spawns in May and June. Female lays up to 300,000 eggs on aquatic plants. Feeds on insects, molluscs and small crustaceans. Golden form also distinguished.

4 Tench *Tinca tinca.* Inhabits stagnant and slow-flowing water in Europe and western Siberia. Also occurs in brackish water of Baltic Sea. Length up to 50 cm., weight about 5 kg. Minute scales, slimy skin. Life span 20 years. Large specimens found only in deep lakes. Spawning time May—July. Female lays about 300,000 sticky eggs which adhere to aquatic plants. Nocturnal fish. Tasty flesh.

5 Roach *Rutilus rutilus.* Occurs in all rivers and in stagnant water in central and northern Europe. Also found in brackish water. Abundant everywhere. Length 15—35 cm., weight sometimes over 1 kg. Spawns near bank in April and May. Female lays 100,000 eggs. Important as food for predacious species, e.g. pike. Valueless in fishponds, in rivers popular with anglers. Lives on river plants, small molluscs, crustaceans and insects.

6 Bream *Abramis brama.* One of largest European freshwater fishes. Length up to 70 cm., weight over 7 kg. High-backed, flat-sided body. Distributed from Urals to west of France and Britain. Inhabits stagnant and slow-flowing water with muddy bed. Spawns in May— July. Female lays 20,000—300,000 eggs at night. Young remain near banks in large shoals. Looks for food (small animals) mainly on bed, surfaces only at night.

7 Silver Bream *Blicca bjoerkna.* High-backed, short, very flat-sided body. Inhabits European rivers and ponds. Usually measures only 30 cm. and weighs less than 1 kg. Spawns in May—June. Female lays about 100,000 eggs among aquatic plants. Of no economic importance. Lives on small animals and partly on aquatic plants.

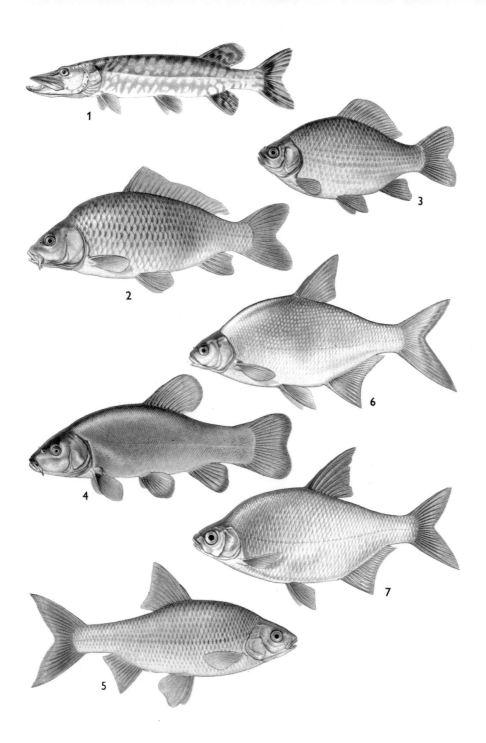

Family: **Carps and Minnows** — *Cyprinidae*

1 Orfe *Leuciscus idus*. Inhabits rivers and river-fed lakes all over Europe. Length 30—45 cm., occasionally up to 70 cm., weight 1—4 kg. Spawns in large shoals near banks from April to June. Female lays 40,000—100,000 eggs on stones and aquatic plants. Lives on insects, worms, small molluscs and crustaceans. Large specimens also eat small fish but orfe not counted as predator. Has very tasty flesh but is comparatively rare.

2 Chub *Leuciscus cephalus*. Commonest fish in slow-flowing European rivers and streams. Length 30 cm. (occasionally up to 70 cm.), weight 0.25—5 kg. Spawning time April and May. Female lays up to 200,000 eggs on aquatic plants. Omnivorous. Eats water plants and small animals, often destructive to young trout populations. Flesh quite tasty.

3 Dace *Leuciscus leuciscus*. Distributed over whole of central and northern Europe. Inhabits fast rivers and streams, also stream-fed ponds. Length 15—20 cm., weight not more than 1 kg. Spawning season March—May. Rival of grayling and trout. Lives on small animals and some plants. Not very popular as food.

4 Asp *Aspius aspius*. Only truly predacious member of carp family. Found near surface of large rivers. Distributed over central and eastern Europe, also found in brackish waters of Baltic Sea. Robust but elongate body. Length 40—60 cm., weight 2—4 kg. (in rare cases up to 1.2 m. and 10 kg.). Spawns from March to beginning of June. Female lays 80,000 to 100,000 eggs on sandy bed. Catches fish, amphibians and occasionally young birds, especially of aquatic species. Very retiring. Has tasty flesh so popular with anglers.

5 *Leucaspius delineatus*. Inhabits central and eastern Europe. Occurs in stagnant and slow-flowing water, also in small ponds and pools. Usually found in shoals. Characterized by silvery sheen and shortened lateral line. Length only 5—6 cm., in exceptional cases up to 12 cm. Spawning time April—May. Female lays about 150 eggs in spirals or rings round stems of aquatic plants. Male guards fry and fans oxygenated water towards them with pectoral fins. Young capable of further reproduction in one year. Lives on algae and small organisms. Important as food for predacious species.

6 *Alburnoides bipunctatus*. Inhabits central Europe. Common in southern and western Germany, elsewhere rare. Lives in shoals in fast, clean rivers, but not at altitudes of over 700 m. Length 9—11 cm. Spawns in April—June. Female lays eggs on sandy bed in flowing water. Fish used by anglers as bait.

7 Bleak *Alburnus alburnus*. Distributed over whole of Europe from Alps as far as Volga. Also found in brackish waters of Baltic Sea, but not in Scotland and Ireland. Inhabits lowland rivers or large river-fed lakes and ponds. Stays near surface. Length 10—15 cm. Spawns from March to June in shallow water near bank, to accompaniment of loud splashing. Female lays eggs at roots of trees extending into water, on aquatic plants, etc. Very abundant fish, important component of diet of predacious fishes. Also significant for destruction of large quantities of mosquito larvae. In addition eats plankton on surface of water. Often employed by anglers as bait in catching predatory fish. In places with very high incidence sometimes used for feeding pigs.

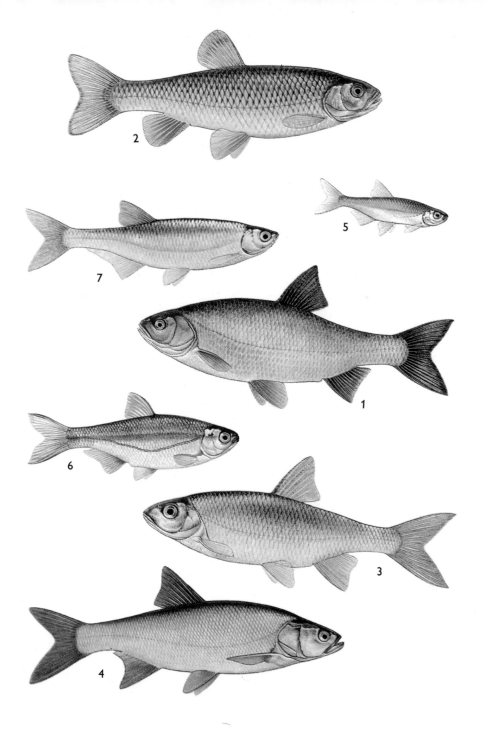

Family: **Carps and Minnows** — *Cyprinidae*

1 *Pelecus cultratus.* East-European fish. Formerly also inhabited bays of Baltic Sea. Often migrates from Black Sea up Danube. Length up to 60 cm. Lives in shoals. Spawns in May and June in salt and fresh water, some individuals in upper reaches of rivers. Female lays about 100,000 eggs on aquatic plants. Lives mainly on plankton.

2 Minnow *Phoxinus phoxinus.* Inhabits fast-flowing streams all over Europe, including mountains. Length 7—14 cm. Males don bright colours in spring. Spawning season May—July. Spawns in daytime, in shoals, in shallow water with sandy bed. Female lays 100—200 large yellow eggs. Fry grows very quickly. Life span 3—4 years. Lives on insect larvae and worms. Found in shoals near surface.

3 Bitterling *Rhodeus sericeus.* Inhabits central Europe north of Alps. Found in stagnant and slow-flowing water. Length 4—10 cm. Male brightly coloured at spawning time, female grows ovipositor. Fish collect in groups in sandy places with bivalves living on bed. Male releases cloud of milt in immediate vicinity of bivalve, which imbibes it together with water. Female inserts ovipositor into shell and lays egg which is fertilized inside shell. Process repeated until all eggs — usually about 40 — have been 'planted'. Shell protects both eggs and fry, which leave shelter after yolk has been consumed. Bitterling largely vegetarian but also eats small crustaceans and worms. Sometimes bred in aquaria.

4 Nase *Chondrostoma nasus.* Once plentiful in most European rivers, especially Oder and Elbe. Still abundant in Danube, Rhine and tributaries. Head produced to snout. Bottom-dweller. Spawning time March—May. Migrates upstream to stony places and spawns in shoals. Female lays up to 100,000 eggs. Adult fish attains up to 50 cm. of length and weighs 2 kg. Lives on water plants and small animals. Flesh not very popular.

5 Barbel *Barbus barbus.* Inhabits whole of central Europe north of Alps, but rare west of Elbe. Lives at bottom of clear flowing water and pools. Length up to 70 cm., weight up to 5 kg. Gather in shoals. Swims upstream in spawning season (April—June). Female lays 5,000—30,000 golden yellow eggs on sandy bed. Eats small animals, e.g. mayfly larvae and eggs and fry of other fishes. Its own roe is regarded as poisonous.

6 Rudd *Scardinius erythrophthalmus.* Inhabits stagnant and slow-flowing waters in Europe, in Alps up to altitude of 2,000 m. Adult fish has bright red abdominal, anal and caudal fins. Length up to 30 cm., weight 1 kg. Spawns in April and May. Female lays up to 100,000 reddish eggs on plants. Feeds on greenstuff and small animals. Has tasty flesh.

7 Gudgeon *Gobio gobio.* Distributed from west of France as far east as central Siberia. Absent in Spain and northern Sweden and Norway. Several subspecies. Single barbel on either side of mouth. Strikingly large fins. Lives at bottom of streams and rivers, also in stagnant water with stony and sandy bottoms. Occurs in brackish water in western part of Baltic. Often found in very large numbers in stream-fed ponds. Length 10—20 cm. Spawns from May to June. Female lays 1,000—3,000 eggs in small clumps on stones and aquatic plants. Young hatch in 10—20 days, according to temperature. Lives on small animals and vegetable debris. Gather in large shoals, often in company of other fishes.

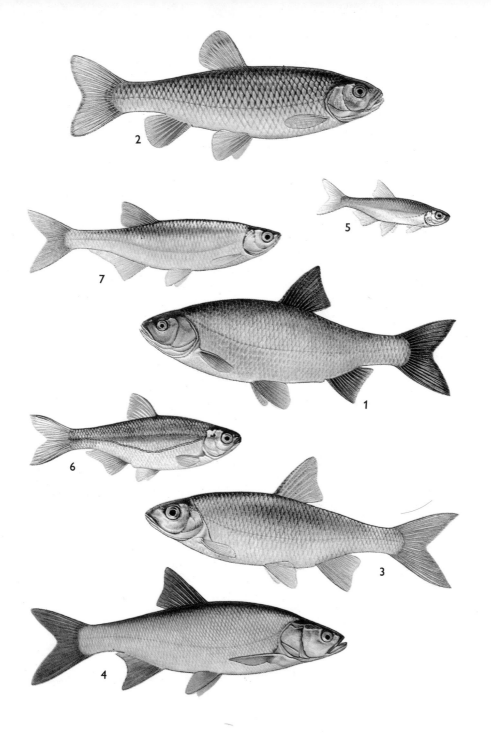

Family: **Carps and Minnows** — *Cyprinidae*

♀

♂ 2

3

1

4

5

6

7

Family: **Carps and Minnows** — *Cyprinidae*

1 Eastern European Bream *Vimba vimba*. Common in central and eastern Europe. Lives near bed. Protruding upper jaw. Length 20—30 cm., weight up to 2 kg. Back often turns black at spawning time. Spawning season April—June. Thousands of fish frequently throng spawning site. Female lays 100,000—200,000 eggs. Lives on small bottom-dwelling animals. Flesh of no great value as food.

Family: **Loaches** — *Cobitidae*

2 Weatherfish *Misgurnus fossilis*. Inhabits greater part of Europe, but absent in England, Norway, Spain and Italy. Lives in mud at bottom of stagnant or slow-flowing water. Ten barbels round mouth help it in search for food. Length 20—30 cm. Spawning season April—June. Female lays up to 10,000 eggs on aquatic plants. Weatherfish has accessory intestinal respiration allowing it to live in oxygen-defficient water. Surfaces, swallows air, forces it down highly vascularized intestine and releases used air through anus. Eats small molluscs and other bottom-dwelling animals, also vegetable debris. Has savoury flesh.

3 Spined Loach *Cobitis taenia*. Inhabits whole of Europe except Norway, Scotland and Ireland. Lives at bottom of clean, slow-flowing or stagnant water with sandy bed. Has 6 short barbels on upper lip and 12—20 round spots on sides. Small, high-set eyes with yellow iris. Length 8—12 cm. Likes to burrow in sand with only head showing. Spawns April—June. Lives on small bottom-dwelling animals. Has accessory intestinal respiration. Below eyes has erectile spine raised when in danger. Hisses if handled.

4 Stone Loach *Noemacheilus barbatulus*. Distributed over whole of Europe except Norway and Sweden. Also abundant in Baltic bays. Lives at bottom of clean, flowing water, less often in lakes and ponds. Smooth snake-like body with scales on sides only. Colouring very variable, but belly always white or bluish. Length 10—15 cm. Spawns from April to June. Female lays about 6,000 eggs on aquatic plants. Eats small bottom-dwelling animals. Once regarded as great delicacy.

Family: **Catfishes** — *Siluridae*

5 European Catfish *Silurus glanis*. Distributed from Rhine as far east as western Asia. Large head with wide snout. Scaleless body. Inhabits deep, slow-flowing rivers, dams and lakes. In deep water may measure up to 3 m. and weigh 250 kg. Solitary fish, occurs in pairs only at spawning time. Spawns from May to June near thickly overgrown banks. Female lays up to 200,000 eggs in shallow water at 18° to 20°C. Stays mainly near bottom, but likes to surface at night. Ungainly in appearance, but swift in action. Predacious. Hunts fish, aquatic birds up to size of goose, small mammals. Young specimens eat insects, molluscs and amphibians. Flesh has excellent flavour.

Family: **North American Catfishes** — *Ictaluridae*

6 Horned Pout *Ictalurus nebulosus*. Originally from U.S.A. Introduced into Europe in 1885 and now bred in rivers and ponds. Length up to 45 cm., weight 1 kg. As distinct from European catfish, has 8 barbels (i.e. 2 more) and adipose fin behind dorsal fin. Stays near bottom, active at night. Spawns in early spring, when found in pairs. Female forms nest-pit between roots, male guards eggs and young fry. Lives on small animals, e.g. fish, etc.

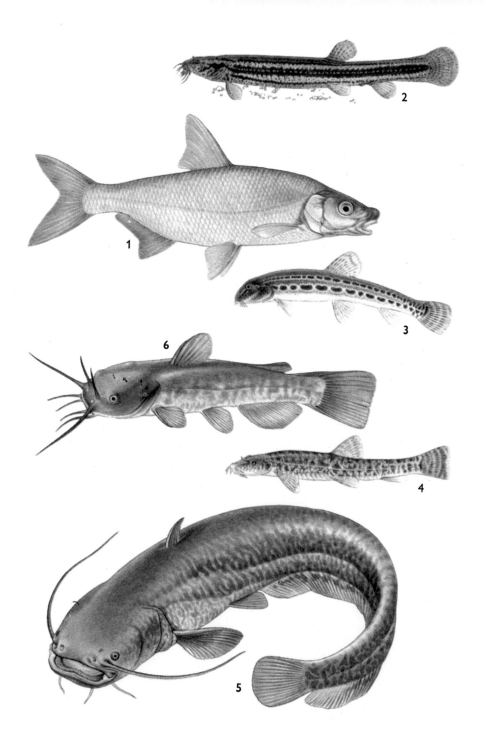

Order: **Eels and Allies** — *Anguilliformes*

Family: **Eels** — *Anguillidae*

1 European Eel *Anguilla anguilla*. Inhabits European coastal waters and rivers. Length over 1 m. (male only 50 cm.), weight up to 5 kg. Eels migrate to western part of Atlantic (Sargasso Sea, east of West Indies), spawn in early spring at depth of 400 m. and temperature of 17°C and then die. Larvae, formerly described as separate species, travel to European coasts with Gulf Stream. At two years measure about 7.5 cm. and reach Europe. At three years acquire typical form and are known as 'elvers'. Invade rivers, develop slowly. Females develop in rivers, males at river mouth. On attaining sexual maturity migrate back to spawning site in sea, taking no food during journey. Male matures at 9, female at 12 years. Predacious fish, lives on different animals. Young bred in ponds.

Order: **Gar Pikes and Allies** — *Beloniformes*

Family: **Gar Pikes** — *Belonidae*

2 Gar Pike *Belone belone*. Lives in shoals in north-eastern part of Atlantic, also in Baltic, Mediterranean and Black Seas. Predacious fish. Lives on swimming crabs, fish, insects. Spawns in shallow water. Female lays eggs from May to June, among aquatic plants. Bones turn green when boiled.

Order: **Lophobranchiate Fishes** — *Syngnathiformes*

Family: **Pipe Fishes** — *Syngnathidae*

3 Narrow-nosed Fish *Syngnathus typhle*. Common in Baltic and North Sea. Length up to 30 cm. Variable colouring. Inhabits shallow water with dense vegetation. Spawns from April to August. Male carries eggs in special abdominal brood pouch, later deposits fry in sea. Eats small crustaceans and fish fry. Suctorial mouth, imbibes prey together with water.

Order: **Perches and Allies** — *Perciformes*

Family: **Sea Basses** — *Serranidae*

4 Sea Bass *Morone labrax*. Inhabits coastal waters of Europe and Africa. Often invades rivers, e.g. Elbe. Length up to 1 m. Spawns at river mouths, also in rivers, from May to July. Sea eggs float, river eggs lie on bed. Fry hatched in 6 days. Predacious fish, pursues pilchard shoals. Has savoury flesh.

Family: **Perches** — *Percidae*

5 Perch *Perca fluviatilis*. Inhabits rivers, lakes and ponds all over Europe. Common fish. Length up to 40 cm., weight 4 kg. For growth over 30 cm. requires 15 years. Consorts in small shoals. Spawning season April to beginning of June. Female lays strings of eggs (total up to 250,000) on aquatic plants etc. Fry hatched in 18 days, take no food up to age of 14 days. Predacious fish, often hunts in shoals. Tasty flesh.

6 Pikeperch *Stizostedion lucioperca*. Distributed over central and north-eastern Europe. Occurs in clean rivers, ponds and brackish water. Length up to 1.3 m., weight 10 kg. Spawns from April to June at depths of 3—5 m. Female lays up to 300,000 eggs in clumps. Predacious fish. When young catches small animals, later different fishes. Flesh has excellent flavour.

7 Pope or **Ruffe** *Acerina cernua*. Inhabits rivers of central and northern Europe. Abundant. Length up to 20 cm. Has preference for deep, clear water and for Baltic bays. Spawning season March—May. Female lays 50,000—100,000 eggs. Predacious fish. Eats insects, worms, crustaceans and eggs and fry of other fishes. Sometimes does serious damage.

8 Streber *Aspro streber*. Occurs only in Danube and tributaries. Lives in flowing water with stony bed. Length only 14—18 cm. Spawns from March to May. Predacious. Lives on worms, insects, small crustaceans and small fish.

306

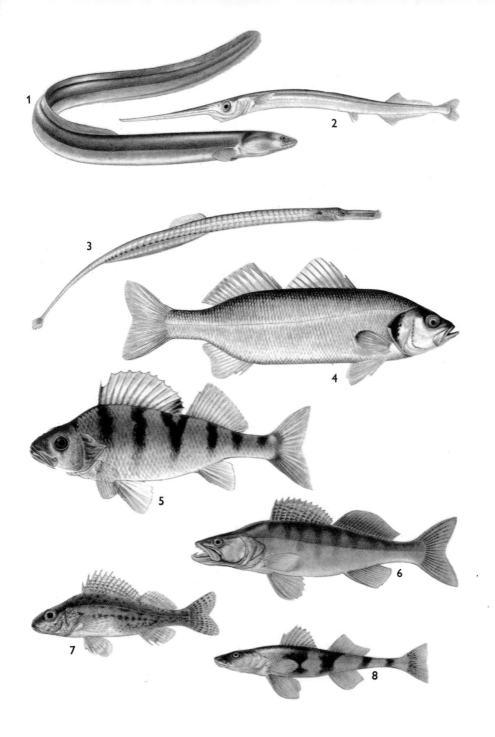

Family: **Mackerels** — *Scombridae*

1 Common Mackerel *Scomber scombrus*. Inhabits Atlantic, Baltic, North Sea, Mediterranean and Black Sea. Length up to 50 cm. In summer frequents shallow coastal water, in winter deep water. Forms huge shoals. Spawns from May to August near coast. Female lays up to 400,000 eggs. At 3 years young mackerel measures 30 cm. and is capable of reproduction. Lives first of all on small crustaceans, later on small herrings, sprats and molluscs. Has excellent flesh. Popular food all over Europe. Caught with nets while migrating.

Family: **Sculpins** — *Cottidae*

2 Miller's Thumb *Cottus gobio*. Inhabits practically whole of Europe. Found in swift-flowing rivers and streams, also in lakes. Stays near bottom and often hides under stones. Length 10—18 cm. Spawning season March—April. Female lays piles of eggs (total 100 to 300) in pits. Eggs guarded by male. Lives on small animals, including trout fry.

Order: **Cods and Allies** — *Gadiformes*

Family: **Cods** — *Gadidae*

3 Burbot *Lota lota*. Distributed over whole of northern hemisphere. Southern limit in Europe northern Italy. Lives in deep, flowing water or river-fed lakes and ponds. Found at quite high altitudes. Length 40—80 cm., weight up to 3 kg. In spawning season (November to beginning of February) swims short distances upstream and looks for sandy site. Female lays up to 1,000,000 eggs in shallow pits or on aquatic plants. Fry hatched in 4 weeks. Nocturnal fish. Predacious, catches smaller fishes and other animals. Flesh regarded as delicacy.

Order: **Flounders** — *Pleuronectiformes*

Family: **Soles** — *Soleidae*

4 Sole *Solea solea*. Found along European coasts of Atlantic, North Sea and part of Baltic. Length up to 50 cm. Colouring adapted to environment. Adults live on sandy bed at depths of not more than 50 m. Active at night. In North Sea spawns from April to August. Young specimens, still symmetrically built, remain near shore up to 2 years and even invade rivers. Eats worms, molluscs, crustaceans and small fishes. Great delicacy. Caught mainly in North Sea.

Order: **Anglers and Allies** — *Lophiiformes*

Family: **Anglers** or **Fishing Frogs** — *Lophiidae*

5 Common Angler Fish *Lophius piscatorius*. Occurs in North Sea, off coast of western Europe and in northern part of Mediterranean. Length up to 2 m. Has isolated, free fin rays on head and anterior part of body. Foremost ray carries leaf-like appendage. Several rows of sharp teeth in mouth. Frequents sea bed, usually found in mud. Spawns in March and April at depths of 1—2 km. Eggs rise to surface. Fry very bizarre in shape. Predacious fish. Lies in wait for prey, 'angling' with long dorsal spines. Lives on fishes, including small sharks and rays. Has very good flesh.

Order: **Sticklebacks and Allies** — *Gasterosteiformes*

Family: **Sticklebacks** — *Gasterosteidae*

6 Three-spined Stickleback *Gasterosteus aculeatus*. Distributed all over Europe, but introduced artificially in many places. Also plentiful along coast. Length 4—7 cm. Care of offspring interesting. At spawning time (April—June) brightly coloured male builds spherical nest from plant fragments and defends surrounding area. Female lays 80—100 eggs in nest and male guards eggs and fry. Several females may lay in one nest and one female may lay 5—6 times in one season. At end of spawning season sticklebacks combine in large shoals. Life span 2—3 years. Very predacious fish. Eats eggs and often fry of other fishes and sometimes does considerable damage. Can be kept in large aquaria with cold water.

Class: **Amphibians** — *Amphibia*

Order: **Tailed Amphibians** — *Caudata* (p. 312). Elongate body with bare, slimy skin. Four short, rather puny limbs used only for crawling. Tail long and well developed.

Family: **Salamanders and Newts** — *Salamandridae* (p. 312). Adults have well developed legs. Eyelids present. Small teeth in both jaws. Swim by means of movements of body and flat-sided tail. High regenerative capacity, i.e. replacement of lost body parts, including bones.

Order: **Tailless Amphibians** — *Salientia* (p. 314). Short, wide body with bare, slimy skin. Strong limbs, hind legs longer and muscular. Digits connected by webbing. Ear drum clearly visible on surface of body. Lay eggs in water, in clumps or strings. Larvae (tadpoles) breathe with gills and remain 2—5 months in water. Adult individuals, after metamorphosis, breathe with lungs.

Family: **Discoglossids** — *Discoglossidae* (p. 314). Small frogs with brightly spotted belly. Skin rough and warty. Pupils round or triangular. Lay eggs in clumps, occasionally singly. Under surface of tongue fixed. Live in water from spring until autumn.

Family: **Spade-footed Toads** — *Pelobatidae* (p. 314). Short, robust frogs with noticeably large head. Slightly resemble true toads, but have smooth skin. Pupils vertical. Large, round tongue, free on one side. Ear drum not visible. Digits of hind limbs extensively webbed. Nocturnal animals, hide in ground during daytime. Have largest tadpoles of whole order. Eggs laid in short, thick strings.

Family: **True Toads** — *Bufonidae* (p. 314). Short, stocky animals. Hind limbs only slightly prolonged. Mouth toothless. Eyelids and ear drums well developed. Skin tough and warty. Secrete fluid containing poison bufotalin. Nocturnal animals, hide during day under stones, in crevices and holes, etc. Eggs laid in long double strings. Take to water only in pairing season, otherwise live on dry land.

Family: **Tree Frogs** — *Hylidae* (p. 316). Small, slender frogs. Tips of digits clubbed. Skin smooth. Upper jaw has fine teeth. Males have single vocal sac below throat. Pupils horizontal and elliptical. Live on trees, in bushes and in grass, etc. Enter water only to lay eggs. Colour of back can change with environment or as a result of some stimulus.

Family: **True Frogs** — *Ranidae* (p. 316). Slender frogs with very long hind limbs. Small teeth in upper jaw. Large ear drums. Front of tongue fixed, indented posterior margin free and can be shot forwards. Males have protrusible vocal sac on either side of head, behind corners of mouth. Pupils horizontal. Eggs laid in clumps.

Class: **Reptiles** — *Reptilia*

Order: **Testudinates** — *Testudines* (p. 318). Distinctive group of reptiles with shell — organ of passive defence. Shell composed of two parts: carapace (on back) and plastron (on abdomen). Carapace usually convex, in most testudinates covered with horny plates. Vision good. Eye has two lids and nictitating membrane. Toothless jaws covered with hard layer of horn as in bird's beak. Horny edge of jaw sometimes very sharp. Tongue fleshy and largely fixed. In terrestrial species limbs adapted for burrowing, in aquatic species for swimming in which case digits are webbed. All testudinates are oviparous. Female lays hard-shelled eggs on dry land, e.g. in sand, humus, etc. Testudinates can go for long periods without food.

Family: **Freshwater** or **Pond Turtles** — *Emydidae* (p. 318). Live in rivers, lakes and ponds, some species also in brackish water, usually in river mouths. Come out to sun themselves and lay eggs. Swim very well but even on land are quicker than tortoises (terrestrial testudinates). Have oval, slightly flattened shell. Mainly carnivorous but eat some plants.

Order: **Scaly Reptiles** — *Squamata* (p. 318). All members of order have scaly body, more or less protrusible tongue and transverse, slit-like cloaca.

Suborder: **Lizards** — *Sauria* (p. 318). Legs usually well developed, but in some species degenerate or even absent. Swift and agile animals. Vision mostly well developed. Eyes generally lidded (apart from exceptions). Tongue rather thin, protrusible and usually with forked tip. When in danger, some species cast off tail which can grow again. Second tail recognizable from different shape of scales. Caudal spine not capable of regeneration, however. Most lizards oviparous. Eggs have usually membraneous shell, in some cases, e.g. geckos, hard shell. Some species ovoviviparous. Live on both animal and vegetable food.

Family: **Skinks** — *Scincidae* (p. 318). Long-bodied, short-legged lizards. Body covered with smooth, glossy scales. Body usually rounded, tail (with exceptions) very long and tapering.

Family: **True Lizards** — *Lacertidae* (p. 318). Well developed limbs. Deeply forked tongue. Body long and cylindrical. Tail easily snapped off, grows again. Most species oviparous, some ovoviviparous.

Family: **Slow-worms** — *Anguidae* (p. 318). Epidermal scales covering body have horny plates underneath. Some species characterized by deep groove along sides. Include species with well-developed limbs and legless species. Some species oviparous, others ovoviviparous.

Suborder: **Snakes** — *Serpentes* (p. 320). Specialized group of reptiles adapted for seizing and swallowing large prey. Legless. Eyelids fused, fixed and transparent. From time to time snakes shed skin, together with epidermis of eyelids. Oviparous or ovoviviparous.

Family: **Colubrid Snakes** — *Colubridae* (p. 320). Largest group of snakes. Majority have no venom fangs. Some species have venom fangs in upper jaw behind normal teeth (back-fanged snakes).

Family: **Vipers** — *Viperidae* (p. 320). Large venom fangs at front of upper jaw, folded back when not in use, erected when snake opens mouth. Venom fangs are hollow and resemble hypodermic needle, with opening on anterior aspect. Venom usually haemolytic and very dangerous.

Class: **Amphibians** — *Amphibia*

Order: **Tailed Amphibians** — *Caudata*

Family: **Salamanders and Newts** — *Salamandridae*

1 Fire Salamander *Salamandra salamandra.* Inhabits whole of central Europe and extends as far as North Africa. Lives in damp moss, among stones near streams and in small rodent holes. Found at altitudes of over 1,200 m. Hibernates deep underground or in caves, often gregariously. Reappears at end of March. In April—May female deposits up to 70 well developed larvae with gills and 4 limbs and measuring about 3 cm., at source of brook. Metamorphosis (transformation to terrestrial form) takes place after 3—4 months. In rare cases larvae spend winter in water. After completing metamorphosis young leave water. Fully grown after 5 years. Length 20 cm. Lives on spiders, worms, gastropods and insects. Skin secretes poisonous substance lethal for small animals. Life span 18 years. Can sometimes be heard squeaking. Most often encountered on forest paths after rain.

2 Alpine Salamander *Salamandra atra.* Glossy black all over. Inhabits Alpine regions (at altitudes of 700—3,000 m) and certain Balkan ranges. Length about 15 cm. Hides under stones and moss and in bushes. Not dependent on water. Female produces two fully developed young which before birth grow to 5 cm. and lose gills. Larvae in female's body live on yolk of eggs which fail to develop. Salamander's diet consists of small insects, spiders, worms and small molluscs. Fully grown after 3—5 years.

3, 4 Crested Newt *Triturus cristatus.* Inhabits whole of central Europe and extends to Urals. Length 14—18 cm. Rarely found at altitudes of over 1,000 m. At pairing time male grows high, doubled crest which starts on forehead and stretches up to tip of tail. Males court females in striking nuptial ceremonies. Crestless female lays over 100 eggs singly on aquatic plants in stagnant water in April or May. Larvae hatch in 2—3 weeks. Metamorphosis after 3 months when larva measures 4.5—9 cm. Adults remain in water long after egg-laying, often until late summer. Newt fully grown at 4 years. Hibernates under leaves and in holes, occasionally under water in mud. Predacious. Catches small crustaceans, insects and molluscs, also eats frog's eggs and tadpoles and larvae of own species.

5 Smooth or **Common Newt** *Triturus vulgaris.* Larva. Distributed over whole of Europe. Length 8—11 cm. Very plentiful. Dorsal crest at pairing time less dentated than in crested newt and continuous at tail base. Female lays 100—250 eggs singly on aquatic plants, usually from beginning of May until June. Larvae hatch in 2 weeks. Metamorphosis after 3 months. Adults visit water only at pairing time. Lives on insects, worms, gastropods and, in water, on tadpoles, etc.

6 Alpine Newt *Triturus alpestris.* Mainly central-European animal, but also extends further west. Length 8—12 cm. At pairing time male wears low dorsal crest and its orange underside turns red. Found at altitudes of up to 3,000 m. Inhabits clear lakes, mountain pools and slow-flowing water. Female lays eggs from March to June. Larvae, hatched in 2—3 weeks, measure about 7 mm. Metamorphosis after 3—4 months when larvae attain 3 cm. of length. Cases of reproduction in larval stage known.

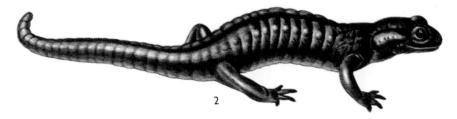

1

2

3

4

5

6

Order: **Tailless Amphibians** — *Salientia*

Family: **Discoglossids** — *Discoglossidae*

1 Red-bellied Toad *Bombina bombina*. Inhabits central and eastern Europe. Occurs mainly in lowlands. Length about 4.5 cm. Lives in ponds, pools, etc. Female lays eggs several times a year but chiefly in May and June. Deposits them in groups on aquatic plants or on bottom. Tadpoles very large. Metamorphosis in September—October. Hibernates in holes, under leaves, etc. Reappears in spring and spends whole of summer in water. Eats small aquatic animals. When in danger, burrows in mud.

2 Yellow-bellied Toad *Bombina variegata*. Inhabits whole of Europe except north and Britain. Eggs laid in June, sometimes later. Tadpoles hatch in 7—9 days. Metamorphosis after 4 months. Hibernates on dry land. From spring, for whole of summer, lives in water. Staple diet mosquito larvae.

3 Midwife Toad *Alytes obstetricans*. Inhabits west of central Europe and south-western Europe. Found in uplands and mountains. Length 5.5 cm. Pairing season early spring to summer. Pairs on dry land. Male winds strings of 20—100 large eggs round legs and carries them until tadpoles are hatched (3—6 weeks). Hatched tadpoles remain in water, undergo metamorphosis in late autumn or following spring. Nocturnal animal. Bell-like call. Lives on insects, worms, spiders, etc.

Family: **Spade-footed Toads** — *Pelobatidae*

4 Spade-footed Toad *Pelobates fuscus*. Distributed over whole of central Europe, extends east to western Siberia. Length up to 8 cm. Nocturnal animal, seldom seen in daytime. From March to May female lays 1,000 eggs in strings 15—50 cm. long, in pools etc. Tadpoles black, measure over 10 cm. After metamorphosis toads measure 3 cm. Crawl out on to dry land. Adults also live on land and leave water after eggs are laid. Hibernate in holes up to 2 m. deep. Eat small animals. Toad emits garlicky odour.

Family: **True Toads** — *Bufonidae*

5 Common Toad *Bufo bufo*. Distributed over whole of Europe and Asia. Length 12 cm., in south up to 20 cm. Abundant everywhere. Occurs in woods, fields, gardens, etc.; often found in cellars. Nocturnal animal. Eats insects, molluscs, worms, occasionally small amphibians. Hibernates in dry holes, etc. Female lays 2 strings of 1,200—6,000 eggs which both parents twine round aquatic plants. Tadpoles, hatched in 12 days, live gregariously. Metamorphosis after 77—91 days; young then leave water. Grow slowly, attain adulthood at 5 years. Life span up to 40 years. Male utters snorting barks.

6 Green Toad *Bufo viridis*. Distributed through western and central Europe as far as Mongolia. Occurs even in dry habitats, in mountains up to altitude of 3,000 m. Digs burrows about 30 cm. deep. Nocturnal animal. Lives on insects, spiders, worms, etc. Hibernates on dry land. In spring female lays two strings of 10,000—12,000 eggs, 3—4 m long, on aquatic plants in shallow water. Male's pairing call in spring is pleasant trill. Metamorphosis after 60—91 days. Fully grown at 4 years.

7 Natterjack Toad *Bufo calamita*. Distributed over western and central Europe. Length 6—8 cm. Crawls, does not jump. Good swimmer, climber and burrower (in winter to depth of 3 m.). In May female lays 3,000—4,000 eggs on aquatic plants. Metamorphosis after only 42—49 days. Young (1 cm.) climb into trees. Nocturnal animal. Loud, craking call. Eats insects, worms, etc.

Family: **Tree Frogs** — *Hylidae*

1 Common Tree Frog *Hyla arborea*. Found all over Europe. Length 3.5—4.5 cm. Takes to water at pairing time. In May female lays up to 1,000 eggs in clumps. Metamorphosis after 90 days. Young frogs crawl out on to land. After egg-laying adults return to bushes and trees. Colouring adapted to environment. Lives on insects and spiders. In autumn frogs retire under stones, into holes, etc. Many hibernate in mud. Males have clear tinkling call.

Family: **True Frogs** — *Ranidae*

2 Edible Frog *Rana esculenta*. Inhabits whole of Europe, Asia and North Africa. Occurs at both low and high altitudes. Found only near water. Male attains 7.5 cm. of length, female up to 13 cm. In May or June female lays 2,000—3,000 eggs in clumps. Tadpoles hatch in 5—6 days. Metamorphosis after 130 days. Tadpoles sometimes hibernate in water. Lives on insects, worms, spiders and small fish. Adults hibernate at water bed in mud, young on dry land. Fond of taking sun-baths. Males have typical croak (crax-crax).

3 Marsh Frog *Rana ridibunda*. Distributed over central and southern Europe, also occurs in south-eastern England, Holland and on Baltic coast. Found near water in warm places in lowlands. Length 15—17 cm. Pairing time April—May. Female lays 5,000—10,000 eggs. Metamorphosis after 83—125 days. Catches insects, worms, small fish and young of small mammals and birds. Very loud call (cray-cray-cray-cray). Hibernates at water bed. Old individuals often hibernate in slow-flowing water.

4 Common Frog *Rana temporaria*. Distributed over most of Europe, extends to eastern Asia. Can be found beyond Arctic Circle. Abundant everywhere. Frequents parks, gardens, woods, etc. In Alps found up to altitude of 3,000 m. Length 10 cm. Often pairs in March, in mountains and north in May and June. Heard only during pairing season. Female lays 1,000—4,000 eggs. Tadpoles hatch in 3—4 weeks. Metamorphosis after 2—3 months but tadpoles sometimes hibernate in water. After egg-laying frog lives on dry land, but in mountains may also remain in water during summer. Nocturnal animal. At end of October returns to water to hibernate but young individuals (up to 3 years) mostly hibernate on land. Eats insects, slugs, spiders and worms.

5 Field Frog *Rana arvalis*. Extends from Belgium across central and northern Europe to Arctic Circle and east to Siberia. Occurs mainly in boggy meadows. Pairs in March and April. Female lays up to 2,000 eggs in 1 or 2 spherical clumps. Spends summer on land, in autumn returns to water to hibernate. Metamorphosis after 2—3 months. Fully grown at 3 years. Nocturnal animal but young also active during day. Lives on insects, molluscs, worms, etc. Deep, muted call. Male turns bluish at pairing time.

6 Dalmatian Frog *Rana dalmatina*. Inhabits central and south-eastern Europe. In north extends to south of Sweden. Lives in damp riverside woods in lowlands. Male attains 6 cm. of length, female 9 cm. Very long hind legs (up to 12.5 cm.). Jumps 1 m. high at distance of 2 m. Pairs at night at end of March and in April. Female lays 600—1,500 eggs in pools, etc. Metamorphosis after 2—3 months. Young frogs crawl out on to dry land. In summer often found far from water. Eats mainly insects. Hibernates chiefly in water. Call barely audible.

Class: **Reptiles** — *Reptilia*

Order: **Testudinates** — *Testudines*

Family: **Freshwater** or **Pond Turtles** — *Emydidae*

1 European Pond Turtle *Emys orbicularis*. Distributed over central and southern Europe, south-western Asia and north-western Africa. Formerly also inhabited England and Rhineland. Length up to 35 cm. Mainly frequents stagnant water, creeks or slow-flowing water with muddy bed and plenty of vegetation. Eats insects, worms, molluscs, small fish and some greenstuffs. Fond of sunning itself beside water. In May or June female lays 3—15 eggs about 3 cm. long in small pit in bank and covers them. Young, hatched in 8—10 weeks, measure 2.5 cm. In October turtle retires to mud to hibernate.

Order: **Scaly Reptiles** — *Squamata*

Suborder: **Lizards** — *Sauria*

Family: **Skinks** — *Scincidae*

2 Snake-eyed Skink *Ablepharus kitaibelii*. Distributed over south-eastern Europe, extends to Hungary and Czechoslovakia in central Europe. Length about 10 cm. Inhabits rocky wooded steppes, deserted vineyards and outskirts of dry, open woods. Lives mainly on small insects. Very quick and agile. Female lays 3—8 eggs.

Family: **True Lizards** — *Lacertidae*

3 Wall Lizard *Lacerta muralis*. Distributed round Mediterranean, extends to western and central Europe. Length up to 20 cm. Expert climber of rocks and trees. Diet consists of insects, spiders and worms. In May or June female lays 2—8 eggs in small pit. Young hatch in 6—8 weeks. Hibernates in holes, crevices, etc. Each animal has own 'preserve'.

4 Sand Lizard *Lacerta agilis*. Very common in Europe north of Alps. Extends west to England and east to central Asia. Length up to 20 cm. and over. Male's back predominantly green, female's grey. Frequents warm, sunny slopes, clearings, etc. Found at altitudes of up to 2,000 m. In May or June female lays 3—15 eggs in shallow pit. Young hatch in 7—12 weeks. Hibernates in holes, under piles of leaves, etc. Each animal has own 'preserve'. Eats insects, spiders and centipedes.

5 Green Lizard *Lacerta viridis*. Inhabits southern and central Europe. Length up to 50 cm. in south, about 30 cm. in central Europe. Frequents warm, rocky places. Expert climber. In spring males fight. In May or June female lays 5—13 (in south up to 21) eggs. Young hatch in 6—8 weeks. Lives on insects, molluscs, small lizards and snakes. Digs burrows up to 1 m. deep. Retires to hibernate in October, reappears in April.

6 Common or **Viviparous Lizard** *Lacerta vivipara*. Distributed over central and northern Europe, occasionally found beyond Arctic Circle. Occurs mainly in mountainous regions but also in plains. Female lays 2—12 eggs at short intervals. Young, hatched immediately, measure about 3 cm. In north young hatched in female's body but in Pyrenees from laid eggs. Lives on insects, spiders, etc. Young also eat plant-lice.

Family: **Slow-worms** — *Anguidae*

7 Slow-worm or **Blind-worm** *Anguis fragilis*. Distributed from England to south of Sweden and across whole of Europe to Algeria. Length up to about 50 cm. Variable colouring. Very abundant in places. Occurs at altitudes of up to 2,200 m. Found mainly under leaves, stones, etc. in deciduous woods with damp soil. Hibernates in holes from end of October, usually gregariously. Ovoviviparous (young hatched from eggs immediately); one female produces 5—26 young. Eats molluscs, worms and insects. Tail easily snapped off but grows again.

Suborder: **Snakes** — *Serpentes*

Family: **Colubrid Snakes** — *Colubridae*

1 Tessellated Snake *Natrix tessellata*. Extends from south-west of France across Germany to central Asia and to eastern part of North Africa. Length up to 1 m., usually less. Spends greater part of life in water. Found at altitudes of up to 2,700 m. Staple diet small fish, occasionally eats amphibians. In some places wreaks havoc among fish fry. Female lays 4—12 eggs at end of June or in July. Disappears in October, often hibernates in rodent burrows near water.

2 Grass Snake *Natrix natrix*. Common all over Europe, extends east as far as Aral Sea. Found mainly near water. Occurs at altitudes of up to 2,000 m. Has distinctive spots on sides of head. In autumn retires to hibernate in crevices, holes, etc., often gregariously. Eats amphibians, occasionally small fish and mammals. Young also eat insects. In July—August female lays 6—30 (in rare cases up to 70) eggs under leaves, in waterside soil or in moss. Young, hatched in 2 months (in south sooner), measure 11—18 cm.

3 Aesculapian Snake *Elaphe longissima*. Inhabits warm parts of Europe and south-western Asia. Length up to 2 m. Largest European snake. Lives in deciduous woods or areas with plenty of bushes. Found in Alps at altitudes of up to 2,000 m. Climbs trees extremely well, plunders birds' nests and devours young. Main diet, however, small rodents and lizards. At end of June or beginning of July female lays 5—8 tough eggs 5.5 cm. long and 3.5 cm. wide in holes, hollow trees and stumps. Young hatch in 6—8 weeks. Snake starts to hibernate in autumn. Uses hollow tree stumps, mammals' burrows, rock crevices, etc.

4 Smooth Snake *Coronella austriaca*. Inhabits practically whole of Europe except Ireland and Mediterranean islands. Extends eastwards into western Asia. Length not more than 75 cm. Very abundant in places. Preference for woods and thickets. Found at altitudes of up to 2,200 m. Lives mainly on lizards, occasionally eats small rodents or birds and sometimes other snakes. Young also eat insects. Ovoviviparous. Female lays 2—15 eggs at end of August or beginning of October and young are hatched immediately. Often mistaken for viper.

Family: **Vipers** — *Viperidae*

5 Common Viper *Vipera berus*. Inhabits central Europe, parts of southern Europe, northern Europe to beyond Arctic Circle and large part of Asia as far as Japan. Length about 80 cm. Variable colouring, typical zigzag line invisible in black specimens. Usually found in mixed forests. Occurs at altitudes of up to 2,700 m. Largely nocturnal, hunts also by day at very high altitudes only. Staple diet small rodents. Potent venom. Does not actively attack man. At end of August or beginning of September female either gives birth to live young or lays 6—20 eggs from which young are hatched immediately. In spring males fight, each attempting to 'flatten' rival but without injuring it. Retires in October. Hibernates gregariously, often together with other snakes, in holes in ground, crevices in rocks, etc.

6 Asp Viper *Vipera aspis*. Distributed over south-western Europe, extends to southern part of Black Forest (Germany). Occurs in rocky places in uplands and on lower slopes of mountains. Nocturnal animal. Lives on small rodents and occasionally small birds. Young catch small lizards. Female gives birth to young in August. Venom very potent, bite fatal in 2—4% of cases. Length not more than 75 cm.

Class: **Birds** — *Aves*

Superorder: **Carinate Birds** — *Carinatae* (p. 326). Birds capable of flight. Fore limbs converted to feathered wings. Secondary loss of flight in a few species.

Order: **Passerine** or **Perching Birds** — *Passeriformes* (p. 326). Highly developed vocal apparatus. In nesting season males announce occupation of nesting area in song. All build proper nests. Young born blind and featherless, covered only with light down; completely dependent on parental care.

Family: **Crows** — *Corvidae* (p. 326). Largest songbirds. Powerful beak with slightly curved tip. Omnivorous. Many species live in colonies.

Family: **Starlings** — *Sturnidae* (p. 328). Smallish birds with large, straight beak and pointed wings.

Family: **Orioles** — *Oriolidae* (p. 328). Moderately large songbirds. Arboreal, build nests in forks of branches. Occur mainly in tropics.

Family: **Tree-creepers** — *Certhiidae* (p. 330). Tiny birds with curved, conical beak. Hard-tipped tail feathers. Strong, curved claws. Climb tree trunks.

Family: **Nuthatches** — *Sittidae* (p. 330). Small, robust birds with strong, straight beak and short tail. Climb trees with agility, often upside down.

Family: **Finches** — *Fringillidae* (p. 330). Small birds with short conical beak. Largely grain-eaters. Live mainly in trees. Build basin-like nests.

Family: **Weavers** — *Ploceidae* (p. 334). Small birds with short conical beak.

Family: **Buntings** — *Emberizidae* (p. 334). Usually up to size of sparrow. Live often on ground. Conical beak.

Family: **Larks** — *Alaudidae* (p. 336). Small, brownish birds with slender beak. Live mainly on ground. Very long claw on hind digit.

Family: **Wagtails** — *Motacillidae* (p. 336). Small, very slim, long-tailed birds. Run nimbly.

Family: **Titmice** — *Paridae* (p. 338). Small birds with short body and thick, awl-like beak. Move with dexterity among branches, often hang upside down. Hole-nesters. Usually insectivorous, in winter also eat seeds. Very useful birds.

Family: *Aegithalidae* (p. 338). Small birds resembling tits. Very long tail.

Family: *Remizidae* (p. 338). Small birds. Hang nest on branches.

Family: **Goldcrests** — *Regulidae* (p. 338). Little birds with delicate, conical beak. Mainly frequent conifers. In winter form small flocks.

Family: **Shrikes** — *Laniidae* (p. 340). Stout birds with strong, hook-tipped beak. Catch insects and small vertebrates. Often collect stock of food by impaling prey on thorns.

Family: **Waxwings** — *Bombycillidae* (p. 340). Largish birds with crested head. Shafts of secondaries terminate in narrow, red, horny plates. Northern birds. Their flocks regularly appear in central Europe in winter.

Family: **Accentors** — *Prunellidae* (p. 340). Small birds with hard beak with wide root. Frequent dense underwood. Large nest made of moss.

Family: **Wrens** — *Troglodytidae* (p. 340). Small, active birds with hard, conical beak and short, erect tail. Lead solitary existence in winter.

Family: **Dippers** — *Cinclidae* (p. 340). Smallish birds with straight, slender beak and very short tail. Live near mountain streams, hunt under water on bed.

Family: **Flycatchers** — *Muscicapidae* (p. 342). Small, insectivorous birds with pointed, slightly flattened beak. Catch insects on wing. Live mainly in trees. Hole-nesters.

Family: **Warblers** — *Sylviidae* (p. 342). Small birds with thin, conical beak. Live in trees and thickets. Mainly insectivorous. Good singers.

Family: **Thrushes** — *Turdidae* (p. 344). Large and small birds with conical beak and long tarsi. Live mainly on insects, worms, etc. Partly also on plant food.

Family: **Swallows** — *Hirundinidae* (p. 348). Small birds with short, flat beak, wide mouth, thin legs and long wings. Insectivorous, catch prey on wing. Build clay nests or make burrows in sandy or clay banks, brick-works, etc.

Order: **Woodpeckers and Allies** — *Piciformes* (p. 350). Moderately large birds with very strong beak. Long, protrusible tongue. On foot, two digits point forwards and two backwards. Very tough tail feathers used as support when climbing.

Family: **Woodpeckers** — *Picidae* (p. 350). Birds specialized for climbing tree trunks. Beak is hacking implement. With some exceptions, carve nests in trees. Live on insects and insect larvae.

Order: **Swifts and Allies** — *Apodiformes* (p. 350). Small to tiny birds (include hummingbirds of South America) with long primaries. Excellent fliers.

Family: **Swifts** — *Apodidae* (p. 350). Smallish birds with short beak with wide root and long, narrow, curved wings. Weak legs used for hanging by. Insectivorous, catch prey on wing.

Order: **Rollers and Allies** — *Coraciiformes* (p. 352). Smallish birds up to size of jackdaw, with short tarsi. Toes partly fused at root. Often brightly coloured.

Family: **Rollers** — *Coraciidae* (p. 352). Robust birds of jackdaw size with beak slightly hooked at tip. Chiefly hole-nesters.

Family: **Bee-eaters** — *Meropidae* (p. 352). Moderately large, very brightly coloured birds with long, pointed, slightly curved beak. Insectivorous. Nest in burrows dug in sand-pits or sandy banks.

Family: **Kingfishers** — *Alcedinidae* (p. 352). Smallish birds (in Europe), with very large head, long, strong, flat-sided beak, short body and extremely short tail. Dig burrows in sandy or clay banks beside water.

Family: **Hoopoes** — *Upupidae* (p. 352). Birds with long, thin, curved beak. Hole-nesters. Agile both on ground and in trees.

Order: **Nightjars** — *Caprimulgiformes* (p. 352). Moderately large birds with strikingly large, wide, flattened head and short, flat, gaping beak with bristly feathers at root. Large eyes. Short, puny legs. Soft feathers like owls'. Nocturnal birds. Lay eggs only in depression in ground. Mainly insectivorous.

Order: **Owls** — *Strigiformes* (p. 352). Large, moderately large and small nocturnal birds. Large head with eyes at front. Soft, fluffy feathers. Beak hooked as in birds of prey. Movable toes with strong, curved claws. Swallow prey in large gobbets. Have no crop and eject undigested remnants of food such as bones, hairs and feathers in form of pellets. Young hatch successively.

Order: **Cuckoos and Allies** — *Cuculiformes* (p. 354). Small and moderately large birds. Beak has slightly hooked tip and cleft corners. Long wings and long, wedge-shaped tail. Short legs with outer toe pointing backwards. Forest-dwellers.

Order: **Birds of Prey** — *Falconiformes* (p. 356). Moderately large to large birds with typical powerful beak. Upper mandible hooked. Sharp-edged jaws. Beak membrane strongly developed. Long, strong, sharp, and in some species curved talons for killing prey. Good and usually swift fliers. Majority carnivorous.

323

Family: **Falcons** — *Falconidae* (p. 356). Robust birds of prey characterized by tooth-like process near tip of upper mandible. One of most rapid fliers. Generally swoop on prey at high velocity. Live on small vertebrates and insects. Nest on rocks, towers, etc.

Family: **Eagles and Allies** — *Accipitridae* (p. 356). Robust to large birds of prey without process on beak. Some belong to largest carinate birds. Several subfamilies. Some species catch live prey, others, e.g. vultures, eat carrion. Vultures do not possess talons but have powerfully developed, strong beak.

Family: **Ospreys** — *Pandionidae* (p. 358). Robust birds of prey with short beak but long, hooked upper mandible. Outer toe can be directed backwards. Very long, curved talons adapted for catching fish.

Order: **Cursory Birds** — *Ciconiiformes* (p. 360). Mostly large birds with long legs and neck. Legs adapted for striding. Beak usually long, straight and hard, but in some species curved (ibises) or widened at tip (spoonbills). Short webbing between toes. Live entirely on flesh. Adults feed young.

Family: **Herons** — *Ardeidae* (p. 360). Moderately large and large birds with long neck and long-toed legs. Beak straight and pointed. Impale or grab prey with sudden thrust of beak. Hold neck in the shape of letter S when flying.

Family: **Storks** — *Ciconiidae* (p. 360). Large birds with long, strong, straight beak. Large, wide wings. Good gliders. Neck extended during flight.

Order: **Pelicans and Allies** — *Pelecaniformes* (p. 362). Aquatic birds with legs adapted for paddling. All four digits point forwards and are webbed. Live mostly on fish. Parents feed young. Beak strong (in some species huge) and can be opened very wide. Pouch often present under lower mandible.

Family: **Cormorants** — *Phalacrocoracidae* (p. 362). Slim, robust birds with elongated beak with hooked upper mandible and small pouch at base of lower mandible. Live on fish, hunt under water. Gregarious.

Order: **Ducks, Geese and Swans** — *Anseriformes* (p. 362). Medium to large birds with short legs adapted for paddling. Long, thick bill with horny lamellae (filter) along inner margin. 'Nail' at tip of upper mandible. Thick plumage, insulating against cold and wet. Uropygial gland ('parson's nose') well developed. Males brightly coloured at mating time. With some exceptions, male and female geese and swans have same colouring. Eggs mostly hatched by female only. Large clutches. Nest lined with down. Some species of ducks dive. Good fliers.

Order: **Divers and Allies** — *Gaviiformes* (p. 366). Medium to large aquatic birds with stout body and slender neck. Short legs adapted for paddling, set far back on body. Wings short, but birds fly well and swiftly. Spend most time in water. Skilled divers.

Family: **Divers** — *Gaviidae* (p. 366). Birds with robust body and long, pointed beak. Build large nests beside northern lakes. When not nesting, live on open sea. In central Europe regularly seen during winter migration.

Order: *Podicipediformes* (p. 366).

Family: **Grebes** — *Podicipedidae* (p. 366). Smallish aquatic birds with slim body and long neck. Toes only fringed with webbing. Build floating nests. Live on small fish and insects. Some species form colonies.

Order: **Doves, Pigeons and Allies** — *Columbiformes* (p. 368). Smallish to moderately large birds with soft swelling (swollen membrane) at base of beak. Short legs, free toes. Mainly arboreal. Parents feed young, first of all with special secretion ('pigeon's milk').

324

Order: **Waders and Allies** — *Charadriiformes* (p. 368).

Family: **Auks, Razorbills and Puffins** — *Alcidae* (p. 368). Medium-sized birds with erect posture. Short, tough tail. Exclusively marine birds. Poor fliers, excellent divers. Form nesting colonies on shore of rocky northern islands. Usually lay single egg. Live on fish, crustaceans and molluscs.

Family: **Gulls and Terns** — *Laridae* (p. 370). Small to moderately large birds with long tapering wings. Live near water. Beak long and flat-sided, often with hooked tip. Toes webbed. Consort in large companies. Parents feed young. Mainly flesh-eaters.

Families: *Charadriidae, Recurvirostridae and Scolopacidae* (p. 372). Small to moderately large birds with rather long legs. Beak long and slender, may be curved down or up. Fly well and swiftly. Frequent muddy and sandy ground by sea, ponds and rivers and sometimes meadows. Always lay 4 eggs. Nest in hollow in ground.

Order: **Cranes, Rails and Allies** — *Gruiformes* (p. 374). Small to large birds with relatively short, rounded wings and short tail. Straight beak. Do not feed young.

Family: **Cranes** — *Gruidae* (p. 374). Large terrestrial birds with long legs, long neck and long, strong, straight, sharp beak like stork's. Males have loud trumpeting call. Perform nuptial dances. At nesting time consort in pairs, otherwise in large communities. Ground-nesting and migratory birds. Fly in typical echelon formation.

Family: **Rails, Moorhens and Coots** — *Rallidae* (p. 376). Small to moderately large birds usually inhabiting sedge and waterside thickets. Body compressed and flexible for wriggling through undergrowth. Long toes. In fully aquatic species (e.g. coot), toes are fringed with webbing. Clumsy flier. Parents carry food to newly hatched young in beak.

Family: **Bustards** — *Otididae* (p. 376). Moderately large to large birds resembling turkeys. Long legs. Only 3 toes (all pointing forwards) with flat claws. Run quickly, fly relatively well. Males larger. Omnivorous.

Order: **Game Birds** — *Galliformes* (p. 376). Small to large birds with strong legs adapted for scratching. Short, thick, blunt-clawed toes. Mainly terrestrial, look for food also on ground. Majority (except steppe species) perch at night in trees. Thick beak with slightly curved tip. Males (cocks) larger and gaudily coloured; in a few species both sexes are same in appearance. Many species polygamous (cock has more than one hen). Mostly ground-nesters. Hen lays several eggs, hatches them unaided. Young independent and learn to fly very soon.

Family: **Pheasants, Partridges and Quails** — *Phasianidae* (p. 376). Birds with unfeathered tarsi and toes. Mainly steppe- and forest-dwellers. Also found at edge of thickets.

Family: **Grouse and Ptarmigans** — *Tetraonidae* (p. 378). Medium to large, stout-bodied birds. Tarsi completely or partly feathered. All forest-dwellers.

Class: **Birds** — *Aves*

Superorder: **Carinate Birds** — *Carinatae*

Order: **Passerine** or **Perching Birds** — *Passeriformes*

Family: **Crows** — *Corvidae*

1 Raven *Corvus corax*. Distributed in Europe, Asia and North Africa. In eastern Europe also lives in villages together with jackdaws, on church towers, etc. In central Europe occurs in vast wooded regions. Builds nest on tall trees or on rocks. Uses and adds to it many years. Building done by female, male fetches material (twigs, moss, hairs, etc.). Female lays 5—6 green-spotted and speckled eggs, often at end of February. Young hatched in 21 days, nest-bound about 40 days. Eggs hatched mainly by female with occasional help from male. Diet consists of small vertebrates, insects, debris of animal origin.

2 Carrion Crow *Corvus corone corone*. Distributed over western and central Europe. Completely black. Inhabits wooded areas interspersed with fields and meadows. Often seen looking for food near water. Builds nest in tall trees, usually in March. Nest made of twigs, moss and diverse materials. At end of March or beginning of April female lays 5—6 greenish, dark spotted eggs. Incubates them 17—20 days, fed by male. Young nest-bound for about one month. In winter families combine in large flocks. Both vegetable and animal diet. Collects seeds and berries etc., catches insects and small vertebrates and also eats carrion.

3 Hooded Crow *Corvus corone cornix*. Distributed in eastern and central Europe. Crossing of two subspecies normal along dividing line, which follows Elbe and Vltava to Vienna and crosses Alps into northern Italy. Biology same as for carrion crow but often also nests in large town parks. Very suspicious and wary. Frequently plunders partridge and pheasant nests and is consequently shot on sight by gamekeepers.

4 Rook *Corvus frugilegus*. Distributed over practically whole of Europe from middle of France and northern Italy, extends east into Asia north of Himalayas. Forms flocks and nests in colonies (often huge). Likes open country, looks for food in meadows and fields. Sometimes nests in towns, e.g. in cemeteries etc. Builds nests on tall trees; large number of nests on one tree quite common. Female lays 3—5 greenish, dark spotted eggs, usually at beginning of April. Young hatch in 17 days and remain about 5 weeks in nest. In winter migrates southwards in flocks and in central Europe is replaced by more northerly population. Mixed diet. Collects seeds, acorns, etc., also feasts on carrion.

5 Jackdaw *Corvus monedula*. Inhabits whole of Europe, northern Asia and north-western Africa. Lives in colonies. Nests on rocky ledges, in towers, hollow trees, etc. Often found in towns. In March builds nest from twigs, straw, moss, feathers, etc. At end of April female lays 4—6 blue-green, grey-speckled eggs. Eggs incubated 17—18 days, mainly by female. Young remain one month in nest and then roam neighbourhood with parents. In autumn jackdaws join flocks of rooks. Lives on insects, spiders, molluscs, worms, only occasionally young of small vertebrates; also seeds, berries, etc. Often calls while flying. Easily tamed.

6 Magpie *Pica pica*. Distributed over whole of Europe, large part of Asia, north-western Africa and North America. Characteristic black and white colouring, long tail. Length about 45 cm. Prefers flat country with small copses and shrubs. Builds nest from twigs, turf, blades of grass, leaves, etc. in trees and small bushes. In April female lays 3—10 greenish, thickly speckled eggs. Young hatch in 17—18 days. Fledged after 26 days and remain with parents through winter. Lives on insects, molluscs, small vertebrates, seeds and berries.

Family: **Crows** — *Corvidae*

1 Nutcracker *Nucifraga caryocatactes*. Distribution area extends from Scandinavia to eastern Asia. In central Europe and Alps inhabits conifer woods, only in mountainous regions. Absent in western Europe. Length over 30 cm. At end of February, in densest branches of tall firs, up to 15 m. from ground, builds nest from broken twigs, moss, lichen, hairs, grass, etc. At end of March female lays 3—4 light green, brown- and grey-speckled eggs. Incubates them alone 16 days, fed by male. Young fledged in 21—25 days, but still remain with parents. Eats insects, occasionally young birds, seeds, acorns, nuts, etc.

2 Jay *Garrulus glandarius*. Distributed over whole of Europe, Asia as far as China and north-western Africa. Lives mainly in deciduous or mixed woods. At beginning of April, in tall trees, sometimes only 2 m. from ground, builds nest of twigs, grass, moss, etc. At end of April or beginning of May female lays 5—7 grey-green, brown-spotted eggs. Incubated by both parents in turn 16—17 days. Jay is very wary at nesting time. Can imitate call of different forest birds. Jays often fly long distances, not in flocks, but singly, with long intervals. Do not call when flying. Raucously announce approach of humans. Live on mixed diet, make stocks of acorns beside tree stumps, etc.

3 Alpine Chough *Pyrrhocorax graculus*. Distributed mainly in Alps, Pyrenees and some parts of central Asia. Length about 37 cm. Occurs at altitudes of over 2,000 m. Seen in lowlands only in winter. Lives in flocks. Builds nest from twigs, hairs, rootlets, etc. in rock crevices. At end of April female lays only 2 green, brown-spotted eggs. Agile mountaineer. Lives on insects, molluscs, small vertebrates and seeds.

Family: **Starlings** — *Sturnidae*

4 European Starling *Sturnus vulgaris*. Distributed over whole of Europe, east into central Asia, also in North Africa. Length 16.5—18.5 cm. Speckled at mating time, otherwise black. In autumn (usually September) migrates to southern Europe and North Africa. Before departing congregates in huge flocks and spends night in sedge. Returns in March. Occasionally resident. Originally nested in hollow trees in deciduous woods, today in orchards, parks and gardens with nesting-boxes. Female builds nest from dry grass, feathers, etc.; male sometimes also fetches material. At end of April female lays 5—6 green-blue eggs, incubated 14 days by both parents. Young fed by parents. After leaving nest form flocks. Lives on insects, worms, cherries and other fruits.

5 Rose-coloured Starling *Sturnus roseus*. Inhabits southern Europe and central Asia. Visits central Europe in flocks and occasionally nests there. Spends winter in northern India. Length about 23 cm. Builds nest in hollows, in piles of stones, in ground or even in open. Lives mainly on locusts, follows them into steppes in huge flocks. Also eats other insects and fruit, in winter rice. Female lays 3—8 pale blue eggs. Young fed by both parents which bring them food at short intervals.

Family: **Orioles** — *Oriolidae*

6 Golden Oriole *Oriolus oriolus*. Widely distributed in Europe, North Africa and western, central and southern Asia. European population migrates to Africa in winter. Length 21—23 cm. Males have high-pitched, fluting call. Inhabits deciduous woods, large parks and gardens. Nest woven from long grass blades, built by female in fork of branch. Female lays 3—5 whitish eggs with small red-brown and mauve spots. Young hatch in 14—15 days. Lives chiefly on insects and insect larvae, spiders and small molluscs, sometimes fruit, e.g. cherries. Migrates from Europe in August.

Family: **Tree-creepers** — *Certhiidae*

1 Common Tree-creeper *Certhia familiaris*. Distributed over most of Europe, central and eastern Asia and North America. Length 11—15.5 cm. Mainly frequents conifer and mixed forests. Usually builds nest behind peeling bark or in stacked timber. Nest made of twigs, grass, moss and feathers. Female lays 6—7 white, red-spotted eggs in April or May. Incubated by both parents in turn 13—15 days. Sometimes nests twice. Climbs tree spiral-wise. Eats small insects and their eggs.

2 Short-toed Tree-creeper *Certhia brachydactyla*. Distributed in central, western (except England) and southern Europe, also Tunisia. Length about 13 cm. Inhabits old deciduous woods, large parks and gardens. Nesting biology as for preceding species. Tree-creepers are resident, i.e. non-migratory birds.

3 Wall-creeper *Tichodroma muraria*. Distributed in mountains of southern and central Europe, e.g. Alps, Pyrenees, Carpathians, and east across Balkans to Himalayas. Length 16—17.5 cm. Mountain-dweller, occurs in lowlands only in winter. At nesting time in couples, otherwise solitary bird. Skilled at climbing rock faces. Builds nest from grass, moss, etc. in crevices. At end of May female lays 3—5 white eggs with red-brown spots and dots. Incubates them unaided. Eats insects, insect larvae and eggs, spiders, etc.

Family: **Nuthatches** — *Sittidae*

4 Nuthatch *Sitta europaea*. Distributed over whole of Europe and Asia (except southern Asia). Body length 13—16 cm. Resident bird. Lives in forests, parks, etc., also in towns. Nests in tree hollows, nesting-boxes, etc., to which it brings scales of pine bark or fragments of dry leaves. If opening too large, fills it with mixture of mud and saliva. Female lays 6—8 white, red-speckled eggs in May, incubates them 15—18 days. Both parents feed young. Diet insects, insect larvae, spiders and seeds stored in cracks.

Family: **Finches** — *Fringillidae*

5 Hawfinch *Coccothraustes coccothraustes*. Distributed over whole of Europe, temperate part of Asia, North Africa. Length 16.5—17.5 cm. Thick beak most characteristic feature. Inhabits deciduous woods, large parks and orchards. Resident bird. Builds nest in April, usually beside trunk, 2—10 m from ground. Nest made of rootlets, grass, hairs, etc., on foundation of thick twigs. At beginning of May female lays 4—6 bluish eggs with grey and mauve spots and streaks. Young hatch in 12—14 days. Eats different seeds and nuts, plus insects at nesting time.

6 Greenfinch *Carduelis chloris*. Distributed over whole of Europe, extends to central Asia and north-western Africa. Length 15—17 cm. Abundant in woods, parks and gardens. In April builds nest from rootlets, dry grass, twigs, etc. in dense branches (chiefly of conifers), 1—20 m. from ground. At beginning of May female lays 5—6 whitish eggs with red-brown spots and blotches. Incubates them 12—14 days, fed by male. Both parents feed young. Diet mainly seeds. Some greenfinches migrate to Italy for winter, others remain behind and live in flocks, together with other birds.

7 Goldfinch *Carduelis carduelis*. Distributed over whole of Europe, Asia Minor, central Asia and North Africa. Length 13—15.5 cm. Inhabits small, open, mixed and deciduous woods, parks, gardens, cemeteries, etc. At end of April builds nest at tip of branch (usually of deciduous tree), 3—10 m. from ground. Nest made of moss, lichen, fluff, horsehair, etc. Nests 2—3 times a year. Lays 4—6 white eggs with violet and reddish speckles and dots. Female incubates eggs 12—14 days. Lives mainly on seeds, in summer also eats insects and insect larvae.

Family: **Finches** — *Fringillidae*

1 Siskin *Carduelis spinus*. Distributed over most of Europe, in east to central Asia. Length 11—13.5 cm. Primarily mountain-dweller but also lives in lowlands. Female builds nest unaided, usually at tip of branch of tall conifer. Nest made of twigs, moss, etc., lined with cocoon silk, hairs, etc. In April female lays 4—6 white eggs with red-brown speckles. Incubates them 12—14 days. Sometimes nests twice. Lives mainly on seeds, in summer also insects. In winter lives in flocks.

2 Linnet *Carduelis cannabina*. Distributed over whole of Europe, in east to western part of central Asia, also in North Africa. Length 13—15.5 cm. Inhabits copses, cemeteries, gardens, etc. Partly migratory. In April builds nest 1.5—2.5 m. from ground in dense bushes, junipers, etc. Nest made of twigs, grass-blades and rootlets, lined with hairs, plant fluff, etc. In April female lays 4—6 whitish eggs thickly speckled with red. Incubates them 12—14 days. Diet seeds and insects.

3 Red-poll *Carduelis flammea*. Distributed in northern Europe, Asia and America, also England. Occasionally nests in central Europe. Length 12—14.5 cm. Seen in central Europe in winter, in large flocks. Builds nest from thin twigs, grass, moss, etc. in bushes or dwarf trees. Lays 4—6 bluish, brown-spotted eggs, incubates them 10—12 days. Lives on seeds, occasionally insects.

4 Serin *Serinus serinus*. Distributed over most of Europe except England and Scandinavia. Length about 11.5 cm. Lives near human communities, in gardens, parks, etc. Migratory bird. Returns at end of March. Male sings from telegraph wires, tall trees, etc. Nest built by female in branches 2—4 m. from ground, from rootlets and grass; lined with feathers, horsehair, etc. Female incubates whitish rusty-speckled eggs 11—13 days. Both parents feed young. After nesting time consort in small groups. Occasionally resident.

5 Bullfinch *Pyrrhula pyrrhula*. Distributed over whole of Europe and temperate parts of Asia. Length 15—19 cm. In central Europe nests mainly in mountains, occasionally in lowlands. Inhabits conifer and mixed forests, also parks and gardens with dense trees and bushes. In April builds nest from twigs, moss, leaves, hairs, etc., relatively close to ground (about 2 m.). Female lays 4—6 pale blue eggs with reddish and violet blotches and black dots. Incubates them 13 days. Lives on seeds, shoots, berries, insects and larvae. In winter frequents lowlands in small troupes.

6 Crossbill *Loxia curvirostra*. Distributed over whole of Europe, temperate parts of Asia, North America. Length 17—18.5 cm. Inhabits conifer forests. Nests at different times of year according to supply of pine and fir cones, seeds of which are food for young. Nest built beside trunk or on forked branch. Winter nests have thick walls and deep basin. Female lays 3—4 greyish white eggs with scattered violet and red-brown spots. Incubates them unaided 14—16 days, fed by male. Newly hatched young have straight mandibles, which begin to acquire typical curved shape after 3 weeks.

7 Chaffinch *Fringilla coelebs*. Distributed over whole of Europe, western Asia, North Africa. Body length 14—18 cm. One of most numerous birds. Lives in woods, gardens and parks. Occurs at altitudes of up to 1,500 m. Many chaffinches resident, joined by others from north. Nest built in trees and bushes 2—10 m. from ground. Rounded woven structure made of rootlets, moss and lichen, thickly lined with hairs, etc. Female lays 6—8 light brown or blue-white eggs marked with red-brown and rusty spots and streaks. Young hatch in 13—14 days. Diet seeds, berries, insects.

Family: **Finches** — *Fringillidae*

1 Brambling *Fringilla montifringilla.* Inhabits northern Europe and Asia. Length 15 to 18 cm. Nests in birch-woods or mixed woods. Nest usually situated low on tree. Made of birch twigs, moss, feathers, etc. Female lays 5—7 eggs like chaffinch's. Seen in central Europe every year from October in flocks. Often visits feeding troughs.

Family: **Weavers** — *Ploceidae*

2 House Sparrow *Passer domesticus.* Distributed over whole of Europe, Asia and North-Africa, also carried to America and Australia. Body length 14—18 cm. Commonest European bird. Lives near human communities. Builds loose nest from straw, fibres, hairs, feathers, etc. on branches or in hollows. Nests up to 4 times a year. Female lays 3—8 blotched and speckled eggs of somewhat variable colouring. Incubates them 13—14 days. Lives on different seeds, buds and, in summer, insects.

3 Tree Sparrow *Passer montanus.* Distributed over whole of Europe and Asia except India. Length 14—16.5 cm. Lives chiefly in open country, gardens, orchards, outskirts of towns and deciduous woods, etc. Builds nest from straw, wool, feathers, etc. in hollow trees, walls or other birds' nests. Nests up to 3 times a year. Female lays 5—6 grey-green, dark spotted eggs, which are incubated by both parents in turn 13—14 days. Eats insects and different seeds. Young fed mainly on insects. Resident bird.

Family: **Buntings** — *Emberizidae*

4 Corn Bunting *Emberiza calandra.* Distributed in Europe from southern Scandinavia, south to North Africa, east to Asia Minor. Length 18—20 cm. Usually inhabits large meadows with shrubs. Builds nest in shrubs on ground, or between tufts of grass. Lines it with grass, leaves, wool, hairs, etc. Female lays 3—6 usually reddish yellow eggs with dark surface spots, deep spots and streaks. Incubates them unaided 12—14 days. Diet seeds, in summer insects.

5 Yellowhammer *Emberiza citrinella.* Distributed over whole of Europe, east to western Siberia. Length 16—20 cm. Abundant in open country or on outskirts of forests. Female builds nest unaided, usually on ground, from blades of grass, horsehairs, etc. At end of April lays 2—5 whitish eggs with numerous dark blotches, spots and streaks. Eggs incubated by both parents 12—14 days. Often nests 3 times. Lives on different seeds, in summer insects, spiders and centipedes. In winter consorts in flocks, often together with other birds.

6 Ortolan Bunting *Emberiza hortulana.* Distributed over whole of Europe and Near East. Length 15—17.5 cm. Inhabits lowlands and uplands, regularly found in orchards. Migratory bird. Winters in southern Europe, returns in middle of April. Ground-nester. Female lays 4—6 whitish grey eggs with dark brown blotches, spots and scrolls. Incubates them 12—14 days. Some couples nest twice. Eats different seeds and, in summer, insects, spiders, etc.

7 Reed Bunting *Emberiza schoeniclus.* Distributed over whole of Europe and temperate parts of Asia. Length 15—17.5 cm. Found in lowlands near ponds, lakes, etc., thickly overgrown with reeds and willows. Nests on or just above ground in grass or bushes. Female lays 4—6 usually brownish eggs with brown-black spots and streaks. Incubates them 12—14 days. Nests twice. Staple diet different seeds. Winters in southern Europe.

8 Snow Bunting *Plectrophenax nivalis.* Nests in most northerly parts of Europe, Asia and North America. Length 15—19 cm. In winter spreads over whole of Europe. Builds feather- and hair-lined nest between stones. In June lays 5—6 bluish white eggs with rusty spots and streaks. Incubates them 14 days. In summer lives on insects, in winter on different seeds. Found in central Europe in winter, in company of bramblings.

Family: **Larks** — *Alaudidae*

1 Crested Lark *Galerida cristata*. Distributed over practically whole of Europe, temperate and southern Asia, south extends up to tropical Africa. Length 18.5—20.5 cm. Found near towns and villages in open, deserted country, fields, etc. Resident bird. Builds nest from grass blades, rootlets, hairs and feathers in depression in ground. Lays 3—5 whitish, dark-spotted eggs, incubates them 13 days. Young fed on insects. Diet seeds and often horse manure remains.

2 Wood Lark *Lullula arborea*. Distributed over whole of Europe, Near East, North Africa. Length 14.5—17.5 cm. Common in pine-woods, also found near towns. Often sings at night. Migratory bird, winters in Mediterranean region, returns in March. Ground-nester. Nest made of grass blades, moss, etc. Female lays 3—5 usually whitish, finely spotted eggs. Incubation period 13—15 days. Diet mainly insects.

3 Sky Lark *Alauda arvensis*. Distributed over whole of Europe, greater part of Asia, North Africa. Length 15—20.5 cm. Always found in fields. Male flutters high in air, singing. Nest lies in depression in ground; lined with fibres, grass blades, hairs, etc. Female lays 3—5 blotched and speckled eggs of greatly variable colouring, incubates them 12—14 days. Lives on insects, spiders, worms, seeds. In autumn migrates in flocks, returns in February. Occasionally resident.

Family: **Wagtails and Pipits** — *Motacillidae*

4 Tree Pipit *Anthus trivialis*. Distributed over whole of Europe, in east extends up to Siberia. Winters in central Africa, returns to nesting area in April. Length 15.5—18 cm. Inhabits conifer, mixed and deciduous woods. Common everywhere, often occurs in mountains. Male sits singing on tall trees or telegraph poles. Ground-nester. Nest woven from grass and moss and lined with hairs, hidden in grass. Female lays 5—6 variably coloured eggs marked with spots and streaks. Incubates them 12—13 days. Diet insects and seeds.

5 Meadow Pipit *Anthus pratensis*. Inhabits practically whole of Europe. Winters in southern Europe and North Africa. Length 15—17 cm. Frequents damp meadows and mountain sides, but also found in lowlands. Male sings while flying. Nest built on ground, from moss, sedge, hairs, etc. Female lays 4—5 light-coloured eggs with dark blotches and streaks. Incubates them 13 days. Lives mainly on insects and spiders, in autumn also seeds. In autumn and spring gathers in flocks in fields. Seldom resident.

6 Yellow Wagtail *Motacilla flava*. Distributed over whole of Europe, in Asia north of Himalayas, North Africa. Winters in Africa. Length 16—19 cm. Inhabits damp lowland meadows. Female builds nest on ground, from grass blades, feathers, hairs, etc. Lays 4—6 whitish to reddish eggs thickly marked with grey-brown speckles. Incubation period 13 days. Eats insects, spiders, worms and small molluscs. Migrates in September, after first forming flocks which spend night in rushes.

7 Grey Wagtail *Motacilla cinerea*. Distributed in Europe, large part of Asia, Africa. European birds winter in Africa. Length 17—20 cm. Occurs in both mountains and lowlands. Found near streams and ponds. Usually builds nest in rocky bank, wall, etc. Lays 4—6 yellowish eggs with reddish and brownish spots and streaks. Incubation period 12—14 days. Sometimes nests twice. Main diet aquatic insects and larvae and water-fleas caught in shallows. Migrates in September.

8 White Wagtail *Motacilla alba*. Distributed over whole of Europe, Asia and Africa. Length 18—20.5 cm. Affinity for water, often found in towns. Builds nest from grass blades, rootlets, moss, etc., lined with feathers and hairs, between stones, in hole in wall, etc. In April or May female lays 5—6 whitish eggs thickly marked with dark spots and streaks. Young hatch in 12—14 days. Lives on various insects and larvae, spiders and worms. In autumn gather in flocks, migrate in September—November. Occasionally resident.

Family: **Tits** — *Paridae*

1 Great Tit *Parus major*. Distributed over whole of Europe except north, Asia and part of North Africa. Length 14—16.5 cm. Inhabits forests, gardens and parks. In winter gathers in troupes in company of other tits. Often found on feeding troughs. Nest built in various hollows, from moss, lichen, hairs, feathers, etc. Female lays 6—14 whitish eggs with red-brown spots. Young hatch in 13—14 days. Nests twice. Parents feed young 15—20 days. Lives mainly on insects and, in winter, seeds. Tempted by lumps of suet on string.

2 Blue Tit *Parus caeruleus*. Distributed over whole of Europe except north, North Africa, in east to Caucasus. Length 11.5—13.5 cm. Inhabits woods, in towns also parks. Nests in hollows, tree stumps, crevices, pipes, etc. Female lays 7—16 whitish eggs thickly sprinkled with rusty blotches and dots. Sits on them 13—15 days. Diet mainly insects and their larvae and in winter seeds. Couples stay together even in winter, often in company of other tits.

3 Coal Tit *Parus ater*. Distributed over whole of Europe, in east to Japan, in south to North Africa. Length 11—12 cm. Resident in central Europe. Inhabits mixed forests, but mainly frequents conifers. Builds nest in tree hollows, from moss and hairs. At end of April lays 7—11 whitish, red-speckled eggs. Young hatched in 14—16 days, fledged at 15 days. Lives mainly on insects, in winter conifer seeds.

4 Crested Tit *Parus cristatus*. Inhabits whole of Europe, in east to Urals. Length 12—13 cm. Found mainly in conifer forests. Builds nest in holes and cracks. Female lays 5—11 whitish eggs with red-brown spots. Young hatched in 15—17 days, fledged at 20 days. Eats insects in all developmental stages. In winter join and lead flocks of other tits.

5 Marsh Tit *Parus palustris*. Distributed in Europe and south of eastern Asia. Length 12 to 14 cm. Inhabits deciduous and mixed woods, parks and gardens. Hole-nester, builds nest from straw, grass, moss, hairs, etc. Female lays 6—10 whitish, red-spotted eggs. Young hatched in 14—15 days, fed by parents 17—19 days. Couples remain together even in winter, but form small troupes. Lives on insects, spiders, in winter also minute seeds.

Family: *Aegithalidae*

6 Long-tailed Tit *Aegithalos caudatus*. Distributed over whole of Europe, in east as far as Japan. Length about 15 cm. Very long tail. Inhabits deciduous woods, parks, etc. When not nesting consorts in small flocks. Nests in trees and bushes, preferably on forked branch. Nest ovoid and closed, with side entrance. Made of moss, lichen, cobwebs, etc. Thickly lined with small feathers. Female lays 7—12 whitish eggs with red blotches and dots, incubates them 13 days. Diet insects.

Family: *Remizidae*

7 Penduline Tit *Remiz pendulinus*. Distributed in southern Europe, south part of central Europe, in east to Japan. Length 10.5—11.5 cm. Found near water, especially ponds. Builds closed spherical nest suspended from tips of terminal willow twigs by fibres made from poplar fluff, etc. Nest has tunnel-like entrance. Female lays 6—8 white eggs, sits on them 12—15 days. Male meanwhile builds new nest. Eats mainly insects and spiders.

Family: **Goldcrests** — *Regulidae*

8 Goldcrest *Regulus regulus*. Distributed over whole of Europe, Asia, North America. Length 8.5—10.5 cm. Smallest European bird, weighs 5—6 g. Inhabits conifer forests. Builds nest from twigs, grass blades, hairs, cobwebs, etc. on dense fir or pine branches. Female lays 8—11 yellowish eggs marked with dark scrolls. Incubation period 16—17 days. Diet small insects and spiders. In winter moves about in tree-tops in small groups, twittering.

Family: **Shrikes** — *Laniidae*

1 Great Grey Shrike *Lanius excubitor*. Distributed in Europe, Asia, North America, North Africa. Length 24—27.5 cm. Inhabits open country, especially with thorny shrubs. Sometimes impales prey (insects and small vertebrates) on thorns. Builds nest from dry twigs, straw, moss, etc. on tall bushes. In May female lays 5—7 whitish, grey- and brown-spotted eggs. Young hatched in 15 days, fed by parents 20 days.

2 Red-backed Shrike *Lanius collurio*. Distributed over practically whole of Europe and Asia. Winters in Africa and southern Asia, returns to Europe in middle of May. Length 18—20.5 cm. Frequents areas with thorny shrubs. Nest hidden in thicket, 1—2 m. from ground, from twigs, straw, rootlets and moss, lined with hairs. Female lays 3—7 pink, red- and brown-spotted eggs. Young hatch in 14—15 days. Leave nest after 2 weeks but remain in bushes. Lives mainly on insects, also young of small birds and rodents. Impales prey on thorns. Imitates call of other birds.

3 Woodchat Shrike *Lanius senator*. Distributed over whole of Europe except England, in east to Poland, in south to North Africa. Winters in Central Africa. Arrives in Europe at beginning of May, leaves in August. Length 19.5—20 cm. Nests on sunny places. Builds nest in bushes like that of red-backed shrike. Lays 5—6 yellowish or greenish, grey- and olive-spotted eggs. Young hatched in 14—15 days, fed by parents 20 days. Eats mainly insects.

Family: **Waxwings** — *Bombycillidae*

4 Waxwing *Bombycilla garrulus*. Distributed in most northerly parts of Europe, Asia and North America. Length 19—23 cm. Visits central Europe only in winter, often in large flocks. Most often seen on rowans or berry-bearing bushes, eating berries. In north nests in conifer and mixed forests. Tree-nester, builds nest from twigs or moss. Female lays 4—6 bluish, black- and violet-spotted eggs, incubates them 14 days. Also eats insects.

Family: **Accentors** — *Prunellidae*

5 Dunnock *Prunella modularis*. Distributed over whole of Europe and north-western Asia. Length 14.5—16.5 cm. Common in central Europe, but very retiring. Inhabits dense conifer woods. In dense branches builds relatively large mossy nest lined with hairs. Lays 4—7 plain blue-green eggs in May. Often nests twice. Young hatch in 12—14 days. Eats mainly insects, in autumn small seeds. In October migrates to Mediterranean region.

Family: **Wrens** — *Troglodytidae*

6 Wren *Troglodytes troglodytes*. Distributed over whole of Europe, temperate parts of Asia, North America, north-eastern Africa. Length 9.5—11.5 cm., weight about 9 g. Resident in central Europe. Solitary bird except at nesting time. Builds spherical nest with side entrance from twigs and moss, lined with hairs and feathers. Lays 5—7 whitish, red-spotted eggs. Young hatch in 14—16 days. Diet insects.

Family: **Dippers** — *Cinclidae*

7 Dipper *Cinclus cinclus*. Distributed over whole of Europe, extends east to central Asia, Himalayas and north-western Africa. Length 17.5—20 cm. Frequents mountain streams and rivers. Resident bird. Hunts for food (insects and insect larvae) under water, on bed. Also collects material for nest under water. Nests in spaces between stones, often at foot of waterfall. Female lays 4—6 white eggs. Young hatch in 15—17 days, leave nest in 3 weeks.

Family: **Flycatchers** — *Muscicapidae*

1 Spotted Flycatcher *Muscicapa striata*. Distributed over whole of Europe, in east to Mongolia, in south to north-western Africa. Winters in tropical and southern Africa. Leaves in September, returns at beginning of May. Length 14—17 cm. Lives on outskirts of forests or in parks. Builds relatively large nest from grass blades and rootlets, lined with hairs and feathers, usually on horizontal branch or overgrown wall, etc. Lays 4—6 bluish white, grey- and russet-spotted eggs. Eggs incubated 13 days by both parents. Eats insects, catches prey on wing.

2 Pied Flycatcher *Ficedula hypoleuca*. Inhabits whole of Europe, western Asia, north-western Africa. Winters in Africa. Length 12.5—14.5 cm. In some regions abundant. Lives in open deciduous woods and parks. Builds nest from moss, fibres, cobwebs, etc. in hollow trees and stumps. Lays 4—8 bright blue-green eggs. Young hatched in 13 days, fed by parents 18 days. Migrates at end of October. Diet insects.

Family: **Warblers** — *Sylviidae*

3 Lesser Whitethroat *Sylvia curruca*. Distributed over most of Europe, in east up to Siberia. European birds winter in central Africa. Leave in August or September, return in second half of April. Length 12.5—13.5 cm. Frequents bushes in woods, gardens and parks. Weaves very loose nest from grass blades and rootlets in tall nettles, shrubs, etc. Female lays 4—6 whitish or yellowish eggs with violet-grey and yellow-brown speckles and black streaks. Young hatch in 11—13 days. Eats insects and spiders.

4 Blackcap *Sylvia atricapilla*. Distributed over whole of Europe, in east to river Ob and in north-western Africa. Winters in Central Africa. Leaves in September, returns at end of April. Length 14—15 cm. Inhabits deciduous woods and parks and gardens with plenty of shrubs. Builds nest from grass blades and cobwebs, in brambles, bushes, etc., usually about 75 cm. from ground. Female lays 4—6 yellowish or greenish, grey- or red-spotted eggs. Young hatch in 13—14 days. Diet chiefly insects, supplemented in autumn by raspberries or bilberries.

5 Garden Warbler *Sylvia borin*. Distributed over most of Europe, in east to western Siberia. Winters in Central Africa. Leaves at end of September, returns in middle of May. Length about 14 cm. Frequents places with shrubs. Weaves nest from stalks among raspberry canes, in brambles, etc., 0.5—3 m. from ground. Lays 4—6 yellowish or greenish eggs with grey and olive spots or marbling. Young hatch in 12 days. Often rears young cuckoos. Eats various insects and their larvae.

6 Barred Warbler *Sylvia nisoria*. Distributed in central Europe, in east to western Siberia. Winters in eastern half of Africa. Leaves in August, returns at end of April. Length 16 to 18 cm. Inhabits large parks, overgrown gardens and margins of forests. Builds nest from grasses, blades, horsehair, etc. in dense bushes, 1—2 m. from ground. Female lays 4—5 yellowish or greenish, grey-speckled eggs. Young hatched in 14—15 days, fed by parents 16 days. Lives mainly on insects, at end of summer also berries.

7 Icterine Warbler *Hippolais icterina*. Distributed in Europe from central France to upper reaches of Ob river. Winters in Africa. Leaves in August, returns early in May. Length 13—16 cm. Inhabits open deciduous woods and large parks. Builds nest from stalks, leaves, rootlets, etc. in deciduous trees or bushes. Masks it with birch bark. Usually lays 5 pink eggs sprinkled with black dots and blotches. Young hatch in 13 days. Eats mainly different insects.

Family: **Warblers** — *Sylviidae*

1 Chiffchaff *Phylloscopus collybita*. Distributed over whole of Europe, in east to Lake Baikal, and north-western Africa. Winters in north-eastern Africa. Leaves in October, male's monotonous song heard soon after return at end of March. Length 12—14 cm. Inhabits deciduous or mixed woods and parks. Female builds closed spherical nest from grass blades and moss in clump of grass on ground. Lays 5—6 white eggs with reddish brown dots. Incubates them unaided 13—14 days. Young fed 2 weeks. Eats only small insects.

2 Wood Warbler *Phylloscopus sibilatrix*. Distributed over whole of Europe except north, and in western Asia. Winters in Central Africa. Leaves in September, returns in middle of April. Male chirps. Length 12—14 cm. Inhabits large woods and parks. Ground-nester. Builds closed, hair-lined nest with side entrance. Female lays 6—8 white eggs with dark brown spots and streaks, incubates them 13 days. Young fledged at 12—15 days. Eats mainly insects.

3 Grasshopper Warbler *Locustella naevia*. Distributed over whole of Europe except north and south, in east up to Mongolia. European birds winter in North Africa. Leaves in August, returns at end of April. Length 13—15 cm. Lives hidden in thick shrubs beside ponds and rivers. Builds deep grass nest on ground under bush. Lays 5—7 pink eggs with rusty blotches and dots. Eggs incubated 13—15 days by both parents in turn. Young leave nest at 10 days, before fully capable of flight. Diet mainly insects.

4 Great Reed Warbler *Acrocephalus arundinaceus*. Distributed over whole of Europe except England and Scandinavia, in east up to Australia, also North Africa. European birds winter in equatorial Africa. Leave in August and September, return in first half of May. Length about 20 cm. High-pitched, screechy song. Inhabits rushes beside ponds, lakes and rivers. Builds basket-like nest between rush stems. Female lays 4—6 bluish eggs with olive green and brown spots. Incubated 14—15 days by both parents in turn. Eats mainly insects.

5 Reed Warbler *Acrocephalus scirpaceus*. Distributed from central Europe to southern England and central Asia. Winters in northern and equatorial Africa. Leaves at end of September, returns in middle of April. Length 15—16 cm. Lives beside water among reeds. Weaves nest from long stalks. Lays 4—5 whitish eggs with olive-coloured surface spots and deep spots. Young hatch in 11—12 days. Male has sweeter song than great reed warbler. Lives on insects and spiders.

Family: **Thrushes** — *Turdidae*

6 Fieldfare *Turdus pilaris*. Distributed in central and northern Europe, in east to Lake Baikal. Length 24.5—28 cm. Migratory bird, northern population comes to central Europe in winter. Weaves nest from grass, twigs, moss, etc., usually reinforced with mud. Often nests in colonies (several nests on one tree) in open conifer woods, also in junipers, sometimes quite low down. Female lays 5—7 greenish white eggs thickly marked with rusty brown spots and streaks. Young hatch in 13—14 days. Eats mainly insects, in winter berries.

7 Mistle Thrush *Turdus viscivorus*. Distributed over whole of Europe, in east to Lake Baikal, in south to north-western Africa. Northern birds migrate south. Length 26—29.5 cm. Prefers conifer woods, occasionally found in large parks. Nest usually situated on pines, about 10 m. from ground, woven from rootlets, grass blades and moss, reinforced with mud. Female builds nest, male fetches material. In April female lays 4—5 blue-green eggs with violet, grey and brown spots, incubates them unaided 13—14 days. Eats mainly insects caught on ground. From autumn onwards roams countryside in small troupes.

Family: **Thrushes** — *Turdidae*

1 Song Thrush *Turdus philomelos*. Distributed over whole of Europe, Asia Minor, in east to Lake Baikal. Winters in southern Europe and North Africa. Leaves in October, returns in March or early April. Length 22—24.5 cm. Inhabits woods, gardens and parks. Builds nest from stalks, twigs, etc., inner side reinforced and faced with mixture of mud and saliva. Nests on bushes, trees and walls. Female lays 4—6 green-blue eggs sprinkled with black dots, incubates them unaided 12—13 days. Young leave nest before fully fledged. Eats insects, worms, molluscs, and in autumn berries.

2 Ring Ouzel *Turdus torquatus*. Distributed in England, Scandinavia, Alps, Pyrenees, Giant Mountains, Caucasus. Winters in North Africa. Leaves in October, returns in April. Length about 27 cm. Inhabits mountain sides. Nests in dense branches of dwarf pines. Lays 4—5 greenish, thickly marbled and streaked eggs. Incubated 14 days by both parents in turn.

3 Blackbird *Turdus merula*. Distributed in whole of Europe, east over narrow zone to China. Part of population resident, part migrates to Mediterranean region. Length 23.5—28 cm. Inhabits forests, parks and gardens near human dwellings. Makes nest from grass blades, rootlets, etc. on trees, bushes and wooden beams, etc. Female lays 4—6 blue-green eggs thickly marked with grey and brown blotches, dots and streaks, incubates them 13—14 days. Young fed by both parents. Sometimes nests three times a year. Lives on insects, worms, molluscs, berries, fruit, etc.

4 Wheatear *Oenanthe oenanthe*. Distributed over whole of Europe, Asia, North America and Greenland. Winters mainly in tropical Africa. Leaves in August or September, returns in April. Length 15—17 cm. Inhabits stony, unwooded slopes, rocky planes or quarries. Builds nest from grass blades, hairs and feathers among stones, in abandoned holes, etc. In May female lays 5—7 greenish eggs, incubates them 14 days. Young leave nest before fully fledged. Diet mainly insects.

5 Whinchat *Saxicola rubetra*. Distributed over most of Europe, in east to western Siberia. Winters in equatorial Africa. Leaves in August or September, in small flocks, returns in April. Length 13—15.5 cm. Frequents uplands with large shrub-strewn meadows. Likes to sit on hummocks. Ground-nester. Nest made of grass blades, moss, etc., lined with grass and plant fluff. In June female lays 5—6 bluish grey eggs, often marked with rusty spots, incubates them 13—14 days. Young leave nest early. Diet mainly insects.

6 Redstart *Phoenicurus phoenicurus*. Distributed over whole of Europe, Asia Minor, in east to western Siberia; also North Africa. Winters mainly in equatorial Africa. Leaves in August or September, returns in first half of April. Length 13.5—17 cm. Lives almost everywhere, in woods, gardens, near human communities. Builds nest from grass blades, rootlets, leaves, hairs, etc. in all sorts of hollows, in walls, between wooden beams, etc. Female lays 5—8 green-blue eggs, incubates them 13—15 days. Nests twice. Eats mainly insects skilfully caught on wing.

7 Black Redstart *Phoenicurus ochruros*. Distributed in central and southern Europe, in west to England, in east up to northern China. European birds winter in North Africa. Leave in October, return at end of March. Length about 15 cm. Originally rock-dweller, now lives in vicinity of man. Builds nest from rootlets, grass blades, hairs, etc. under shed roofs, in barns, on cornices. Female lays 5—6 white eggs, incubates them 14 days. Young leave nest before fully fledged and go into hiding. Diet mainly insects.

Family: **Thrushes** — *Turdidae*

1 Nightingale *Luscinia megarhynchos*. Distributed in western, central and southern Europe, in east to central Asia, in south to North Africa. Winters chiefly in equatorial Africa. Leaves in August, returns at end of April. Migrates only at night. Length 18—20 cm. Inhabits margins of deciduous or mixed woods, thickets beside rivers and ponds, etc. Male sings during day as well as at night. Song carries long distances. Builds nest from grass blades, rootlets, moss, rush stems, etc., lined with hair, in branches of impenetrable bushes. Female lays 4—6 olive brown, sometimes thickly speckled, eggs, incubates them unaided 13 days. Young leave nest early. Diet mainly insects and worms.

2 Bluethroat *Luscinia svecica*. Distributed over whole of Europe except England and Mediterranean region, in east as far as Mongolia. Winters in North Africa. Length about 15 cm. Seldom nests in central Europe, but often found in large numbers in riverside shrubs during migration. Builds nest from dry grass blades on or near ground, in bushes near stretches of reeds. Female lays 5—6 bluish eggs sprinkled with brown spots. Young hatch in 13 days, leave nest after 2 weeks. Eats small insects and their larvae.

3 Robin *Erithacus rubecula*. Distributed over whole of Europe, Asia Minor, in east to western Siberia. Most birds migrate to North Africa in October, but old males often remain behind. Length 13—16 cm. Frequents thickets in woods, parks and gardens. Ground-nester, hides nest under clump of grass, between stones, in holes, etc. Nest made of moss, rootlets, grass blades, hairs, etc. Female lays 5—7 yellowish eggs marked with red blotches and dots, incubates them unaided 13—14 days. Young fed by both parents. Some birds nest twice. Lives mainly on insects, in autumn and winter supplemented by berries and forest fruits.

Family: **Swallows** — *Hirundinidae*

4 Swallow *Hirundo rustica*. Distributed over whole of Europe, most of Asia, North America, North Africa. European birds winter in Africa south of Sahara. Leave in September, return in first half of April. Length 18—23 cm. Basin-like nest built by both partners from small lumps of clay mixed with saliva and from grass blades lined with hairs and feathers. Female lays 4—6 whitish, red- and violet-spotted eggs. Incubates them 14—16 days, fed by male. Young fed 3 weeks by both parents. When young are fledged, birds spend night in flocks in sedge beside ponds. Eats mainly insects caught on wing.

5 House Martin *Delichon urbica*. Distributed over whole of Europe, most of Asia, North Africa. European birds winter in Africa south of Sahara. Leave in September, return in second half of April. Length 15—16.5 cm. Builds clay nest on vertical wall, under eaves or cornices. Nest completely closed except for side entrance on top. Birds often form large colonies. Female lays 4—5 pure white eggs. Incubated 12—13 days by both parents in turn. Young fed 20—23 days. Some birds nest again in July. Eats mainly insects caught in air.

6 Sand Martin *Riparia riparia*. Distributed over whole of Europe, large part of Asia, North America, north-western and north-eastern Africa. European birds winter in equatorial and southern Africa. Leave in August, return in second half of April. Length 12.5—14.5 cm. Lives preferably near rivers, lakes and ponds, also in sand-pits with sheer walls, in which it makes burrows 1.5 m. long. Nest chamber lined with feathers and grass blades. Nests in colonies. Female lays 5—7 pure white eggs in middle of May. Eggs incubated 15 days by both parents in turn. Young fed in nest 23 days. Lives on insects caught in air.

Order: **Woodpeckers and Allies** — *Piciformes*

Family: **Woodpeckers** — *Picidae*

1 Green Woodpecker *Picus viridis*. Distributed over whole of Europe except most northerly parts, in east to Ukraine. Length 33—37 cm. Resident, but after nesting season roams long distances. Has predilection for open woods, parks and orchards. Both partners hack hole in rotting tree trunks, finished in 14 days. Line hole only with splinters. Female lays 6—8 white eggs, incubated 15—17 days by both parents in turn. Young leave nest after 17—20 days. Birds live mainly on larvae of different wood beetles, also rake open anthills and collect pupae and adult ants on their long, sticky, protrusible tongue. Occasionally visit beehives, especially in winter.

2 Great Spotted Woodpecker *Dendrocopos major*. Distributed over whole of Europe, extends east in narrow zone to Japan, in south to North Africa. Length 22.5—26.5 cm. Inhabits woods, parks and large orchards. Resident bird, but in winter roams countryside round birthplace. Hacks hole in deciduous trees and conifers 2—10 m. from ground, lines it with small splinters. Female lays 4—8 glossy white eggs in April or May. Young hatch in 13 to 15 days. Lives on beetle larvae (e.g. on bark beetles), wedges hazelnuts in crevice, cracks shell and eats kernel, also eats seeds of conifers. In winter often consorts with nuthatches or tits.

3 Black Woodpecker *Dryocopus martius*. Distributed over whole of Europe except England and southern parts, in east extends as far as Japan. Length 42—48.5 cm. Mainly inhabits large conifer forests in lowlands and mountains, but also encountered in deciduous woods where it nests in strong beeches or birches. Like other woodpeckers, in spring drums on dry branch stumps. Usually nests over 4 m. above ground. Both partners hack hole about 50 cm. deep in 2 weeks, making pile of splinters at foot of tree. Female lays 4—5 white eggs. Young hatch in 12—14 days, leave nest after 24—28 days. Eats mainly wood beetle larvae and ants and their nymphs.

4 Wryneck *Jynx torquilla*. Distributed over whole of Europe, in east to Japan. Migratory bird. Winters in northern and eastern Africa. Usually leaves in August, returns in second half of April, immediately utters typical plaintive call. Length 18.5—19.5 cm. Inhabits outskirts of deciduous woods, parks, orchards and large gardens. Does not make own nesting hole, often content with crack in wall. Does not line nest. In May—June female lays 7—10 white eggs. Parents incubate eggs 13—14 days, feed young 24—26 days. Feeds on caterpillars, ant pupae, etc. Wryneck can turn long, flexible neck by up to 180 degrees.

Order: **Swifts and Allies** — *Apodiformes*

Family: **Swifts** — *Apodidae*

5 Common Swift *Apus apus*. Distributed over whole of Europe, in east to China, in south to north-western Africa. Migratory bird. Leaves at beginning of August (sometimes end of July), winters in Africa south of Sahara, returns at end of April or beginning of May. Length 18—21 cm. Builds nest under eaves of tall houses, on steeples, towers, etc., from pile of plant debris and feathers snapped up during flight and stuck together with saliva. Female lays 2—3 white eggs, incubates them 18 days, fed by male. Young leave nest at 6 weeks, immediately able to fly. Eats insects caught on wing. Swifts like to consort in darting, screeching flocks. Rapid fliers, cover about 900 km. a day.

Order: **Rollers and Allies** — *Coraciiformes*

Family: **Rollers** — *Coraciidae*

1 Roller *Coracias garrulus.* Distributed in Europe except England and north, in east to India, in south to north-western Africa. Migratory bird. Leaves at end of August, winters in Africa south of Sahara, returns at beginning of May. Length 30—34 cm. Nests in tree hollows. Female lays 3—5 pure white eggs. Eggs incubated by both parents in turn, young leave nest at 28 days. Keeps look-out for prey, catches it mainly on wing. Lives on insects, small vertebrates, in Africa mainly locusts.

Family: **Bee-eaters** — *Meropidae*

2 Bee-eater *Merops apiaster.* Distributed in southern Europe, Asia as far as India, north-western Africa. Nests in central Europe in Slovakia, Moravia and Hungary, in recent years also in Sweden, Denmark and Holland. Migratory bird, winters in Africa south of Sahara. Frequents places with sandy or clay banks, in which it makes burrow with beak (in about 3 weeks). Lives in small colonies. Lays 5—6 white eggs, incubated 22 days by both parents in turn. Eats mainly hymenoptera, especially bees and wasps.

Family: **Kingfishers** — *Alcedinidae*

3 Kingfisher *Alcedo atthis.* Distributed over whole of Europe except north, in east to Asia, and north-western Africa. Resident bird, but northerly population shifts somewhat south. Nomadic during winter. Length 16.5—18.5 cm. Inhabits places with clean water and sheer banks. Makes burrow about 1 m. long above waterline, lines nest-chamber with fish scales and bones. Female lays 6—8 white eggs. Young hatch in 21 days. Kingfishers catch prey — small fish — by swooping into water.

Family: **Hoopoes** — *Upupidae*

4 Hoopoe *Upupa epops.* Distributed over whole of Europe and Asia except northern parts, and practically whole of Africa. Migratory bird. European population leaves in August or September, winters in equatorial Africa, returns in April. Length 28—32.5 cm. Prefers open country with meadows and pastures, also found in old avenues near ponds, or in open deciduous woods. Nests in tree hollows or piles of stones. In May female lays 4—8 greyish or brownish white eggs, incubates them unaided 16 days, fed by male. Eats chiefly beetle larvae. Name expresses typical call.

Order: **Nightjars** — *Caprimulgiformes*

5 Nightjar or **Goatsucker** *Caprimulgus europaeus.* Distributed over most of Europe, in east to central Siberia, also in north-western Africa. Migratory bird. Leaves in September, winters mainly in Africa south of Sahara, returns in first half of May. Length 26—28 cm. Nests in bare depression in ground. Female lays 2 whitish, grey-speckled eggs indistinguishable from background. Eggs incubated 16—19 days by both parents in turn. Young fed only at night. By day, nightjar perches lengthwise on branch. Goes hunting after sundown. Lives on insects — mostly moths and beetles — caught on wing.

Order: **Owls** — *Strigiformes*

6 Snowy Owl *Nyctea scandiaca.* Distributed in European, Asian and North American tundra. Flies south in winter and occasionally appears in central and southern Europe. Length 56—65 cm. Mainly diurnal bird. Likes high perches. Skilful flier. Nests on ground or in cleft rocks. Lays 3—8 white eggs with staggered hatching. Catches mainly rodents, sometimes small birds, occasionally fish.

Order: **Owls** — *Strigiformes*

1 Eagle Owl *Bubo bubo*. Distributed over whole of Europe except England, whole of Asia except southern and northern parts, North Africa. Resident bird, not nomadic during winter. Length 62—72.5 cm., female slightly larger. Inhabits extensive forests, wooded rocks and ravines. Occurs at both low and high altitudes. Nests in tree hollows, in ruins and on ground. Female lays 2—5 white eggs at end of March, incubates them unaided 35 days. Hides during day, flies only at night, fairly close to ground. Hunting radius 15 km. Catches mammals up to size of hare, birds, occasionally fish.

2 Long-eared Owl *Asio otus*. Distributed over most of Europe, in east as far as Japan, North America, North Africa. Resident bird in Europe, sometimes migratory. Length 35 to 39 cm. Abundant in forests, preserves and parks. Nests in old nests of other birds or squirrels. Female lays 4—6 white eggs, usually in April, incubates them unaided 27—28 days, fed by male. Eats mainly voles, also maybugs and other beetles caught after dark. During day hides in dense branches. In winter often roams countryside in troupes, looking for rodents.

3 Little Owl *Athene noctua*. Distributed over whole of Europe except north, in east as far as Korea, North Africa. Resident bird. Length 23.5—27.5 cm. Inhabits outskirts of woods, ruins, parks, avenues; likes to perch on roofs, behind chimneys. Nocturnal bird, but also hunts in afternoon of dull days. Plaintive call often heard at night near human dwellings. During day hides in holes and hollows. Nests in similar places. Female lays 4—7 white eggs, incubates them 28 days. Catches small rodents, occasionally small birds, especially sparrows, often also insects, chiefly beetles.

4 Tawny Owl *Strix aluco*. Distributed over whole of Europe except north, parts of Asia, north Africa. Resident bird. Length 41—46 cm. Goes hunting after dark. During day hides in dense branches, usually in same place, piles of ejected pellets to be found under tree. Inhabits forests, parks, large gardens and avenues, at both low and high altitudes. Nests in tree hollows, under wooden beams, etc. Female lays 2—5 white eggs, incubates them 28 days. Young fully fledged after 3 months. Catches mainly small rodents, also small birds, amphibians and insects.

5 Barn Owl *Tyto alba*. Distributed over whole of Europe, southern Asia, Australia, Africa and America. Resident bird. Length 33—39 cm. Originally rock-dweller, in Europe now lives in vicinity of man. Nests in attics, below eaves, in ruins, towers or dovecots. Female lays 4—6 white eggs on bare base, incubates them 30—34 days, fed by male. Young fledged after 50 days. In years of vole plagues nests several times. In addition to voles and mice catches moles, shrews, sparrows and insects. Young birds often fly far afield.

Order: **Cuckoos and Allies** — *Cuculiformes*

Family: **Cuckoos** — *Cuculidae*

6 Common Cuckoo *Cuculus canorus*. Distributed over whole of Europe, most of Asia, Africa. European birds migrate in August or September, winter in Africa south of Sahara, return at end of April when male immediately makes itself heard. Length 31—39 cm. Has preference for open woods with undergrowth. Female lays eggs (average 18) one by one in nests of small birds. Young hatch in only 12 days, after 10 hours throw all other occupants (eggs or young) out of nest. Young cuckoo remains in nest 23 days and is fed by foster-parents 3 more weeks. Eats mainly caterpillars (even hairy ones), spiders, etc.

Order: **Birds of Prey**— *Falconiformes*

Family: **Falcons** — *Falconidae*

1 Peregrine Falcon *Falco peregrinus*. Distributed in Europe, Asia, Africa, North America, Australia. Length 41—50 cm. Wings long and pointed at flight. Nests in cleft rocks, towers, or nests abandoned by other birds of prey. In April lays 3—4 eggs with red-brown spots. Young hatch in 28—29 days. Male hunts for young, female feeds them. Hunts primarily in air. Swoops on prey at velocity of up to 200 km. an hour. Catches mainly birds — pigeons, crows, starlings, gulls, etc. Formerly trained for hunting. Young birds migratory, old birds sometimes resident.

2 Hobby *Falco subbuteo*. Distributed over whole of Europe, temperate parts of Asia, North Africa. Migratory bird. Winters in southern Africa, returns to nesting places in April. Length 32—36 cm. Nests in deserted nests of crows or other birds. Frequents small woods. Female lays 2—4 eggs with red-brown spots. Young hatch in 28 days. Male brings prey for young, female feeds them. Catches small birds or insects in air. Can even catch swifts and swallows. Devours prey on tree. Protected.

3 Kestrel *Falco tinnunculus*. Distributed over whole of Europe, Asia and Africa. Length 31—38 cm. Nests on jutting rocks, in abandoned nests of other birds, in towers and hollows. Sometimes nests in colonies. In May female lays 3—8 eggs with red-brown spots. Young hatch in 28 days. Prefers to hunt in open country, fields and meadows. Hovers in air, swoops on prey, mainly small rodents and insects. Migrates in autumn to North Africa, but some birds remain behind.

Family: **Eagles and Allies** — *Accipitridae*

4 Golden Eagle *Aquila chrysaetos*. Distributed in Europe, Asia, North America, North Africa; in Europe mainly Alps, Pyrenees and Scotland. Length 82—92 cm., wing span about 2 m. Long tail spread during flight. Nuptial flights held in March. Builds nest on rocks, from sticks, clumps of grass, hairs, etc. Female lays 1—3 brown-spotted eggs, incubated 45 days by both parents in turn. Male mostly fetches prey for young, female prepares it for them. Catches mammals and birds up to size of small chamois or goat.

5 Lesser Spotted Eagle *Aquila pomarina*. Distributed in central Europe, in east to southern Asia. Length 61—65 cm., wing span about 150 cm. Nuptial flights in spring. Builds nest in trees, from twigs, grass, etc. Female usually lays 2 spotted eggs, occasionally relieved by male while incubating them. Parents generally rear only one young. Catches rodents, reptiles, birds and insects. Migrates in winter to southern Africa. Locally abundant in Europe.

6 Marsh-harrier *Circus aeruginosus*. Distributed over whole of Europe, across Asia to Far East, Africa, Australian region. Length 49—60 cm. Frequents large ponds and lakes. Locally abundant. Builds nest from piled rush stems in large reed beds. Female lays 3—6 greenish white eggs in May. Young hatch in 32—33 days. Both parents hunt for food, only female feeds young. Catches young gulls, voles, frogs, etc. Winters in tropical Africa, returns in March.

7 Buzzard *Buteo buteo*. Distributed over most of Europe, extends east as far as Japan. Length 46—55 cm. Very variable colouring, from black-brown to pure white. Nests in trees in small woods near hunting ground in open country. Builds nest from small sticks 8—15 m. from ground. Female lays 2—5 eggs with brown and violet spots. Eggs incubated 30 days by both parents, but more by female. Catches voles, mice, occasionally birds. Likes to sit on high perches. Resident bird, nomadic in winter. Some individuals fly to North Africa.

Family: **Eagles and Allies** — *Accipitridae*

1 Rough-legged Hawk *Buteo lagopus*. Distributed in north-European, Asian and American tundra. Always winters in central and southern Europe. Length 53—60.5 cm. Wears feather 'trousers'. Arrives in central Europe in October and remains until March. Often forms large flocks. Catches voles and, in times of shortage, partridges. In native habitat nests in trees, lays 2—7 eggs and lives mainly on lemmings.

2 Black Kite *Milvus migrans*. Distributed in Europe, Asia, Africa and Australia. Length about 56 cm. Inhabits regions with rivers, lakes or ponds. Also frequents human communities in role of scavenger. Builds nest in tree top or uses nests of other birds. Female lays 2—3 eggs, incubates them 30 days, occasionally relieved by male. Lives on small vertebrates, but likes to collect scraps on ground or water surface. Winters in Africa.

3 White-tailed Eagle *Haliaeetus albicilla*. Distributed in central and northern Europe, whole of Asia except southern parts. Also nests in Scotland. Length 75—98 cm., wing span up to 230 cm. Inhabits coast, lakes or large ponds and rivers. Makes nest from branches, usually in tall trees, occasionally on rocks. Uses same nest for years, adds to it. Female lays 2—3 whitish eggs, incubated 6 weeks by both parents in turn. Catches mainly fish, also birds up to size of heron, but chiefly weak individuals.

4 Goshawk *Accipiter gentilis*. Distributed over whole of Europe, Asia except southern parts, and most of North America. Length of male 52—56 cm., female 60—64.5 cm. Colouring often variable. Inhabits small woods, often settles near villages. Radius of nesting area about 5 km. Builds nest from twigs and green sprays on tall trees, adds to it every year. Female lays 3—5 grey-green eggs, often with brown spots, incubates them 38 days, mainly unaided. Catches squirrels, rabbits, birds (mainly jays, pigeons, crows, etc.). Useful bird in falconry.

5 Sparrow-hawk *Accipiter nisus*. Distributed over whole of Europe, most of Asia except north, north-western Africa. Length of male 31—34 cm., female 37—41 cm. Resident and nomadic, some birds migratory. Forest-dweller with preference for conifer woods. Builds nest from dry twigs, preferably in tall spruces, beside trunk. In May female lays 4—6 bluish green eggs with brown-red spots, incubates them unaided 31—36 days, fed by male. Male fetches food for young, female feeds them. Catches mainly small birds, especially sparrows, but also blackbirds, finches, etc.

6 Honey Buzzard *Pernis apivorus*. Distributed in Europe except north and south, in east as far as Urals. Migratory. Leaves in October, winters in western and central Africa, returns in April. Length 50—57 cm. Prefers deciduous and mixed lowland woods. Frequents chiefly places inhabited by wasps which are its staple diet. Nests in abandoned nests of other birds of prey near clearings or margins of forests. Female usually lays only 2 whitish eggs with red-brown spots. Young hatch in 30—35 days. Digs out wasps' broods, but also eats soft fruits.

Family: **Ospreys** — *Pandionidae*

7 Osprey *Pandion haliaetus*. Distributed in central, northern and southern Europe, Asia, Australia and America. Migratory bird. European population leaves in September, winters in Africa, returns in April. Length 56—61.5 cm. Inhabits basins of large rivers, area round ponds and lakes or coastal regions. Builds nest from twigs, clumps of grass, turf, etc. in tall trees, especially pines and oaks. Female lays 2—3 bluish eggs with red-brown spots. Young hatch in 29 days. Lives mainly on fish. Hovers above water, then dives after prey.

Order: **Cursory Birds** — *Ciconiiformes*

Family: **Herons** — *Ardeidae*

1 Heron *Ardea cinerea*. Distributed over most of Europe, Asia as far as Japan, Africa. European birds winter in Africa, return at beginning of April. Length about 90 cm. Inhabits regions with ponds and lakes. Builds nest from dry twigs in tall trees. Lives in colonies. Female lays 4—5 blue-green eggs, incubated 25—28 days by both parents in turn. Young hatch in same order as eggs were laid. Catches small fish, amphibians, molluscs, insects, small rodents and birds. Flocks of northern herons often seen in central Europe in winter.

2 Purple Heron *Ardea purpurea*. Distributed in southern, eastern and occasionally central Europe, southern Asia, Africa. European birds winter in Africa, leave at end of September. Length about 80 cm. Inhabits large reed beds round ponds and lakes. Builds nest from grass blades and twigs on flattened rushes. Usually nests in colonies. Female lays 7—8 bluish green eggs, incubated 24—28 days by both parents in turn. Lives mainly on fish, frogs and insects.

3 Night Heron *Nycticorax nycticorax*. Distributed in southern Europe, southern parts of central Europe, south-eastern Asia, whole of Africa, America. European birds winter in Africa, leave at end of August or in September. Length about 55 cm. Inhabits regions with ponds, swamps, etc. Builds nest from small sticks in trees or bushes. Lives in colonies. Female usually lays 4 green-blue eggs, incubated 21—23 days by both parents in turn. Lives mainly on valueless fishes, hunts over wide area.

4 Little Bittern *Ixobrychus minutus*. Distributed in Europe except England, in east to Siberia, most of Africa, Australia. European birds migrate in August, winter in Africa, return at end of April. Length about 35 cm. Inhabits sedge round ponds, pools, creeks, etc. Builds nest on flattened reeds near water level. Female lays 5—6 whitish eggs, incubated 16—19 days by both parents in turn. Young climb rushes at one week. Eats small fish, frogs and insects.

5 Bittern *Botaurus stellaris*. Distributed over whole of Europe to south of Sweden, in east to Japan, also in Africa. European birds migrate in October to equatorial Africa, return in March. Occasionally resident. Length about 70 cm. Lives secretively in large reed beds round ponds and lakes. Booming call. Builds nest on flattened rushes. Lays 4—6 green-grey eggs in April or May. Young hatch in 25—26 days. Catches frogs, small fish, insects, etc. Freezes with beak held to sky if disturbed.

Family: **Storks** — *Ciconiidae*

6 White Stork *Ciconia ciconia*. Distributed in Europe, central and eastern Asia including Japan, North Africa. European birds migrate to Africa at end of August, return in first half of April. Length about 1 m. Builds large nest on tall trees, roofs and chimneys. Female lays 2—6 white eggs, incubated 30—34 days by both parents in turn. Parents fetch food for young, regurgitate it on to nest. Catches insects, amphibians, small mammals and birds. Voiceless, clatters beak.

7 Black Stork *Ciconia nigra*. Distributed in central and eastern Europe, south of Sweden, Iberian peninsula, in east across China to Sakhalin. European birds migrate in September, winter in Africa south of Sahara, return at beginning of April. Length about 1 m. Inhabits wooded regions at both low and high altitudes. Has large nesting area. Builds nest on tall tree close to trunk. Female lays 2—5 bluish white eggs, incubated by both parents 28—32 days. Lives mainly on fish, but also catches amphibians or small vertebrates and insects. Flies far afield. Does not clatter beak, but utters hoarse hissing sounds.

Order: **Pelicans and Allies** — *Pelecaniformes*

Family: **Cormorants** — *Phalacrocoracidae*

1 Great Cormorant *Phalacrocorax carbo*. Distributed in Europe, Asia, Africa, Australia, North America. Central-European birds migrate in September to Mediterranean region, return at beginning of March. Length 80—90 cm. Nests in colonies. Builds nest in trees, from small sticks. Female lays 3—4 blue-green eggs. Young hatch in 28—30 days, remain 8 weeks in nest. Lives mainly on fish, hunts under water. Often hunts together with pelicans, which do not dive.

Order: **Ducks, Geese and Swans** — *Anseriformes*

2 Whooper Swan *Cygnus cygnus*. Distributed mainly in northern parts of Europe and Asia. In winter often seen on rivers or ice-free lakes in central and southern Europe. Length 155—170 cm., wing span up to 2.5 m., weight about 10 kg. In native habitat lives beside lakes or bays surrounded by rushes, in which it builds large nest. Female lays 4—6 eggs, incubates them mainly unaided 35—40 days. Lives on small aquatic animals and green-stuff. In severe winters migrates southwards in large flocks.

3 Mute Swan *Cygnus olor*. Distributed in northern Europe and central Asia; in recent years lives in halfwild state on many lakes and ponds in central Europe. Length about 160 cm. Builds nest from twigs, reeds, etc. in reed beds or on ground. Female lays 5—9 white, green-tinged eggs. Incubates them mainly unaided. Male keeps watch but occasionally relieves female. Young hatch in 35 days, on second day take to water with female. Swan with young aggressive. Mainly vegetarian but also eats insects etc.

4 Grey Lag-goose *Anser anser*. Distributed in Scotland, Scandinavia, in central and eastern Europe, across Asia to Far East. Migrates south at end of October (northern birds winter in England), returns to nesting areas at end of February or beginning of March. Length 78—92 cm. Builds nest from rush stalks and other material, usually in reed beds, but sometimes in small willows. Lines nest with down. Female lays 4—7 whitish eggs, incubates them unaided 28 days. Eats seeds, grass, shoots, etc.

5 Bean Goose *Anser fabalis*. Distributed in northern parts of Europe and Asia, coast of Greenland. Length 73—90 cm. Winters from September in central, western and southern Europe. Frequents ice-free water. In some years appears in huge flocks. Very wary bird. Looks for food in meadows and fields. Returns to nesting area in May. Builds nest from grass blades etc. Female lays 3—6 eggs, incubates them about 26 days. Vegetarian.

6 Brant Goose *Branta bernicla*. Distributed over coasts of northern Asia and North America. Length 58—88 cm. In winter migrates along west coast of Europe to Spain and Morocco. Some flocks stray far inland, into central Europe. Builds nest from grass blades in dry parts of tundra. Female lays 3—6 eggs, incubates them about 25 days. Lives on grass, seeds, lichen.

7 Sheld-duck *Tadorna tadorna*. Distributed over coasts of northern and western Europe, round Black Sea, in east as far as Mongolia. Length about 65 cm. In winter (sometimes in spring) appears on rivers and ponds in central Europe. Nests in holes and hollows, also uses deserted foxes' earths. Sometimes nests in rocks. Female lays 6—16 plain yellowish eggs, incubates them unaided. Young hatch in 28 days. Lives on greenstuff, insects, worms, small crustaceans, etc.

Order: **Ducks, Geese and Swans** — *Anseriformes*

1 Mallard *Anas platyrhynchos*. Distributed in Europe, Asia and North America, in winter also North Africa and India. Length 49—63 cm. Inhabits overgrown pools, ponds, lakes and rivers. Often nests on small ornamental ponds in town parks. Nest usually built on ground, in clump of grass or under bush, occasionally in tree. Female lays 8—14, generally green-grey eggs, incubates them unaided 26 days. When dry, young follow female to water. Young promptly dive if in danger. Mixed diet. Like all ducks, males have same colouring as females during summer.

2 Widgeon *Anas strepera*. Distributed in southern England, central Europe, in east as far as Amur, and North America. Length about 48 cm. European birds migrate in October to Mediterranean region, return in March. Mainly inhabits overgrown ponds. Nest hidden in reed-grass, nettles, etc. In May or June female lays 8—14 creamy eggs, incubates them unaided 26 days. Mixed diet.

3 European Teal *Anas crecca*. Distributed over whole of Europe except Spain, temperate and northern Asia, large parts of North America. Length 30.5—38 cm., weight about 0.3 kg. European birds migrate in August, winter in southern Europe and North Africa, return in April. Inhabits thickly overgrown ponds. Nests on ground in meadows etc., often far from water. In May female lays 8—10 eggs. Mixed diet. Form flocks in autumn. Swift flier.

4 Garganey *Anas querquedula*. Distributed in Europe, extends east as far as Japan. Length 34—40 cm. In September European birds migrate in flocks to North and Central Africa. Inhabits places with thickly overgrown water. Nests in dense clumps of grass or under bushes. At end of April female lays 8—12 eggs, incubates them about 23 days. Mixed diet.

5 Shoveller *Anas clypeata*. Distributed in western, central and northern Europe, in east across Asia to North America. In September migrates to Mediterranean region, returns in second half of March. Length about 45 cm. Inhabits regions with ponds and meadows. Nests in grass in meadows and fields. Lines nest with dry reed-grass and down. Female incubates 9—12 greyish eggs 23—24 days. Catches mainly small animals in shallows. Wide bill acts as sieve.

6 Red-crested Pochard *Netta rufina*. Distributed in parts of central Europe, western and central Asia. In recent years has spread to many places in central Europe. Migrates in September to southern Europe, returns in April. Length about 60 cm. Nests on small islands or right beside water. Female incubates 7—10 grey-yellow eggs 27 days. Gathers food on surface of open water.

7 Pochard *Aythya ferina*. Distributed mainly in central Europe, in east to western Siberia, North America. Both migratory and resident. Length about 40 cm. Very common. Inhabits large ponds and lakes surrounded by reed beds. Lives mostly on water. Builds nest near water, on clumps of reed-grass or small islands. Female incubates 8—14 relatively large, yellow-green eggs about 24 days. Seeks food — aquatic animals and plant shoots — mainly under water.

8 Tufted Duck *Aythya fuligula*. Inhabited originally northern Europe, Asia and Iceland, but has begun to move south. Today common in England and central Europe. European birds winter on coasts of western Europe and Mediterranean. Leave in October. Length about 38 cm. At end of May builds nest in clump of reed-grass or on ground, close to water. Female incubates 6—9 green-grey eggs 25—26 days. Young completely black. Mixed diet, gathered mainly under water. Excellent diver.

Order: **Ducks, Geese and Swans** — *Anseriformes*

1 Golden-eye *Bucephala clangula*. Distributed in northern parts of Europe, Asia and North America, recently parts of central Europe. Migrates in October to coasts of western and southern Europe, returns to central Europe at end of March. Length about 40 cm. Builds down-lined nest in tree hollows or nesting-boxes, often at great height. Female incubates 8—18 greenish eggs about 30 days. Mixed diet, gathered mainly in water.

2 Eider Duck *Somateria mollissima*. Distributed in most northerly arctic regions of Europe, Iceland, Greenland, North America and north-eastern Siberia. Length about 58 cm. In autumn and winter regularly appears on ice-free rivers in central Europe. Builds nest near sea, in grass, among stones, etc. Female lays 4—5 greenish eggs, packed in finest down, incubates them 24—27 days. Lives mainly on small animals but also eats some plants.

3 Goosander *Mergus merganser*. Distributed in northern parts of Europe, Asia and North America. Regularly appears on ice-free rivers in central Europe, frequently in large flocks, from November to April. Length about 65 cm. Nests inland, often far from water, usually in tree hollows. Female incubates 7—12 dull green eggs 35 days. Young hop out of nest unaided. Lives on small fish, water snails, aquatic insects, etc.

Order: **Divers and Allies** — *Gaviiformes*

Family: **Divers** — *Gaviidae*

4 Black-throated Diver *Gavia arctica*. Distributed in northern parts of Europe, Asia and North America. Also nests in Scotland and north of Poland. Occasionally appears on central-European rivers from October to April. Length 70—74 cm. Inhabits lakes, mainly in tundra and taiga belt. Nests beside water. Each couple has own nesting 'preserve'. Both parents incubate 1—3 spotted eggs about 25 days. Lives on fish, supplemented by molluscs, large insects, small crustaceans, etc.

Order: **Grebes and Allies** — *Podicipediformes*

Family: **Grebes** — *Podicipedidae*

5 Great Crested Grebe *Podiceps cristatus*. Widely distributed over whole of Europe and Asia except most northerly parts, whole of Africa and Australia. Winters in western and southern Europe and often on rivers in central Europe. Migrates by night. Length 54 to 61 cm. Inhabits lakes and large ponds thickly overgrown with rushes. Builds nest from aquatic plants among reeds. Nest sometimes floats. Female usually lays 3—4 dingy greenish eggs, incubated by both parents 25 days. Parents often carry dark-striped young on back and push food down their beak. Catches small fish and insects.

6 Black-necked Grebe *Podiceps nigricollis*. Distributed over whole of Europe except Scandinavia, in east to western Siberia, west to North America, eastern Africa. Migrates in October or November to western and southern Europe, returns in April. Length 31—33.5 cm. Inhabits thickly overgrown ponds and lakes. Often nests in colonies of up to several hundred couples. Builds nest in rushes. Female incubates 3—4 (occasionally up to 6) dull white or greenish eggs 20—21 days. Lives mainly on insects.

7 Little Grebe or **Dabchick** *Podiceps ruficollis*. Distributed over whole of Europe, southern and south-eastern Asia, Australia, whole of Africa. Length about 23 cm. Very common, but shy and secretive. Inhabits small ponds, pools, creeks, etc., overgrown with reeds. Arrives in April. From fragments of aquatic plants builds floating nest among rushes, close to open water. Female lays 4—9 white, green-tinged eggs, incubated 20 days by both parents in turn. Eats mainly aquatic insects. Often resident on ice-free parts of rivers.

Order: **Doves, Pigeons and Allies** — *Columbiformes*

Family: **Doves and Pigeons** — *Columbidae*

1 Wood Pigeon *Columba palumbus*. Distributed over whole of Europe except most northerly part, Asia Minor, north-western Africa, in east to central Asia and Himalayas. European birds migrate in September or October to southern Europe and north-western Africa, return in middle of March. Length about 40 cm. Mostly inhabits conifer and mixed woods, but also encountered in large parks. Builds loose, untidy nest from dry twigs, usually 5—30 m. from ground, on spreading branch. Female lays 2 white eggs in April, sometimes second clutch in June. Young hatch in 16—18 days. Lives on seeds of forest plants, but also raids crops.

2 Stock-dove *Columba oenas*. Distributed over whole of Europe except Scandinavia, in east to central Asia, in south to north-western Africa. European birds migrate in September or October to southern Europe and North Africa, return in middle of March. Length about 34 cm. Chiefly inhabits deciduous woods with old beeches and oaks, in hollows of which it builds nest. Also uses nesting-boxes. Female lays 2 white eggs in April and again in June. Young hatch in 17—20 days. Lives mainly on various seeds.

3 Turtle Dove *Streptopelia turtur*. Distributed over whole of Europe, in east to central Asia, whole of North Africa. In September—October migrates to Africa north of equator, returns in April. Length about 30 cm. Inhabits young woods and overgrown hillsides with fields and meadows in vicinity. Builds nest in thick undergrowth, in tall, dense bushes, etc., 1—7 m. above ground. Female lays 2 white eggs. Young hatch in 14—17 days. Lives on seeds (especially of weeds), small molluscs, etc.

4 Collared Turtle Dove *Streptopelia decaocto*. Inhabited originally southern Asia, Asia Minor and southern part of Balkans. A few decades ago started to spread west, now inhabits whole of Europe and is one of commonest birds. Resident bird. Frequents human communities, lives in town parks, gardens, orchards, etc. and accepts titbits left outside window. Nests several times a year, from early spring to autumn. Winter nesting and laying also known. Builds nest from sticks and grass blades in dense tree tops or tall bushes. Has preference for spruces and ornamental trees in parks. Lays 2 white eggs. Lives on various seeds, molluscs and insects, in winter will eat scraps and chopped meat. Has loud call.

Order: **Waders and Allies** — *Charadriiformes*

Family: **Auks, Razorbills and Puffins** — *Alcidae*

5 Guillemot *Uria aalge*. Distributed over coasts of northern Europe, England, north-eastern Asia, north-western part of North America. Length about 45 cm. In winter frequents coasts of western Europe and Mediterranean countries. Rock-dweller. On ledge of rock female lays single large, spotted egg, incubated 35 days by both parents in turn. Lives on small fish, crustaceans, etc., caught in sea.

6 Puffin *Fratercula arctica*. Distributed mainly over coasts of Scandinavia and northern islands, west coast of England, Iceland, Greenland. Length 30—36 cm. In winter appears along coasts of western Europe and Mediterranean countries. Builds nest in burrow up to 3 m. long. Female lays single egg, incubated 35 days by both parents in turn. Catches mainly small saltwater fish.

Family: **Gulls and Terns** — *Laridae*

1 Black-headed Gull *Larus ridibundus*. Distributed in Europe, extends to Far East. Length 33.5—43 cm. In nesting season has black-brown head, in winter white. European birds winter mainly in western and southern Europe, but many remain behind on ice-free rivers in central Europe. Arrives in nesting area in second half of March. Nests in large colonies on small islands in ponds. Nest made of grass blades, twigs, leaves, etc. Female usually lays 3 spotted eggs of very variable colouring. Young hatch in 22—24 days. Lives on insects, small fish, fruit, e.g. cherries, etc. Follows plough and snaps up grubs and worms.

2 Black-backed Gull *Larus canus*. Distributed in England, northern Europe, northern Asia, north-western part of North America. Winters along coasts of western Europe, often flies inland to rivers of central Europe. Returns to nesting areas in April. Length 38—48 cm. Nests in grass on small islands, etc. Female lays 3 spotted eggs. Young hatch in 25—26 days. Fed by parents 35 days. Eats insects, molluscs, other birds' eggs, fruits and seeds.

3 Herring Gull *Larus argentatus*. Distributed over coasts of northern and southern Europe, northern Asia and North America. Length 55—69 cm. Nests on ground on shore, in Balkans also on roofs of houses. Female lays 2—3 spotted eggs. Young hatch in 26 days, fully fledged after 8—9 weeks. Lives on small animal, scraps, etc. In autumn also roams inlands to rivers, particularly Danube.

4 Great Black-headed Gull *Larus marinus*. Distributed over coasts of Scandinavia, Iceland, England and North America. Length 61—76 cm. In winter lives nomadically along coasts of northern and western Europe. Often accompanies ocean-going liners out to sea, hoping for scraps. Otherwise eats fish, crustaceans and birds' eggs and young. Nests on cliffs. Usually lays 3 spotted eggs. Both parents incubate eggs 29—30 days and then feed young.

5 Arctic Skua *Stercorarius parasiticus*. Inhabits Arctic waters and coasts of northern Europe, Asia and North America. Length about 46 cm. In winter comes to African coast. Common on coast but strays to rivers in central Europe. Nests in colonies. Female lays 2 spotted eggs on bare ground, between clumps of grass. Young hatch in 25—26 days. Lives on different animals caught in sea, also hunts lemmings and eats berries. Chases gulls, forces them to drop food, snaps it up in air.

6 Common Tern *Sterna hirundo*. Distributed over whole of Europe, temperate parts of Asia, North America. Length 34—40 cm. Migrates in August to southern Africa, returns at beginning of May. Nests in colonies. Makes nest on ground, from a few sticks, roots, shells, etc. Female lays 2—4 spotted eggs of somewhat variable colouring. Young hatch in 20—22 days. Diet small fish. Hovers in air looking for prey, dives after it at high speed.

7 Black Tern *Chlidonias niger*. Distributed over large part of Europe, in east to central Asia, part of North America. Length 24—27 cm. European birds migrate at end of July to equatorial Africa, return in May. Lives in small colonies. Builds nest on floating aquatic plants. Female lays 2—3 spotted eggs. Young hatch in 14—17 days. Lives mainly on aquatic insects, small crustaceans and fish, but also often travels several miles to look for insects in fields.

Families: *Charadriidae, Scolopacidae*

1 Lapwing *Vanellus vanellus*. Distributed over whole of Europe, in east to temperate parts of Asia as far as Korea. Length about 30 cm. Very common. Skilful flier. Winters in western and southern Europe and North Africa, often returns at end of February. Inhabits damp meadows and fields near ponds and lakes. Builds nest on small hummock, lines it with blades of grass. Female lays 4 olive brown speckled eggs, incubated by both parents 24 days. After 2 days, young disperse and hide in surrounding grass. In autumn forms flocks round ponds. Eats insects, worms, molluscs, seeds.

2 Golden Plover *Pluvialis apricaria*. Inhabits northern Europe, England, Iceland, east coast of Greenland. Winters in west and south-west of Europe and in North Africa. In September to October always migrates across central Europe, can be seen there mainly in fields, usually in small flocks. Length 25—30 cm. Inhabits swampy areas in north. Builds nest like lapwing's on ground. Lays 4 eggs, young hatch in 20 days. Catches insects, worms, etc.

3 Little Ringed Plover *Charadrius dubius*. Distributed over whole of Europe except England and Scandinavia, most of Asia, North Africa. European birds migrate in September— November to equatorial Africa, return in middle of April. Length 16—19 cm. Likes sandy ground beside lakes, ponds and rivers. Nests in small depression in pebbles. Female lays 4 yellowish, dark-spotted eggs, incubated by both parents 22—24 days. Eats insects, insect larvae and worms.

4 Sea Plover *Charadrius alexandrinus*. Distributed along all European coasts except most northerly regions, whole of temperate and southern Asia, whole of Africa, Australia, southern U.S.A. and west of South America. European birds winter on African coast south of equator. Length 16—18.5 cm. Prefers sandy shores beside sea or salt lakes. Female lays 4 spotted eggs in depression in stones, incubates them 24 days. Catches insects, small crustaceans, worms and molluscs. Migrating birds often seen in central Europe.

5 Dunlin *Calidris alpina*. Distributed in England, north coast of Germany, Scandinavia and northern parts of Asia and North America. Winters on coasts of western Europe, Mediterranean region and Africa. Migrating birds seen in large numbers beside ponds from end of August. Length 19—22.5 cm. Nests mainly in tundra belt, builds nest in peat moors. Female lays 4 eggs, incubated by both parents. Lives on insects, worms and molluscs.

6 Ruff (female **Reeve**) *Philomachus pugnax*. Distributed over northern parts of Europe and Asia, but also nests in central Europe, e.g. Poland, Holland and Belgium. Winters in Africa. Appears in flocks beside ponds over whole of central Europe during migration. Length 23—33 cm. Male's colouring very variable. During nesting season males wear 'ruff' and fight duels. Female builds nest lined with grass blades and leaves in small pit. Lays 4 eggs, incubates them unaided 20—21 days. Eats mainly insects, worms and molluscs.

7 Redshank *Tringa totanus*. Distributed over whole of Europe and across temperate belt of Asia to Far East. Migrates in August—October, return at end of March. Length 27—31 cm. Inhabits flat ground beside large ponds and lakes. Builds grass-lined nest in depression in ground. Female lays 4 grey, dark-speckled eggs, incubated 22—25 days by both parents in turn. Young fledged at 25 days. If enemy approaches nest or young, parent birds fly up, screeching. Lives on insects, worms, molluscs, crustaceans and small fish.

Families: *Scolopacidae, Recurvirostridae*

1 Black-tailed Godwit *Limosa limosa.* Distributed in northern part of western Europe except England, Iceland, northern Germany, central and eastern Europe, across Asia to Far East. European birds migrate in August or September to northern and equatorial Africa, return in first half of April. Length 39.5—49.5 cm.; female always much larger. Inhabits water-logged meadows beside ponds and lakes. Makes nest in shallow depression in thick grass or on clod, lines it with a little grass. Female lays 4 dark-spotted eggs, incubated 24 days by both parents in turn. If enemy approaches, flies up into air, uttering piercing, piping cries. Eats insects, insect larvae, worms, small molluscs.

2 Avocet *Recurvirostra avosetta.* Distributed in southern Spain, coast of Germany, occasionally swampy ground round lakes and ponds in central Europe, in east to Mongolia. European birds winter in southern Africa. Length 42—47.5 cm. Builds nest among plants in depression in mud of drained ponds, etc., lines it with a few plants. Female lays 4 olive green eggs with grey-brown spots. Eggs incubated 24—25 days by both parents in turn. Lives on insects, insect larvae, crustaceans and molluscs found in shallow water and mud.

3 Curlew *Numenius arquata.* Distributed in Europe except south, Iceland, in east to western Siberia. European birds winter in eastern Africa, return at end of March. Length 54—69 cm. Inhabits large, wet meadows or steppe country in vicinity of water. Builds nest in small depression in ground, among grass. Female lays 4 spotted eggs, often strewn with dark dots and streaks. Eggs incubated 26—28 days by both parents in turn. Female responsible for care of young. Lives on insects, insect larvae, seeds of aquatic plants, etc.

4 Woodcock *Scolopax rusticola.* Distributed over whole of Europe except most northerly parts, in east forms belt across Asia to Japan, also found on Azores and Canaries. European birds winter in southern Europe and North Africa, return at end of March. Migrate by night. Length 34—38 cm. Inhabits deciduous or mixed woods where it frequents large, damp, grassy spaces, streams, etc. Nests in a small leaf- or moss-lined depression under a bush. Female lays 4 spotted eggs of somewhat variable colouring, incubates them unaided 22 days. Eats insects, worms and molluscs.

5 Common Snipe *Gallinago gallinago.* Distributed over whole of Europe except south, in east across temperate parts of Asia to Japan. European birds winter mainly in Africa, return in March. Occasionally resident. Length 24.5—31 cm. Inhabits swamps, damp meadows and peat-bogs. Nests in deep depression in dense grass. Female lays 4 eggs with olive and green spots, incubates them unaided 19—21 days. Lives on insects, spiders and worms. In autumn congregates in flocks. At mating time male flies high into air and dives with spread tail feathers, vibrations of which produce bleating sound.

Order: **Cranes, Rails and Allies** — *Gruiformes*

Family: **Cranes** — *Gruidae*

6 Crane *Grus grus.* Distributed in northern Europe and Asia. Occasionally nests in north and east of central Europe. European birds winter in North Africa and along Nile, return in April or May. Length 105—120 cm. Inhabits extensive swamps and marshes. Flies in typical V-formation. Couples remain together. Female builds large nest in swamp, from reeds and aquatic plants. Usually lays 2 grey-green, dark-spotted eggs. Young hatch in 29—30 days. Eats mainly greenstuffs, but also insects, molluscs and occasionally small vertebrates.

Family: **Rails, Moorhens and Coots** — *Rallidae*

1 Water Rail *Rallus aquaticus*. Distributed over whole of Europe, in east across temperate Asia to Japan, also North Africa. Winters in southern Europe and North Africa, returns in middle of April. Length about 28.5 cm. Mainly nocturnal bird. Inhabits fishpond regions. Nests on swampy ground under bush etc. Nest made of grass, reed-grass, leaves, etc. Female lays 6—12 yellowish, rusty-spotted eggs, incubated 20 days by both parents. Newly hatched chicks are black. Parents push food into their beak. Lives on insects, worms and small leaves.

2 Spotted Crake *Porzana porzana*. Distributed over most of Europe, in east to central Asia, north-western Africa. Migrates to southern Europe and North Africa in October, returns in middle of April. Length 21—25 cm. Leads secretive existence. Builds nest from grass and leaves on clump of reed-grass in swamp. Female lays 6—8 spotted eggs. Young hatch in 18—21 days. Eats insects, spiders, molluscs, seeds and parts of aquatic plants.

3 Moorhen *Gallinula chloropus*. Distributed over most of Europe, central and eastern Asia, America, Africa. European birds occasionally resident, but mostly winter in North Africa. Length about 32 cm. Inhabits overgrown lakes, ponds and pools. Makes deep-basined nest from reeds and aquatic plants on surface of water among rushes. Female lays 6—8 yellowish eggs with rusty brown spots. Young hatch in 19—22 days. Lives on insects, worms, seeds and parts of plants.

4 Coot *Fulica atra*. Distributed over whole of Europe, across temperate parts of Asia to Japan, Australia, north-western Africa. European birds winter in western and southern Europe, but often occur in flocks on rivers of central Europe. Return to nesting places in March. Length 38—45 cm. Inhabits any type of overgrown stagnant water. Builds nest on surface of water, at margin of vegetation, from rush stems, sedge, etc., often with a connecting 'bridge'. Female lays 5—15 mauvish, black-spotted eggs. Young, hatched in 22 days, have orange-coloured head. Lives on small aquatic animals, seeds and parts of plants.

Family: **Bustards** — *Otididae*

5 Great Bustard *Otis tarda*. Distributed in southern and central Europe, in east to China, north-western Africa. Length of male about 100 cm., female about 80 cm. Inhabits steppes and vast fields. Female lays 2—3 brownish spotted eggs in depression in ground, incubates them about 30 days. Large nesting sites near Berlin and in southern Slovakia. Lives on insects, worms, small vertebrates, seeds and parts of plants.

Order: **Game Birds** — *Galliformes*

Family: **Pheasants, Partridges and Quails** — *Phasianidae*

6 Partridge *Perdix perdix*. Distributed over most of Europe except northern Scandinavia, in east to central Asia. Length about 26 cm. Inhabits steppes, in Europe mainly fields. Usually at beginning of May female lays about 15 olive brown eggs in pit in ground, incubates them unaided 23—25 days, but male also cares for young. Eats mainly plants, supplemented in summer by insects, spiders and molluscs. In autumn gathers together in small flocks. Highly prized game bird in Europe.

7 Quail *Coturnix coturnix*. Distributed over most of Europe, temperate parts of Asia as far as Japan, North and South Africa. European birds winter mainly in Africa. Leave in October, return at end of April. Length about 18 cm. Inhabits steppes, meadows and fields. Male polygamous. Female digs small pit, lays 6—18 eggs, usually marked with dark brown blotches and dots, incubates them unaided 18—20 days. Lives on seeds, shoots, small molluscs, worms and insects.

Family: **Pheasants, Partridges and Quails** — *Phasianidae*

1 Common Pheasant *Phasianus colchicus*. Originally distributed in a few races in central and eastern Asia, but introduced into many parts of Europe and North America. Known in central Europe since 14th century. European races now thoroughly crossed. Length of cock about 80 cm., hen about 60 cm. Inhabits copses, wooded slopes, etc. in lowlands and uplands. Female lines depression in ground with leaves and grass, lays 8—15 plain brownish eggs, incubates them unaided 23—27 days. Cock polygamous. Lives on plants, shoots, seeds and various small animals. Important game bird.

2 Rock Partridge *Alectoris graeca*. Distributed in mountainous regions from southern Europe east to China. Abundant in Balkans and on southern slopes of Alps. Introduction attempted in many places in central Europe. Length about 35 cm. Inhabits rocky slopes. In summer ascends to dwarf timber belt, in winter descends into valleys. In May or June female lays 10—15 light brown, often thickly spotted eggs in depression in rock or in clump of grass. Lives on seeds, grass, insects, etc.

Family: **Grouse and Ptarmigans** — *Tetraonidae*

3 Ptarmigan *Lagopus mutus*. Distributed in tundras in northern Europe, Asia and North America, also England, Spain and Alps. Length about 35 cm. In summer brownish with white wings, in winter completely white except for black tail. White colouring makes it blend with snow. Female usually lays 7—10 russet-speckled eggs in depression among stones or in clump of grass, etc. Eats shoots, buds (e.g. of willows, birches, etc.), seeds and, in summer, insects, spiders and small molluscs. In winter spends night in holes in snow.

4 Black Grouse *Lyrurus tetrix*. Distributed over whole of Europe except south, whole of temperate Asia, but mainly more northerly regions, primarily taiga. Length of cock about 65 cm., hen about 45 cm. Cock weighs about 1.5 kg. Likes deciduous and mixed woods with damp meadows in vicinity. Early in spring birds congregate on special 'parade grounds', in clearing, on moor, in meadow, etc., where cocks fight duels. Cock polygamous. Hen lays 6—10 yellowish, dark-spotted eggs in moss- and grass-lined pit, incubates them unaided about 26 days. Lives on seeds, berries, shoots, insects, worms, etc.

5 Capercaillie *Tetrao urogallus*. Distributed in northern England, central and northern Europe, eastwards to Sakhalin. Length of cock about 100 cm., hen 70 cm. Cock can weigh up to 6 kg. Inhabits large forests. Males perform interesting nuptial rites. 'Song' divided into three parts: knocking, trilling and slurring. Hen lays 5—12 yellowish, brown-spotted eggs in shallow depression lined with leaves, conifer needles, etc., incubates them unaided 24—27 days. Lives on shoots, conifer needles, whole tips of conifer branches, insects, molluscs, etc. Most highly prized game bird.

6 Hazel Hen *Tetrastes bonasia*. Distributed over whole of central and northern Europe, extends east to eastern Siberia and south-eastern China. Now scarce in mountains of central Europe, but still abundant in Scandinavia. Length about 38 cm. Inhabits mixed forests, especially with birches and dense undergrowth including bushes, cranberries and bilberries. Female lays 8—12 yellowish, dark-spotted eggs in shallow depression at foot of tree, incubates them 25 days. Lives on seeds, shoots, berries, insects, small molluscs, etc. Flesh very savoury.

Order: **Insectivores** — *Insectivora* (p. 382). All small, short-legged mammals. Walk on whole surface of palm and sole. Complete dentition, large number of sharp teeth, canines barely distinguishable from incisors. Live mainly on insects, some species also eat small vertebrates. Huge appetite. Some species hibernate.

Family: **Hedgehogs** — *Erinaceidae* (p. 382). Back and sides covered with spines. Can curl up, making spines stand erect. Short tail. Eat insects, worms, small vertebrates and birds' eggs. Nocturnal animals. Hibernators.

Family: **Moles** — *Talpidae* (p. 382). Small mammals with cylindrical body, short legs and short thick coat. Fore legs like shovels for digging. Small eyes. Vestigial ears hidden by fur. Live mostly underground. Eat worms and insects.

Family: **Shrews** — *Soricidae* (p. 382). Small mammals resembling mice. Head tapers off into pointed snout. Rather long tail. Nocturnal animals, hide during day. Fairly common.

Order: **Bats** — *Chiroptera* (p. 384). Distinctive group of mammals with typical, sharp-pointed teeth. Patagial (wing) membrane stretched between digits of forelimbs, trunk and hindlimbs and often tail. Digits of hindlimbs clawed for hanging upside down. Clawed thumb only free digit on hand. Female gives birth to 1 or 2 young. Fluttering flight. Silky fur. Small eyes. Well developed sense of smell and touch. Very large ears. Bats have specific, radar-like system enabling them to fly accurately in dark. During flight emit supersonic sounds inaudible to human ear, which rebound from objects and are perceived by bat's sensitive ear in form of echo. Some bats have membraneous appendages on snout. In cold regions hibernate, body temperature drops to almost 0°C. Nocturnal animals. Live mainly on insects.

Family: **Horseshoe Bats** — *Rhinolophidae* (p. 384). Ear uncovered. Membraneous appendages on snout.

Family: **Typical Bats** — *Vespertilionidae* (p. 384). Ear furnished with long lid. Smooth snout.

Order: **Hares and Rabbits** — *Lagomorpha* (p. 384). Largish mammals with long ears, short tail and long hind legs. Two small teeth behind incisors, i.e. total of 4 incisors, in upper jaw.

Order: **Rodents** — *Rodentia* (p. 386). Small to comparatively large mammals with only two incisors in upper jaw, which grow as they are worn down. Terrestrial, arboreal and aquatic animals. Many pests. Others valuable for fur.

Family: **Squirrels** — *Sciuridae* (p. 386). Arboreal species have long bushy tail, terrestrial species short ears and short, hairy tail.

Family: **Dormice** — *Gliridae* (p. 386). Small to tiny arboreal rodents with long, bushy tail. Nocturnal animals. Hibernators.

Family: **Old World Rats and Mice** — *Muridae* (p. 388). Small terrestrial rodents with relatively short legs. Include many pests. Long, hairless tail. Round-cusped molars.

Family: **Hamsters** — *Cricetidae* (p. 388). Largish rodents with stout body and short legs and tail. Have facial pouches.

Family: **Voles** — *Microtidae* (p. 390). Incurving, non-cusped molars. Short tail and ears.

Family: **Beavers** — *Castoridae* (p. 390). Moderately large aquatic rodents with webbed hind feet. Flattened, scaly tail. Strong teeth. Thick fur.

Family: **Nutrias** — *Myocastoridae* (p. 390). Moderately large aquatic rodents with blunt head and large incisors. Webbed feet. Introduced into Europe for fur, bred on farms, in some places wild.

Order: **Beasts of Prey** — *Carnivora* (p. 392). Mostly terrestrial animals of varying size, with powerfully developed teeth and long-clawed toes. Long tail (except bears). Mostly carnivorous, some species omnivorous.

Family: **Cats** — *Felidae* (p. 392). Moderately large to large, lithe carnivorous mammals with short jaws, long tail and rough tongue. Claws usually retractile. Very keen vision, excellent hearing. Jump on prey. Run swiftly, some species can also climb or swim. Mostly nocturnal.

Family: **Dog Tribe** — *Canidae* (p. 392). Long-legged beasts of prey with 5 toes on forelimbs, 4 toes on hindlimbs and non-retractile claws. Tapering, fanged jaws. Run swiftly. Excellent hearing and smell. Many species go around in packs or troops.

Family: **Mustelids** — *Mustelidae* (p. 392). Smallish flesh-eaters with long body, short legs and short, sharp claws. Rounded head. Majority secrete pungent substance. Some species arboreal, others terrestrial, also aquatic.

Family: **Bears** — *Ursidae* (p. 396). Some of largest flesh-eaters. Robust body, wide head, tapering jaws, short tail. All legs have 5 digits with strong, blunt claws. Walk on whole of sole. Omnivorous. Only one species in Europe.

Order: **Pinnipeds** — *Pinnipedia* (p. 396). Large aquatic mammals with short, thick coat. Paddle-like limbs. Digits webbed and with rudimentary claws. Spindle-shaped body. Nostrils can be closed. Degenerate tail. Pointed teeth. Live mainly on fish. Some species travel long distances to breeding beaches on rocky islands.

Order: **Whales** — *Cetacea* (p. 396). Large to gigantic mammals completely adapted to aquatic existence. Fish-shaped body. Jaws usually long. Only toothed whales *(Odontoceti)* have teeth. Produce 1—2 young. Live in sea, but occasionally stray into rivers.

Order: **Even-toed Ungulates** — *Artiodactyla* (p. 398). Large ungulates with even number of digits. Third and fourth toe most developed, carry hoofs.

Non-ruminants — *Nonruminantia* (p. 398). Omnivorous, with complete dentition and one stomach.

Family: **Pigs** — *Suidae* (p. 398). Large mammals with long snout for rooting in soil.

Ruminants — *Ruminantia* (p. 398). Moderately large to large mammals with incomplete dentition (incisors, and usually also canines missing in upper jaw). Chew cud. Herbivorous. Stomach divided into 4 or 3 compartments.

Family: **Deer** — *Cervidae* (p. 398). Large, graceful mammals with long legs. Males grow antlers (in rare cases females also). Antlers have branches (tines); regularly shed, grow again.

Family: **Hollow-horned Ruminants** — *Bovidae* (p. 400). Moderately large to large mammals with genuine horns (hollow formations of thick horn covering boss on frontal bone). Horns are permanent fixture. Male's horns larger than female's (females of some species hornless). Herbivorous.

Class: **Mammals** — *Mammalia*

Order: **Insectivores** — *Insectivora*

Family: **Hedgehogs** — *Erinaceidae*

1, 2 European Hedgehog *Erinaceus europaeus*. Two races — western *(E.e. europaeus)* with brown underside and dark bands round eyes, and eastern *(E.e. roumanicus)* with white underside. Dividing line from Oder along upper reaches of Elbe and Vltava. Hedgehog inhabits deciduous and mixed woods with dense undergrowth and town parks. Likes dry places. In Alps up to 2,000 m. Makes nest in hole, under pile of leaves, etc., usually with two entrances. Female gives birth to 3—8 (in rare cases up to 10) young with soft white spines. Young open eyes at 14 days. Nocturnal animal. Hibernates from end of October to March under pile of leaves, in burrow, etc. Lives on worms, insects, small vertebrates, birds' eggs. Also kills venomous snakes without getting bitten and eats them. Almost immune to snake venom. Length up to 30 cm., weight over 1 kg. Newborn young weigh 12—25 g. Life span 8—10 years.

Family: **Moles** — *Talpidae*

3 Common Mole *Talpa europaea*. Abundant in whole of central Europe and western Asia. In Alps up to 2,400 m. Lives underground in damp places with loose soil. Digs burrows with chambers and passages. Length 13—17 cm., weight 70—120 g. Twice a year female gives birth to 3—9 tiny young which grow very quickly. Open eyes at 3 weeks, suckled 4—6 weeks, independent at 2 months. Life span 2—3 years. Non-hibernator.

Family: **Shrews** — *Soricidae*

4 Common Shrew *Sorex araneus*. Abundant in whole of Europe except Mediterranean region and Ireland. Frequents damp places with undergrowth. In Alps up to 2,000 m. Occurs mainly in damp woods and peat-bogs, also in ditches. Inhabits vole and mole burrows, but sometimes digs own. In winter found in houses and outbuildings. Length 6.2—8.5 cm., weight 7—15 g. Newborn young weigh only 0.4—0.5 g. Between April and September female produces up to 4 litters of 5—7 hairless, blind young. Coat grows from 6th day, open eyes at 18—25 days. Active mainly after sundown and before sunrise. Non-hibernator.

5 European Water Shrew *Neomys fodiens*. Inhabits whole of central Europe. In Alps up to 2,500 m. Frequents rivers, streams, ponds and pools. Inhabits rodent burrows and makes own burrow beside water. Likewise found in flooded cellars. Also nests in tree hollows, up to 0.75 m. above ground, but always near water. Swims well. Catches insects, worms and small fish. Length 7—11 cm., weight 10—20 g. Female gives birth 2—3 times yearly to 4—10 hairless, blind young, which are suckled 5—6 weeks and reach adulthood at 3—4 months. Nocturnal animal, active mainly in early morning. Life span not more than 1.5 years. Non-hibernator.

6 Common European White-toothed Shrew *Crocidura russula*. Inhabits western, southern and parts of central Europe. Occurs up to altitudes of 1,600 m. Lives in open country, less often on margins of forests, but chiefly in gardens and parks. In winter often frequents human dwellings, cowsheds, cellars, etc. In wild surroundings lives in mouse-holes or digs own burrow. Length 6—8.5 cm., weight 6—7.5 g. Female gives birth to 3—10 young 2—3 times a year. Young open eyes at 13 days, suckled about 20 days, are adult at 4 months. Life span usually about 1.5 years, in rare cases up to 4 years. Non-hibernator. Lives on insects and worms. Nocturnal animal.

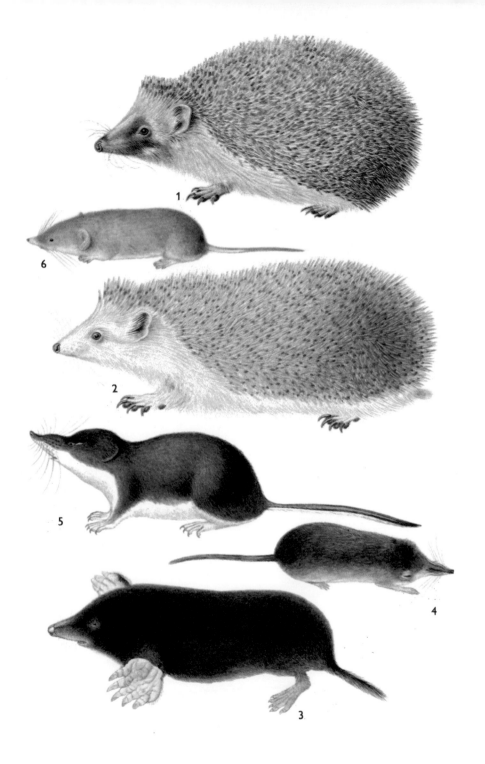

Order: **Bats** — *Chiroptera*

Family: **Horseshoe Bats** — *Rhinolophidae*

1 Lesser Horseshoe Bat *Rhinolophus hipposideros*. Inhabits south of central Europe. In Alps up to 2,000 m. During day shelters in attics, steeples, caves, etc. Slow and ungainly in flight. Comes out well after dark and only in warm, calm weather. Hibernates in deep caves, mines, etc. Hangs from roof in groups of up to 100, in long rows. One litter of 1—2 young annually. Young open eyes at one week, are adult at one year. Born in colonies of females. Hibernates from October to April. Life span 14—15 years.

Family: **Typical Bats** — *Vespertilionidae*

2 Brown Bat *Myotis myotis*. One of commonest European bats. Shelters during day in attics, towers or cellars. Hibernates in caves, mines, etc., often in vast numbers. Goes hunting after dark. Flies slowly and clumsily, at height of 5—8 m., over gardens, parks, etc., at 15 km. an hour. Known to migrate distances of over 200 km. in spring and autumn. Has one young yearly, in May or June, born in colonies of 100—2,000 females. Young grows quickly, can fly at 5—6 weeks. Hibernates from October to April. Maximum life span 14.5 years.

3 Fringed Bat *Myotis nattereri*. Inhabits most of Europe. Lives in small colonies of up to 30 individuals, males singly. During day shelters in tree hollows, nesting-boxes, etc. Hibernates in mines, caves and cellars. Circles low and slowly round trees. Catches insects sitting on branches. Hunts from dusk to dawn, but not in windy weather. Female gives birth to single young. Long hibernation period. Life span up to 15 years.

4 Noctule Bat *Nyctalus noctula*. Distributed over whole of Europe. During day shelters in small groups in tree hollows. Hunts in woods, parks, over water, etc. Starts early in evening and flies until dawn. In autumn appears in afternoon. Migrates 750—1,500 km. south or south-west to hibernate, but sometimes remains in hollows, cowsheds, etc. Female gives birth to 1—2 young, which open eyes at 6—7 days and can fly at 45 days. Flies quickly, 50 km. an hour. Hibernates from October to April.

5 Long-eared Bat *Plecotus auritus*. Distributed in Europe, Asia and North Africa. Strikingly large ears. Abundant near human communities. Appears after dark. Flies low, frequently veering. Hunts on outskirts of forests, in parks and also within woods. In June female gives birth to 1—2 young which are independent at 6 weeks. Hibernates in caves, cellars, etc. from October to end of March, alone or in groups of 2—3 individuals.

Order: **Hares and Rabbits** — *Lagomorpha*

6 Snow Hare *Lepus timidus*. Inhabits Ireland, Scotland, northern Europe, Asia, North America. One subspecies also in Alps. In summer ascends to 3,400 m., in winter comes down below 600 m. In winter shelters in snow, marmot burrows, etc. Weighs up to 3.5 kg. In summer grey-brown, in winter pure white. Between May and August female gives birth to 2—5 young with open eyes, suckles them about 3 weeks. Life span 8—13 years. In Europe protected.

7 Common or **European Hare** *Lepus europaeus*. In Europe distributed over cultivated grasslands, other races inhabit large areas of Asia and Africa. In Alps up to 3,000 m. Also lives in forests. Weighs up to 8 kg. Between February or March and September female produces 3—5 litters of 2—7 young with open eyes. Suckles them only 2—3 weeks. Active after dusk and at night. Hides in bushes during day. Herbivorous. In some regions important as game.

Order: **Hares and Rabbits** — *Lagomorpha*

1 European Wild Rabbit *Oryctolagus cuniculus*. Originally from west of Mediterranean region. Since Middle Ages introduced into other parts of Europe; now relatively abundant everywhere. In mountains seldom found above 600 m. Inhabits open woods, parks, etc. Weighs up to 2 kg. (rarely 3 kg.). Digs burrows. Between March and September female produces 3—6 litters of 5—12 or even 15 blind young which open eyes at 10 days, are suckled 4 weeks and attain adulthood at 6—8 months. Life span 10 years. Forms colonies (warrens). Hunted for flesh. Can become pest. Ancestor of domestic rabbits.

Order: **Rodents** — *Rodentia*

Family: **Squirrels** — *Sciuridae*

2 Red Squirrel *Sciurus vulgaris*. Distributed over whole of Europe, extends across Asia as far as Japan. Forest-dweller, occurs in mountains up to limit of tree belt. Builds large spherical nest from twigs, leaves, moss and hairs, in trees; also uses deserted birds' nests and tree hollows. From January to August female produces 2—5 litters of 3—7 blind young. Lives on tree seeds, fruits, mushrooms, insects, birds' eggs and young; also gnaws shoots. In August lays in stocks of food under moss. Non-hibernator.

3 European Ground Squirrel *Citellus citellus*. Inhabits eastern part of central Europe as far as China. Does not live in western Europe. Steppe-dweller. Occurs on grassy slopes up to altitude of 700 m. Digs burrow 1—4 m. deep and up to 7 m. long. Female gives birth to 6—11 young which open eyes at about 4 weeks. Lives on grass, fruit and insects. Hibernates in burrow from October to April. Does not lay in food stocks.

4 European Alpine Marmot *Marmota marmota*. Inhabits Alps, Carpathians and mountains in Asia. Frequents rocky slopes at 800—3,000 m. Digs burrows 1.5—3 m. deep and up to 10 m. long, with several entrances. Lives in colonies. For winter digs special burrow and blocks entrances. Hibernates from end of September until April. Builds up body fat deposits in autumn. Female gives birth to 2—6 blind young which open eyes at 20 days. Active both during day and at night. Very cautious, utters warning whistles. Lives on grass, seeds, berries, insects. Does not store food. Life span up to 18 years.

Family: **Dormice** — *Gliridae*

5 Fat Dormouse *Glis glis*. Distributed from north of Spain across central Europe to Asia Minor. Inhabits deciduous woods at altitudes of up to 1,500 m. Common in orchards and parks, frequents also buildings. Length up to 19 cm. Between June and August female gives birth to 2—9 blind young which open eyes at 20 days. Nocturnal animal, lives on buds, shoots, seeds, fruit, insects and occasionally young birds. Hibernates from end of August until May. Makes moss-lined nest in hollows or nesting-boxes.

6 Garden Dormouse *Eliomys quercinus*. Distributed from Portugal across central Europe to Urals, in south to North Africa. Mainly inhabits conifer woods with undergrowth, but also parks. Builds spherical nest in rock crevices, tree hollows, etc. Litter comprises 2—8 young which open eyes at 18 days. Nocturnal animal, excellent climber. Lives on shoots, berries, fruit and insects. In autumn enters human dwellings. Hibernates in hollows, nesting-boxes, squirrels' nests and attics, from September to April.

7 Common Dormouse *Muscardinus avellanarius*. Distributed in Europe as far as central Sweden, part of England, in south to Italy. Absent in Spain. In mountains up to 2,000 m. Inhabits dense thickets, especially young undergrowth. Sometimes found in gardens. In summer builds spherical nest up to 12 cm. across with side entrance, usually 1—1.5 m., but sometimes 20 m., above ground. Lives on seeds, berries, buds and insects. Hibernates from October to end of March in tree hollows, cleft rocks or under pile of leaves. Body temperature drops to 1°C. Litter comprises 3—9 young which open eyes at 16 days.

386

Family: **Old World Rats and Mice** — *Muridae*

1 House Mouse *Mus musculus*. Distributed over whole of Europe, originally from Asian, North-African and Mediterranean steppes. In Alps at up to 2,700 m. Lives in dwellings, outbuildings, woodpiles, etc. Good climber. Makes nest in holes, skirting-boards, walls, etc. Female produces litters of 4—8 (occasionally up to 12) blind, hairless young several times a year. Young open eyes at 12—14 days, become mature at 6—7 weeks. Life span about 1.5 years, in captivity up to 4 years. Does not hibernate. Lives on waste matter, seeds, etc. In large numbers does damage to food stocks.

2 Harvest Mouse *Micromys minutus*. Distributed in Europe, in east to south-eastern Asia, but not very abundant. Lives on margins of forests, in reed beds beside ponds, in oat- and other fields. Builds spherical nest with side entrance between stalks, 40—80 cm. above ground. Female produces 2—3 litters of 3—12 blind young a year. Young open eyes at 7 days. Also builds sleeping nest with two entrances. In winter visits barns, outbuildings, etc. Climbs and swims very well. Active mainly at night. Lives on seeds and insects. Non-hibernator. Life span 4 years.

3 Long-tailed Field Mouse *Apodemus sylvaticus*. Distributed over whole of Europe, in north to Iceland, in south to Crete. Very abundant. In Alps up to 2,500 m. Inhabits dry conifer and mixed woods, thickets and fields, in winter appears in houses, but only on ground floor. Nesting burrow has 2—3 entrances. Female produces up to 4 litters of 2—9 young a year. Young open eyes at 12 days. Climbs well and can jump distances of up to 80 cm. Can also swim. Nocturnal animal. Non-hibernator. Lives on seeds, roots, shoots, insects. Maximum life span 6 years, average 1.5 years.

4 Black Rat *Rattus rattus*. Originally from tropical belt of Old World, spread by ships all over globe. European incidence now localized (usually near large rivers, in harbours and towns). Frequents attics and storehouses. Climbs and jumps well. Female produces up to 6 litters of 4—15 (rarely 20) naked and blind young a year. Grow coat in 7 days, open eyes at 13—16 days. Lives mainly on vegetable matter and household scraps. Non-hibernator. Life span up to 7 years.

5 Brown or **Norway Rat** *Rattus norvegicus*. Originally from north-eastern Asia, has been carried all over globe. Very common in whole of Europe. Important pest, carrier of many diseases. In mountains up to 1,600 m. Frequents places with water, canals, sewers, rubbish dumps, etc. Via waste pipes enters cowsheds, cellars and buildings, mainly in winter. Lives in groups. Builds nest in burrows. Digs well and can swim and dive. Female produces 2—7 litters of 6—9 (or even 22) young a year. Young open eyes at 13—17 days. Non-hibernator. Omnivorous. Also attacks small vertebrates. Life span 4 years.

Family: **Hamsters** — *Cricetidae*

6 Common Hamster *Cricetus cricetus*. Distributed from France across central Europe as far as Yenisei river. Inhabits cultivated lowland steppes. Digs burrows (30—60 cm. deep in summer, over 2 m. in winter) with several exits, nest chamber and storeroom. Female produces 2—3 litters of 6—18 young a year. Young open eyes at 14 days. Nocturnal animal. Hibernates from October to March, body temperature falls to 4°C. Wakes every 5 days and eats from stocks, which can weigh up to 15 kg. Omnivorous. Eats plants, seeds, invertebrates and small vertebrates. Carries food to burrow in facial pouches.

Family: **Voles** — *Microtidae*

1 Musk Rat *Ondatra zibethica*. Originally from North America. Introduced into Europe near Prague in 1905, has spread over whole of Europe, advancing 25 km. a year. Lives in lakes, ponds, pools and rivers, in mountains up to 1,000 m. Digs burrow about 1 m. deep in bank with one or more entrances. In large numbers can do considerable damage to earthworks. Builds winter structures 1 m. high and 2 m. in diameter over water, from rushes and sedge. Female produces up to 4 litters of 5—14 young a year. Young open eyes at 11 days and leave nest at 3 weeks. Good swimmer and diver. Active mainly at night and in morning. Non-hibernator. Lives on aquatic plants, molluscs, occasionally fish. Life span about 5 years.

2 Bank Vole *Clethrionomys glareolus*. Distributed over whole of Europe except south, Asia as far as Yenisei river. Similar form in North America. In Alps up to 2,200 m. Abundant. Lives on outskirts of forests, in bushes, etc. Ground-dweller. Builds spherical nest from grass, moss, etc. in bushes, up to 1 m. above ground, otherwise underground. Female produces 3—4 litters of 3—8 young a year. Young open eyes at 9 days. Climbs well and can jump. Non-hibernator. Lays in food stocks, e.g. seeds, covers them with leaves. Lives mainly on vegetable matter, occasionally insects. Life span 1.5—2.5 years.

3 Common Vole *Microtus arvalis*. Distributed in Europe except England and Scandinavia, in east as far as China. Inhabits cultivated steppes, fields, dry meadows and open woods. Often occurs in large colonies. Digs branching passages in surface soil and nest chamber at depth of about 0.5 m. In winter tunnels under snow. Female produces up to 12 litters of 3—13 young a year. Young open eyes at 8—10 days. Active mainly at night. Non-hibernator. Lives on grass, shoots and field crops. Life span 1.5—4 years. Important pest.

Family: **Beavers** — *Castoridae*

4 European Beaver *Castor fiber*. Once inhabited whole of Europe, now almost completely exterminated. Today found in only a few parts of Europe, mainly in north and east. Extends east as far as Mongolia. Lives beside stagnant and slow-flowing water. Digs burrows in bank, with shaft leading below water level. Also builds 'lodges' 2—3 m. high on water. Lodges are made of branches and small trunks which beaver fells by gnawing and drags to building site. Builds dams across flowing water, from branches, grass, etc. Couples live in colonies. Very good swimmer and diver. At end of April female gives birth to 2—7 fur-coated young with open eyes, suckles them about 8 weeks. Nocturnal animal. Not true hibernator. Lives on plants and tree shoots. Lays in winter stocks, e.g. willow branches, etc., under water. Life span up to over 30 years. Very valuable fur.

Family: **Nutrias** — *Myocastoridae*

5 Nutria or **Swamp Beaver** *Myocastor coypus*. Comes from South America. Bred in Europe on farms. Now also found wild there (descendants of escapees). Weighs up to 8 kg., sometimes more. Spends much time in water. Digs burrows in bank, 6 m. long and 3 m. deep. Also builds nest in waterside shrubs. Excellent swimmer but poor diver. Female produces 2—3 litters of 4—7 open-eyed young a year, suckles them 8 weeks, but young start to take solids after only 10 days. Lives on grass and aquatic plants. Active after dusk and during day. Non-hibernator.

Order: **Beasts of Prey** — *Carnivora*

Family: **Cats** — *Felidae*

1 Common Wild Cat *Felis silvestris*. Distributed in Europe, Near East, central Asia, North Africa. Lives only in deep forests, chiefly in mountains. Shelters in tree hollows, old badger sets, etc. Female gives birth in shelter to 3—7 blind young, which open eyes at 9—11 days. Suckles them 4 months, but at 6 weeks young can already take hunted food. Cat has clearly demarcated 'preserve', but in mating season or times of food-shortage roams up to 100 km. afield. Except for mating season lives singly. Does not hibernate. Active at night. Catches small vertebrates and insects. One of its subspecies may be ancestor of domestic tabby cat.

2 Northern Lynx *Lynx lynx*. Distributed over eastern and northern Europe and Balkan mountains. In central Europe still abundant in Czechoslovakia. Also occurs in French Alps. Inhabits wooded, mountainous country up to 2,500 m. Solitary animal except at mating time. Nocturnal. Hide during day in cleft rocks, hollows, etc. Weighs up to 30 kg., occasionally 45 kg. Excellent vision and hearing. Climbs well, runs swiftly. In May female gives birth to 2—3 (rare up to 5) spotted young which open eyes at 16 days and are suckled 2 months. Life span up to 17 years. At night catches mammals up to size of roe deer and birds (chiefly game birds). Lies in wait for prey and pounces on it.

Family: **Dog Tribe** — *Canidae*

3 Wolf *Canis lupus*. Once inhabited whole of Europe, but was practically exterminated. Still to be seen in north-eastern Europe. In central Europe quite common in Czechoslovakia and Poland. Occurs at altitudes of up to 2,500 m. Lives in large forests and shrub-grown steppes. In spring and summer lives in families, in autumn forms large packs. Weighs up to 50 kg. (in rare cases 70 kg.). Gestation period 60—65 days. In April or May female gives birth to 4—8 blind young which open eyes at 10 days. Nocturnal animal. Travels long distances (up to 70 km.) in search of prey, catches it by 'round-up' system. Can run up to 160 km. during night. Pack takes on large domestic animals, but gives man wide berth. Eats different vertebrates, insects, molluscs and even fruit. Perhaps only ancestor of domesticated dogs.

4 Red Fox *Vulpes vulpes*. Commonest European member of this family, also occurs in Asia and North America. In Alps up to 3,000 m. Inhabits forests, game preserves, large parks, etc. 'Snoops' round human communities and steals small livestock. Digs 'earth' with several exits. Sometimes occupies it together with badger. Gestation period 51—54 days. Between February and May female gives birth to 4—12 blind young which open eyes at 12—15 days. Eats voles, other small mammals, birds, insects and molluscs, but also forest fruits. Life span 10—12 years. Useful animal rather than nuisance, unless too numerous.

Family: **Mustelids** — *Mustelidae*

5 Common Otter *Lutra lutra*. Originally common in whole of Europe, Asia and North Africa, but exterminated in many parts of central Europe. Inhabits stagnant and flowing water with unregulated banks. Adapted for aquatic existence. Excavates lair in banks, or uses various types of hollows. Lair has entrance 50 cm. below surface and 1 or 2 ventilation shafts. Swims and dives extremely well, can stay under water 6—8 minutes. Gestation period 61—63 days. Female gives birth to 2—6 young which do not open eyes for 4 weeks. Eats mainly fish, also crustaceans, amphibians, etc. Life span 10—18 years. Valuable for fur. In central Europe protected.

1 Pine Marten *Martes martes*. Distributed over practically whole of Europe, in east as far as Asia Minor. Forest-dweller. Climbs trees extremely well and leaps from tree to tree over distances of up to 3.5 m. Makes lair in tree hollows, deserted birds' and squirrels' nests and sometimes owls' nests. Female gives birth to 2—7 young which do not open eyes for 34 days. Catches small mammals (especially squirrels), birds and insects; in autumn also eats fruits and berries. Life span 8—14 years.

2 Stone or **Beech Marten** *Martes foina*. Distributed over whole of Europe except British Isles and Scandinavia, in east across Asia to Himalayas and Mongolia. In Alps up to 2,000 m. Fairly common. Frequents vicinity of human dwellings and often settles in attics, even in towns. Makes grass lair under roofs, in ruins, in cleft rocks and often in hole in ground. In spring female gives birth to 3—7 young which open eyes at 34 days. Suckles them 3 months, but young can already take solids at 6 weeks. Active at night. Catches birds, steals poultry and eggs, also likes fruit, e.g. plums.

3 Common Stoat or **Ermine** *Mustela erminea*. Distributed in Europe; southern limits Pyrenees, Alps and Carpathians. In Alps up to 3,000 m. Found in both dry and damp environments, in steppes and woods or in gardens near dwellings. Mostly red-brown in summer, white with black-tipped tail in winter. Makes lair in holes in ground, in walls, under outbuilding floors, etc. In April or May female gives birth to 3—7 young which do not open eyes for 40 days. Climbs well and can swim. Lives on small rodents and birds, occasionally eats invertebrates and fruit. Life span 5—10 years.

4 Weasel *Mustela nivalis*. Distributed over whole of Europe except Ireland, North Africa, northern and temperate parts of Asia. In Alps up to 2,700 m. Commonest member of this family. Very slim, can slip through narrow holes, e.g. of ground squirrels and rats, etc. Inhabits forests, hedges, parks and gardens. In winter approaches dwellings and shelters in cowsheds, barns, haystacks, cellars, etc. Female gives birth to 3—7 (rarely up to 12) young which open eyes at 21—25 days. Suckles them 6—7 weeks. Very useful animal; catches mice, voles, young rats and ground squirrels. Occasionally eats also invertebrates. Life span 4—7 years.

5 European Polecat *Mustela putorius*. Distributed over practically whole of Europe, temperate parts of Asia, Morocco. Lives in woods and fields, but also frequents dwellings. In winter shelters in barns, sheds, etc. Makes lair in rabbit burrows, tree hollows or pipes. Locally abundant. Mainly terrestrial; does not like climbing, but swims well and can dive. In April or May female gives birth to 3—11 white-coated young which open eyes at 30—37 days. Nocturnal animal. Eats small mammals, birds and their eggs, invades chicken-roosts, steals eggs and bites hens.

6 Ferret *Mustela furo*. Domesticated form of polecat, used for catching wild rabbits. Can be crossed with polecat. Has similar colouring, from pure white to dark. When ferret is placed in rabbit burrow, rabbits rush out and are snared in nets. Easily tamed if caught young.

7 Common Badger *Meles meles*. Distributed in Europe and temperate parts of Asia. In Alps up to 2,000 m. Mainly inhabits woods, also shrub-strewn hillsides and sometimes town parks. Digs 'set' composed of chamber, several passages and ventilating shafts. Likes warm, dry places. Female gives birth to 2—6 blind young which open eyes at 3—4 weeks. Nocturnal animal. Not genuine hibernator, wakes up every few days. Omnivorous, eats anything from insects to small vertebrates and forest fruits. Life span 10—15 years.

Family: **Bears** — *Ursidae*

1 Brown Bear *Ursus arctos*. Several races, from Europe to Asia and North America. Rare in central Europe. In recent years has multiplied in Czechoslovakia and neighbouring Poland. Inhabits wooded, mountainous regions. Found at altitudes of up to 2,600 m. Makes lair in hole in ground, under uprooted tree or in cave. Males larger than females; in Europe weigh up to 350 kg. Female gives birth to 2—5 very small, blind young which open eyes at 4—5 weeks. Littering period December to February. During this time female lies in den, not eating, and warms young by holding them close to body with paws. In spring, at 4 months, young follow mother and remain with her 2 years. Long winter sleep (November to March), but not true hibernation as body temperature does not fall. Life span 35—60 years. Omnivorous, eats practically anything — insects, worms, reptiles, birds, mammals up to size of deer. In times of shortage attacks sheep or even cows. Catches fish and has weakness for honey. In autumn eats forest fruits, berries, etc.

Order: **Pinnipeds** — *Pinnipedia*

2 Harbour or **Hair Seal** *Phoca vitulina*. Distributed in coastal waters of North Atlantic and North Pacific. Strays up rivers, e.g. up to 700 km. inland up Elbe. Occasionally seen in western Baltic. Gregarious, lives in herds. Diurnal animal. Males weigh up to 150 kg. Gestation period about 340 days. At beginning of June or in July female gives birth to 1—2 young weighing 10—15 kg. and measuring 90 cm. Suckles them 4—6 weeks. When weaned, young live 6 weeks on shrimps. Can dive as soon as they are born. Adult at 3—4 years. Can stay under water 5—6 minutes, in exceptional cases up to 15 minutes. Sleeps under water, floats up to surface with closed eyes for air. Swims at about 17 km. an hour (at 35 km. when hunting). Lives mainly on fish. Life span up to 30 years.

Order: **Whales** — *Cetacea*

3 Common Porpoise *Phocaena phocaena*. Distributed in North Sea, Baltic, Mediterranean, Black Sea, Atlantic and North Pacific. Still fairly common off coasts of Europe, especially Germany. Often swims inland up rivers, e.g. Rhine, Elbe, Thames, etc. Consorts in small groups. Gestation period 10—11 months. Female gives birth to one young weighing 6—8 kg. Adult weighs up to 80 kg. Huge appetite. Lives on fish such as herrings, mackerels and salmon. Unpopular with fishermen as often tears nets when caught in them. Its flesh is edible.

4 Bottlenose Dolphin *Tursiops truncatus*. Distributed in Baltic, North Sea, Mediterranean, Black Sea and Atlantic. Length 2.5—3 m. Has long jaws. Gregarious, communities often large. Female gives birth to single young late in summer, suckles it very long. Swims extremely well, up to 35 km. an hour. Predacious animal. Both jaws armed with strong teeth. Lives mainly on fish frequenting upper layers of sea. Also eats octopus, squid, sea snails and other marine animals. In places where there are few fish often does great damage and is mercilessly destroyed by fishermen. Males fight each other at mating time. Bottlenose likes to leap out of water while swimming.

Order: **Even-toed Ungulates** — *Artiodactyla*

Family: **Pigs** — *Suidae*

1 Wild Boar *Sus scrofa*. Widespread in Europe, Asia and North Africa. Inhabits forests with undergrowth. Lives in families and herds, but old boars are solitary. Hides in thickets during day, comes out to feed at night. Gestation period 16—20 weeks. Sow gives birth to 3—12 striped young in bed of moss and grass. Young attain adulthood at 5—6 years. Life span 10—12 years. Omnivorous, but prefers berries, fruit, roots, grass, etc. Roots in soil for worms, insects and small vertebrates. In large numbers can severely damage potato and sugar beet crops, etc. Boar weighs up to over 200 kg. Game animal. Excellent flesh. Ancestor of domesticated pigs.

Family: **Deer** — *Cervidae*

2 Common Fallow Deer *Dama dama*. Originally inhabited Mediterranean region and Asia Minor. Brought to Europe in 10th and 11th century and bred for hunting. Later escaped from preserves and today, in some parts of Europe, is found in large forests. Lives in small herds or singly. Occurs chiefly in lowlands, but also in uplands. Males have palmated antlers. Weight of male up to 125 kg., female 50 kg. Rutting (mating) season from middle of October to November. Gestation period about 230 days. In June or July doe gives birth to one (occasionally 2—3) young. Nocturnal animal. Lives on grass, field crops, acorns, bark, shoots, etc. Game animal. Life span 20—25 years.

3 Red Deer *Cervus elaphus*. Several subspecies distributed in Europe, Asia, North Africa and North America. Inhabits both plains and mountains. Found in Alps at altitudes of up to 2,000 m. Forms herds of about 6—12 animals (rarely up to 80) led by old female (hind). These herds contain hinds and calves. Except at rutting time, old males (harts) live alone or combine in small herds led by strongest. Hide during day, come out at night to feed in clearings, at forest margins, in meadows and fields. Keep within fixed limits and use regular tracks. In rutting season (September—October) males separate and strongest wage battles for herd of hinds. Gestation period 231—238 days. Hind gives birth to one (occasionally 2) young which joins herd with mother on 8th day. Hart weighs up to 225 kg., hind 120 kg. Game animal. Antlers are prized trophy.

4 Sika Deer *Cervus nippon*. Originally native of northern China and Japan. Imported and bred in Europe in preserves, now found there even wild. European animals mostly outcome of crossing of several races. Lives in plains and hills. Spotted during summer. Male weighs up to 55 kg., female 45 kg. Few tines on antlers. Rutting season October—November. One or two young born in June. Life span about 20 years. Same diet as other deer; grass, field crops, shoots, acorns, bark, twigs, etc.

5 Roe Deer *Capreolus capreolus*. Distributed over most of Europe and large part of Asia. In Alps up to 2,400 m. Inhabits forests with undergrowth, copses, meadows with bushes, etc. Lives within specific limits. In summer occurs singly or in small groups, in winter in large herds led by old dams. Except for rutting time, males lead solitary existence, however. Weight 15—30 kg. Primary rutting season July to beginning of September, secondary season November and December. Longer gestation period after summer fertilization. Female gives birth to 1—3 young in May or June. Lives on grass, shoots, forest fruits, etc. Life span 10—17 years. Important game animal.

Family: **Deer** — *Cervidae*

1 Elk *Alces alces*. Distributed in northern Europe, Asia and North America. Not resident in central Europe, but seen there many times in recent years (from Poland). Lives in large, dank forests, swampy scrublands, beside lakes and pools, etc. In summer lives alone or in families. In winter forms herds of 10—15 animals, but without old males. One of largest European animals. Weighs up to 600 kg. Male has huge, palmated antlers. Rutting season end August to October. Gestation period 35—38 weeks. At end of April or beginning of May female gives birth to 1—2 (seldom 3) young which accompany her after 3—4 days. Grazes towards evening and early in morning. Lives on shoots, aquatic plants (gathered standing in water), twigs, etc. Life span 20—25 years. Game animal, but protected in central Europe.

Family: **Hollow-horned Ruminants** — *Bovidae*

2 Chamois *Rupicapra rupicapra*. Inhabits high European mountains, extends east to Caucasus. In some places brought down to lower altitudes. Found in Alps up to 3,000 m. In summer ascends to snowline, in winter comes down to lower altitudes. Lives on steep, rocky slopes with little vegetation. Climbs nimbly and can leap 8 m. Except for old males lives in herds, usually led by female. If startled, utters warning whistle. Male weighs up to 60 kg., female 40 kg. Horns curved at tip, thicker in males than in females. In rutting season (October—December) males wage fierce duels. In April or June female gives birth to one (rarely 2 or 3) young which remains with mother 2 years. Diurnal animal. Grazes on grass, leaves, shoots, etc. Life span 15—20 years.

3 Ibex *Capra ibex*. Distributed in high parts of Pyrenees, Alps, Caucasus and central Asia. In Alps above forest belt. Even in winter usually remains at altitude of 2,300—3,200 m. Herd consists of females, young and young males. Except at rutting time, adult males live in separate communities of up to 30 animals, old males singly. Males weigh up to 110 kg., females 50 kg. Rutting season from middle of December to beginning of January. Gestation period 22—23 weeks. At end of May or beginning of June female gives birth to one (rarely 2) young which follows her only a few hours after birth. Ibex leaps and climbs extremely well. Lives on mountain plants, leaves, lichen, etc. Life span up to 30 years.

4 Mouflon *Ovis musimon*. Originally native of Sardinia, Corsica and Cyprus. Introduced into many parts of central Europe. Inhabits dry, rocky places in wooded uplands and hills. Lives in herds of usually 10—20 animals, in winter over 30. Found mainly in deciduous and mixed woods. Old rams in separate troupes, very old rams solitary. Male weighs up to 50 kg. Rutting season October—December. Gestation period 21—22 weeks. Between end of March and beginning of May ewe gives birth to one (seldom 2) young. Primarily nocturnal animal, rarely active in daytime. Lives on various grass, leaves, shoots, etc. Life span 20 years.

5 European Bison or **Wisent** *Bison bonasus*. Wild European stock exterminated at end of 18th century. Now bred in a few national parks and zoos. Caucasian race completely extinct. Frequents mixed forests with dense undergrowth. In summer prefers damp localities, forest meadows and peat-bogs, in winter drier places. Lives in herds of 6—40 animals led by old cows. Only very old bulls are solitary. Male weighs up to 1,800 kg. Rutting season August and September. Gestation period 40—41 weeks. In May or June cow gives birth to usually one calf (occasionally 2). Both diurnal and nocturnal animal. Grazes mainly in evening and morning. Lives on leaves of bushes and trees, twigs, grass, bark, etc. Life span 30—40 years.

BIBLIOGRAPHY

ACWORTH, W. BARBARA: Trees for Towns. London, 1960

AUSTIN, O.L.: Birds of the World. London, 1963

BANNERMAN, D.A.: The Birds of the British Isles. Edinburgh, 1954

BEAN, W.J.: Trees and Shrubs Hardy in the British Isles (8th edition revised). London, 1970

BEAUFOY, S.: Butterfly Lives. London, 1947

BENSON, S.V.: The Observer's Book of British Birds. London, 1937

BRIMBLE, L.J.F.: Trees in Britain. London, 1946

BRINK, VAN DEN, F. H.: A Field Guide to the Mammals of Britain and Europe. London, 1967

BROCKMAN, C.F. and ZIM, H.S.: Trees of North America. New York, 1968

BRUUN, B. and SINGER, A.: The Hamlyn Guide to Birds of Britain and Europe. London, 1970

BUTCHER, R.W.: A New Illustrated British Flora. 2 vols. London, 1961

CAIN, S. A. and DE OLIVEIRA CASTRO, G.M.: Manual of Vegetation Analysis. New York, 1959

CHRISTIAN, G.: Countryman's Pocket Book. London, 1967

CLAPHAM, A.R., TUTIN, T.G. and WARBURG, E.F.: Flora of the British Isles. 2nd edition. Cambridge, 1962

CLAPHAM, A.R., TUTIN, T.G. and WARBURG, E.F.: Excursion Flora of the British Isles. 2nd edition. Cambridge, 1968

COLYER, C.N. and HAMMOND, C.O.: Flies of the British Isles. London, 1951

CORBET, G.B.: Terrestrial Mammals of Western Europe. London, 1966

DAUBENMIRE, R.F.: Plants and Environment. A Textbook of Plant Autoecology. New York, 1947

EDLIN, H.L.: Tree Planting and Cultivation. London, 1970

EDLIN, H.L.: Trees, Woods and Man. London, 1956

ELWES, H.J. and HENRY, A.H.: The Trees of Great Britain and Ireland. London, 1969

ESAU, K.: Plant Anatomy. New York, 1953

FORD, E.B.: Butterflies. London, 1946

GROSSMAN, M.L. and HAMLET, J.: Birds of Prey of the World. London, 1965

HADFIELD, MILES: British Trees: A Guide for Everyman. London, 1957

HANSON, H.: Dictionary of Ecology. London, 1962

HARLOW, W.H. and HARRAR, E.S.: Textbook of Dendrology. New York, 1958

HIGGINS, L.G. and RILEY, M.D.: A Field Guide to the Butterflies of Britain and Europe. London, 1970

HUTCHINSON, J.: Evolution and Phylogeny of Flowering Plants. London and New York, 1969

IMMS, A.D.: Insect Natural History. London, 1950

KRAMER, P.J.: Plant and Soil Water Relationships. New York, 1949

LEUTSCHER, A.: Tracks and Signs of British Animals. London, 1960

LLOYD, CHRISTOPHER: Shrubs and Trees for Small Gardens. London, 1966

LONGFIELD, C.: Dragonflies of the British Isles. London, 1949

MAKINS, F.K.: The Identification of Trees and Shrubs. London, 1948

MCCLINTOCK, D. and FITTER, R.S.R.: The Pocket Guide to Wild Flowers. London, 1956

MELDERIS, A. and BARGENTER, E.B.: A Handbook of British Flowering Plants. London, 1955

MENNINGER, EDWIN A.: Fantastic Trees. New York, 1967

NEWMAN, L.H. and MANSELL, E.: The Complete British Butterflies in Colour. London, 1968

OOSTING, H.J.: The Study of Plant Communities. An Introduction to Plant Ecology. San Francisco, 1958

PERRING, F.H. and WALTERS, S.M. ed.: Atlas of the British Flora. London, 1962

PETERSON, R., MOUNTFORT, G. and HOLLOM, P.A.: A Field Guide to the Birds of Britain and Europe. London, 1967

POKORNÝ, J.: Trees of Parks and Gardens. 2nd edition. London, 1970

PRIME, C.T. and DEACOCK, R.J.: Trees and Shrubs: Their Identification in Summer and Winter. London, 1951

RILEY, N.D.: Insects in Colour. London, 1963

SAVILE, D.B.O.: Collection and Care of Botanical Specimens. Ottawa, 1962

SCOTT, P.: The Swans, Geese and Ducks of the British Isles. Annual Report of the Wildfowl Trust. Slimbridge, 1950-51

SINNOTT, E.W. and WILSON, K.S.: Botany: Principles and Problems. 5th edition. New York, 1955

SOUTH, R.: Butterflies of the British Isles. London, 1924

SOUTHERN, H.N.: A Handbook of British Mammals. Oxford, 1964

STOKOE, W.J.: The Observer's Book of Butterflies. New York, 1969

TANSTEY, A.G.: Introduction to Plant Ecology. London, 1946

TANSTEY, A.G. and EVANS, E.P.: Plant Ecology and the School. London

TUTIN, T.G. ed.: Flora Europaea. Vol. I, 1964, Vol. II, 1968, London

VAN DYNE, G.M. ed.: The Ecosystem Concept in Natural Resource Management. New York, 1969

VESEY-FITZGERALD, B.: British Bats. London, 1949

VOOUS, K.K.: Atlas of European Birds. London, 1960

WALKER, D. and WEST, R.G. ed.: Studies in the Vegetational History of the British Isles. London, 1970

WALKER, E.P.: Mammals of the World. Baltimore, 1964

WEISZ, P.B. and FULLER, M.S.: The Science of Botany. New York, 1962

WITHERBY, H.F.: The Handbook of British Birds. London, 1949

Plants

Animals

411

416

417